Teaching Climate Change in the Humanities

Climate change is an enormous and increasingly urgent issue. This important book highlights how humanities disciplines can mobilize the creative and critical power of students, teachers, and communities to confront climate change. The book is divided into four clear sections to help readers integrate climate change into the classes and topics they are already teaching as well as to engage with interdisciplinary methods and techniques. *Teaching Climate Change in the Humanities* constitutes a map and toolkit for anyone who wishes to teach valuable lessons that engage with climate change.

Stephen Siperstein has a PhD from the University of Oregon and teaches English and Environmental Humanities at Choate Rosemary Hall in Wallingford, Connecticut, USA.

Shane Hall is a doctoral candidate in the Environmental Studies Program and Department of English at the University of Oregon, USA.

Stephanie LeMenager is Moore Professor of English at the University of Oregon, USA. She is widely involved in outreach projects and regularly engages with the press.

Teaching Climate Change in the Humanities

Edited by Stephen Siperstein,
Shane Hall and Stephanie LeMenager

Routledge
Taylor & Francis Group

LONDON AND NEW YORK

First published 2017
by Routledge
2 Park Square, Milton Park, Abingdon, Oxon OX14 4RN

and by Routledge
711 Third Avenue, New York, NY 10017

Routledge is an imprint of the Taylor & Francis Group, an informa business

© 2017 Stephen Siperstein, Shane Hall, and Stephanie LeMenager

British Library Cataloguing-in-Publication Data
A catalogue record for this book is available from the British Library

Library of Congress Cataloging-in-Publication Data
A catalog record for this book has been requested.

ISBN: 978-1-138-90712-6 (hbk)
ISBN: 978-1-138-90715-7 (pbk)
ISBN: 978-1-315-68913-5 (ebk)

Typeset in Bembo
by FiSH Books Ltd, Enfield

Printed and bound in Great Britain by
TJ International Ltd, Padstow, Cornwall

For our students, teachers, and mentors

Contents

Illustrations

Figures

Tables

Contributors

Stacy Alaimo is Professor of English, Director of Environmental and Sustainability Studies, and Distinguished Teaching Professor at the University of Texas at Arlington. She has published widely in environmental humanities, science studies, and eco-cultural studies on such topics as gender and climate change, queer animals, sustainability, new materialism, and ocean ecologies. Her books include *Undomesticated Ground: Recasting Nature as Feminist Space*; *Bodily Natures: Science, Environment, and the Material Self*, which won the 2011 ASLE Award for Ecocriticism; and the co-edited collection *Material Feminisms*. She is currently completing two books, *Blue Ecologies: Science, Aesthetics, and the Creatures of the Abyss* and *Protest and Pleasure: New Materialism, Environmental Activism, and Feminist Exposure* and she is also editing the volume *Matter* (forthcoming).

Peder Anker is Chair of the Department of Environmental Studies and Associate Professor at the Gallatin School of Individualized Study at New York University. His teaching and research interests lie in the history of science, ecology, environmentalism and design, as well as environmental philosophy. He is the co-author of *Global Design: Elsewhere Envisioned* (2014) together with Louise Harpman and Mitchell Joachim. He is also the author of *From Bauhaus to Eco-House: A History of Ecological Design* (2010), which explores the intersection of architecture and ecological science, and *Imperial Ecology: Environmental Order in the British Empire, 1895–1945* (2001), which investigates how the promising new science of ecology flourished in the British Empire.

Swayam Bagaria is currently a PhD student in the Anthropology Department at Johns Hopkins University. His interests lie in questions of law and religion in India as they appear in ritual sacrifice, religious iconography, and the imbrication of myth and memory.

J. Baird Callicott is the co-editor-in-chief of the *Encyclopedia of Environmental Ethics and Philosophy* and author or editor of a score of books and author of dozens of journal articles, encyclopedia articles, and book chapters in environmental philosophy and ethics. Callicott has served the International Society for Environmental Ethics as President; Yale University as Bioethicist-in-Residence;

and the National Socio-environmental Synthesis Center as Visiting Senior Research Scientist (funded by the National Science Foundation). His research proceeds simultaneously on four main fronts: theoretical environmental ethics, comparative environmental ethics and philosophy, the philosophy of ecology and conservation policy, and climate ethics. He taught the world's first course in environmental ethics in 1971 at the University of Wisconsin–Stevens Point. His most recent book is *Thinking Like a Planet: The Land Ethic and the Earth Ethic* (2013), and he is currently writing a textbook on Presocratic natural philosophy.

SueEllen Campbell is Professor of English at Colorado State University. She is co-director (with John Calderazzo) of Changing Climates @ Colorado State, a multidisciplinary education and outreach initiative, and she runs the website 100 Views of Climate Change (http://changingclimates.colostate.edu); both projects are supported by CMMAP (the Center for Multiscale Modeling of Atmospheric Processes, an NSF-funded Science and Technology Center). Her most recent book is *The Face of the Earth: Natural Landscapes, Science, and Culture* (2011).

Mark Carey is Associate Dean and Associate Professor of History in the University of Oregon's Robert D. Clark Honors College, as well as Associate Professor of Environmental Studies. He has published widely on the history of glaciers, climate change, water, mountaineering, and health, including three books: *The High-Mountain Cryosphere: Environmental Changes and Human Risks* (2015), edited with Christian Huggel, John Clague, and Andreas Kääb; *Glaciares, cambio climático y desastres naturales: Ciencia y sociedad en el Perú* (2014); and *In the Shadow of Melting Glaciers: Climate Change and Andean Society* (2010), which won the Elinor Melville Award for the best book on Latin American environmental history. He is co-director with Kathy Lynn of the UO's Climate Change and Indigenous Peoples Initiative, and co-founder of the Transdisciplinary Andean Research Network. He served as a contributing author for two chapters of the most recent intergovernmental Panel on Climate Change (IPCC) assessment report.

Jan Dietrich is an Associate Professor and Old Testament scholar at Aarhus University working in the fields of Old Testament and Ancient Near Eastern anthropology, including the history of mentalities, ritual studies, wisdom, law, and iconography. One of his research interests is social and cognitive coping strategies in relation to disasters and other traumatic events.

Wai Chee Dimock is the William Lampson Professor of English and American Studies at Yale University. She is best known for *Through Other Continents: American Literature Across Deep Time* (2006). Editor of PMLA, and a film critic for the *Los Angeles Review of Books*, her essays have also appeared in *Critical Inquiry*, the *Chronicle of Higher Education*, *The New Yorker*, and the *New York Times*.

James Engell has taught at Harvard since 1978, chairing the Department of English from 2004 to 2010. He earlier chaired the Degree Program in History and Literature as well as the Department of Comparative Literature, and he served on the Committee on the Study of Religion. A faculty associate of the Harvard University Center for the Environment and Fellow of the American Academy of Arts and Sciences, he has taught environmental courses at Harvard, the National Humanities Center, and Waseda University. In 2008 he conceived and co-edited *Environment: An Interdisciplinary Anthology*. His other books include *The Creative Imagination: Enlightenment to Romanticism* (1981); *The Committed Word: Literature and Public Values* (1999); and, with Anthony Dangerfield, *Saving Higher Education in the Age of Money* (2005), which won the 2007 Association of American Colleges & Universities Ness Book Award for best book on liberal education.

Robert Melchior Figueroa is Associate Professor of Philosophy in the School of History, Philosophy, and Religion at Oregon State University. His combined pedagogy and research on the philosophy of environmental justice extends and reconfigures dimensions of justice to address a broad range of issues. Some examples include climate change, climate refugees, Latin@ issues, critical disability studies, indigenous issues, critical tourism studies, and interspecies justice. He and Sandra Harding co-edited *Science and Other Cultures: Issues in the Philosophies of Science and Technology* (2003), as part of their three-year grant from the National Science Foundation. He is the director of the Environmental Justice Project in the Center for Environmental Philosophy and co-director of the Program in Ethics, Society, and the Environment at OSU. Among his forth-coming works is *Environmental Justice as Environmental Ethics: A New Introduction*, a manuscript-text to teach environmental philosophy with environmental justice as an interpretive centerpiece.

Janet Fiskio is Associate Professor of Environmental Studies and Comparative American Studies at Oberlin College, where she teaches classes on climate change, environmental justice, food studies, and environmental humanities. Her pedagogy emphasizes an interdisciplinary, community-based approach to ques-tions of environment and social justice. Her projects include a book about climate justice entitled *Counter Friction* and collaborative research projects on urban farming and race in the Rust Belt. Her articles have appeared in *American Literature, Race, Gender, and Class*, and *The Cambridge Companion to Literature and the Environment*. She serves on the Executive Council for The Association for the Study of Literature and Environment (ASLE) and as book review editor for *Resilience: A Journal of the Environmental Humanities.*

Stephanie Foote is Professor of English and Gender and Women's Studies at the University of Illinois at Urbana-Champaign. She is the author of *Regional Fictions, The Parvenu's Plot*, the editor of two reprints of Ann Aldrich's classic 1950s lesbian pulps for the Feminist Press, and with Elizabeth Mazzolini, the co-editor of *Histories of the Dustheap* (2012). With Stephanie LeMenager, she is the co-founder and co-editor of *Resilience: A Journal of the Environmental Humanities*, a peer-reviewed digital journal. She is currently at work on several projects that bring together her interests in American Studies and environmentalism, including one on the fate of deaccessioned print artifacts from the late nineteenth century to the present.

Greg Garrard is Sustainability Professor at the University of British Columbia and a National Teaching Fellow of the British Higher Education Academy. He is a founding member and former Chair of the Association for the Study of Literature and the Environment (UK and Ireland). He is the author of *Ecocriticism* (2004, 2nd edition 2011) as well as numerous essays on eco-pedagogy, animal studies, and environmental criticism. He has recently edited *Teaching Ecocriticism and Green Cultural Studies* (2011) and *The Oxford Handbook of Ecocriticism* (2014) and become co-editor of the journal *Green Letters: Studies in Ecocriticism*.

William Gleason is Professor and Chair of English at Princeton University, where he is also affiliated with the Program in American Studies, the Center for African American Studies, the Program in Urban Studies, and the Princeton Environmental Institute. He is the author of *The Leisure Ethic: Work and Play in American Literature, 1840–1940*, and *Sites Unseen: Architecture, Race, and American Literature*, and co-editor (with Joni Adamson and David Pellow) of *Keywords for Environmental Studies* (forthcoming).

Cheryll Glotfelty is Professor of Literature and Environment at the University of Nevada, Reno. She co-edited *The Ecocriticism Reader: Landmarks in Literary Ecology*, which helped open the field of ecocriticism. Her most recent co-edited editions are *The Bioregional Imagination: Literature, Ecology, and Place* and *The Biosphere and the Bioregion: Essential Writings of Peter Berg*. She has won numerous teaching awards, including the CASE-Carnegie Professor of the Year award for Nevada.

Shane Hall is a doctoral candidate in the University of Oregon's Environmental Science, Studies, and Policy Program. His research investigates the impacts of climate change, international development, and militarization on social and environmental justice. Shane teaches courses in both the environmental studies program and the English department. He has designed innovative upper-level environmental studies courses such as "Imagining Environmental Futures," which focuses on literary representations of apocalypse, dystopia, and utopia, and "Cultures of Coal," which examines the human and environmental history of burning coal. Shane is the first Graduate Student Teacher-Scholar for the University of Oregon's campus-wide Teaching Effectiveness Program. In this role Shane helps instructors across ranks and disciplines develop their pedagogy in dialogue with one another and with national and scholarly conversations about excellence in higher education. He has established and implemented a university-wide professional development program for graduate student teachers.

Steven Hartman is Professor of English Literature at Mid Sweden University, where he has been active in developing the interdisciplinary EcoHumanities Hub. He is also a founding member and present chair of the Nordic Network for Interdisciplinary Environmental Studies (NIES). NIES has been active in a number of public humanities and environmental humanities projects, including "Inscribing Environmental Memory in the Icelandic Sagas," a major interdisciplinary research initiative that examines environmental memory in the medieval Icelandic sagas, with a prominent focus on historical processes of environmental change and adaptation.

Kevin Hatfield is an Adjunct Assistant Professor with the Department of History and affiliated faculty member of the Robert D. Clark Honors College at the University of Oregon. He specializes in the history of the American West, environment, and immigration, with a particular emphasis on the intersections of race/ethnicity, property, and community in the Northern Great Basin. His research and scholarship focuses on the Bizkaian Basque community of eastern Oregon, Western Idaho, and northern Nevada; and the Northern Paiute communities of the Confederate Tribes of Warm Springs and Burns Paiute Tribe, with publications in the *Nevada Historical Society Quarterly* and *The Journal of the Society of Basque Studies in America*. He has also developed an undergraduate curriculum engaging students in decolonizing pedagogy and community-based research with indigenous and ethnic community course partners.

Mogens S. Høgsberg is a curator, PhD, and an archaeologist at Moesgård Museum in Aarhus with special interests in the North Atlantic and particularly in the Greenland Norse from their initial settlement around 1000 AD to their eventual demise in the mid-to-late-fifteenth century. Human responses to, and agency in, environmental changes have been a key factor in this debate. In addition, one of his major research interests has been the development of the dwellings of the Greenland Norse.

Heather Houser is an Associate Professor of English at The University of Texas at Austin. Her research areas include the contemporary novel, environmental media and criticism, affect studies, and science and technology studies. She is the author of *Ecosickness in Contemporary U.S. Fiction: Environment and Affect* (2014) and of essays appearing in *American Literary History*, *Public Culture*, *American Literature*, and *Contemporary Literature*, among other venues. Her current project, "Environmental Art and the Infowhelm," examines the aesthetics of information management in recent environmental literature and new media.

Hsinya Huang is Professor of American and Comparative Literature and Dean of the College of Arts and Humanities, National Sun Yat-Sen University, Taiwan. Her book publications include *(De)Colonizing the Body: Disease, Empire, and (Alter)Native Medicine in Contemporary Native American Women's Writings* (2004) and *Huikan beimei yuanzhumin wenxue: duoyuan wenhua de shengsi (Native North American Literatures: Reflections on Multiculturalism)* (2009), the first Chinese essay collection on Native North American literatures. She edited the English translation of *The History of Taiwanese Indigenous Literatures* and is currently editing two essay volumes, *Aspects of Transnational* and *Ocean and Ecology in the Trans-*

Pacific Context. She is editor-in-chief of *Sun Yat-sen Journal of Humanities*. She serves on the Council of the American Studies Association, Advisory Board of *The Journal of Transnational American Studies, JTAS*, U.C. Berkeley e-scholarship and Advisory Board of Routledge Research in Transnational Indigenous Perspectives. Her current research projects investigate Native American and Pacific Islanders' literatures, radiation ecologies in the Pacific, and Chinese railroad workers in North America.

Matthew Kearnes is an Australian Research Council Future Fellow and Associate Professor based in the Environmental Humanities at the School of Humanities and Languages, University of New South Wales. Matthew's research is situated between the fields of Science and Technology Studies (STS), environmental sociology, human geography, and environmental humanities. His current work is focused on the social and political dimensions of technological and environmental change, and he has published widely on the ways in which the development of novel and emerging technologies is entangled with profound social, ethical, and normative questions. His most recent volume is the co-edited book *Remaking Participation: Science, Environment and Emergent Publics* (2016). For more information about Matthew's research please visit https://research.unsw.edu.au/people/dr-matthew-benjamin-kearnes.

Naveeda Khan teaches anthropology at Johns Hopkins University. She is the author of *Muslim Becoming: Aspiration and Skepticism in Pakistan* and editor of *Beyond Crisis: Re-evaluating Pakistan* and special journal issues on "Number as Inventive Frontier," and "The Fate of Our Corruption." Her interests lie at the intersection of climate science, religious imagination and everyday life in riverine settings in Bangladesh.

Uwe Küchler studied English and American Studies, French and Sociology at Berlin's Humboldt-Universität, the University of London's Goldsmiths' College and at Georgetown University in Washington DC. He received an MA in English, American and French Studies, as well as Sociology in 2001 and has worked in the publishing house *Berlin Verlag* and for the *Literary Scouting Agency Maria B. Campbell Associates* in New York City. In his dissertation, he pursued questions of intercultural learning and teaching in the context of internationalizing higher education. From 2006 to 2013, he worked as Assistant Professor at Universität Halle-Wittenberg (Germany). Avocationally, he taught English at a local high school. In February 2013, Küchler was appointed *Juniorprofessor* (Teaching English as a Foreign Language) at Universität Bonn (Germany), where his current research focuses on the topic of nature, environment, and sustainability in foreign language teaching.

Nicholas Lawrence teaches American literature and critical theory at the University of Warwick. He is co-author, with members of the Warwick Research Collective, of *Combined and Uneven Development: Towards a New Theory of World-Literature*.

Stephanie LeMenager is Barbara and Carlisle Moore Professor of English and Professor of Environmental Studies at the University of Oregon. Her publications include the books *Living Oil: Petroleum Culture in the American Century*, *Manifest and Other Destinies* and (as co-editor) *Environmental Criticism for the Twenty-first Century*. Her forthcoming book, *Weathering: Toward a Sustainable Humanities*, treats the role of the Humanities in the era of global climate change. She is a founding editor of *Resilience: A Journal of the Environmental Humanities*.

Anthony Lioi is Associate Professor of Liberal Arts and English at the Juilliard School in New York City. He teaches contemporary American literature, rhetoric and composition, and green cultural studies. His essays have appears in many journals, including *ISLE, Feminist Studies, Journal of Ecocriticism, ImageTexT,* and *CrossCurrents.* He is the media review editor of *Resilience: A Journal of Environmental Humanities.*

Kathy Lynn is a faculty research assistant in the Environmental Studies Program at the University of Oregon. She is a practitioner and applied researcher with experience in working with rural, resource-based communities and Native American tribes in the Pacific Northwest to address social, environmental and economic issues associated with climate change. Kathy coordinates the Tribal Climate Change Project, a collaboration with the USDA Forest Service Pacific Northwest Research Station. Her research focuses on understanding the impacts of climate change on tribal culture and sovereignty, and the federal trust responsibility in an era of climate change. Kathy also facilitates the Pacific Northwest Tribal Climate Change Network, which is comprised of tribes, tribal organizations, public agencies, and non-governmental groups throughout the Northwest and from across the country.

Graeme Macdonald is Associate Professor in the Department of English and Comparative Literary Studies at the University of Warwick, UK, where he teaches modern and contemporary literature and drama and critical and cultural theory. He has authored various articles and essays on nineteenth to twenty-first century literature and culture, and is editor of *Post-Theory: New Directions in Criticism* (1999) and *Scottish Literature and Postcolonial Literature* (2011). He has recently edited and introduced a new edition of John McGrath's 1973 play *The Cheviot, the Stag and the Black, Black Oil* (2015), and is part of the Warwick Research Collective (WreC) who have just published a collective monograph, *Combined and Uneven Development: Towards a New Theory of World-Literature* (2015). He has published articles on oil, energy resources, and culture, the most recent being an article on SF, energy and future fuel, in *Paradoxa: SF Now* (2015). He teaches a graduate class on Petrofiction and is at present engaged on a monograph project on oil and world literature.

Darragh Martin is a Core Lecturer at Columbia University, where he received his PhD in Theater in 2013. His work has featured in *Teaching Shakespeare Beyond the Centre* and *Magic! New Irish Fairy Tales.* He is a founding member of Columbia Divest for Climate Justice.

Bill McKibben is an author and environmentalist who in 2014 was awarded the Right Livelihood Prize, sometimes called the 'alternative Nobel.' His 1989 book *The End of Nature* is regarded as the first book for a general audience about climate change, and has appeared in 24 languages. He has gone on to write a dozen more books. He is a founder of 350.org, the first planet-wide, grassroots climate change movement, which has organized twenty thousand rallies around the world in every country save North Korea, spearheaded the resistance to the Keystone Pipeline, and launched the fast-growing fossil fuel divestment movement. The Schumann Distinguished Scholar in Environmental Studies at Middlebury College and a fellow of the American Academy of Arts and Sciences, he was the 2013 winner of the Gandhi Prize and the Thomas Merton Prize, and holds honorary degrees from 18 colleges and universities. *Foreign Policy* named him to their inaugural list of the world's 100 most important global thinkers, and the Boston Globe said he was "probably America's most important environmentalist." A former staff writer for *The New Yorker*, he writes frequently for a wide variety of publications around the world, including the *New York Review of Books*, *National Geographic*, and *Rolling Stone*.

Nicole Merola is an Associate Professor of Ecocriticism and American Literature in the Literary Arts & Studies Department at the Rhode Island School of Design. In addition to teaching the course on climate change cultures described in this collection, she teaches courses on the Anthropocene, contemporary ecological fiction, green film, narratives of evolution, and theories of natureculture, as well as a fieldwork-based course focused on arts, humanities, and sciences approaches to biodiversity. Her recent publications include "Materializing a Geotraumatic and Melancholy Anthropocene: Jeanette Winterson's *The Stone Gods*," in *The Minnesota Review* (2014); "T. C. Boyle's Neoevolutionary Queer Ecologies: Questioning Species in 'Descent of Man' and 'Dogology'," in *America's Darwin: Darwinian Theory in U.S. Culture* (2014); and "*Cosmopolis*: Don DeLillo's Melancholy Political Ecology," in *American Literature* (2012).

Upamanyu Pablo Mukherjee is a Professor of English and Comparative Literary Studies at the University of Warwick. He is the author of *Natural Disasters and Victorian Imperial Culture: Fevers and Famines* (2013), *Postcolonial Environments: Nature, Culture and Contemporary Indian Novel in English* (2010) and *Crime and Empire: Representing India in the Nineteenth Century* (2003). His current projects include two large-scale research projects on the novel form in the Indian ocean world and the relationship between science policy and science fiction in post-colonial South Asia.

Patrick D. Murphy is a Professor in the Department of English at the University of Central Florida. He has authored *Transversal Ecocritical Practice* (2013), *Ecocritical Explorations in Literary and Cultural Studies* (2009), *Farther Afield in the Study of Nature Oriented Literature* (2000), *A Place for Wayfaring: The Poetry and Prose of Gary Snyder* (2000), and *Literature, Nature, and Other: Ecofeminist Critiques* (1995).

Persuasive Aesthetic Ecocritical Praxis is forthcoming. He has also edited or co-edited such books as *The Literature of Nature: An International Sourcebook* (1998), and *Ecofeminist Literary Criticism and Pedagogy* (1998), with a Chinese translation of the latter published in 2013. He was the founding editor of *ISLE: Interdisciplinary Studies Literature and Environment*. His ecocritical work has been translated into Chinese, Danish, Italian, Japanese, Korean, and Spanish. He teaches critical theory, modern and contemporary American literature, comparative literature, ecocriticism, and ecofeminism.

Esben B. Niels is Assistant Professor of Rhetoric at the Department of Aesthetics and Communication, Aarhus University. He has worked on contemporary secularized brands of apocalyptic rhetoric and how these are used in political discourse, social activism, and popular culture. The main focus of this research has been on the international climate change debate. Other research interests include environmental rhetoric in general, narrative rhetoric, rhetorical criticism, contemporary activism and the rhetoric of popular culture.

Mathias V. Nordvig is Visiting Assistant Professor in Nordic Studies at the Department of Germanic & Slavic Languages & Literatures, University of Colorado, Boulder. In his doctoral dissertation he studied how eco-mythological aspects permeate Old Icelandic sagas, in particular how observations of, and lessons derived from, seismic activity and volcanic eruptions have shaped deities and narratives. He specializes in pre-Christian Nordic mythologies, Scandinavian folklore, Nordic memory studies, myth and disaster studies, North Atlantic and Greenlandic literature, reception history of the Viking Age, and Neo-paganism.

Jennifer O'Neal is the University Historian and Archivist at the University of Oregon, and affiliated faculty with the Robert D. Clark Honors College, History Department, and the Native Studies program. She specializes in American West and Native American history, with a specific emphasis on decolonizing methodologies and social movements. Her research and scholarship are dedicated to the intersections between social, cultural, and historical contexts in which archives exist for marginalized or underrepresented communities and developing frameworks and guidelines for the post-custodial stewardship of collections, with recent publications in the *Journal of Western Archives* and *Journal of Critical Library and Information Studies*. In collaboration with Kevin Hatfield, she has developed an undergraduate curriculum engaging students in decolonizing pedagogy and community-based research with indigenous and ethnic community course partners. She is a member of The Confederated Tribes of Grand Ronde in Oregon.

Emily Potter is a Senior Lecturer in Literary Studies at Deakin University. She has published widely on questions of literary and cultural engagements with the environment and climate change. Her publications include the co-edited collection *Ethical Consumption: A Critical Introduction* (2010) and the co-authored book *Plastic Water: The Social and Material Life of Bottled Water* (2015).

Felix Riede is an archaeologist with particular interest in the relationship between humans and the environment at the intersection between the Arts and the Sciences. In particular, he has been researching the impact of extreme events such as volcanic eruptions on human communities in the deep past. He is currently Associate Professor and Head of Department, and is coordinating PI of the Climate | Culture | Catastrophe Network (http://c3net.au.dk), a hub for the Environmental Humanities at Aarhus University.

Stephen Rust is Instructor at the University of Oregon and Adjunct Instructor at Oregon State University. He teaches courses in cinema studies and composition. Stephen is co-editor of *Ecomedia: Key Issues* (2015) and *Ecocinema Theory and Practice* (2013) and site moderator of EcomediaStudies.org. His work has appeared in such journals as *ISLE* and such collections as *The Cambridge Companion to Literature and Environment*.

Stephen Siperstein has a PhD in English from the University of Oregon and currently teaches English and Environmental Humanities at Choate Rosemary Hall in Wallingford, CT. His research focuses on environmental education, climate change cultures, and contemporary North American literature, and his work on teaching climate change has appeared in the *Journal of Sustainability Education* and the volume *Learner-centered Teaching Activities for Environmental and Sustainability Studies* (Springer, 2016). His poetry has been included most recently in *The Hopper, saltfront, Poecology, ISLE*, and the collection *Winds of Change: Short Stories about Our Climate* (Moon Willow Press, 2015). He is involved in climate education projects in both secondary and higher education.

Jonathan Skinner is Associate Professor and teaches on the English and Comparative Literary Studies program at the University of Warwick. His interests include contemporary poetry and poetics; ecocriticism and environmental studies; ethnopoetics; sound studies; critical theory; and translation. He is founder and editor of *ecopoetics,* a journal which features creative-critical intersections between writing and ecology.

Scott Slovic is Professor of Literature and Environment and Chair of the English Department at the University of Idaho. He served as founding president of the Association for the Study of Literature and Environment (ASLE) from 1992 to 1995, and since 1995 has edited the journal *ISLE: Interdisciplinary Studies in Literature and Environment.* He has written, edited, or co-edited twenty-two books, including most recently *Ecocriticism of the Global South, Currents of the Universal Being: Explorations in the Literature of Energy*, and *Numbers and Nerves: Information, Emotion, and Meaning in a World of Data.*

Annette Højen Sørensen is an Assistant Professor and Classical archaeologist who has worked with several aspects of the Bronze Age Eastern Mediterranean cultures. During recent years she has primarily been focusing on the impact of natural elements and events in the iconography of Aegean cultures. Through her many research partners in the natural sciences Annette has been involved in several projects and publications concerning the chronologies of the Eastern Mediterranean and the iconography of nature and natural settings.

Julie Sze is an Associate Professor and the Director of American Studies at U.C. Davis. She is also the founding director of the Environmental Justice Project for U.C. Davis's *John Muir Institute for the Environment*, and in that capacity is the Faculty Advisor for *25 Stories from the Central Valley*. Sze's research investigates environmental justice and environmental inequality; culture and environment; race, gender and power; and urban/community health and activism and has been funded by the Ford Foundation, the American Studies Association and the U.C. Humanities Research Institute. Her book, *Noxious New York: The Racial Politics of Urban Health and Environmental Justice*, won the 2008 John Hope Franklin Publication Prize, awarded annually to the best published book in American Studies. She is currently on the managing board of *American Quarterly* and *Boom: A Journal of California*.

Imre Szeman is Canada Research Chair of Cultural Studies and Professor of English, Film Studies, and Sociology at the University of Alberta. His most recent books include the co-edited collections *Fueling Culture: Energy, History, Politics* (2016), *A Companion to Critical and Cultural Theory* (2016), and *Energy Humanities: A Reader* (2016) and the co-written book *Popular Culture: A User's Guide* (4th revised edition, 2016). He is currently working on *On Empty: The Cultural Politics of Oil*.

Karen Thornber is Professor, Chair, and Director of Graduate Studies in the Department of Comparative Literature, Harvard University, where she is also Chair of Regional Studies East Asia and a member of the Department of East Asian Languages and Civilizations. Her research and teaching focus on world literature and the literatures and cultures of East Asia and the Indian Ocean Rim (South and Southeast Asia, the Middle East, Africa). She is author of two multiple international-prize winning books – *Empire of Texts in Motion: Chinese, Korean, and Taiwanese Transculturations of Japanese Literature* (2009) and *Ecoambiguity: Environmental Crises and East Asian Literatures* (2012), and more than fifty articles and chapters, many of which focus on environmental criticism. Also a published translator of Japanese poetry, Thornber is currently working on several projects, including a book on world literature and global health, a book on networking environments, and a global history of leprosy.

Anthony Vital, born in South Africa, teaches at Transylvania University, a liberal arts college in Kentucky. Through his varied research and teaching interests, he puzzles over the relation of text, society, and planet – and the language we use in daily life-building. In the late 1990s, he began presenting conference papers that explored a postcolonial ecocriticism of South African literature, one alert to how, during the transition to democracy, the country's environmental culture began to emphasize environmental justice. From these papers, he has been publishing articles exploring how criticism might attend to the interconnection of literary form and language, environmental justice, ecology, and the postcolonial condition. Recent work links these topics with the planetary and the global and, in relation to these, climate change.

Gillen D'Arcy Wood is Nicholson Professor of English, and Director of the Sustainability Studies Initiative in the Humanities at the University of Illinois, Urbana-Champaign. He is the author of two books on Romanticism, *The Shock of the Real: Romanticism and Visual Culture, 1760–1860* (2001) and *Romanticism and Music Culture in Britain, 1770–1840: Virtue and Virtuosity* (2010), and an historical novel, *Hosack's Folly,* about yellow fever in 1820s New York (2005). His new book, *Tambora: The Eruption that Changed the World* (2014), reconstructs on a global scale the period of drastic climate change and social devastation arising from Mt. Tambora's eruption in Indonesia in 1815. *Tambora* has received significant critical and media attention, and has been reviewed by *The Wall Street Journal, The Times Literary Review, Nature,* and *The South China Morning Post,* among others.

Robert Wilson is associate professor of geography at Syracuse University and a recent fellow at the Rachel Carson Center for Environment and Society in Munich. His current project examines the development of the climate movement in the United States, which focuses on the coalition of disparate groups that comprise the movement and activists' use of social media and other digital tools for organizing.

Preface

The Work Ahead

It's not so difficult, we tell our students,
not so difficult that you should despair
or forget dreaming. There are others here
in this room and beyond who will gather,
humans and non-humans alike,
though you may not know them yet,
may not know their stories or their lives.
Yet don't expect the task to be easy;
do not assume it will take less
than a lifetime. It will take more.
Hope is like that: sometimes a sunken stone,
sometimes a silver maple leaf slipping
across currents, sometimes a mallard
rising fast and jewel-like in the morning,
another drop in the great watershed of things.
Your choice is whether to imagine:
the leaf, the light, the green sheened feathers,
the sounds of a river, the stories—
our choice is whether to work.

(Stephen Siperstein, 2015)

Introduction

Stephen Siperstein, Shane Hall and
Stephanie LeMenager

The story of this book began in a classroom. Well, many classrooms actually.

In the winter of 2014, the co-editors, along with a small group of other scholars and educators, took part in a graduate seminar at the University of Oregon titled "The Cultures of Climate Change" and conceived by Stephanie LeMenager. The course aimed to take "global anthropogenic climate change as a case study through which to explore the interdisciplinary axes of the environmental humanities" (LeMenager) and to do so by addressing a range of media and texts, from climate change fiction (cli-fi) to public art projects to radical hacktivism to the education system itself. But more than advancing these stated aims, the course became a laboratory for teaching and learning about climate change.[1] Quickly it became clear that expertise was distributed widely across the seminar—that Stephen Siperstein, for example, had embarked upon what may be the first university dissertation to address climate change pedagogy in literary and cultural studies, and that Shane Hall had earned recognition and awards as an experimental, inspiring teacher of climate change in the humanities.[2] The professor stepped down from her proverbial podium to enter a vibrant community of fellow learners and educators. As in any successful collaborative research venture, we left every class meeting with more burning questions than when we had entered. Often, these questions were not just about specific readings or assignments, but about the enterprise itself.

For instance, we wondered: how can we imagine effective, transformative climate change pedagogy in a literature, history, philosophy, or media studies course? Do the cultures of climate change belong in a boutique upper-division elective or does the topic necessitate a perspectival shift across various humanities courses and curricula? Does climate change demand we rethink what departments look like and how faculty interact with one another and with students? Should such education include opportunities for activism? Should it inspire hope, combat despair? What kind of humanities teaching is possible, and necessary, in the era of climate change?

These multiple and interlocking questions continued to direct our discussions long after our seminar ended. We grappled with them as each of us proceeded to develop and teach additional courses. While we explored through our course design and classroom practices some tentative answers, we also came to understand that these same kinds of questions were being asked, and provisionally answered, by other humanities educators around the world. At conferences, through emails, and by word of mouth, we were hearing about remarkable educational experiments in teaching climate change within the humanities. We recognized the need to gather some of these experiments that, taken together, represent a fast-growing community of scholars and educators working to bring the humanities into climate change discourse and vice-a-versa. The 34 chapters and afterword gathered in this collection approach some of our questions, and in turn pose a number of their own. This book is an artifact of collective questioning and collaborative work. In a manner that is often personal and reflective of classroom experiences, our authors consider mentorship, pedagogical method, and course design. All serve as models, challenges, or guides. We hope this collection appropriately honors those whose commitments to teaching climate change in the humanities precede and accompany our own. We also hope the book calls forth a growing community of educators new to the conversation.

The planetary provocation

As the slow-rolling disasters of climate change continue to unfold, the question is no longer *if* anthropogenic climate change will come to be the defining issue of our time, but rather *how* anthropogenic climate change defines our present, and how it will shape our individual and collective futures. Today, the ubiquity of climate change, its causes and effects, entangles virtually every human endeavor and action with ecological and geophysical processes. Every mote of carbon dioxide or other greenhouse gas emitted through the vast web of the global economy contributes to climate disruption, as does every carbon sink filled, destroyed, or diminished. The social effects of climate change are just as widespread and convoluted, from childhood malnutrition in Arctic Canada, where changes in seasonal migratory patterns radically affect the hunting economy, to debates about whether official "refugee" status can be given to migrants fleeing sinking Pacific island states. Even real estate values in coastal California and Florida, havens of global wealth, respond to sea level rise, as the insurance industry well knows. The ubiquity of climate change implicates all of us in the wealthy world as both perpetrators and victims, while its most negative impacts continue to be distributed unevenly and unjustly.

The omnipresent yet uneven imbrication of ourselves and our students in climate change leads us to consider perhaps the first provocation of climate education in the humanities. We summarize this first provocation as the ecological, planetary provocation. Likewise offered as a foundational maxim of environmental education, it is eloquently voiced by famed naturalist John Muir: "When we try to pick out anything by itself, we find it hitched to everything else in the Universe" (248).

Climate change is "hitched" to so many aspects of our lives as human animals, just as our lives have always been deeply interwoven into the vagaries of climate. As Richard C. Foltz notes, one of the first tenets of teaching environmental history is that "we should remind ourselves that humans interact not only with each other, but in all times, places and contexts with the non-human world as well" (10). Integrative approaches developed over almost two decades through teaching environmental history, philosophy, and literary and cultural studies are well-suited to climate change education. Yet humanists have lagged behind their colleagues in the natural and social sciences in developing curricula around climate change. This is due largely to the understandable tendency in higher education for teaching to follow research. Technical and scientific reports for decades have emphasized the tremendous challenges of unmitigated climate change—rising sea levels, extreme weather events, crop failure, and social unrest, among others—and thus there has been more focus on teaching the technical and scientific dimensions of these issues. Climate science is taught to graduate and undergraduate students in courses, integrated into a host of internships and extracurricular opportunities, and even acknowledged by the White House as crucial for developing nation-wide climate literacy.[3] Although educators have pointed to the necessity of including the humanities in climate change curricula, far more scholarship has attended to teaching climate change in science and policy disciplines.[4]

Over the past fifteen years, many working in the humanities have been changing this dynamic. For one, scholars and educators in the humanities have long addressed environmental issues, and particularly how to teach such issues in their classrooms. Those working in the field of environmental literary and cultural studies, for instance, have always been, as the ecocritic Greg Garrard puts it, "preoccupied with pedagogy" (1). Crucial scholarship about teaching and learning has also come out of the fields of environmental philosophy and environmental history.[5] More recently, the interdisciplinary field known as the Environmental Humanities developed in part as a response to climate change and its corollaries, such as ocean acidification and mass extinction. The magnitude of these changes has rallied international, interdisciplinary collectives like the Mellon-sponsored Humanities for the Environment observatories, for instance, and the Extinction Studies Working Group, which brings humanities scholars and artists into conversation with natural and social scientists.

Still, even with this emerging emphasis within the humanities on global environmental concerns, the way that humanities teaching is seen from the outside is significantly framed by its relation to scientific disciplines. We do not deny the central importance of technological innovation and policy intervention in response to climate change, and we recognize the wisdom of some of our contributors' calls to begin any humanities course focused on climate change with a brief foundational unit in climate science. Technical analyses in the academy, as in popular culture and political discourse, have publically cast climate change as an engineering problem best suited for study in the fields of applied science or policy-making. In this vein, the humanities may play an important role in making the science and policy histories of climate change accessible through fluent communication skills. Yet as our contributors show, the humanities can do much more than this. The diverse spatial and temporal scales of this "wicked problem" demand more of the humanities than the mere translation of climate science for lay readers. Climate change is wicked in the social planning sense of being a messy, reactive, and difficult-to-define problem, resistant to attempts at tidy, linear solutions. It is also a wicked problem in the moral sense. Consider the profound and fraught questions of meaning, value, and justice provoked by climate change and its diverse effects, from applied ethical problems such as how to distribute reservoir waters in regions affected by drought to social concerns like how to conceptualize indigenous sovereignty when a tribe's physical territory is lost to rising seas or even how to experience pleasure beyond consumerism. Several of our contributors remind us that questions of social justice and the equitable distribution of environmental burdens and goods should be at the center of the concept of sustainability.

Humanities disciplines long dedicated to exploring counterfactuals—the if/then imagination of alternate possible worlds—can be powerful vehicles for navigating the ethical conundrums and cultural unease that come with shifting ecological parameters. In partnership with the social sciences, which are to some degree represented in this volume, the humanities provide an imaginative space and set of critical tools for grappling with issues of power, representation, and materiality. Historical knowledge and interpretive skills help us untangle the oftentimes invisible connections between ordinary structures of feeling, habit, and the political facts of the modern carbon economy that fuels climate change.

All of us include exercises in our classrooms that help students visualize both what might be and map the often invisible infrastructures that organize their material lives. For example, LeMenager gives students the basic research tools for tracing the life cycle of a favorite consumer item. Students use web databases, industry journals, and interviews with company spokespersons to determine their chosen object's impact on climate, workers, and ecosystems. This research becomes the basis of a scholarly detective narrative. Sometimes the student "detective" comes out of the project with a desire to act differently, and to love different, more sustainable things. We recognize that informed consumerism will not save the planet, but learning to research and create narratives about the supply chains and transport systems that structure our worlds fosters a point of view into modern systems that seem opaque to many young people. Simply being able to tell a coherent story about such systems performs a modest social intervention.

From the perspective of the humanities, some of the most pressing questions about climate change have to do with justice and sociality: *who* survives, *who* gets to live well, *how* do we live well together? Climate change is the defining provocation of our time. In homage to the nonfiction writer and activist Naomi Klein, we believe that, indeed, it changes everything. Like it or not, we humans are facing a profound change of story. To live in a world of climate change is to live in a state of disorientation. The mercilessly indifferent forces of physics are challenging taken-for-granted ways of viewing and living in the world. Chief among these worldviews is the assumption that fossil fuels can power our economies indefinitely and without consequence. The familiar landmarks of Western modernity and postmodernity—progress, science, common humanity and material prosperity—are obscured by stranger and stranger weather, leaving us unsure of where we are and where we should go.

Of course, the problem of where to go is a literal one for populations fleeing sinking communities and drought-ridden states. The increasingly visible limits to Earth's carrying capacity and the socio-political unrest that ensues present a strong conceptual dilemma of how to envision peaceful, survivable futures. In this time of climate chaos, we need to transform social, economic, and political systems, and to do so with creativity and strong ethical grounding. Humanities classrooms are important transformative spaces.

Cultivating student agency

By challenging the material and ideological underpinnings of an increasingly global marketplace through profound physical changes, climate change seems a universal and threatening provocation. Yet provocations are also invitations. Students cannot be properly "instructed" in the *correct* education. They can only learn if they freely find truth or falsity in new experiences (materials, questions, subjects). Hence, climate change can be an invitation to both new experience and new thinking, should one be willing to consider and dwell together in its profound implications.

The sociologist and pedagogical theorist Jack Mezirow dubs educational occasions such as these "disorienting dilemmas" (86). Disorienting dilemmas spark initial feelings of discomfort or other unsettled emotions that provide the raw material of productive reflection and re-orientation through a process of planning, experimentation, and adaptation. From such dilemmas can grow transformative learning, through which students question and change taken-for-granted assumptions and forge new beliefs. This dynamic educational process allows one to make meaning by elaborating on existing beliefs, to change perspectives and approaches to beliefs, or to take up new beliefs entirely (Mezirow 84). On the other hand, as Kari Norgaard's groundbreaking work on climate change denial makes clear, these same unsettled emotions can cause well-informed people to minimize or ignore climate change. We find the tension between climate change's motivating and demotivating forces crucial to understanding the interventions the contributors to this volume make to engage students across humanities disciplines. That is, the distressing realities of climate change constitute both obstacle and incitement to student engagement.

This central challenge climate change poses to student learning became clear to Shane Hall when he administered to his introductory environmental studies students a survey at the start of a term. In response to the survey questions, "What concerns do you have at the start of this course? What obstacles do you foresee yourself facing?" one fifth of the 60 students surveyed noted that they were concerned that the "depressing" nature of the topic of study would cause them to disengage from the class and stop learning. These "depressed" souls were by and large first year students who had elected to take Hall's class. Similar examples of crisis fatigue came up in Stephen Siperstein's "Intro to Cli-Fi" course, which also included mostly first year students new to the social and political impacts of climate change. Throughout the term, students posted to a public class blog. Many of their posts captured the general mood of the course, with titles like "Is There Any Hope?", "Why Global Warming Scares Me" and "The Pits of Despair." Yet in these and other assignments, students did not merely dwell in their negative feelings. They used them as spurs to new forms of agency and action, which they tried out in the classroom community.

These anecdotes are indicative of the intellectual curiosity and fortitude of our students. They elected to take our courses and to engage in them. In their frank admissions of fear or hopelessness, we see teaching and learning opportunities. The same aspects that make climate change at first glance difficult to teach—its multi-scalar and multi-temporal complexity, its political and ideological baggage, its plethora of ugly feelings—are precisely what makes it relevant and meaningful to a wide range of students. In this volume, many of our contributors speak directly to why they feel motivated to continue working with students to find a moral compass and an imagined, livable future within this wicked problem that is widely recognized—most recently by the Catholic church—as the leading social, ecological, and spiritual crisis of our time. The relevance of climate change to students' lives and interests makes learning about it intrinsically valuable.

Much as we might hope that the college or university classroom offers our students a primary context for making meaning, we realize that often they identify more with groups outside of the academy, for example with their places of worship, athletic teams, or Reserve Officers' Training Corps (ROTC) units. Using course materials about how to redress the effects of climate change that are generated by non-academic authors, like the U.S. Navy, the insurance industry, or a consortium of evangelical churches, may give such students license to think seriously about climate change and to remain consonant with their core values, as one of our contributors demonstrates in his discussion of culturally conservative source materials. These unexpected sources serve as models of how climate change can be understood outside of polarizing political debate. As several of our other contributors suggest, there is also great potential in engaging students with creative texts that aren't explicitly about climate change, like environmentally themed Hollywood films, science fiction novels, and comics series. Popular culture that approaches climate change indirectly is crucial for connecting climate change and related issues to students' interests in entertainment and the arts.

However, it is not enough for a student to recognize the enormity of climate change and its import to their personal communities or values in order for that student to engage meaningfully, for instance to continue thinking or taking action once a particular course comes to an end. While humanities classrooms often brim with the playful energies endemic to disciplines in which counterfactual thinking is valued, nonetheless we find ourselves, when teaching about climate change and contemporary culture, shadowed by despair—sometimes that despair is our students', and sometimes it is our own. Despair dampens the desire to teach and to learn, as it challenges empowerment as well as communal efficacy. Doris Sommer, a scholar of Latin American Studies at Harvard, has described her development toward the socially committed pedagogy she calls "the Engaged Humanities" as stemming from the realization that "teaching despair to young people seemed to me not only tedious but irresponsible compared to making a case for [their becoming] cultural agents" (6). Yet precisely because despair undermines the self, or at least the comfortable habits through which we live our everyday lives, it is often a precondition for fresh thought, new habits, and rethinking the kinds of socio-ecological relationships that generate livable futures.

Fear, anger, and shame are another suite of emotions familiar to teachers of environmental issues in our current moment. Like despair, these emotions can be the raw material out of which knowledge is fashioned. When coupled with dialogue and reflection, they can incite us to take up approaches to engaging our students as cultural agents with the capacities to create small shifts of perspective and practice (Sommer 4). Many contributors remind us that climate change represents only one among many current causes of our students' fear, anger, and shame. Two of our contributors who co-taught a religious studies course note how their Baltimore classroom responded to the murder by police of a young African American man, Freddy Gray. The murder occurred in Baltimore while the class was exploring the relation of climate change to religious experience. What might have been a semester of frustration in which climate change seemed a far-away problem evolved into a searching discussion about the connections between racism, ecological loss, and insufficiently regulated capitalism, with a consideration of what roles religion and spirituality might play in leading us out of the morass.

The success of this particular example of positive learning in the face of multiple forms of oppression was encouraged by a supportive, courageous learning environment created by both faculty and students. Given that the goal of all transformative learning is "to maximize students' potential for intellectual and emotional growth" (Slavich and Zimbardo 591), course environments need to be considered holistically, including the "intellectual, social, emotional, and physical" space in which learning occurs (Ambrose 170). Several of our contributors speak to this point. Students often face forms of marginalization in and out of the higher education classroom, which may create conditions hostile for their learning. Even small oversights by a teacher can reinforce such marginalization and stifle the learning environment, especially if students do not feel free to express their points of view (Cranton 175–6). One measure by which a supportive course environment can be recognized is the degree to which students are encouraged to steer discussion, or even push back against a professor's lessons. In a recent discussion of cli-fi that emphasizes the sociological problem of "manufactured risk," Stephanie LeMenager stopped her lecture to listen to a student from a tribal community in central Oregon, who raised her hand to suggest that the North America being discussed by the novelist and the professor did not reflect her own cultural history and values. The discussion then turned to intergenerational memory and the ways in which stability, rather than risk, might be considered—and made—norms. The student's comments may have interrupted the lecture, but they expanded the discussion. Since the class already was structured as three mini-lectures with designated stopping points to invite student participation, it had become fairly common for students to raise their hands. In this case, the intervention couldn't wait for the designated discussion period, and that turned out to be good. We want our classrooms to be places where students challenge our own and each other's assumptions about culture, history, and ecology. This example points to the fact that students are never *tabulae rasa*—and, too, that their efforts to teach us, and each other, are invaluable.

At the University of Oregon, we encounter many undergraduates with keen environmental interests. Yet these interests stem from diverse sources, for instance from family businesses in logging, ranching, and fishing, from hunting with their families or tribal members, or from countercultural environmentalism. We understand that each of these ways of caring about the environment merits our respect. If treated as valuable on its own terms, each can generate conversation about how best to live together as we endure regional climate shifts that already affect our snowpack, rivers, farms, and coastal fisheries. These encounters underscore the need to take care to know who our students are and where they come from, and to recognize that instructional methods must vary depending upon answers to these questions.

In and out of the classroom, students themselves maintain the vibrancy of the cultural practices central to the humanities. Yet it is the educator's role to scaffold curricular objectives to encourage students to develop and practice their cultural agency. One method of supporting cultural agency that we editors are committed to is storytelling. Stephen Siperstein even co-developed a digital climate storytelling project (The Climate Stories Project) and related curriculum that showcases witness accounts of climate change throughout the world. Encouraging students to craft and share publically their own stories is important for promoting their recognition of themselves as scholars and planetary citizens. All three of the editors have invited students into exercises of collective storytelling about what life might be like in an altered climate future, using the transmedia storytelling project FutureCoast, which was created by the game designer Ken Eklund through the Columbia University Climate Center's Polar Partnership. Undergraduates composed and published "voicemails from the future" on the FutureCoast website. The voicemails are spoken narratives that imagine local climate shifts and playfully think through means of mitigation, remediation, and endurance. LeMenager incorporated FutureCoast into a two-hundred student Introduction to Environmental Studies, and the project allowed students in Siperstein's and Hall's smaller seminars a first foray into writing cli-fi. Hall uses the "utopia" concept as a prompt to help his students think critically as they write fictional blueprints for an ecologically and socially sustainable world, and to reflect on the ethical grounding of such worlds. Since "perfect" worlds are never actually perfect, critical thinking about utopia helps us trouble-shoot possible futures. Many of our contributors speak to how such motivating, creative activities can be offered across different disciplinary contexts and course designs.

The stories that students and teachers co-create can begin to build alternatives to the doomsday narratives or delusional techno-optimisms often associated with climate change in popular culture. If the world is indeed unraveling, what will we (re)weave with the threads? Will such future tapestries be sustainable, resilient, and just? Will they be encompassing enough to welcome all creatures into their compassionate folds? This work of re-making is well-suited to the humanities. Teaching can be a kind of weaving, a stitching together of communities both within and beyond the classroom. Teaching climate change in the humanities, with attention to representations and mediations, histories and ethics, material artifacts and cultural forms, can push us through despair, perhaps, and toward the social practice of caring—a practice not identical to hope but at the least embedded in relationships with other humans and other life, relationships that compel us to place questions of justice and of collective survival at the forefront of our thinking.

A guide to the volume

We have organized the chapters in this collection to make navigation practical and user friendly. In particular, we recognize that readers may be coming to this book with different backgrounds and experiences in teaching climate change. For example, one reader might be looking for ways to incorporate climate change or any relevant environmental content into a course for the first time. Another reader might approach this volume as an inveterate teacher of environmental topics and themes and yet want to rethink approaches to teaching climate change as its effects and threats become more visible and encompassing.

The volume's first part, Who We Are, showcases exemplary versions of a kind of academic writing that we, at least, had rarely encountered in our careers prior to editing this book. The chapters in this section reflect upon what it means to be a teacher in the era of climate change, about how professional careers, understandings of expertise, and even the emotions present in the classroom are affected. The contributors to this section write about curricular and program building around global climate change, as SueEllen Campbell has done, about the ways in which their own privilege entangles them in the structures of petro-capitalism that undergird climate collapse, as Imre Szeman suggests in a wry "letter" on the subject, and about how professors need to act as mentors to our students and seek out mentors for ourselves, perhaps in the sciences or within communities of activism—this latter being the topic of James Engell's eloquent chapter. Indeed, we confront climate change as teachers, students, mentors, mentees, privileged subjects, oppressed subjects, or entangled subjects, a term that might please Stacy Alaimo, who found her intellectual insights entangled, for her students, with the fate of an European newt. Cultural geographer Robert Wilson turns his undergraduates' apparent apathy about climate change into a soul-searching investigation into how to combat the paralyzing emotions that come into play as students learn more about climate change. The contributors in this first section write with reflective, personal voices, sometimes with multiple voices in the same chapter, as with the group of scholars who write for us from the University of Warwick. Doing this gives them space to step back from specific courses or texts and consider larger questions of what it means to be a teacher and student in a climate change classroom, or, even more broadly, what it means to teach and learn climate change within institutional environments still largely invested in fossil fuels and in unjust structures of student debt and part-time faculty labor.

While the chapters in this first section reflect movingly on what it means to be a teacher in this unprecedented ecological moment, the second two sections of the volume speak to teaching and learning climate change directly and indirectly in specific curricula and course contexts. Readers interested in developing or rethinking classes focused upon global climate change will appreciate the chapters in the part Teaching and Learning Climate Change Head On. The chapters in this section treat methods, classes, and case studies involving teaching climate change in the humanities. This part offers our widest range of disciplinary approaches, from J. Baird Callicott's sharp thinking about how climate change alters his approach to ethical philosophy to Felix Reide et al.'s multidisciplinary, team-taught class on eco-cultural collapse to Heather Houser's careful guidance about how humanities teachers might use climate data visualizations. The work of Mark Carey, Kathy Lynn, Kevin Hatfield, and Jennifer R. O'Neal to decolonize climate change research by partnering with indigenous thinkers and communities presents a powerfully innovative model for climate change education. Individually, these essays provide fascinating case studies of the ways climate change can be taught using different methods and approaches in the humanities and in educational contexts ranging from Greg Garrard's large undergraduate generalist course to Nicole Merola's design studio, where she teaches climate change through literary study and material fabrication. Collectively, these essays offer a glimpse of how climate change as a wicked problem has prompted creative thinking and teaching across humanities curricula.

Teaching Climate Change Sideways presents contributors who write about how to include climate change in courses and disciplines that are not directly "about" climate change per se. As climate change becomes a more central topic within popular and academic culture, it spreads across disciplines and demands notice within educational contexts that long precede widespread concern about it. Contributors to this section have found ways to bring climate change into disciplinary and topical discussions that could easily exclude it, thereby enriching students' understanding of both climate change and other topics of study within— in this section—anthropology, American studies, classics, film and media studies, and literary and cultural studies. For Swayam Bagaria and Naveeda Khan, the anthropological study of religious experience in European and South Asian contexts became an almost accidental means of addressing the effects of climate change on cultures in the global south, whereas Darragh Martin deliberately seeks out means of making his Classics courses ecologically relevant by incorporating climate-change-related themes into the reading of texts such as Ovid's *Metamorphoses* and the Book of *Genesis*. By contrast, Cheryll Glotfelty, who has long experience in teaching how literary texts reflect and generate environmental meaning, chooses to teach climate change indirectly because she finds that restoration, as an environmental and aesthetic project, offers a more manageable scale of action, and hope, for her students. Similarly, Stephanie Foote's innovative course about the environmental impacts of garbage connects relatively familiar and manageable practices of waste disposal to global-scale economic imperatives that are drivers for climate change. All of the authors in this section suggest ways to make climate change a part of curricula designed for other purposes.

While the preceding chapters offer up a plethora of useful texts, case studies, assignments, and curricular models, the contributions that constitute our final section emphasize rich archives for climate change teachers. The chapters in Archives and Contexts offer up texts that prompt strong discussion and historical contexts critical to understanding climate change as a problem of social resistance, global extinction, and environmental injustice to the world's indigenous communities and its poor. Patrick Murphy makes an invaluable contribution by outlining an archive of texts that have proven successful in culturally conservative student communities, including military documents treating climate change response strategy. Wai Chee Dimock uses the classic environmental text *Walden* by Henry David Thoreau to launch a tour de force exploration of how bio-acoustic archives can help us measure rates of extinction, while Hsinya Huang and Emily Potter examine how indigenous communities consider climate change within centuries of colonialist threats to their sovereignty, in East Asia and Oceania. The archive of world literature that both Huang and Potter address, from Taiwan and Australia respectively, becomes the broad topic of Karen Thornber's chapter, while Peder Anker further internationalizes the collection with an historical account of how Norway's oil culture contributes to contemporary understandings of sustainability.

Looking forward

We hope these essays offer ideas and inspiration for more interdisciplinary and international work across the humanities on the problem of how to address and respond to climate change. While the examples put forth by our contributors are relevant to educators across the humanities, no volume can be fully representative. We recognize that voices from literary and cultural studies are present in greater numbers than those from other humanities fields—and yet even this strong showing does not capture the many potential iterations of teaching climate change in these subjects. We recognize, too, that a collection like ours invites further response from pedagogical theorists.

We want this volume to spur more innovation and dialogue, to call forth questions and experiences that will continue expanding what we call the culture of climate change, by which we mean the culture of our contemporary moment and, we imagine, our future.[6] We hope that the cultural knowledge of the humanities can help us to anticipate what is not yet known and to endure it with civility, justice, and grace. Finally, as Bill McKibben reminds us in his Afterword to the volume, we write to spur thinking and acting outside of the classroom—to make clear that the work of higher education opens into contexts of protest, advocacy, and world building.

Notes

1   When *New York Times* reporter Richard Pérez-Peña expressed interest in doing a story about the course, subsequently sat in on a weekly seminar meeting, and later featured the course in his article "College Classes Use Arts to Brace for Climate Change," we

recognized what others perhaps had been feeling for quite some time already: that climate change education needed the humanities.

2   We would also like to acknowledge the contributions of seminar members April Anson, Aylie Baker, Anna-Lisa Baumeister, Timothy Chen, Jenny Crayne, Liz Curry, M Jackson, Tyler McGuire, Taylor McHolm, Mike Ossiff, Jaleel Reed, Rachel Rochester, and Harrison Stevens.

3   The Obama administration's recent Climate Education and Literacy initiative doesn't mention the humanities (or for that matter, the social sciences) as playing a large or important role in such education.

4   Notably, the recent volumes *Universities and Climate Change: Introducing Climate Change to University Programmes* (Walter Leal Filho, Springer 2010), *Education and Climate Change: Living and Learning in Interesting Times* (Fumiyo Kagawa and David Selby, Routledge 2010), and *Climate Change Education Knowing, Doing and Being* (Chang Chew Hung, Routledge 2014) usefully nod to the importance of the humanities in developing climate change curricula, but do not explore its sub-disciplines or pedagogical approaches in depth.

5   Ecocriticism, or green cultural studies, has a long history of research focused specifically on teaching, with Garrard's edited volume being only the most recent in a long line of important teaching-focused work, such as the landmark 2008 volume edited by Laird Christensen, Mark C. Long, and Frederick O. Waage, *Teaching North American Environmental Literature*. Important publications about teaching environmental history include Foltz, Stroud, and Stewart's "Environmental History: Profile of a Developing Field"; Schwartz's "Teaching Environmental History: Environmental Thinking and Practice in Europe 1500 to the Present"; Corey's "Pedagogy and Place: Merging Urban and Environmental History with Active Learning"; and Stroud's "Under the Field: Dead Bodies in the Classroom." Finally, see the pedagogical contributions to *The OAH Magazine of History* special issue "Environmental History Revisited" 25:4 (2011). One of the most important teaching-focused works in the field of environmental philosophy is the 2006 volume *Teaching Environmental Philosophy*, edited by Clare Palmer.

6   This idea of the "culture of climate change" originated in a graduate seminar titled "Cultures of Climate Change" and taught by Stephanie LeMenager at the University of Oregon in Winter 2014.

References

Ambrose, Susan A. *How Learning Works: Seven Research-based Principles for Smart Teaching*. San Francisco, CA: Jossey-Bass, 2010. Print.

Chew Hung, Chang. *Climate Change Education Knowing, Doing and Being*. New York: Routledge, 2014. Print.

Christensen, Laird, Mark C. Long, and Frederick O. Waage. *Teaching North American Environmental Literature*. New York: Modern Language Association of America, 2008. Print.

Corey, Steven H. "Pedagogy and Place: Merging Urban and Environmental History with Active Learning." *Journal of Urban History* 36.1 (2010): 28–41. Print.

Cranton, Patricia. *Understanding and Promoting Transformative Learning: a Guide for Educators of Adults*. San Francisco, CA: Jossey-Bass, 2012. Print.

Foltz, Richard C. "Does Nature Have Historical Agency? World History, Environmental History, and How Historians Can Help Save the Planet." *The History Teacher* 37.1 (2003): 9–28. Print.

Foltz, Richard C., Ellen Stroud, and Mart A. Stewart. "Environmental History: Profile of a Developing Field." *The History Teacher* 31.3 (1998): 351–368. Print.

Garrard, Greg. *Teaching Ecocriticism and Green Cultural Studies*. New York: Palgrave Macmillan, 2012. Print.

Kagawa, Fumiyo and David Selby, Eds. *Education and Climate Change: Living and Learning in Interesting Times*. New York: Routledge, 2010. Print.

Klein, Naomi. *This Changes Everything: Capitalism vs. the Climate*. New York: Simon & Schuster, 2014. Print.

Leal Filho, Walter. *Universities and Climate Change: Introducing Climate Change to University Programmes*. Berlin: Springer, 2010. Web.

LeMenager, Stephanie. *The Cultures of Climate Change syllabus*. 2014. English Dept., University of Oregon, Eugene, OR. PDF file.

Mezirow, Jack. "Learning to Think Like an Adult: Core Concepts in Transformation Theory." *Handbook of Transformative Learning*. Eds Edward Taylor and Patricia Cranton. San Francisco, CA: Jossey-Bass, 2012. 73–96. Print.

Muir, John. *My First Summer in the Sierra*. 1911. New York: Dover Publications, 2004. Print.

Norgaard, Kari. *Living in Denial: Climate Change, Emotions, and Everyday Life*. Cambridge, MA: MIT UP, 2011. Print.

Palmer, Clare, Ed. *Teaching Environmental Ethics*. Boston: Brill Publishing, 2006. Print.

Slavich, George M. and Phillip D. Zimbardo. "Transformational Teaching: Theoretical Underpinnings, Basic Principles, Core Methods." *Educational Psychology Review* 24.4 (2012): 569–608. Print.

Sommer, Doris. *The Work of Art in the World: Civic Agency and Public Humanities*. Durham, NC: Duke UP, 2014. Print.

Stroud, Ellen. "From Six Feet Under the Field: Dead Bodies in the Classroom." *Environmental History* 8.4 (2003): 618–627. Print.

Part I
Who we are

1 Making climate change our job

SueEllen Campbell

4%

I want to begin with a number. As of March 2015, only 4% of Americans hear a friend or relative talk about climate change at least once a week (Leiserowitz 10). Four percent.

Imagine yourself in a grocery store with another hundred shoppers. This week, ninety-six of them won't hear about this topic from anybody they know. In an average group of twenty-five students, only one talks about it once a week. Only four do so once a month.

Why is this? Our brains aren't wired for this topic: it's abstract, seemingly distant, too big. We worry we can't answer important questions or deal with misinformation. We avoid touchy issues of politics, ideology, religion, and cultural and personal identity. Above all, we find it deeply unsettling.

Climate change, therapist Rosemary Randall writes, is "a disturbing subject that casts a shadow across ordinary life." Like other social taboos, it can cause conflict and embarrassment; it "can raise fears and anxieties that people feel have no place in polite conversation." It provokes many defense mechanisms. In the words of another therapist, Renee Lertzman, these include "denial (it's not going to affect me or my kids; the science is not settled), projection (it's their fault, not mine), paralysis, apathy and disavowal (I know this is happening, but I am going to continue doing what I do anyway). When we trigger anxieties we almost always inadvertently trigger defenses—and when it comes to climate change these defenses act on everyone from greenie urban liberals to climate science naysayers." Note Lertzman's "everyone."

No wonder we don't like to talk about it. And yet it is certainly our greatest global problem.

We must help break this silence.

Learn a lot and take it personally

Once I heard Susan Joy Hassol talk about climate change communication, a field in which she is a leader. When she finished, someone asked a version of the most common question after climate change talks: "What do you say to people who ask you what they can do to help?" She answered, "I tell them to learn a lot and take it personally."

Perhaps this answer resonated for me because it describes my own path. Elizabeth Kolbert's 2005 *New Yorker* series and subsequent book, *Field Notes from a Catastrophe* (2006) shocked me into serious attention. By the time the 4th assessment of the Intergovernmental Panel on Climate Change appeared, my husband and English-department colleague John Calderazzo shared my concern, and one day that spring of 2007 we found ourselves sitting at our kitchen table trying to think how we could help. Within days we'd started planning what turned into an education and outreach program we called Changing Climates @ CSU.

Right away, we decided to work around the institutional edges. We gathered friends, acquaintances, and folks we'd only heard about for a pair of brainstorming sessions—and collected way too many ideas. Then we planned a semester-long lecture series, faculty speaking to faculty, sixteen speakers covering topics like how the climate system works, diseases that will spread with warmer temperatures, and potential impacts on farmers in the US and East Africa. We scheduled these talks for late Tuesday afternoons, advertised them only on campus, and averaged eighty listeners per talk—some of whom, to our surprise, were key climate researchers from different departments who were just then meeting each other. The next year we ran a revised series, advertised widely as Thursday-evening public lectures, "Climate Change: What We All Need to Know," eight speakers on climate science, biological and ecological effects, economics, the literary imagination, effects on people, politics and policy making, and energy solutions. This time our audiences averaged 250.

Late that first fall we started getting forwarded emails about a national climate change teach-in to be held in late January. After some resistance, we organized two days of talks that year and the next, adding other topics: visual art, national security, impacts in the Rocky Mountains, how to talk to skeptics, and so on. A few events since have brought our total to nearly 120 talks given by over 110 different speakers—speakers from twenty-eight academic departments and every college on campus, plus other entities at CSU, in town, in the region, and farther away. We've counted well over six thousand heads in our audiences.

How could two English professors pull this off? It just took time, energy, and commitment. You can read the details in our essay "Changing Climates @ Colorado State: A 'How To' Guide." Short version: it helped that we knew our way around campus; that several of John's former students worked in administration and PR; that he is comfortable on the phone while I can organize topics into logical sequences and create complicated schedules. It helped, we heard, that we had no scientific turf to protect; one scientist friend told us he was embarrassed that it took English teachers to make these conversations happen.

We kept things simple, did a lot by ourselves, and manna fell from heaven: people like our dean, the vice president for research, and the university president's assistant gave us money or helped us get funds we didn't know existed. More important, many people helped us without charge. Almost all our speakers donated their work. We paid to print posters, but a friend designed them. Modest refreshments and a few rooms cost us, but most rooms on campus didn't. The student center and the campus teaching and learning center donated videotaping. We relied heavily on the university's PR apparatus—and on word-of-mouth advertising. Our total expenses were so low that virtually any university or college could afford them.

We also found the leaders of a climate research center (CMMAP, the Center for Multiscale Modeling of Atmospheric Processes) that happened to be headquartered on our campus. They wanted to expand their education and outreach activities, and their excellent long-term funding from the National Science Foundation allowed them to adopt us after our first year. By buying us course release time, they helped us find the time and energy to keep going after those first two exhausting, rewarding years.

We've stopped running lots of lectures now; others on campus have taken on this job. Instead, we've been helping scientists who want to speak more clearly to the general public. And, with targeted help from colleagues, we (mostly I) run a multidisciplinary climate change website, *100 Views of Climate Change*, intended primarily for college teachers, their students, and interested non-specialist adults. This collection of annotations and links crosses the curriculum, from climate science to art, ecology to activism, misinformation to wild weather. The sources are accessible and reasonably lively, with college-level content and primer-level clarity. This is one good place to learn a lot.

I also still recommend Kolbert's book, along with the comprehensive, user-friendly website for the 2014 U.S. National Climate Assessment; Robert Henson's excellent primer, *The Thinking Person's Guide to Climate Change* (2014); Tim Flannery's *The Weather Makers* (2005) for a southern hemisphere focus and lots about biology; and Mike Hulme's *Why We Disagree about Climate Change* (2009), a heady consideration of just how "wicked" the problem is. I point to the *Skeptical Science* website and to *The Psychology of Climate Change Communication*, a 2009 report from Columbia University's Center for Research on Environmental Decisions. Having learned that universities are full of people happy to answer questions, visit classes, and otherwise share their knowledge, I also consult colleagues across campus.

There is *so* much knowledge available to us, once we step through evasion into curiosity and determination.

One key thing to learn is how enormous the difference is between our possible futures. If, collectively, we do nothing different, if we stick with what is called BAU, or business as usual, then we face a global temperature rise during this century of perhaps 5°C. (As my climate scientist friend Scott Denning explains, for inland, temperate-zone, northern-hemisphere places like Colorado, this means roughly 14°F: hot summer days of 109°, not 95°.) Globally, the World Bank reports, "A 4°C world is likely to be one in which communities, cities and countries would experience severe disruptions, damage, and dislocation, with many of these risks spread unequally" (World Bank 19). More severe floods, droughts, heat waves, and hurricanes; biodiversity and crop losses; inundated coasts, acidified oceans, and dead coral reefs: such problems might be beyond our adaptive capacity.

If we act aggressively, though, we might see a rise of just 2°C (or about 6°F in Colorado), not good, but much, much better. Perhaps more to the point, a very large space divides these two scenarios. The choice of what we do, and thus the world we will be living in, this choice is ours—ours collectively, as a gathering of individuals.

And taking all this information personally? I suspect that this next step is inevitable. Climate change is, after all, everybody's business.

Still, there are so many versions of evasion. It is so easy to think, or feel, that it can't be real, then be blindsided by a piece of news. One day last year, for instance, I read (in a World Wildlife Fund report) that in just the last forty years, the number of mammals, birds, amphibians, and fish on Earth has dropped by over half. Habitat loss and human hunger are the first two culprits, but climate change is the third. Another day I was shown a map of the western states illustrating projected increases in area burned every year for each degree Celsius in global temperature rise (National Research Council 41). The space around my own home in Colorado— where in 2012 one huge wildfire stopped a half mile away—was split between the scarlet of 393%, for the grassy plains, and the brown of 658%, for the forested mountains. At such moments, my stomach clenches, my heart pounds, and I can't catch my breath. I try to sit still, let my feelings unfold, and remind myself that real caring encompasses fear and grief. I think about what courage and authentic hope might entail. Then I get back to work.

This is what taking climate change personally means to me.

That's not my job

A few years ago, my friend Nina Bjornsson went to a talk given by cultural theorist Slovaj Žižek at the University of Iceland. He spoke about the damaged climate and how simplistic thinking will eventually doom the human race. After he finished, she waited in line to ask, not surprisingly, "What can we do?" His answer? "That's not my job."

Like many others in the academic humanities, Žižek saw his job as illuminating the problem, not trying to solve it. In departments of English and in cultural studies, at least, this premise is central to our BAU. We so often focus on what is wrong. We analyze, critique, interrogate, problematize. We blame gigantic faceless forces: corporations, capitalism, neoliberalism. We talk about how everything is constructed—by faceless forces. As another cultural critic, Bruno Latour, points out, "entire PhD programs are still running to make sure that good American kids are learning the hard way that facts are made up, that there is no such thing as natural, unmediated, unbiased access to truth, that we are always prisoners of language, that we always speak from a particular standpoint, and so on, while dangerous extremists are using the very same argument of social construction to destroy hard-won evidence that could save our lives" (227). When we emphasize critical thinking, we may do so at the expense of thinking that is practical, compassionate, and creative.

Climate change is a problem for our BAU in other ways, too. My department's core subjects are language and texts, not greenhouse gases, international negotiations, or carbon pricing. We typically focus on individuals and small groups of people, not populations, species, or social and political institutions. We tend to discuss rather than lecture, to emphasize interpretation over fact, personal responses over worldly effects. We may feel more comfortable teaching the "controversy" than teaching the facts, a bad idea when controversy is manufactured to obscure the facts. We aren't trained to help students understand climate change or prepare to cope with a disrupted planet—never mind how to transform economies, infrastructures, politics. This hasn't been our job.

If on a global scale BAU is a recipe for very big trouble, can we be complacent about ours? I think we need to admit that sticking to BAU is a kind of denial. We must imagine new job descriptions.

We don't have to start from scratch, but we may want to return to some basics. We can think about and employ the power of words and stories. We don't expect people to always act rationally. We understand about personal identity, how hard it is to change, how much it directs what we do. We know how deeply enmeshed it is with such things as gender, sexuality, race, ethnicity, class, social and cultural structures, ideology, our physical environment. We have learned to talk about these things, even when doing so is scary. We feel comfortable with emotions, beliefs, and values, things numbers can't adequately capture. We pay attention to how people find or make meaning, and how meaning can change. We care about the lived experiences of individuals and communities. We nurture empathy for those who are different from us. We imagine other people's lives, in other places and other times, and other ways of living. We have distinctive ways of thinking that we can bring to the climate change conversation. Once we turn our minds to the task, we too have important things to offer.

We can do this work indirectly. I have asked students to observe how characters in wartime novels respond to crisis, how they adapt to the need to live differently. I have pointed to the way novels like Leslie Marmon Silko's *Ceremony* understand that impersonal disruptions such as prolonged drought also disrupt personal, familial, and cultural identity. In a course on the Dust Bowl, we tried to put ourselves in the place of the real and fictional people we read about. What was it like to watch a farm dry up and blow away, a child suffer with dust pneumonia? Would we have stayed home or taken off for some place the rain still fell? Would our hope have been realistic, our disappointments paralyzing? What would it be like to become a refugee in an unwelcoming place—or watch our own towns fill with strangers needing housing and jobs?

Hundreds of literary works, I now see, offer sites for contemplating what happens when the world changes around us, shaking our understandings of who we are and what we should do. Many suggest ways to find strength and resilience in ourselves and in others. Some show us how cultural changes actually occur, despite opposition and inertia; they can teach us what it means to be agents for change. We can easily add ideas relevant to climate change to a wide variety of literature courses.

In writing classes, both expository and creative, we can urge students to think creatively and rigorously about how to make a better future. One of my colleagues,

Tom Conway, gives his advanced composition classes a "spaceship Earth" assignment based on work by Buckminster Fuller and Paul Hawken. His students research, design, and write about life on a city-sized spaceship "with the overall goals of sustainability and flourishing in mind"—and then they consider how their best ideas might be enacted on *this* Earth.

In my environmental literature courses, I tackle the subject of climate change directly. Starting at midterm in my most recent such course, we worked our way in this order through the following. First, *Chasing Ice*, a powerful documentary film about photographer James Balog's project tracking receding glaciers. When the film ended, my students sat in stunned silence, and I promised I would help them move past that state of shock. Second, *Field Notes from a Catastrophe*, for solid information. Third, Doug Fine's *Farewell, My Subaru*, a short, funny account of going off the grid that lightens the mood and suggests how small personal actions can lead to larger, more effective ones. Fourth, biologist Carl Safina's account of a year spent mostly on the tip of Long Island, *The View from Lazy Point*. With its impressive mix of personality, science, philosophizing, polemic, and lyricism, with its balance of good news and bad, this book energizes students.

Finally, we read some essays I think of when I feel worst about climate change: two pieces that confront its emotional impact, Rosemary Randall's "The Id and the Eco" and Ray Scranton's "Learning to Die in the Anthropocene"; pieces about citizen activism by Terry Tempest Williams, Bill McKibben, and Audrey Shulman; essays about ethics by Dale Jamieson and Michael P. Nelson, who suggest we should act not with success in mind but in ways we feel are right; and Paul Hawken's heartening "To Remake the World," with which I showed (on his interactive website) photographer Chris Jordan's "E Pluribus Unum," an image of Hawken's index of grassroots groups working toward a better world. All these texts offer traditional literature-class topics. But they do much more that matters today.

In these ways and in others, thinking about what I and my students can do about climate change is now the center of my job.

Tell the truth

One day last year I was chatting with a young woman whose name I don't remember. She mentioned how rarely she hears solid information about climate change that isn't sugar-coated. I replied that the research about communicating this topic shows that too much bad news, however accurate, makes listeners shut down, and so, hoping to be heard, many people soften their messages. She cut in with words that I keep hearing: *Tell the truth!*

The truth has many parts. In this case, the setting is important. It was September 2014, and we were painting signs on a rooftop in Brooklyn, working with volunteers from all over the country to prepare for a climate change march. She had come from Utah, I from Colorado. She was a snowboarder and an activist; I an introverted English professor. She must have been less than half my age. We were two tiny points in a very large gathering.

The People's Climate March turned out to be enormous, a gathering of not the thirty or forty thousand the New York City police expected, not the hundred thousand the organizers dreamed of, but something like four hundred thousand people. Those who carried the signs we had painted, bright orange life rings stenciled with the names of communities hit hard by Superstorm Sandy, led the march. So many people filled the streets of downtown Manhattan that it was hours before the end of the line could begin to walk.

The optimism, energy, and commitment in that gathering were stunning and contagious. And they remain critical parts of the unfolding story of climate change: the agency we can own, the power of creativity and community. So I keep learning this story. I keep taking it personally. I try to tell the truth. And I make it my job to talk about it.

References

Campbell, SueEllen, and John Calderazzo. "Changing Climates @ Colorado State: A 'How To' Guide." Posted on 100 Views of Climate Change: http://changingclimates.colostate.edu/docs/ChangingClimatesHowTo.pdf.

Conway, Thomas. "Writing Arguments: Spaceship Earth Assignment." Posted on 100 Views of Climate Change: http://changingclimates.colostate.edu/humans2.html.

Hawken, Paul. "To Remake the World." *Orion*, May–June 2007. Web.

Jamieson, Dale. "A Life Worth Living." *Moral Ground*. Eds Moore, Kathleen Dean and Michael P. Nelson. San Antonio, TX: Trinity University Press, 2010, 183–88. Print.

Latour, Bruno. "Why Has Critique Run out of Steam? From Matters of Fact to Matters of Concern." *Critical Inquiry*, 3.2, 2004, 225–48. Web.

Leiserowitz, Antony, E. Maibach, C. Roser-Renouf, G. Feinberg, and S. Rosenthal. *Climate Change in the American Mind: March 2015*. Yale University and George Mason University, New Haven, CT: Yale Project on Climate Change Communication. Web.

Lertzman, Renee. "Breaking the Climate Fear Taboo." *Sightline Daily*, 12 March 2014. Web.

McKibben, Bill. "Something Braver Than Trying to Save the World." *Moral Ground*. Eds Moore, Kathleen Dean and Michael P. Nelson. San Antonio, Texas: Trinity University Press, 2010, 174–77. Print.

National Research Council. *Climate Stabilization Targets: Emissions, Concentrations, and Impacts over Decades to Millennia*. Washington, DC: National Academies Press, 2011. Web.

Nelson, Michael P. "To a Future Without Hope." *Moral Ground*. Eds Moore, Kathleen Dean and Michael P. Nelson. San Antonio, Texas: Trinity University Press, 2010, 458–62. Print.

Randall, Rosemary. "The Id and the Eco." *Aeon*, December 2012. Web.

Schulman, Audrey. "How to Be a Climate Hero." *Facing the Change: Personal Encounters with Global Warming*. Ed. Steven Pavlos Holmes. Salt Lake City: Torrey House Press, 2013, 152–58. Print.

Scranton, Roy. "Learning How to Die in the Anthropocene." *The Stone, New York Times*, 11 October 2013. Web.

Williams, Terry Tempest. "Climate Change: What Is Required of Us?" *Moral Ground*. Eds Moore, Kathleen Dean, and Michael P. Nelson. San Antonio, Texas: Trinity University Press, 2010, 429–33. Print.

World Bank. "Turn Down the Heat: Why a 4°C Warmer World Must Be Avoided." Washington DC: World Bank. 2012. Web.

World Wildlife Fund. *Living Planet Report 2014*. Web.

2 Climate disruption involves all disciplines

Who becomes a mentor?

James Engell

> Thou art no slave
> Of that false secondary power by which
> In weakness we create distinctions, then
> Deem that our puny boundaries are things
> Which we perceive, and not which we have made.
> (William Wordsworth, *Prelude* 1805, Book II, ll. 220–24)

> Lisa and I have discovered that using one discipline to address the environment is not going to work. You have to use them all.
> (William D. Ruckelshaus, first Administrator of the EPA, 1970–73, 1983–85, speaking with EPA Administrator Lisa Jackson, "Living on Earth", Public Radio International, April 16, 2010)

> The ongoing explosive growth of knowledge, especially in the sciences, has resulted in a convergence of disciplines and created the reality, not just the rhetoric, of interdisciplinary studies.
> (Edward O. Wilson, "On General Education at Harvard", 2004)

> "Interdisciplinary" is a ladder-like word created by humanists to climb out of a hole they never should have fallen into in the first place.
> (Wilfred Cantwell Smith, scholar of comparative religions and of Islam, in conversation, c. 1988)

The teaching and research needed to understand and mitigate climate disruption touches many environmental concerns—e.g. biodiversity, energy use, geoengineering, ocean acidification, deforestation, human rights. It involves multiple disciplines—e.g. atmospheric chemistry, oceanography, politics, history, economics, computer modeling, agricultural science, conservation biology, ethics, urban planning. Their "separate" nature erodes. How, then, to approach climate disruption, harnessing the expertise of specialties yet integrating them into the whole of their interactions? The great transition that must occur in the next few decades, weaning humanity off fossil fuels and establishing low-to-zero carbon economies, requires an unprecedented coordination of science, politics, international relations, culture, technology, the arts, religious stewardship, and education.

Who, in this welter of activity, can act as a mentor? To this challenge confronting everyone who engages—from whatever angle—climate disruption, mitigation, and the need to lessen dependence on fossil fuels, this essay offers one answer: we must act as mutual, reciprocally subservient co-mentors. Multiple mentorship pays great benefits, and we need it.

This essay I dedicate to F. Gene Hampton, my first mentor in environmental studies. One of the pioneering teachers in Kansas to teach evolution and ecology, he taught my biology class in 1966–67 at Shawnee Mission South High School in Overland Park. Years before the first Earth Day or national legislation on air, water, and endangered species, he convinced the school district to buy land near the high school as an ecological field station. He taught what was not yet called conservation biology. That year my father died, and Gene Hampton helped me through a difficult time, too. Later, he won awards, including Kansas Teacher of the Year, and almost fifty years later we remain in touch. Much of what I do comes from his inspiration. Despite being worth vast sums, with office parks and housing estates a stone's throw away, the land that he persuaded taxpayers to buy was, when I revisited it in 2014, still a field station.

What, after all, is a mentor? Where does the word come from? Its origin is female, from the goddess of wisdom and the arts, Athena. Even though the historical record of ancient Greece gives scant credit to women for knowledge or education, its mythology and literature, embedded in earlier practices, tell another story. Athena transforms herself into a man named Mentor. With Odysseus away, slowly returning to Ithaka, s/he advises Telemachus, his son. Appearing in Homer's poem, Mentor becomes central in *Les Avantures de Télémaque* (1699) by François Fénelon. Widely translated, it was popular for two centuries. Mentors have much to fulfill: "le sage Mentor" is wise, possesses a capacious mind, tenacious memory, and loves connections between different kinds of knowledge. In short, s/he is interdisciplinary. Loyal over decades, Mentor nurtures, partners with, but doesn't smother youth. When Odysseus returns, Mentor re-establishes peace and accord by running institutional interference and wisely playing academic politics. Whatever we mean by "mentor" stems from an ancient story retold three centuries ago, but relevant as ever.

Today, facing global climate change, peers become mentors. James McCarthy, oceanographer and climate scientist, former president of the American Academy for the Advancement of Science and current Chair of the Union of Concerned Scientists Board of Directors, first talked with me about administrative turbulence at our university. Conversations soon engaged "climate shock" (a phrase we prefer to "climate change"), education, and action. As co-chair of the Intergovernmental Panel on Climate Change (IPCC) Working Group II and a lead author of its 2001 Report, he helped me understand intricacies of climate science and international negotiations that I could not grasp alone. He was key in persuading an organization to which we belong to divest fossil fuel holdings (without financial loss). At a seminar I organized on environmental issues at the National Humanities Center, he showed how climate data involving many elements (e.g. volcanic eruptions, sun cycles, oscillations of ocean temperatures and currents) could be disaggregated to reveal that no element or combination of them accounts for the elevation of global mean temperature. The only reasonable conclusion is that it is causally linked to increased atmospheric carbon dioxide emitted by human activity. Another colleague, James Anderson, opened my eyes to feedback effects of global warming on Earth's cryosphere, the ice systems in Arctic, Antarctic, Greenland, and glacial areas. Jim Anderson also related how thawing land areas in northern high latitudes release methane (he measures this directly), and how climate disruption in North America is newly responsible for loss of stratospheric ozone. Jim Anderson advocates radically revamping science education to show students how chemistry and physics are being played out in Earth's climate system with the highest stakes possible.

Ben Friedman, an economist, co-teaches with me a course on growth, inequality, technology, and evolution. With issues such as climate change, he keenly recognizes that "the net outcome will probably hinge to a large extent on the role played by policy. Even when economic growth fostered by globalization causes living standards to rise, the environment will not simply take care of itself" (Friedman 390). Yet, Ben emphasizes that actual costs of mitigation are reasonable—if we act now. Jim McCarthy outlined risks of rising sea levels in the northeast United States, an area whose geology, ocean currents, and variations in Earth's gravity produce sea level rise faster than many other locations. After Jim presented cost estimates for mitigation over the next decades, Ben calculated that these were feasible and for each person amounted to one cup of coffee per week. No one was reassured, however, when a few months later voters in Massachusetts defeated a sensible measure to peg the state gasoline tax to inflation. It remains at a figure established years ago. As inflation takes its toll the gas tax will decrease—a lesson in politics.

Naomi Oreskes studied the purveyors of skepticism concerning any connection between smoking and poor health. She has found that similar forces, often the same people and politicians, have tried to discredit the link between fossil fuels and climate disruption. She co-authored *Merchants of Doubt* (2010) and, more recently, *The Collapse of Western Civilization: A View from the Future* (2014). The former reveals how organized, highly funded groups try to sabotage even conservative, consensus conclusions of science. This opened my political eyes wider: her research is specific, factual, and, in the case of *The Collapse of Western Civilization*, imaginative, too. That book treats, from a futuristic retrospect, how so many sectors of western society in the twenty-first century ignored the writing on the wall about climate disruption. She made me realize why Aristotle calls politics the master science. Naomi has written, too, about the questionable hope that natural gas will be a decades-long "green bridge" to an economy with lower greenhouse gas emissions.

Students become mentors, too. Courageous, eloquent, and optimistic, Chloe Maxmin, led the movement for fossil fuel divestment at Harvard—as an undergraduate. Tim DeChristopher served time in federal prison, then came to Harvard Divinity School. We appeared on a panel together and so I came to know his work and action. His crime was successfully bidding but not paying for energy contracts (see the film *Bidder 70*). He called attention to giveaways and insufficient regulation of drilling on federal lands. Chloe and Tim, passionate, willing to suffer consequences of civil disobedience, are outspoken in this truth: climate disruption is the overriding, world-historical issue of their generation and, if not addressed, will pass a sentence on all posterity infinitely more harsh than the one Tim served. These are some of my current mentors, individuals whom I met where I teach and write—McCarthy, Anderson, Friedman, Oreskes, Maxmin, DeChristopher—and there are more, including my co-editors of *Environment: An Interdisciplinary Anthology* (2008), Glenn Adelson, Brent Ranalli, and K. P. Van Anglen. Together, they cover science, law, history, including the history of science, and literature.

The point is this: we become a community of mutual, reciprocal mentors, collaborators, when we listen to—and teach, and teach with—those outside our own training and bailiwick. We meet the magnitude of the problem that we face only with the magnanimous dedication of teaching and learning from each other. It's strenuous, and it takes time. But it's exhilarating, and it's now necessary. The end is knowledge; the end of that knowledge is action—establishing a price on carbon, breaking the political capture of the fossil fuel industry, restoring ecosystems, building more efficient cities, enhancing environmental education. With climate disruption, then, we are not mentored singly, but by co-mentors, older and younger, in a process that doesn't end.

Certain designations and fields did not exist a generation ago—some not even a decade ago. Yet, they are anchored in observed phenomena: for example, "environmental restoration," "cultural geography," "environmental justice," and "conservation biology," the last sometimes assumed to originate with a conference in the United States that founded a journal with that name. Yet, such a discipline and publication with that name already existed in Europe—showing that different groups often discover independently an identical need (let credit be spread around). "Ecological economics" is a natural combination. The two words share one origin, *oikos*, ancient Greek for "house." Many fields yoke the results of science with public policy and government. Global climate disruption inflects each one, and each one is needed to deal with that disruption.

The challenge of climate change forces a reconceptualization of disciplines. A discipline, defined with respect to environmental study and, in many ways, with respect to all natural and human activity, is itself a collection of knowledge and skills fused and focused in order to address particular aspects of a total environmental reality that actually forms a continuum. A discipline then has no definitive borders and *can have none*. It has instead zones of contact, multiple interfaces. A single discipline may be said to be like a character in a play: distinct, individual, with a given name, developing over time, clearly one actor, yes, yet ultimately meaningless and without true identify or interest unless witnessed in dramatic interaction with all the other characters, with facts and actions not of its own making, and in its own actions affecting others.

In 2004 I taught a summer course at the University of Colorado on environmental visions in the United States, from Lewis and Clark through Thoreau, Louis Agassiz, Teddy Roosevelt, and Rachel Carson. I could never have done it alone, but was joined by Glenn Adelson, a conservation biologist who now heads the environmental studies program at Lake Forest College, and Patty Limerick, then director of the Center of the American West at the university in Boulder. Only working together could each one of us feel adequate. In 2010, starting online and then in Tokyo, I taught in a seminar on sustainability for college students from North America and Asia with an emphasis on the U.N.'s year of biodiversity. Flying solo was impossible. We had a marine biologist, a terrestrial biologist, and an environmental economist from, respectively, the U.S., Singapore, and Beijing. Interdisciplinary means international, too.

Edward O. Wilson suggests that the way to teach any subject, especially one with many interconnections, is precisely *not* by starting with one small corner and then adding another and another, trying, as it were, to master a jigsaw puzzle by emptying the box and randomly trying to fit pieces together—an ideal way to get discouraged and give up. Wilson says,

> If I learned anything in my 41 years of teaching, it is that the best way to transmit knowledge and stimulate thought is to teach from the top down. Address questions such as "the nature and origin of life, the meaning of sex, the basis of human nature, the origin and evolution of life, why we must die, the origins of religion and ethics, the cause of aesthetic response" and then peel off layers of causation as currently understood, in order to teach and provoke, and in growing technical and philosophically disputatious detail.
>
> (121)

Solving the puzzle means getting the big picture first: look for corner pieces, ask tough questions, study that image on the box cover, get students excited about what the big questions and problems are, *then* drill into detail. Most young people, given a chance and support, will instinctively ask hard questions and seek answers. The more that knowledge *accelerates,* a verb first applied to discovering knowledge in the later eighteenth century (at the dawn of the industrial age and high energy use), the more that refashioning of our teaching should take place at speed, and accelerate, too.

The simple point seems often overlooked. As the conduct of our lives is the arrow point of interacting disciplines, so improvement of that conduct can come *only* from an awareness of how those disciplines interpenetrate, an imaginative projection of how new knowledge and new disciplines interact, finally judged according to values and beliefs. Is such imaginative projection possible? The filmmaker Frank Capra, who studied science in college, made *You Can't Take It With You* in 1938, which includes Jimmy Stewart's character passionately advocating large-scale solar energy. Capra produced *The Unchained Goddess* in 1958, with serious talk of climate disruption from greenhouse gas emissions! The film has animation that shows parts of Florida under water.

In "Why Environmental Studies?" an essay that my co-editors and I wrote, we urge that engaging environmental study means nothing less than "to re-envision liberal education in the arts and sciences" (Adelson et al. 4). Climate disruption makes this more urgent. While we each pursue distinct paths in research and teaching, their *combined* profile redraws the meaning of liberal education; it actually *becomes* one, and this is why it is important to cultivate in colleges the liberal arts *and* sciences, where the conjunction really means connection, not mere addition.

What we are doing can face institutional hurdles, structural impediments, and skeptics. (We missed the boat at Harvard when our General Education program failed to require—did not even mention—environmental education.) The traditional set-up of departments can be a barrier. We need to realign our disciplines, which is hard work, lobbying, and academic politics. If I've learned anything about this process, it's that you've got to stick your neck out. It's largely up to tenured professors to make the case. In conversation, I heard Paul Ehrlich say he didn't want his office to be next to the office or lab of another biologist, and that the worst thing would be for his office to be next to another biologist doing work similar to his own. He envisioned a building where he'd meet a person from political science across the hall, bump into another from cultural studies, take coffee with an historian, and see a nanotechnologist in engineering not far away.

Despite institutional hurdles and the effort needed to run an interdisciplinary program with team teaching, it *is* happening more and more. Environmental education is beginning to occupy the place in curricula it should hold: part of graduation requirements, something every student should study. It's no shame that interdisciplinary education and the sustainable humanities lead to jobs, varied and increasing. This doesn't sully a liberal education; it confirms it. Because environmental study can be inflected many ways—conservation, health, law, teaching, industry and business, engineering, architecture, scientific research, journalism, government and public policy—environmental study favors no one vocation or profession.

This relevance is not personally selfish. As Gus Speth urges near the end of *Red Sky at Morning*, it is needed to create a new environmental *movement,* one with a home in colleges and universities. It means changing teaching, even changing the academic profile of institutions, and certainly changing ourselves. Just as there is what Andrew Beattie and Paul Ehrlich call in their book, *Wild Solutions, How Biodiversity is Money in the Bank,* a natural internet of connection between creatures in ecosystems, so by analogy we can bring our human (and virtual) internet to bear on climate disruption. It's more than the connection of one body of knowledge with others; it's also the connections among groups of people and communities, the networks of nature echoed and replicated in transformed networks of people who will manage and protect those natural networks. The humanities and arts play a significant role. Athena is goddess of the arts.

Any new mission for the academic world, any reconsideration of what it means to be human, any movement to alter human values, is informed by the arts *and* the sciences, by what was once the synonym of "culture" before that word came to mean anything we practice, including the culture of unsustainability. We're in the process of changing ourselves; we're changing our sense of mentors, colleagues, and students. This change won't happen overnight. As with any movement that achieves lasting impact, it must work for decades, though with climate disruption an alarm clock ticking with no snooze button to hit: Athena, a.k.a. Mentor, knew with Telemachus that no minute could be wasted. To such a task each one of us is radically inadequate. Let us mentor one another.

References

Adelson, Glenn, et al., eds. *Environment: An Interdisciplinary Anthology.* New Haven: Yale University Press, 2008. Print.

Beattie, Andrew, and Paul Ehrlich. *Wild Solutions, How Biodiversity is Money in the Bank.* New Haven: Yale University Press, 2001. Print.

Capra, Frank. *The Unchained Goddess*, fourth Capra film in the Bell Telephone Series, 1958. Motion picture. Web. www.youtube.com/watch?v=sqClSPWVnNE&list=PLR9gfw ZcOGtE8nOiF_r_Bmr-nL02gVGla.

Capra, Frank. *You Can't Take it With You.* Screenplay by Robert Riskin, based on the play by George S. Kaufman, Columbia Pictures Corporation, 1938. Motion picture.

Fénelon, François de Salignac de la Motte. *Les Avantures de Telemaque, Fils d'Ulysse.* London: J. Tonson and J. Watts, 1719 (1st edn 1699). Print.

Friedman, Benjamin M. *The Moral Consequences of Economic Growth.* New York: Knopf, 2005. Print.

Gage, Beth, and George Gage. *Bidder 70.* Gage and Gage Productions, 2012. Documentary film.

Oreskes, Naomi. "Wishful Thinking About Natural Gas: Why Fossil Fuels Can't Solve the Problems Created by Fossil Fuels." *TomDispatch*, 27 July 2014. Web. www.tomdispatch.com/blog/175873.

Oreskes, Naomi, and Erik M. Conway. *Merchants of Doubt: How a Handful of Scientists Obscured the Truth on Issues from Tobacco Smoke to Global Warming.* New York: Bloomsbury Press, 2010. Print.

Oreskes, Naomi, and Erik M. Conway. *The Collapse of Western Civilization: A View From the Future.* New York: Columbia University Press, 2014. Print.

Speth, James Gustave. *Red Sky at Morning: America and the Crisis of the Global Environment.* New Haven: Yale University Press, 2004. Print.

Wilson, Edward O., "On General Education at Harvard." *Essays on General Education in Harvard College*, 120–21. Cambridge, MA: President and Fellows of Harvard College, 2004. Print.

3   When the newt shut off the lights

Scale, practice, politics

Stacy Alaimo

Several years ago, before there was much engaging literature on climate change available, I included Mark Lynas's 2004 non-fiction travel narrative, *High Tide: The Truth about Our Climate Crisis* in a few undergraduate environmental literature and film courses. In the prologue Lynas explains that while he understood the science behind climate change, he found it all "a bit too abstract" and "difficult to connect to [his] everyday reality" (xxix). So he embarks upon a three year journey across five contents, "searching for the fingerprints of global warming," interviewing "Mongolian herders, Alaskan Eskimos, Tuvaluan fishermen, American hurricane chasers and a whole Army of scientists" (Lynas xxxiii). While students found much within *High Tide* to be thought-provoking, as well as disturbing, one section in particular stood out. Explaining that there are "serious practical reasons why natural ecosystems can't simply move with a shifting climate," Lynas gives this example: "The great crested newt couldn't move north even if it wanted to—it can't cross the M4 motorway." Somehow it was this sentence—the predicament of one English newt—that had the strongest impact on students in this particular environmental literature course in north Texas. Indeed, it could be said that the newt switched off the classroom lights for the rest of the semester (see Figure 3.1).

The plight of the newt who couldn't cross the road provoked the students to insist that we conduct class in such a way as to minimize our impact on the climate, which suddenly seemed to be the newt's climate. We turned off the lights when we entered the room, pulling up the long, dusty shades and letting the daylight, or the cloudy ambiance, in. Admittedly, this may seem a ridiculously minute incident, a pedagogical moment that would be better served as an anecdote for the pub rather than as an essay. But consider that many of the pedagogical, epistemological, and political challenges of climate change, extinction, and the Anthropocene are, precisely, about scale and the human inability to shift between, connect, and make sense of multiple, interconnected dimensions. Ursula Heise, in her influential book, *Sense of Place, Sense of Planet: The Environmental Imagination of the Global*, argues for an "eco-cosmopolitanism," which envisions "individuals and groups as part of planetary 'imagined communities' of both human and nonhuman kinds" (61). Instead of fostering an "ethic of proximity," eco-cosmopolitanism investigates "by what means individuals and groups in specific cultural contexts have succeeded in envisioning themselves in a similarly concrete fashion as part of the global biosphere"

Figure 3.1 Great crested newt
Source: © Dirk Ercken

(Heise 62). Lynas's tale of the newt was one such means of inciting a stance of eco-cosmopolitanism for one group of students. This infinitesimal yet impassioned action of turning off the lights in the classroom suggests that climate change entails a reconsideration of the ethical and political, as even the smallest actions take place within multiple, scrambled, and interconnected scales. Was the focus on one newt and one light switch a way to gain a conceptual grasp on complex, nearly unfathomable forces and systems? Or was it merely a way to contain the uncontainable, domesticate the devastatingly unthinkable results of climate change and extinction? How can instructors encourage everyday modes of activism, and, at the same time, help students understand the epistemological and political problems posed by interacting, emergent forces that cannot be captured by the plight of say, just one species of newt? And how can climate change pedagogies foster an eco-cosmopolitanism that makes sense of the relations between small, simple practices and the larger domains of politics, policy, and global environmental processes?

In the same chapter that the newt appears, Lynas discusses how everyone who drives a car is complicit in climate change, adding that even worse, the flights he took for this book alone "produced over fifteen tonnes of carbon dioxide" (27). In the sprawling urban, suburban, exurban, and somewhat rural landscapes of north Texas, driving across rather long distances, usually in massive trucks or SUVs, is the norm. Within that wider geography, across which most of us had driven to campus, was the space of our classroom, a fleeting utopian space where business would not go on as usual. Our "enlightened" class often took place in a noticeably dark room.

That sense of the classroom, as a place to experiment with and cultivate alternative modes of being that do not conform to normal routines, to practice even the most minute forms of resistance, is, I think, invaluable for social change. To learn about climate change while wasting electricity is to reassert the assumption that education consists of boxed up bits of knowledge that don't really change anything, that don't really matter. It is to divorce reason from sympathy, analysis from action, ideas from practices, concepts from material realities. And yet, turning off the lights was terribly easy. We did not suffer. We did no community outreach or activism. It would be outrageous to say that turning off the lights for roughly 40 hours in a semester did anything for the crested newt or any other species or particular group of people.

Rather than attempting to deliver a solution to these problems, it would be more valuable, pedagogically, to provide multiple frameworks from ecocultural theories and environmental activism, and then to encourage students to place themselves within these quandaries and develop their own positions and practices. I have occupied several positions regarding similar questions, starting with my critique of the "what you can do at home to save the earth" movements of the early 1990s that I discussed in *Undomesticated Ground: Recasting Nature as Feminist Space* (2000), as a kind of domestication of environmental politics, which placed the burden of environmental crises on "housekeepers," short circuiting wider political engagement and ignoring industry, corporations, and the military, all of which are massively destructive. Forms of direct, everyday environmentalism have burgeoned in the early-twenty-first century, diverging into different modes, from sustainability movements, which tend to be expert-driven, managerial, and depoliticized; to DIY environmentalisms, such as urban chicken keeping or biofuel hacking; to carbon footprint analysis conducted within multiple scales and venues. I have been critical of the anthropocentric, bland, managerial flavor of mainstream sustainability discourse, decrying its construction of "nature" as an inert resource existing for human use. But I did serve as the Academic Co-Chair for the President's Sustainability Committee (while teaching the class) and was charged, among other things, with finding ways to reduce the amount of water and electricity that was used across campus. The university undertook many projects, from Leadership in Energy and Environmental Design (LEED) certified new buildings, to xeriscaping, green roofs, meatless Mondays in the cafeteria, and new academic programs and initiatives. While the university spent millions on new electricity-saving systems, which soon paid for themselves in savings, it was often more difficult to find ways to ensure that simpler things be done, such as switching off classroom lights. Despite the stickers placed next to every light switch on campus, telling people to turn them off, a stroll through nearly any instructional building would reveal the maddening glare of fluorescent light—and its invisible carbon footprint—streaming from most classrooms.

Perhaps the pedagogical moment when the newt turned off the lights reveals a key weakness in mainstream campus sustainability discourses, which attempt to cleanse themselves of the political: they seek to change behavior from the top down, by invoking only the most dry, bloodless, anthropocentric discourses that assume everyone is already on board with the wisdom of saving resources or slow-ing climate change. There is rarely any discussion of such things as species extinction, toxins, environmental racism, or climate injustice. This sort of discourse attempts to hail faculty, staff, and students into obedient, ostensibly non-ideologi-cal practices, but more often, perhaps, sparks disobedience, or fortifies apathy. This is Texas, not Sweden. Individual freedom trumps the broader social or environ-mental good. The campus nickname is, tellingly, the "mavericks." While it would be foolish to draw broad conclusions from one tiny moment, it may be useful to consider that newt again, in the sense that the rational, anthropocentric, expert-driven, resource-based versions of sustainability may not be as appealing as a compelling depiction of the plight of one nonhuman species facing extinction. This not only suggests the value of the humanities, the arts, the imagination, and the potentially transformative nature of the classroom, but also the value of a non-anthropocentric, biophilic, multispecies approach to climate change. Even as Western politics and ethics have been defined exclusively as the domain of the human, it may well be that empathy, compassion, and concern for nonhuman crea-tures may fuel climate change politics, activism, and practices, at least for those of us who are, as Joy Williams calls us, "animal people" (123). The newt, not the command of the official sticker, turns off the lights.

While this pedagogical tale underscores how eco-cosmopolitanism can be moti-vated by concern for nonhuman species, and, at the same time, illustrates the value of the humanities in climate change pedagogy, the question of what constitutes meaningful or significant action remains. Turning off the lights was a sort of private action, enclosed by the classroom—not a political rally, wider campus initiative, or an accessible digital campaign. Could turning off the lights be a sort of environ-mentalist version of neoliberalism in which, as Wendy Brown puts it, "citizenship itself loses its *political* valence" (39). Brown explains that "neoliberal rationality disseminates the model of the market to all domains and activities—even where money is not at issue—and configures human beings exhaustively as market actors, always, only, and everywhere as *homo oeconomicus*" (31). Saving electricity, already associated with saving money, is a domestic(ated) sort of action which positions the subject as an economic actor, even if, following Brown here, the domain is not at all economic, but rather, about decreasing one's carbon footprint or increasing one's cache of environmentalist karma. Is this too cynical or not cynical enough? Like most questions, it could be fruitfully debated by students. But to complicate things further, or to turn back to where we were earlier, we should note that Brown's *Undoing the Demos: Neoliberalism's Stealth Revolution* focuses on rationality, lauding the "powers of knowledge, reason and will for the deliberate making and tending of our common existence" (222). Her perspective is, not surprisingly, quite anthro-pocentric, even when critiquing industrial, GMO and pesticide-laden agriculture that was forced on Iraqis by the U.S. after the war. While climate change and species extinction are mentioned in passing, Brown's conception of the human here is untouched by posthumanism, new materialisms, material feminisms, or environmentalist thought: "With the vanquishing of *homo politicus*, the creature who rules itself and rules as part of the demos, no longer is there an open question of how to craft the self or what paths to travel in life" (41). This humanist notion of discrete, disembodied, rational subjectivity is all too familiar, and readily occupied, as the entire world of environments, ecosystems, xenobiotic substances, interior intra- acting material agencies, and a multitude of nonhuman species become invisible once again, enabling the ascendant human to "rule." The ideal of crafting a self seems immaterial, especially in the face of climate change, extinction, pollution, ocean acidification, social injustice and other planetary crises.

My concern that everyday environmental practices may domesticate environmental politics remains, but it has been joined by another, perhaps contradictory perspective, that environmentalism, environmental justice, environmental health, climate change, and extinction demand immersed, material feminist, new materialist, and post-humanist modes of recasting ethics and politics. I wrote *Undomesticated Ground* from a theoretical position influenced by (feminist) poststructuralism, the post-Marxism of Ernesto Laclau and Chantal Mouffe, and the method of discursive contestation and rearticulation within cultural studies, including that of Stuart Hall. These positions reflect the wider linguistic turn of the 1980s and beyond. My next book, *Bodily Natures: Science, Environment, and the Material Self*, insisted that it was crucial for both environmentalism and feminism to conceive of how discursivity and materiality are interconnected. My conception of transcorporeality in *Bodily Natures* does not separate the domestic from the political, but instead, envisions a crisscrossing, scale-shifting sense of the human as immersed in intra-active material agencies. Transcorporeality disperses "politics" widely and unpredictably across all sorts of spaces and practices. And even across time. Astrida Neimanis and Rachel Loewen Walker propose a "temporal frame of 'thick time'—a transcorporeal stretching between present, future, and past," as an alternative to the "neoliberal progress narratives of controlling the future or sustainability narratives of saving the past" (558). If we find ourselves within thick time, neither fleeting pedagogical episodes nor the vast time scales of climate change are something to leave behind, but instead, become the very temporalities of that which we already are. Practices, as seemingly inconsequential as turning off the lights, become embodied, crystalizing through time, which means that both environmental politics and environmental pedagogies may be extended—even without continual intention and reflection—in ways that are difficult to predict. Do any of those students still turn off the lights?

Postscript

Perhaps those who were in that class have entirely forgotten about that newt by now, or perhaps they are curious about its status. The IUCN Red List places the newt in the "least concern" category, based on data from 2008, noting that water pollution, habitat fragmentation, and collectors (for the pet trade) are threats, with no mention of climate change. However, the May 2012 report "Climate change modelling of English amphibians and reptiles: Report to Amphibian and Reptile Conservation Trust," predicts that, "the vast majority of the country becomes unsuitable with central England becoming unsuitable in the 2050s, followed by the

North and West in the 2080s," adding that "the only gains in climate space are in small pockets of central northern England and in Scotland" (Dunford and Berry 18). No specific highways are mentioned, but the report does recommend increasing "habitat connectivity" so that the newt will be able to survive (Dunford and Berry 20).

References

Alaimo, Stacy. *Bodily Natures: Science, Environment, and the Material Self.* Bloomington, IN: Indiana University Press, 2010.

Alaimo, Stacy. "Sustainable This, Sustainable That: New Materialisms, Posthumanism, and Unknown Futures." *PMLA* 127.3, May 2012: 558–564.

Alaimo, Stacy. *Undomesticated Ground: Recasting Nature as Feminist Space.* Ithaca, NY: Cornell University Press, 2000.

Brown, Wendy. *Undoing the Demos: Neoliberalism's Stealth Revolution.* Cambridge, MA: Zone Books, 2015.

Dunford, R.W. and Berry, P. M. "Climate change modelling of English amphibians and reptiles: report to Amphibian and Reptile Conservation Trust." Oxford: Environmental Change Institute, May 2012, www.eci.ox.ac.uk/research/biodiversity/downloads/ARCTrustFINALReport.pdf.

Heise, Ursula. *Sense of Place and Sense of Planet: The Environmental Imagination of the Global.* New York: Oxford University Press, 2008.

IUCN Redlist. "Triturus Cristatus." www.iucnredlist.org/details/22212/0.

Lynas, Mark. *High Tide: The Truth about Our Climate Crisis.* New York: Picador, 2004.

Neimanis, Astrida and Rachel Lowen Walker, "Weathering: Climate Change and the Thick Time of Transcorporeality." *Hypatia* 29.3, Summer 2014: 558–575.

Williams, Joy. *Ill Nature.* New York: Vintage, 2002.

4 Knowing and not knowing climate change

Pedagogy for a new dispensation

Matthew Kearnes

Introduction

As I draft this paper in a hotel room overlooking the Jardin du Luxembourg in the 6th arrondissement of Paris, a few kilometres away in Le Bourget negotiations for the United Nations Framework Convention on Climate Change (UNFCC) Conference of the Parties (COP 21) are once again occupying the collective imagination. While the world watches, and even dares to hope for ambitious multi-lateral efforts on decarbonisation, climate negotiators are locked away in conference rooms finalising the text of a joint statement, with only the faintest rumours emanating about draft agreement texts. Aside from the official negotiations across the city there are numerous fringe events organised by a plethora of scientific, environmental and cultural organisations. On the way to one such event, I happened to walk past another, an installation by the artist Olafur Eliasson and geologist Minik Rosing entitled *Ice Watch*. Around the Place du Panthéon twelve large blocks of ice, originally harvested from free-floating icebergs in a fjord outside Nuuk, Greenland, were arranged in clock formation, slowly melting in the crisp early December air.[1] Crowds mingled around the ice formation, some touching their surface while others listened to the ice as it creaked and groaned, as the melting formed cracking patterns through these immense hunks of frozen water.

As I listened to Eliasson explain his motivation for the installation I was struck by the theatricality of the work. The slow violence of melting ice and the disappearance of frozen landscapes – with their multitude implications for both human and nonhuman inhabitants – sit alongside what Donna Haraway terms the "tragicomedic" narratives of apocalypse (in this case the ticking of the doomsday clock) as now-familiar tropes in the political aesthetics of climate change (Haraway 1997). Kathryn Yusoff writes that images of melting ice and stranded polar bears have "become mythic and biophysical storyteller[s], figuring the complexities of changing climates and habitat loss, and conjoining the biophysical and emotional worlds of humans and animals" (Yussof 2010, p. 74). These images have, she continues, "become a prosthetic emotional device for testing the water of loss" (Yussof 2010, p. 76). The pathos of the scene in Place du Panthéon is accompanied by the installation's website, which outlines a series of 'climate facts' and their implications for sea ice and glacial ice.

In addition to being an artwork, *Ice Watch* is also perhaps a mode of public education. Overlooked by the Sorbonne and the stateliness of the nearby *grandes écoles*, passing *Ice Watch* was a reminder that the Conference of the Parties (COP) meetings are also sites of intense (and at times overwhelming) pedagogy. The facts of climate change, and their political, economic, and social ramifications are on display all over the city, on billboards, posters, and magazine covers. Indeed a series of 'anti-ads', that ironically mock major world leaders and the greenwashing of major corporations, are plastered over the city's bus shelters.[2] Paraphrasing Brian Wynne, both climate science and politics have become "political art" (Wynne 2010, p. 289), at times playful and at times educative. In the case of *Ice Watch*, the artist's twitter feed invites visitors to come to Place du Panthéon and "Listen to what the ice is telling us!".[3] At the same time, the use of emergency powers, enacted in the wake of a mass shooting only two weeks before the COP21 negotiations and used to place climate activists and campaigners under house arrest and to proscribe where protests and public marches would be permitted (Neslen 2015), is a sober reminder that climate pedagogies are always entangled with climate politics. The stakes are high when performing alternative climate knowledges.

In this brief chapter my contention is that approaching climate change teaching from the perspective of the Environmental Humanities – an emergent disciplinary formation at the interface between the humanities, social sciences and environmental practice (Rose et al. 2012) – is situated in the shadow of these intense pedagogies of climate science, knowledge and politics. Climate teaches us and is being taught to us. Though these pedagogies overlap, a particular disciplinary dispensation – in which the humanities and social sciences have been largely segregated from the science global warming and confined to questions of the 'human dimensions' of environmental change – has largely dominated the pedagogic imagination of climate change (Proctor 1998; Urry 2011).[4]

While this disciplinary dispensation has been the focus of substantial critical reflection (see for example: Castree et al. 2014) that the separation of climate science from climate research in the humanities and social sciences is a work of incredible institutional traction – effectively undergirding the bureaucratic complex of contemporary climate knowledge, politics and policy – with an explicit educational mandate, underlies the challenge for carving out a climate pedagogy from the perspective of the environmental humanities. However, the argument that I hope to develop over the coming pages is that in the difference between the expressive potentialities of environmental change – the fact that climate itself is an agent of embodied and affective pedagogy – and the institutionally segregated pedagogies of global change research we might identify both the space and opportunity for a more satisfying and cosmopolitan dispensation.

Climate pedagogies

Approaching climate change teaching from the perspective of the environmental humanities is situated in the shadow of ways in which an "intensely scientific primary framing of the issue" is combined with an equally intense "economistic imagination and framing of the appropriate responses" (Wynne 2010, p. 291. See also Urry 2011). The educative frame of much climate pedagogy is one in which the publics of climate change are presented as publics that need to be taught, whose attitudes need to be changed, and whose behaviours need to be modified (Chilvers and Kearnes 2015; Shove 2010).

This pedagogic frame is also manifest in the disciplinary breakdown of climate knowledges, which have tended to distinguish 'climate facts' from the 'human dimensions' of environmental change, while shielding from scrutiny the central commitments of contemporary climate politics and policy; i.e. technological substitution and the commodification of carbon (Proctor 1998; Rayner and Malone 1998). This dispensation is most clearly evident in the separation between research concerning the "physical scientific aspects of the climate system and climate change," the "vulnerability of socio-economic and natural systems to climate change," and "options for mitigating climate change through limiting or preventing greenhouse gas emissions" in the three core working groups of the Intergovernmental Panel on Climate Change (IPCC).[6]

Where a more integrated assessment of the entanglement of environmental change with human social orderings and value systems might once have been possible (See for example: Rayner and Malone 1998), this three-way distinction has had the effect of largely separating research efforts along disciplinary lines, while at the same time assuming "an autonomous, reified social world, with inputs and outputs, whose causal mechanisms can be understood from outside" (Palsson et al. 2013, p. 6). While the humanities and interpretive social sciences have recently been embraced in climate pedagogy and practice (Blue 2015; Castree et al. 2014; Hulme 2011), in practice the disciplinary dispensation between the humanities and sciences has continued to exert exceptional influence in framing climate knowledge and the largely techno-economic responses adopted in mainstream climate policy. In recent climate pedagogy (see for example: Adger et al. 2013) the concept of culture performs a mediating role, shaping social responses to environmental change, while explaining public deviance from scientific consensus and simultaneously obscuring the implicit cultural commitments of climate science and politics. In this guise, culture is mobilised for distinctly pedagogic purposes, to institutionalise climate knowledge assessments that are presented as floating free of their historical and normative moorings.

Apocalypse and providence

This disciplinary dispensation – with its heavy reliance on the physical sciences of climate change and largely implicit political, economic and value commitments – matters. As Hulme argues, the partiality of contemporary climate assessment processes set the frame of "what exactly is the climate change 'problem' that needs to be 'solved', and they set the tone for the human imaginative engagement with climate change" (Hulme 2011, 177). Approaching climate change from the perspective of the humanities is therefore not simply an additive move, of adding one more disciplinary perceptive to an already-crowded climate scene. Rather work in Environmental Humanities is oriented toward an opening-up of climate change pedagogy to more diverse and cosmopolitan knowledges, and begins from an acknowledgement of the ways in which the 'idea' of climate – and of climate change – is deeply interwoven with a nested set of social, cultural, and mythological meanings.

Climate and weather are, for example, deeply interwoven with the religious thematics of providence and order. Changes in weather, and climatic instability more generally, are associated with the withdrawal of divine favour and judgement, while the ability to control, predict, and circumvent climatic patterns (often for political or economic gain) is associated with mythical figures afforded the power to control atmospheric phenomena and with miraculous displays of divine omnipotence and pastoral care (Kearnes 2015; Szerszynski 2014).What we see in installations such as *Ice Watch* is the ways in which these narratives of apocalyptic destruction and technologically-mediated resolution continue to be neatly interwoven through the political aesthetics of climate change. Narratives of apocalyptic projection and the promises of technological deliverance are invoked in a globalising project of planetary management and climatic regulation (Lövbrand and Stripple 2006). For example, in their respective histories of the development of climate modelling, both Elichirigoity (1999) and Edwards (2010) demonstrate that the development of contemporary climate knowledge is dependent on and reinforces a projection of the globe as a scale of technocratic management and regulation. Contemporary climate knowledge functions to sustain a uniquely "global knowledge infrastructure" (Edwards 2010, p. 8) while at the same time "becoming deeply enmeshed in the constitutional structure of global environmental governance" (Miller and Edwards 2001, p. 3).

Similarly, when viewed in a longer historical context, the potential for controlling and manipulating climatic systems, for both strategic and military purposes, has remained implicit, and at times explicit, in weather modification research and the development of meteorology and climate science more generally (Cox 2002; Harper 2008). Recent histories of meteorology paint a picture of the field as propelled by a desire to transform itself – from a "guessing science" (von Kármán, quoted in Harper 2008, p. 2) to a modern, predictive and calculative technoscientific enterprise. Throughout the 1940s-60s, in both US and Soviet research institutes, seemingly far-fetched plans for the military use of weather modification were developed alongside strategic civilian projects designed to secure agricultural productivity by influencing rainfall patterns and the onset of tornadoes. The names of these projects – *Project Cirrus*, *Project Climax*, *Project Stormfury* and the ambitious *Meteorology Project*, led by the famously hawkish mathematician John von Neumann at Princeton's Institute for Advanced Study – are indicative of the scale and intention of these initiatives. Writing in 1946, von Neumann outlined his vision of a confluence of information science, advances in computational capacity, and the development of a properly predictive form of meteorological science, suggesting that the *Meteorology Project* would take the "first steps toward influencing the weather by rational, human intervention... since the effects of any hypothetical intervention will have become calculable" (quoted in Harper 2008, p. 4).

What these historical studies demonstrate is that global climate knowledge is not simply knowledge *about* climate. Rather climate knowledge – and the ambitious attempt to model the relations between atmospheric, earth and ocean systems – operates at the intersection between the political-economic regimes of globalisation and a technoscientific orientation toward manipulation and control. And as the settlement agreed in Paris signals a renewed an intention to "hold the increase in the global average temperature to well below 2°C above pre-industrial levels and to pursue efforts to limit the temperature increase to 1.5°C above pre-industrial levels" (Conference of the Parties 2015, p. 2), notions of climatic mastery and technologically-enabled destiny continue to appear as central figures in our contemporary meanings of climate. That this commitment will likely see decarbonisation efforts augmented by a range of (largely untested) strategies designed to remove carbon from the atmosphere through the use of largely untested negative emissions and carbon sequestration technologies (Anderson 2015) underlies the continuing salience of the "ideological freightage we load onto interpretations of climate and our interactions with it" (Hulme 2009, p. 28).

In this co-productionist frame, climate is as much a physical manifestation of processes of greenhouse gas concentrations and radiative forcing as it is a carrier of cultural, moral and theological meanings. The idea of climate and of climate change operates as a lens for making sense of the world, and contemporary scientific projections of possible climate futures continue to be riven with cultural, theological, and mythical sensibilities.

Learning to be affected by climate change

By dwelling with a culturally rich concept of climate – that insists that climate change is "inescapably entangled with human ways of being in the world, and broader questions of politics and social justice" (Rose et al. 2012, p. 1) – the goal of contemporary climate pedagogy might therefore be to develop a space for more cosmopolitan climate subjectivities. In place of climate pedagogies wedded to a diffusionist model of global climate knowledge, this requires the cultivation of an ironic disposition toward projections of human mastery and technological deliverance and a more humble assessment of how climatic change will always and inevitably exceed our attempts to tame it. In short, this is a form of climate learning that refuses the false comfort of a climate politics that suggests we might "return to living with a simply natural climate" (Hulme 2010, p. 120). Instead, such learning insists on a decentred account of the 'anthropos' in anthropogenic global warming; that though we are influential, we are not the central players in our own story.

Writing in the context of recent debates concerning the Anthropocene – a geological epoch of 'our making', defined by the 'cumulative impact of civilisation' (Syvitski 2012) climatic and environmental systems – Latour argues that "not only do we have to swallow the news that our very recent development has modified a state of affairs that is vastly older than the very existence of the human race, but we have also to absorb the disturbing fact that the drama has been completed and that the main revolutionary event is behind us, since we have already crossed a few of the nine 'planetary boundaries' considered by some scientists as the ultimate barrier not to overstep!" (Latour 2014, p. 1). For Latour, the Anthropocene portends both a future-to-come and a threshold that has *already* been crossed. The realisation of the collective human interference with environmental and climatic systems is in this sense an ironic one, as it is also a realisation of our own insignificance in the face of earth processes that are both literately and figuratively beyond human imagination and control. Nigel Clark writes of an earth "that remains largely indifferent in the face of our interventions" and that while "our catastrophes may be mere contingencies for the earth … the fallout of the planet's rumblings is for us potentially catastrophic" (Clark 2011, p. 214). Though the record of current global warming reveals the extent to which humans have already influenced environmental the spectre of abrupt climatic change and threshold change underscore our helplessness in the face of an indifferent earth. Techno–utopian fantasies of reflecting sunlight away from the earth, or burring carbon in the ground, appear in this light as mere child's play.

The paradox of this asymmetry is beautifully satirised by Maarten Hajer's critique of the assumption, implicit in much recent commentary on environmental change, of the idea that "the planet has a cockpit, and in that cockpit, *we* can change course" (Hajer 2012). In more recent work Hajer et al. (2015) refer to this condition as 'cockpit-ism', the "illusion that top-down steering by governments and intergovernmental organizations alone can address global problems" (Hajer, p. 1652). While cockpit-ism has been central to the architecture of global climate knowledge (Edwards 2010) if, as Latour suggests, the threshold between the Holocene and the Anthropocene has *already* been crossed, current systematic consideration of the collective human impacts on planetary systems reveal that 'we' were never really in control (Clark 2014). In Hajer's terms, though the recently signed Paris agreement has been cast as representing a new era of global climatic consensus – as a success of diplomacy over politics – we must recognise the radical possibility that there really never was a cockpit (nor a pilot) guiding the path of spaceship earth.

In this light, in place of simply humanities teaching *about* climate, pedagogy in the Environmental Humanities might be re-characterised as cultivating dispositions toward what Chakrabarty portrays as the entanglement of the species histories of humanity and the earthly histories of the world. We are already living in and with dramatic climatic and environmental changes. The challenge of climate pedagogy is therefore to allow climate change to teach us, to cultivate an affective form of bodily learning together with an Anthropocene subjectivity alive to diverse forms of sense making necessary to reconstruct our own entanglements with processes of environmental change (Cameron et al. 2011). Paraphrasing Latour (2004), climate pedagogy might be cast as learning to be affected by climatic and environmental change. This affective disposition will of course be riven with all the contradictions and lacunae of a post-ecological condition that couples "an unprecedented recognition of the urgency of radical ecological policy change, on one hand, [with] an equally unprecedented unwillingness and inability to perform such change, on the other" (Bluhdorn 2011, p. 36). However, rather than representing a definitive endpoint for ecological thinking it is tragi-comic narratives of apocalypse and progress – strange "bedfellows in the soap opera of technoscience" as Haraway (1997) writes – that represent the raw materials from which we might construct an ironic more-than-human pedagogy of climate and environmental change (see Szerszynski 2007).

Notes

1   See: http://icewatchparis.com.
2   www.theguardian.com/artanddesign/gallery/2015/nov/30/anti-advertising-the-hijacked-bus-stops-of-paris-brandalism-climate-change-in-pictures.
3   https://twitter.com/olafureliasson/status/672444714113740801
4   The notion of the "Human Dimensions of Environmental Change" has a longer and wider history than climate change, having been central to the formation of the 'Committee on the Human Dimensions of Global Change' of the US Academy of Sciences in the early 1990s, and with continuing legacies in structuring social science and humanities research in this area (Hackmann and St. Clair 2012; IHOPE 2005; see also Castree 2015 and Lövbrand et al. 2009).
5   www.ipcc.ch/working_groups/working_groups.shtml.

References

Adger, W. N., Barnett, J., Brown, K., Marshall, N., and O'Brien, K. 2013. Cultural dimensions of climate change impacts and adaptation. *Nature Climate Change* 3(2): 112–17.

Anderson, K. 2015. Duality in climate science. *Nature Geosci* 8(12): 898–900.

Blue, G. 2015. Framing Climate Change for Public Deliberation: What Role for Interpretive Social Sciences and Humanities? *Journal of Environmental Policy & Planning*: 1–18.

Bluhdorn, I. 2011. The politics of unsustainability: COP 15, post-ecologism and the ecological paradox. *Organisaton and Environment* 24(1): 34–53.

Cameron, J., Manhood, C., and Pomfrett, J. 2011. Bodily learning for a (climate) changing world: registering differences through performative and collective research. *Local Environment* 16(6): 493–508.

Castree, N. 2015. Changing the Anthropo(s)cene: Geographers, global environmental change and the politics of knowledge. *Dialogues in Human Geography* 5(3): 301–16.

Castree, N., Adams, W. M., Barry, J., Brockington, D., Buscher, B., Corbera, E., Demeritt, D., Duffy, R., Felt, U., Neves, K., Newell, P., Pellizzoni, L., Rigby, K., Robbins, P., Robin, L., Rose, D. B., Ross, A., Schlosberg, D., Sörlin, S., West, P., Whitehead, M., and Wynne, B. 2014. Changing the intellectual climate. *Nature Climate Change* 4(9): 763–68.

Chilvers, J., and Kearnes, M., eds. 2015. *Remaking Participation: Science, Environment and Emergent Publics*, London: Routledge.

Clark, N. 2011. *Inhuman Nature: Sociable Life on a Dynamic Planet*. London: Sage.

Clark, N. 2014. Geo-politics and the disaster of the Anthropocene. *The Sociological Review* 62(S1): 19–37.

Conference of the Parties. 2015. *Adoption of the Paris Agreement*. FCCC/CP/2015/L.9/Rev.1: United Nations Framework Convention on Climate Change.

Cox, J. D. 2002. *Storm Watchers: The Turbulent History of Weather Prediction from Franklin's Kite to El Niño*, Hoboken, NJ: John Wiley & Sons.

Edwards, P. N. 2010. *A Vast Machine: Computer Models, Climate Data and the Politics of Global Warming*. Cambridge, MA: MIT Press.

Elichirigoity, F. 1999. *Planet Management: Limits to Growth, Computer Simulation and the Emergence of Global Spaces*. Evanston, IL: Northwestern University Press.

Hackmann, H., and St. Clair, A. L. 2012. *Transformative Cornerstones of Social Science Research for Global Change*, International Social Science Council.

Hajer, M., A. 2012. *Rethinking Environmental Governance*. Presentation to the Stockholm Resilience Centre, Stockholm University, 13 September 2012. Video available at www.stockholmresilience.org/21/news—events/seminar-and-events/seminar-and-event-videos/9-13-2012-maarten-hajer—-rethinking-environmental-governance.html (accessed 20 September 2012).

Hajer, M., Nilsson, M., Raworth, K., Bakker, P., Berkhout, F., de Boer, Y., Rockström, J., Ludwig, K., and Kok, M. 2015. Beyond Cockpit-ism: Four Insights to Enhance the Transformative Potential of the Sustainable Development Goals. *Sustainability* 7(2): 1651–60.

Haraway, D. J. 1997. *Modest Witness@Second_Millennium.FemaleMan©_Meets_OncoMouse™: Feminism and Technoscience*, London: Routledge.

Harper, K. C. 2008. *Weather by the Numbers: The Genesis of Modern Meteorology*. Cambridge, MA: MIT Press.

Hulme, M. 2009. *Why We Disagree About Climate Change: Understanding Controversy, Inaction and Opportunity*. Cambridge: Cambridge University Press.

Hulme, M. 2010. Learning to live with recreated climates. *Nature and Culture* 5(2): 117–22.

Hulme, M. 2011. Meet the humanities. *Nature Climate Change* 1(4): 177–79.

IHOPE. 2005. *Developing an Integrated History and Future of People on Earth: Research Plan*, Stockholm. IGBP Report No. 59. IGBP Secretariat.

Kearnes, M. 2015. Miraculous engineering and the climate emergency: climate modification as divine economy. In: C. Deane-Drummond, S. Bergmann and B. Szerszynski (eds) *Nature, Technology & Religion – Transdisciplinary Perspectives*. London: Ashgate, 219–37.

Latour, B. 2004. How to talk about the body? The normative dimension of science studies. *Body & Society* 10(2–3): 205–29.

Latour, B. 2014. Agency at the Time of the Anthropocene. *New Literary History* 45(1): 1–18.

Lövbrand, E., and Stripple, J. 2006. The climate as political space: on the territorialisation of the global carbon cycle. *Review of International Studies* 32(02): 217–35.

Lövbrand, E., Stripple, J., and Wiman, B. 2009. Earth System governmentality: Reflections on science in the Anthropocene. *Global Environmental Change* 19(1): 7–13.

Miller, C. A., and Edwards, P. N. 2001. Introduction: the globalisation of climate science and climate politics. In: C.A. Miller and P. N Edwards (eds) *Changing the Atmosphere: Expert Knowledge and Environmental Governance*. Cambridge, MA: MIT Press, pp. 1–30.

Palsson, G., Szerszynski, B., Sörlin, S., Marks, J., Avril, B., Crumley, C., Hackmann, H., Holm, P., Ingram, J., Kirman, A., Buendía, M. P., and Weehuizen, R. 2013. Reconceptualizing the 'Anthropos' in the Anthropocene: Integrating the social sciences and humanities in global environmental change research. *Environmental Science & Policy* 28: 3–13.

Proctor, J. D. 1998. The meaning of global environmental change: retheorising culture in human dimensions research. *Global Environmental Change* 8(3): 227–48.

Rayner, S., and Malone, E. L. (eds) 1998. *Human Choice and Climate Change*. Vol. I-IV. Columbus, OH: Battelle Press.

Rose, D. B., van Dooren, T., Churlew, M., Cooke, S., Kearnes, M., and O'Gorman, E. 2012. Thinking through the environment, unsettling the humanities. *Environmental Humanities* 1: 1–5.

Shove, E. 2010. Beyond the ABC: climate change policy and theories of social change. *Environment & Planning A* 42(6): 1273–85.

Syvitski, J. 2012. The Anthropocene: An epoch of our making. *Global Change* 78: 12–15.

Szerszynski, B. 2007. The Post-ecologist Condition: Irony as Symptom and Cure. *Environmental Politics* 16(2): 337–55.

Szerszynski, B. 2014. *Geoengineering and Religion: A History in Four Characters.* Opinion Article, Geoengineering Our Climate Working Paper and Opinion Article Series.

Urry, J. 2011. *Climate Change and Society.* London: Polity.

Wynne, B. 2010. Strange Weather, Again: Climate Science as Political Art. *Theory, Culture & Society* 27(2–3): 289–305.

Yusoff, K. 2010. Biopolitical Economies and the Political Aesthetics of Climate Change. *Theory, Culture & Society* 27(2–3): 73–99.

5 Energy, climate and the classroom

A letter

Imre Szeman

Dear x,

You asked me the other day: what does it feel like to teach about the environment? You wanted to know: does teaching about the environment ... well, does it *work*?

As you know, for the past decade I've been trying to make sense of the ways in which we have come to understand—or more to the point, have failed to truly grapple with and comprehend—the nature and character of our petro-modernity. We could never have been modern except for our access to coal, oil, and gas, which provide us with an unprecedented amount of cheap energy. Everything we have come to associate with modernity—from its characteristic speed and contraction of space, to its technologies and infrastructures—is possible only as a result of our access to these remnants of ancient life. I've described modern culture as a *petro-culture* to emphasize the role of the *ur*-commodities that form the all too real base on which the superstructure of everything else has been built—even those elements of the mode of production that are typically identified as the base! (A new map of base and superstructure would have everything floating on a top of a rapidly diminishing sea of oil, an Atlantis that the gods don't submerge as punishment but leave stranded on a dry ocean bed.) Despite the fact that we have shaped ourselves in relation to these specific sources of energy, until recently, we have largely failed to name them in theory or culture. It is important that we start thinking about our—and by 'our' I do mean all of us, the whole globe—culture as a petroculture because we need to understand all of the ways we are subjects of oil. We need to understand this because our major source of energy, now and for the near future, which fuels global society in a fundamental way, is also the principle cause of global warming and of other forms of environmental damage. Our petro-culture—which is to say, what and who we are—is what generates global warming, every day and in every way.

It's impossible to address global warming without significant changes in our use of fossil fuels. This is widely known. Making these changes means becoming different subjects who embrace a different collectivity and sociality—subjects who decide to no longer be creatures of petroculture. This is less well known. We don't just need to find new sources of energy and cut down on our use of fossil fuels. We need to invent new ways of being, belonging, and behaving—and to do so quickly. It's an intimidating proposition. It means that we not only need to change the energy source on which we depend, but also need to change everything else. We have no models of such intensive and extensive social transformation, especially not in a short time frame (necessitated by global warming) and in a society in which almost everything is geared, with the help of fossil fuels, to produce more and more … and more.

In winter 2014, I taught a graduate class in environmental studies called "Resource Culture: Oil in Fiction and Theory." In this seminar, the students and I took the challenge of interrogating the petro-fictions that animate our petrocultures head on. We examined a range of recent essays and books that re-narrate the history of petroculture or which strive to uncover its animating philosophies, including Timothy Mitchell's *Carbon Democracy*, Dipesh Chakrabarty's "The Climate of History," Allan Stoekl's *Bataille's Peak*, Stephanie LeMenager's *Living Oil*, and Andrew Nikiforuk's *The Energy of Slaves*. A key, early intervention into the cultural politics of oil was novelist Amitav Ghosh's "Petrofictions," an essay in which he laments the lack of attention in American fiction to all things related to oil (Ghosh 1992). While not wishing to deny the reality or importance of Ghosh's basic insight—the United States in the twentieth century is also a Middle Eastern country, and yet there is nothing in its fiction of its tragic, ongoing misadventures in the region—my students and I also looked at those few fictions that *have* attended to the social importance of oil.[1] That these are all *science* fictions wasn't lost on us; the continued lack of 'normal' fictions dealing with oil was telling about how we still view the stuff (out of sight, out of mind!). We ended the course by examining two provocative essays on the role of oil in contemporary fiction as well as in broader narratives and rhetorics of social and cultural life at the present time: Peter Hitchcock's "Oil in an American Imaginary" and Graeme Macdonald's "The Resources of Fiction" (Hitchcock 2010; Macdonald 2013).

The big take away? More information, more science, more certainty about global warming isn't what will do the trick. Macdonald's essay starts with a prophetic epigraph from Italo Calvino's 1974 short story, "The Petrol Pump": "I should have thought of it before, it's too late now" (Calvino 1974 [1966], p. 170). One of the central issues that we had to address in the course was how we stand in relation to crisis. We asked ourselves: how do we think, understand and narrate the social significance of fossil fuels in order to avoid multiple crises, and two in particular: the socio-political crisis that will undoubtedly attend the declining availability of oil and coal, and the environmental crisis of global warming that is the outcome of burning the stuff even when we know we shouldn't? One of the intriguing developments in contemporary critical theory has been attention to the socio-psychological figures and mechanisms we use to avoid confronting our political realities. As much a component of modernity as oil—distinct psychic and linguistic modes of being that accompany the scale and complexity of the modern that fossil fuel engenders—there are multiple mechanisms through which we have learned to disarticulate (or, indeed, never allow to concatenate) the link between knowledge and action that shapes political possibility (or should shape it). It is plainly not enough to identify the relation of oil to the environment to produce change. It was important in the course to attend to the insights about our intellectual and affective relation to crisis, and the challenges this poses to our common understanding of the function of our knowledge systems. And so we spent time thinking and talking about cruel optimism through Lauren Berlant and petro-melancholia via LeMenager, and also pondered the specific difficulties of figuring global warming through encounters with Timothy Morton's hyperobjects and Rob Nixon's idea of "slow violence" (Berlant 2011; LeMenager 2011; Morton 2013; Nixon 2011). Indeed, for students in literary and cultural criticism, one of the most productive sites at which to probe the operations of our resource fictions was through an assessment of the modes of being and behaving generated by cultural narratives. In *Small is Beautiful*, E.F. Schumacher notes, "it is always possible to dismiss even the most threatening problem with the suggestion that something will turn up" (Shumacher 2010 [1973], p. 29). Many of the students' seminars attended to (de)formation of subjectivity that pairs an indefinite teleology with such disinterest, inaction or incapacity.

What was it like for the students to throw themselves into these texts, these ideas? It was tremendously empowering for them. The class was held in a building at the University of Alberta overlooking the deep North Saskatchewan River valley that cuts Edmonton in half. The city's presence near the Alberta Oil Sands means that it is impossible to live there and not be alive to the realities of the fossil fuel industry and how it shapes work and life. The students in my class had been longing to address and assess fossil fuel culture as part of their graduate studies, to connect it to the texts and concepts they had encountered in literary and cultural studies, and to make it part of their broad assessment of the politics of contemporary society and the operations of power. Through critical discussion and debate, "Resource Culture" gave them the opportunity to put some issues of the day directly on the table. The texts we read argued convincingly that our relationship to fossil fuels is less scientific and technological than cultural and social. The role of narratives of being and belonging, of imaginaries and desires, and of hopes and fears in shaping our understanding of and relation to oil and the environment gave legitimacy and strength to the investigations undertaken by my students. Their skills as literary and cultural critics were needed to plot next steps on the difficult road ahead. There was nothing special about the way that I organized this course; in many ways, because I didn't know how the students might treat the content, I was timid about messing about with its form. The excitement for the students came from recognizing how important—indeed, essential—the humanities were to figuring out the past, present, and future of petro-modernity.

This, at least, is part of the story.

It might seem as if what I'm about to say stands as a contradiction to the feelings of capacity and possibility that my students experienced when they turned their attention to oil. But I'll say it anyway. Each and every class began abuzz with intellectual energy; three hours later, however productive our analysis and discussion might have been, our critical interrogations drawing up flashes of insight, we ended up grim and silent, a despondency that we pushed aside with sharp, sarcastic meta-comments and promises to work hard on next week's readings. As we learned about resource culture in each class, we slid from possibility to impossibility, from an opening to closure, and from the capacity to makes changes to the way we exist in relation to oil to feelings of impotence in the face of the detailed maps about oil modernity that we drew together, which seemed to make such changes improbable.

I know that this affective slide was partially my fault. In each class, I pushed my students to think about what we might learn from how each writer frames our relationship to oil modernity. All too often, those writers who attended to the trauma of our dependence on fossil fuels were as capable of outlining, productively and insightfully, the characteristics of oil modernity as they were in arguing that there's not much we can do to change the direction in which we're heading. It was—it is—important to insist on the all too real significance of fossil fuels in shaping contemporary culture. We can name the problems and consequences of continuing to depend on oil to the degree that we do. And we can also identify the ways in which contemporary society *doesn't* react to analyses of both the impact of its use and of looming energy limits. From different starting points, whether reading Morton or Berlant, my students and I moved, maybe too quickly, to the same conclusion: though we were able to identify what's what about oil, power, and society, and did so with ever greater precision and specificity, we didn't always add to our knowledge about what we could do to change our relationship to oil. Instead, more often than not, we repeated the breaks between knowledge and political possibility that haunt our relationship to oil and to global warming. What is to be done? We didn't have the slightest idea.

From hope to despair, from optimism to pessimism. A thrilling and exhausting class! If we were able to return the next week with renewed energy it was in part due to the fact that we treated the class itself as an exception. The rhythms, patterns, and codes of everyday life outside of class made it seem as if all was okay. While in class, we went after the tendency to which Schumacher points. Outside of class, we made due with the collective shrug of the shoulders that lets us fill up the tank of our cars and treat this strange mechanical act as the most normal thing in the world.

If we have come to believe that our social being constitutes something of an error through and through—a traumatic discovery, to say the least!—the only possible solution is that we become something completely other. It's a nigh impossible demand. We don't want the outcome of a fuller insight into the character of our societies as petro-societies to result in a feeling that genuine political change is impossible. That's not much of a politics. In "Petrofictions," Ghosh notes that, for the most part, oil culture is "a Problem that can be written about only in the language of Solutions" (Ghosh 1992). Part of the problem in the class was that we all wanted to read for immediate, direct and simple solutions to the problem of oil. How could we not, given all that is at stake, and given that time is of the essence? We learned that limiting knowledge to pure utility is one of the principle protocols of petroculture, and a big reason why we find ourselves in the predicament we're in. Isn't this way of knowing encapsulated in Martin Heidegger's idea of "standing reserve"—a theoretical concept materialized in the vast oil farm of tanks at Cushing, Oklahoma? (Heidegger 1977). Cushing has as much right to be named the capital of the twenty-first century as places like Shanghai or Dubai.

There's another way to think about petrocultures, I think, one that doesn't minimize the significance of oil to modernity and to our social and environmental future, but which nevertheless generates political capacity rather than paralysis. This year, I had an opportunity to re-read a text that I hadn't cracked for some time: Fredric Jameson's *Postmodernism, or, The Cultural Logic of Late Capitalism*. Jameson doesn't talk about oil and energy *at all* when talking about late capitalism, which to my mind constitutes a limit to his narrative of political, social and cultural shifts and transformation. Near the beginning of the book, Jameson points to problem that can arise when one tries to paint the big picture. He writes:

> The more powerful the vision of some increasingly total system or logic—the Foucault of the prisons book is the obvious example—the more powerless the reader comes to feel. Insofar as the theorist wins, therefore, by constructing an increasingly closed and terrifying machine, to that very degree he loses, since the critical capacity of his work is thereby paralyzed, and the impulse of negation and revolt, not to speak of those of social transformation, are increasingly perceived as vain and trivial in the face of the model itself.
>
> (Jameson 1991, pp. 5-6)

Jameson insists that we need to identify and analyze a "cultural dominant," since without it "we fall back into a view of present history as sheer heterogeneity, random difference, a coexistence of a host of distinct forces whose effectivity is undecidable" (Jameson 1991, p. 6). However, the identification of a cultural dominant need not rule out political possibility. At the outset of a book that will outline in great detail the forces and dimensions of late capitalism, and which might thus come across as naming a total system from which there is no escape, Jameson connects a political project to his endeavor: "to project some conception of a new systematic cultural norm and its reproduction in order to reflect more adequately on the most effective forms of any radical politics today" (Jameson 1991, p. 6). It is hard to draw an exact or easy parallel between the project of identifying a cultural dominant and the project of (for lack of a better way of describing it) naming an *energy* dominant; the forces and significance that one might want to assign each dominant are distinct, to say the least. Everything we read in "Resource Culture" could be seen as making a total system even *more* total. (You think we live in a biopolitical society? Well guess what? It's not just biopolitical, it's an *oil* biopolitical society!). Fossil fuels *are* a cultural dominant, even if rarely named as such. What reading Jameson again reminded me is the reason why we map cultural dominants, which is to better "grasp our positioning as individual and collective subjects and regain a capacity to act and struggle which is at present neutralized by our spatial as well as our social confusion" (Jameson 1991, p. 6). Even in the face of global warming and a petroculture in which it is (in some sense) oil all the way down, this remains a laudable and important goal. The point of naming an energy dominant is to understand our social confusion so we can begin the task of acting, struggling, becoming something new, together.

Were I to teach a class on "Resource Culture" again, I'd do it differently. I'd have students read texts about petrocultures, so as to have them learn about the depths of our interpellation with fossil fuels. But I'd also have them read and think about the ways in which live collectively today, and how we might live together differently in the future. No course can do everything it needs to do—I get that. Still, I think that I should have focused not only on an investigation of the oil and energy in shaping petroculture, but also on an exploration of the ways in which we understand *collectivity*. I would add texts such as Ursula K. LeGuin's *Dispossessed* (1974) or Naomi Oreskes and Erik Conway's *The Collapse of Western Civilization* (2014), two accounts of futures in which energy is figured differently than it is today, both of which keep the problem of collectively front and center (LeGuin 1994 [1974]). I think, too, that I would move away from 'big picture' theoretical framings of oil as a determinant resource and include works such as Kolya Ambramsky's edited collection, *Sparking a Worldwide Energy Revolution: Social Struggles in the Transition to a Post-Petrol World* (2010), which discusses collective actions taking place around the world. Finally, if attitude, affect, and sentiment are key to environmental change (whether to enabling or disabling it), I would focus even more directly on exploring these in my course design, by turning (for example) to the work of the scholars writing in the Public Feelings project,[2] and from there, to a consideration of the ways in which women have been interpellated within petro-modernity in a specific manner that needs more critical attention than it has received to date.

I said it before: energy shapes our ways of being, and being together. The way we have wanted to think about oil is to come up with a substitute energy source that would effectively allow us to paint oil out of the picture while keeping our current forms of subjectivity and collectivity. This is our most dangerous environmental fantasy *and* our most dangerous political one as well. If we need to change *everything* in the way that I have suggested in this letter, then we need resources to imagine and figure the changes that we'll need to make. If I teach a course about oil and global warming again, I'll make sure to provide my students with some of those resources, so that the capacities and possibilities that energize them don't collapse into uncertainty and despair. Let me put it this way: if global warming is about how we live together, shouldn't we be learning about just that: interrogations of the process of social and political change, analyses of the systems that produce late capitalist collective life? Could one not imagine a class on energy and the environment that spent most of its time knee deep not in the muck of oil, but in the political theory and utopian imaginings of new social forms?

I'd better go. I have to get ready to go and teach.

Take care,

Imre

Notes

1   These fictions included: J.G. Ballard, *Concrete Island* (New York: Harper, 2008); Steven Amsterdam, *Things We Didn't See Coming* (New York: Anchor, 2011); and Paolo Bacigalupi, *The Windup Girl* (San Francisco: Night Shade Books, 2009).

2   Books in the Public Feelings project include Ann Cvetkovich, *Depression: A Public Feeling* (Durham: Duke, 2012); Berlant, *Cruel Optimism*; and José Esteban Muñoz *Cruising Utopia: The Then and There of Queer Futurity* (New York: New York University Press, 2009).

References

Ambramsky, K. 2010. *Sparking a Worldwide Energy Revolution: Social Struggles in the Transition to a Post-Petrol World*. Oakland, CA: AK Press.

Berlant, L. 2011. *Cruel Optimism*. Durham, NC: Duke University Press.

Calvino, I. 1996 [1974]. "The Petrol Pump." *Numbers in the Dark and Other Stories*. Trans. Tim Parks. London: Vintage.

Chakrabarty, D. 2009. "The Climate of History: Four Theses," *Critical Inquiry* 35: 197–222.

Ghosh, A. 1992. "Petrofiction." *New Republic* 2 March 1992: 29–34.

Heidegger, M. 1977. "The Question Concerning Technology," *The Question Concerning Technology and Other Essays*. New York: Harper Torchbooks: 3–35.

Hitchcock, P. 2010. "Oil in an American Imaginary." *New Formations* 69.4: 81–97.

Jameson, F. 1991. *Postmodernism, or, the Cultural Logic of Late Capitalism*. Durham, NC: Duke University Press.

LeGuin, U. 1994 [1974]. *Dispossessed*. New York: Harper.

LeMenager, S. 2011. "Petro-Melancholia: The BP Blowout and the Arts of Grief." *Qui Parle* 19.2: 25–55.

LeMenager, S. 2013. *Living Oil: Petroleum and Culture in the American Century*. Oxford: Oxford University Press.

Macdonald, G. "The Resources of Fiction." *Reviews in Cultural Theory* 4.2 (2013): 1–24.

Mitchell, T. 2011. *Carbon Democracy: Political Power in the Age of Oil*. New York: Verso.

Morton, T. 2013. *Hyperobjects: Philosophy and Ecology after the End of the World*. Minneapolis, MN: University of Minnesota Press.

Nikiforuk, A. 2012. *The Energy of Slaves*. Vancouver: Greystone Books.

Nixon, R. 2011. *Slow Violence and the Environmentalism of the Poor*. Cambridge, MA: Harvard University Press.

Oreskes, N. and Conway, E.M. 2014. *The Collapse of Western Civilization: A View from the Future*. New York: Columbia University Press.

Schumacher, E.F. 1973 [2010]. *Small is Beautiful: Economics as if People Mattered*. New York: Perennial.

Stoekl, A. 2007. *Bataille's Peak: Energy, Religion, and Postsustainability*. Minneapolis MN: University of Minnesota Press.

6 Will the end of the world be on the final exam?

Emotions, climate change, and teaching an introductory environmental studies course

Robert Wilson

For the past decade, I have annually taught GEO 103 Environment and Society, my university's introductory environmental studies course. It is a large class of 75 to 150 students with graduate teaching assistants leading weekly smaller discussion groups. The bulk of students in the course are not geography majors or even humanities or social science majors. Rather, they are visitors from other fields and far-flung parts of campus: engineering, computer science, elementary education, finance and entrepreneurship, broadcast journalism, sports management, and fashion design. In short, they are neither budding environmentalists nor would-be environmental studies majors—not by a long shot. This course is likely the first, and last, environmental studies class they will ever take. But since they are enrolled in this course to fulfill a liberal arts distribution requirement, they enter my class somewhat under duress, and most likely, the course is the lowest priority among the four to six classes they are taking that semester. Sparking interest in environmental policy and the Environmental Humanities in such an audience is challenging, both for myself and the teaching assistants who work with me.

By and large, many of the students approach this course, and perhaps their other classes, with a very instrumental outlook. Given this situation, it is not surprising that they lack enthusiasm taking courses outside their major. What many want from this course, is the highest possible grade with the minimum amount of effort. The instrumental outlook of contemporary college students is a familiar lament among academics (Nathan; Arum and Roksa), but it seems quite troubling in a course such as this given that it focuses so much on climate change—and climate change, to put it mildly, is something students will have to contend with for the rest of their lives, regardless of their major or chosen career. While the course focuses on the cultural, political, and economic dimensions of a number of environmental issues, climate change is a major topic in the class, and it has become even more so throughout the past ten years. While it is not a natural science course per se, I do devote a week to the science and consequences of climate change. Whether it is the rise of atmospheric temperature, the loss of sea ice in the Arctic, or the growth of wildfires in the western United States, the findings about climate change published in the Intergovernmental Panel on Climate Change (IPCC) reports or National Climate Assessment have grown more dire and worrisome with each passing year (Mann and Lee; U.S. Global Change Research Program). Despite my best efforts to contain this section of the course, my discussion of climate change now takes up more and more of the class.

Confronted with the dire predictions of climatologists, the students by and large have one reaction: indifference. The cavalier attitude of students toward their future and that of fellow people around the world was brought home to me a few years ago in an email by one of my teaching assistants leading a discussion section about climate change. "My soul is crushed," she began. "I thought we were going to have this fabulous conversation about framing arguments, the role of science, finding allies and figuring out how to effectively communicate [climate science to the public]. The class—and I don't just mean two or three vocal people—basically came up with this: all of Bangladesh could die, the temperature could increase six degrees, tons of species could die, and people in other places could suffer from drinking water and crop shortages, and we wouldn't care at all." She went on: "On one hand, it's sort of confusing—they're super cynical and at times seem morally bankrupt, but they also sort of want something to happen ... They won't care about species loss (even polar bears!) until they believe it will economically hurt them. They don't care about people in any other place. They will only care about drought when they don't have enough drinking water or when food is really expensive ... And if NYC becomes like Houston? Whatever. That's what air conditioning is for. And if poor people can't afford it? Go to the mall" (Green).

Dealing with such a reaction posed challenges for my teaching assistant and me, and I would argue, raises important questions for those of us in the environmental humanities. A generation of scholarship in the Environmental Humanities and allied fields such as political ecology, environmental history, and environmental sociology have urged scholars to highlight the injustice of climate change for poor and marginal communities, both within the United States and in the Global South, and how a warming world could deepen inequality (Nixon; Robbins; Perrualt, Bridge, and McCarthy). Imparting this knowledge about climate justice is a core intellectual, political, and ethical pillar of teaching climate change in the Environmental Humanities. Yet how should we react when students respond to the science and ethics of climate change with a shrug and a "meh"?

My initial response to my dispirited teaching assistant was to remind her that as much as we would like students to share our concern about climate change and the consequences for people around the world, we cannot make them care. Our role is to teach them the fundamentals of environment-society geography and pose the policy and ethical questions raised by climate change, but ultimately, what lessons they draw from that are their own. I also wanted to meet with the students in the discussion section, and fortunately, this is something they suggested them-selves. We had a productive conversation about climate change—which, truth be told, some still doubted was even happening. Most seemed unconvinced it was much of a problem or that we owed much to those most affected by the rising seas, fiercer storms, and searing droughts that come with it.

A recent book by sociologist Kari Norgaard on emotions and climate change sheds light on their reactions. Drawing on ethnographic work in Norway and in-depth interviews with students in the United States, she sought to unravel the puzzle of nonparticipation in addressing climate change. Why do people fail to tackle climate change even when they know the science and the potential consequences of global warming? She argues that when faced with the reality of climate change, people in these countries have three dominant emotional reactions: guilt, fear, and helplessness (Norgaard 187–97). They feel guilt because as residents of industrialized countries, they realize they contribute to climate change through the energy they use and greenhouse gas emissions produced. Confronted by a warmer and stormier future, people are incapacitated by fear. Finally, climate change seems so immense and abstract they felt utterly helpless to do anything about the problem. The indifference and resignation many of my introductory environmental studies course students express may simply be how these feelings of guilt, fear, and helplessness manifest themselves. Yet if my environmental studies course fosters feelings of powerlessness and indifference among my students, what is the solution? And what different emotions would I want to elicit in my course? Instead of guilt, fear, and powerlessness I try to provoke feelings of *anger*, *entitlement*, and *empowerment*.

Anger

One of the more baffling aspects of teaching this environmental studies course is the students' lack of anger about climate change and the collective failure of governments to tackle the problem. While students might feel guilt about how their high-energy-use lifestyles contribute to climate change, they are not the ones who set energy policy; governments and the fossil-fuel companies that lobby them do. As scholars have amply shown, fossil-fuel companies have undertaken a decades-long campaign to foster doubt about climate change and how the burning of fossil fuel contributes to global warming (Oreskes and Conway). More recently, investigative journalists have shown how companies supporting climate-change skepticism, such as Exxon-Mobil, clearly understood the science of climate change and did peer-reviewed research on the topic decades ago, yet chose to fund climate-change skeptic groups instead of lowering emissions (Banerjee, Song, and Hasemyer). Such scholarship and investigative reports assume a more prominent place in my lectures and the readings I assign in the course. They show, among other things, how powerful interests in our society have launched a sustained campaign to manufacture doubt about climate change and bully or harass climate scientists. This should foster feelings of anger, rather than guilt, among my students.

Entitlement

Of the three emotions I hope to elicit, this may appear the most unusual and controversial. Millennial college students are often depicted in the media (unfairly,

I would say) as pampered and privileged—in a word, entitled. Urging my students to feel more entitled might seem as only amplifying their supposedly worst tendencies. But if my students do feel entitled, they probably feel entitled about the wrong things. I want my students to feel entitled to the same sort of stable climate their ancestors enjoyed for much of the past 10,000 years. Scholarship from a number of disciplines argues that the rise of agricultural societies and modern civilizations was partly due to the relatively stable global climate that has endured since the end of the Pleistocene (Brooke). While historians and climate science have shown that the climate has changed, especially on the regional scale, over the Holocene, the magnitude of change is nothing compared to the degree of climate change anticipated over the next century, especially if greenhouse gas emissions continue to rise in coming decades. Without people realizing it, a relatively stable climate, and the stable sea levels that came with it, were a fixture of human life for much of the past ten millennia. Now we are entering a period of profound climate instability. I encourage my students to consider the consequences of the loss of a stable climate for themselves and others of their generation and consider who had the right to take that sort of climate away from them.

Empowered

For most of the past decade, when I asked students if anything could be done to cope with climate change and reduce greenhouse gas emissions, they said "no." Since they feel guilt, fear, helplessness, and indifference about climate change, it comes as no surprise they doubt whether politicians or citizens can do much to address the problem. To counter this, I make a point to lecture and assign readings on the growth of the environmental movement of the 1960s and 1970s and the many achievements of that era. As historian Adam Rome shows in the *The Genius of Earth Day*, the environmental movement was a disparate coalition comprised of liberals, middle-class women, counterculture youth, and others whose efforts led to many legislative achievements (the Clean Air Act, the Environmental Protection Agency, the Endangered Species Act) as well as a greening of higher education and journalism (Rome). Of course, there were many serious shortcomings to this movement, especially the fact that it was overwhelmingly white, suburban, and middle- to upper-middle class. But I also discuss the development of the environmental justice movement from the 1980s to the present and how people of color and less affluent supporters of this movement challenged corporate polluters, indifferent bureaucrats, and mainstream environmentalists to deal with the disproportionate siting of toxic waste dumps and facilities in poor and minority communities. As a scholar, it is imperative that I acknowledge the shortcomings of these movements, especially the mainstream environmental movement which has not done enough to diversify its membership or address environmental justice concerns. Yet since my students assume nothing can be done to cope with any environmental issue, least of all climate change, it is also essential to highlight the successes of these efforts toward environmental reform and social justice as well as their limitations.

In past years when I taught the course, most of the environmental achievements I cited came from events and movements in the past. More recently, I have been able to show the development of the climate justice movement in the United States and elsewhere (McKibben; Klein). As with the environmental movement over forty years ago, the climate justice movement is also a coalition that includes familiar supporters of environmental causes along with a much stronger voice for indigenous peoples, African Americans, and other groups not always identified as environmentalists (Wilson). Millenials have been among the most influential members of this vibrant movement, and they have demanded politicians and corporations make substantive commitments to lower greenhouse gas emissions. Perhaps the most prominent and innovative climate justice group in the United States is 350.org, which was founded by seven Middlebury College students and Bill McKibben in 2007. Employing their organizational skills, 350.org leaders have helped plan and lead demonstrations, civil disobedience actions, and countless protests. They represent a new generation of student leaders able to harness digital tools, especially social media, to build a movement.

Now I can also point to achievements on my own campus. As students have at many other colleges, some students at Syracuse University have embraced the fossil-fuel divestment movement. Beginning in 2012, a small group of students circulated petitions calling on the university to divest its endowment from fossil-fuel companies and they met with the administration to plead their case. Over the next three years, they held rallies and marches, organized teach-ins on climate change, lobbied the student government to pass a resolution favoring divestment, and along with faculty allies, pressured the University Senate vote in favor of divestment as well. They forged alliances with other groups on campus advocating greater support for campus sexual assault victims on campus, those seeking recognition for the needs of disabled students, and those standing in solidarity with Black Lives Matter. Together, representatives of these various interests occupied the university administration building for two weeks and demanded action. Eventually, the university agreed to some of their concerns, most notably, divesting the endowment from fossil fuels. I hope students leave my class empowered by the history of environmental achievements and the efforts of climate activists on their campus and elsewhere. The point is not for students in the course to all become environmentalists or slavishly support the climate justice movement. Rather, it is to recognize that organized, committed citizens can effect change.

Should we structure courses in the Environmental Humanities to elicit emotions? Certainly, seeking to foster emotions is a more nebulous "learning outcome" than understanding key course-related terms and concepts. But as Environmental Humanities scholars have shown, the predominant ways we present climate change to our students commonly generate profoundly unempowering emotions among those in our classes. Instead of resigning ourselves to this fate, we should carefully consider what emotions we hope our courses will evoke and structure our lectures, readings, and discussions in the best way to induce them.

References

Arum, Richard, and Josipa Roksa. *Academically Adrift: Limited Learning on College Campuses.* Chicago, IL: University of Chicago Press, 2010. Print.

Banerjee, Neela, Lisa Song, and David Hasemyer. "Exxon's Own Research Confirmed Fossil Fuels' Role in Global Warming Decades Ago." *Inside Climate News* 16, September 2015. Web, accessed 9 December 2015.

Brooke, John L. *Climate Change and the Course of Global History: A Rough Journey.* New York: Cambridge University Press, 2014. Print.

Green, Barbara. "My soul is crushed." Email to the author, 5 November 2009.

Klein, Naomi. *This Changes Everything: Capitalism vs. the Climate.* New York: Simon & Schuster, 2014. Print.

Mann, Michael E., and Lee R. Kump. *Dire Predictions: Understanding Climate Change.* 2nd edn. New York: DK Publishing, 2015. Print.

McKibben, Bill. "It's Time to Fight the Status Quo." *Solutions Journal* 3.3 (2012). Web, accessed 9 December 2015.

Nathan, Rebekah. *My Freshman Year: What a Professor Learned by Becoming a Student.* New York: Penguin Books, 2006. Print

Nixon, Rob. *Slow Violence and the Environmentalism of the Poor.* Cambridge, MA: Harvard University Press, 2011. Print.

Norgaard, Kari M. *Living in Denial: Climate Change, Emotions, and Everyday Life.* Cambridge, MA: The MIT Press, 2011. Print.

Oreskes, Naomi, and Erik M Conway. *Merchants of Doubt: How a Handful of Scientists Obscured the Truth on Issues from Tobacco Smoke to Global Warming.* New York: Bloomsbury Press, 2010. Print.

Perreault, Tom, Gavin Bridge, and James McCarthy, eds. *The Routledge Handbook of Political Ecology.* New York: Routledge, 2015. Print.

Robbins, Paul. *Political Ecology: A Critical Introduction.* 2nd edn. Malden, MA: Wiley-Blackwell, 2011. Print.

Rome, Adam. *The Genius of Earth Day: How a 1970 Teach-In Unexpectedly Made the First Green Generation.* New York: Hill and Wang, 2013. Print.

U.S. Global Change Research Program. *Third National Climate Assessment (2014).* Web, accessed 9 December 2015.

Wilson, Robert. "The Necessity of Activism." *Solutions Journal* 3.4 (2012). Web, accessed 9 December 2015.

7 Teaching climate crisis in the neoliberal university

On the poverty of Environmental Humanities

Upamanyu Pablo Mukherjee, Graeme Macdonald, Nicholas Lawrence, and Jonathan Skinner

'Greenwashing' the neoliberal university (Upamanyu Pablo Mukherjee)

Two trends since the 1970s have resulted in a drastic re-tooling of university space. The first is *marketization*, defined as 'the process by which the state uses market principles and disciplinary apparatuses to create greater efficiencies in non-market institutions' (Canaan and Shumer 4).[1] The second is a step-change in the production of *academic capitalism*, understood as the way in which university faculty increasingly are made to adopt market-like behaviours – in particular, internecine competition for funding provided by bodies external to the university, and (self-) branding as a way of academic life (Slaughter and Leslie).

Both trends have had profound effects on the three kinds of labour conventionally associated with universities: teaching and learning, research, and administration. The most dramatic effect can be seen in the conversion of students into 'consumers,' which, while conferring upon them certain 'rights' and powers, severely curtails their engagement with the kind of critical thinking that is fundamental to higher education. As Thomas Docherty and others have argued in the UK context, the paranoid focus on 'student experience' works to foreclose the possibility of any meaningful learning. A similar effect can be seen on the teaching side of the equation, perhaps most obviously in the area of examination. Docherty suggests that in today's university, exams operate more as tactics of 'containing' intellectual enquiry and 'managing' information than of genuinely testing knowledge (7, 20).

Instrumentalization of teaching is mirrored in instrumentalization of research. Even or especially when research money is dispensed by the state, the research agenda itself is pre-defined along narrow, 'manageable' contours. The UK Research Excellence Framework (REF), which determines the amount of funding to be awarded to HE institutions for the research conducted by faculty, typically does so by setting government-identified interdisciplinary 'themes' – often geared toward partisan government objectives – as the precondition for such awards (Docherty 15). Such instrumentalization has been streamlined by the turn to 'managerialism' that characterizes universities in the Global North (Readings 22). This can be seen in the disproportionate hiring of non-academic administrators and the rapid absorption of faculty into a 'complex administrative lattice' that makes the measurement and documentation of staff and student 'performance' a major feature of academic life (Slaughter and Leslie 1–2; Canaan and Shumer 6).

Our home institution, the University of Warwick, has built a well-deserved reputation as a 'market leader' in academic capitalism over five decades. Bill Readings once described the slogan of 'excellence' as one telltale feature of the neoliberal university (22). Such slogans are hardwired into our university's declared strategic goals:

> Warwick has a reputation for excellence. But a world-class institution has to continue to strive for excellence, in all disciplines. We're committed to doing this, ensuring that our research makes a distinctive, competitive impact on the world.
>
> (University of Warwick)

In fact, each of the university's aims embody core values of marketized education – provision of 'best employability outcomes,' developing management and leadership skills, 'significantly increas[ing] the percentage of research and development income from the commercial and related sectors,' etc. (University of Warwick).

Although these goals were publicized relatively recently, they have been part of Warwick's DNA since its foundation in 1965. E. P. Thompson rightly diagnosed the nexus between British higher education and a shifting model of historical capitalism as a *general* feature of the postwar period, but also noted that it was the concentration of business interests at the top of the university's chain of command that made Warwick a pioneering institution (32). It is instructive to note the future Thompson had predicted for Britain and British higher education five decades ago:

> It is a febrile, wasteful, publicity-conscious world, whose prosperity floats upon hire-purchase and the shifting moods of the status-conscious consumer; a [...] world of expense-account living, lavish salesmanship [...] and of refined managerial techniques and measured day-work.
>
> (16–17)

The fact that the University of Warwick today appears commonplace in its commitments to 'refined managerial techniques' signals the accuracy of Thompson's predictions. If today's universities are best understood as distinctive versions of neoliberal corporations, and if climate change presents the most fundamental challenge to the corporate agenda, what in this context can we expect of Environmental Humanities?

Teaching petroculture (Graeme Macdonald)

Nowhere is the neoliberal university more compromised than in its entanglements with the carbon economy. Even as the divestment movement gains serious traction, forcing leading universities to drop their portfolio of investments in fossil fuels, the public support given to fossil fuel research continues unabated. As Ellen Young notes in the UK context, 'Universities, research councils and government departments all play their part in assisting oil and gas companies to find better ways of extracting more fossil fuel more cheaply from increasingly hard to get reserves' (43). What has become clear in this process is both the symbolic resonance of the act of divestment *and* its exposure of the overt and covert relations between some of the most culpable agents of global warming and the higher education system. There continue to be substantial financial benefits derived from fossil fuel corporations across the university sector. Universities in turn reciprocate with accolades for such companies in the naming of buildings, business-friendly research projects, and the awarding of executives with prestigious honorary degrees.

In addition to exposing this nexus, the divestment campaign draws attention to the tensions between the university's mandate of enriching social and natural life and its function as a driver of industrial policy. The embedding of the university in 'the economy' owes much to the large-scale turn to a petrolic life after World War II, a shift that Mathew Huber has argued helped create and sustain neoliberalism as a political, economic, and cultural project. From geologic modelling to oil-based financial algorithms, universities have provided a steady stream of useful research for oil and gas companies, whose centrality to the world economy, as Timothy Mitchell has shown, underpins the neoliberal order. In the UK, the symbiotic relations between higher education and petroleum were further consolidated with the privatisation of energy firms and the orientation of state research councils and funding streams toward meeting the challenge of 'energy security' in a post-peak oil scenario. It was perhaps not coincidental that the recent controversial raising of tuition fees was recommended after a report by Lord Browne, a former chairman of BP and high profile advocate of shale gas exploitation.

So to teach a course on petrocultures, as I do, requires some initial outlining of the extent to which our activity as university subjects is predicated on fossil fuels, including how they saturate the books we read and the material spaces we inhabit. Part of my pedagogic strategy is to encourage students to consider the degree to which their 'energy unconscious' is both environmentally bound and politically sealed. To analyse our naturalization as petro-subjects is a key object of our lessons – and this we undertake through a cognitive mapping of our manifold petro-spaces, ranging from clothes and smart phones to campus infrastructure, revealing in the process that the university is as much an endangered, and endangering, ecological niche as a grassland or a river delta.

If the divestment campaign is a symbolic exercise in delegitimation, then the content of petrofiction provides a route into understanding the cultural and social productions of hydrocarbon regimes. I ask my students to think about the discursive patterning of oil's speculative promise over the history of modern petroculture and to consider how fiction offers a distinctive way to think about the narrative strategies and representative techniques that oil companies have excelled at since their inception. The university features heavily, for example, in one of the first key works of petro-fiction, Upton Sinclair's 1927 novel *Oil!* The relationship between the 'oiligarch' father and the errant son is strained by the latter's determination to pursue further education instead of joining the family business. Further paternal ignominy results from the son's choice of a humanities degree instead of one in engineering or science, which might have served him well as the heir to an oil empire. The son's experience at university results in the awakening of his political conscience, glimpses of which were already visible in the conservationist instincts he exhibits at the beginning of the novel. In this plotline, *Oil!* seems to present the university as a space of resistance to the despoliation of the environment by the previous generation's 'pioneering recklessness.' At the same time, Sinclair chronicles oil companies' early infiltration of higher education, as they grasp the business expediency of subtending university research.

Ellen Young argues that 'the fossil fuel industry is thoroughly embedded in the public structures of science and any serious attempt to mitigate climate change must be more ambitious about challenging this' (43). I would go further, and ask my students to realise the complete immersion of all sectors across the university within neoliberal carbon culture. This is why it is a fundamental task of the university – in teaching as well as research – to disentangle us from what it has helped create.

Toward ecopraxis (Nicholas Lawrence)

Despite the prevalence of courses bearing the prefix 'eco-', the profile presented at many universities on both sides of the Atlantic is one in which ecological concerns represent at most a subfield specialty, a technical challenge to be 'solved' by the application of university resources, or an aspect of university strategy indistinguishable from branding and publicity campaigns. This disconnect between rhetoric and ground-level reality matches the wider field of struggle within which climate politics is routinely shunted aside or pitted in opposition to more pressing considerations – economic growth, 'employability,' entrepreneurial innovation. Ultimately, the gap stems – as Val Plumwood among others has argued – from the legacy of a Cartesian worldview in which 'nature,' on the one hand, and 'society' or 'humanity' on the other, occupy functionally distinct worlds, the former serving as passive agent for the latter's active principle (115). Hence the force of anthropologist and activist David Graeber's point:

> We seem to be facing two insoluble problems. On the one hand, we have witnessed an endless series of global debt crises. ... On the other, we have an ecological crisis, a galloping process of climate change. ... The two might seem unrelated. But ultimately they are the same.[2]

Our students, who face historic levels of personal debt while tracking the new-normal turbulence of extreme weather and endemic joblessness as a matter of course, grasp the implications of this relation far better than their administrators.

Given the neoliberal university's propensity to invoke eco-awareness while practically ignoring its implications, it has become increasingly clear that a central mission of green studies must be to scrutinize the production of human mediascapes as a specifically environmental issue. How, for example, might we grasp the material force of the apparently frictionless world of corporate communications in ecological terms? What are the implications for a theory of (world-) ecology that accepts the constituent role of linguistic practices in the production of the (worldwide) web of life?

In pursuing these questions, the course I teach, 'Literature, Environment, Ecology,' considers a range of case studies, from Rachel Carson's critique of the legitimating rhetoric surrounding pesticide use in the mid-C20, to the media reception of Naomi Klein's *This Changes Everything*, to the discursive haemorrhaging occasioned by the Deepwater Horizon oil spill. In each case, the dangers apparent in distinguishing too cleanly between 'natural' and 'humanly made' systems confirm Jason Moore's contention that 'we don't yet have an adequate language to talk and act and analyze as if humans and the rest of nature mutually constitute each other' ('Wall Street' 40). The lack of a non-Cartesian vocabulary for considering climate change – widely understood as the central challenge bequeathed us by the Anthropocene, but, Moore argues, better conceived as more specifically a crisis of the 'Capitalocene' (*Capitalism* 169–192) – in turn becomes a provocation for field-trip investigations into corporate environment-making.

It's often said that ecocritics would rather be hiking than sitting in class. Our venture outside the classroom has a different purpose: we visit Dungeness, a quasi-desert strip of peninsular shingle on Britain's southeastern coast, in order to take a tour of the nuclear power station situated on the headland. The French state energy company EDF, which runs the power station, shut down tours for security reasons after the September 11th attacks, but revived them after the Fukushima meltdown in 2011 triggered – as our tour guide candidly acknowledged – 'a PR problem for the industry.' How the PR problem became incorporated into the presentational form of EDF's Visitor Centre serves as the real occasion of our site research. My students are savvy enough not to dismiss the rhetoric used by the corporation as secondary to its undeniably material impact on the local and national environment; the sharp questions they ask of company representatives indicate their awareness of this rhetoric's environment-shaping capacity. Following the money, in this instance, means following the power, including the power of words.

In addition to the reactor, Dungeness is the site of a wildlife preserve and also the last residence of filmmaker, designer and poet Derek Jarman, who died of an AIDS-related illness in 1994. Jarman's book *Modern Nature* documents his work on the area outside Prospect Cottage, the fisherman's home he made his own during the final decade of his life, using indigenous plants, driftwood and detritus from the beach in order to fashion a sea garden responsive to the environment and his own aesthetic promptings. To take in, dialectically, the relations between this enigmatic work of landscape art, the bird sanctuary around it, and the cooling tower looming nearby affords the opportunity to grasp how ecopraxis might run counter to official narratives of disarticulation and disavowal. 'There is more sunlight here than anywhere in Britain: this and the constant wind turn the shingle into a stony desert where only the toughest grasses take hold' (Jarman 2).

Ecopoetics as feral communication (Jonathan Skinner)

I rarely feel as exposed to the contradictions built into a neoliberal carbon economy as when I walk from the bus stop to the Warwick Writing Programme to
teach ecopoetics, a 'creative writing' workshop with an ecological emphasis. A
motto emblazoned on hoarding erected around the construction of a £150 million
National Automotive Innovation Centre reminds me that my institution's 'Future
is Automotive.' In such an environment, my pedagogy feels like a form of feral
communication, conducted in the shadow of this hoarding. Graduates of creative
writing programmes, most of whom will not seek employment in higher education and for whom the digital maze of the culture industry offers no stable point
of entry, will sooner or later learn such feral communication – self-authorizing
modes of knowledge capable of scavenging from, and transporting knowledge
between, the institutions that ultimately fail them.

I also contribute to interdisciplinary modules with titles like 'Challenges of
Climate Change,' lecturing on greenwashing in the media to expose the contradiction in narratives that equate 'nature' with 'freedom' and use both to sell
petroleum. Although popular, these modules remain structured as units of information delivery, with slides and debates over 'solutions.' As the contributing faculty
have little time to share notes, there is scant reflection on cross-disciplinary
contexts, on the fact that students may want to articulate the units into a useable
pattern made of disparate epistemologies. There is limited response, in fact, to a
global circumstance that changes all perspectives. The other option for tackling
climate change lies in disciplinary specialization, as in the focus on 'ecological'
reading known as ecocriticism within the Environmental Humanities. Here the
research of other disciplines, often acquired through reviews in the popular literature, must be imported as expertise in ways that only get debated by peers internal
to the humanities. In neither case does teaching climate change change teaching:
disciplines do not benefit from the proximity of *other* disciplines to reshape their
theories of knowledge and teaching methods, with the goal of forging new
communicational capacities.

The underfunded contact zones between disciplines remain an area of benign
neglect, a kind of 'third' institutional landscape. When enshrined in 'programmes,'
such spaces can become the entropic (or sometimes profitable) zone of 'studies' –
as in the study of ecology without statistics, say, or literature without rhetoric, or
of practice-led studies like 'creative writing' – and viewed with suspicion by those
who see them as cover for institutional reprioritizing. These 'third landscapes,'
which represent parked capital to the university management, can also offer cover
for resurgence and resistance, however, where pedagogical risks might be taken and
hard questions asked of 'eco' speak (Skinner 22). Such spaces are vulnerable to
quick takeover as capital gets reallocated and are thus best approached as 'temporary autonomous zones' where feral communications might develop (Bey).

Students in my creative writing workshops are challenged to develop a poetics,
i.e. to carry out site-based research, to theorize, and to activate findings in the
mode of unknowing integral to their writing, an imagination scaled to the world

ecology of climate change. Such generalist skills will be as vital as expertise to the feral citizens of a failed state. In Ecopoetics, the Automotive Innovation Centre's construction site, once a green pitch for field sports, becomes a 'zero panorama' occasioning discussion of Robert Smithson's concept of 'ruins in reverse,' as we articulate the entropy of development, and write our own tour of its monuments (Smithson 72). The fake 'future' painted on its hoarding comes in for *détournement* along with its language of 'opportunities in the sector.' On another day, we turn compost at the student allotment and read from the canon of garden literature, exploring poetry's role in composting language, as we compose poems with what we learn about the vegetables that taste good to us.

A serious playfulness is encouraged: student portfolios develop a variety of site-specific cases, from dorm recycling, the rhetoric of mapping, or slow violence in the time of disasters, to invasive species, third landscapes at the urban-rural interface, wind power, and the ethics of cosmetics. The work takes off in new directions for these writers, versed in the successes and failures of recent experimental writing, and is placed in ways that challenge the usual circuits of poetry. Ecopoetics at its most provocative bends 'creative' writing as we know it – inspiring confidence that my students are resilient enough to create the jobs that don't yet exist for them. I am less confident that the institution can learn from these feral communications occurring in the shadow of its monuments to planetary ruin.

Notes

1   Canaan and Shumer make a distinction between commodification and marketization, viewing the former as a feature of U.S. higher education and the latter as more characteristic of Europe.
2   Graeber continues: 'Saying that global debt levels keep rising is simply another way of saying that, as a collectivity, human beings are promising each other to produce an even greater volume of goods and services in the future than they are creating now. But even current levels are clearly unsustainable.'

References

Bey, Hakim. *TAZ: The Temporary Autonomous Zone, Ontological Anarchy, Poetic Terrorism*, New York: Autonomedia, 1991.
Canaan, Joyce E. and Wesley Shumer. "Higher Education in the Era of Globalization and Neoliberalism." *Structure and Agency in the Neoliberal University*. Eds Joyce E. Canaan and Wesley Shumer. New York: Routledge, 2008. 1–32.
Docherty, Thomas. *For the University*. Huntingdon, UK: Bloomsbury Academic, 2011.
Graeber, David. 'A Practical Utopian's Guide to the Coming Collapse,' *The Baffler*. http://thebaffler.com/salvos/a-practical-utopians-guide-to-the-coming-collapse.
Huber, Mathew. *Lifeblood: Oil, Freedom and the Forces of Capital*. Minneapolis, MN: University of Minneapolis Press, 2013.
Jarman, Derek. *Modern Nature*, London: Vintage, 1991.
Mitchell, Timothy. *Carbon Democracy: Political Power in the Age of Oil*. London: Verso, 2011.
Moore, Jason W. 'Wall Street is a Way of Organizing Nature.' *Upping the Anti: A Journal of Theory and Action* 12 (May 2012): 39–53.

Moore, Jason W. *Capitalism in the Web of Life: Ecology and the Accumulation of Capital*. London: Verso, 2015.

Plumwood, Val. *Feminism and the Mastery of Nature*. New York: Routledge, 1993.

Readings, Bill. *The University in Ruins*. Cambridge, MA: Harvard University Press, 1996.

Skinner, Jonathan. 'Thoughts on Things: Poetics of the Third Landscape.' *The Ecolanguage Reader*. Ed. Brenda Iijima. New York: Nightboat Books, 2010. 9–51.

Slaughter, Sheila and Larry Leslie. *Academic Capitalism: Politics, Policies and the Entrepreneurial University*. Baltimore, MD: The Johns Hopkins University Press, 1997.

Smithson, Robert. *The Collected Writings of Robert Smithson*. Ed. Jack Flam. Berkeley, CA: University of California Press, 1996.

Thompson, E. P., Ed. *Warwick University Ltd: Industry, Management and the University*. Harmondsworth: Penguin, 1970.

University of Warwick website. www2.warwick.ac.uk. Accessed 30 November 2014.

Young, Ellen. 'Science, Universities and The Fossil Fuel Industry: How the Public Structures of Science and Engineering Fuel Oil and Gas Company Research.' *Potential Energy: The Politics of Energy in Scotland*. Edinburgh: The Post Collective, 2015. 40–43. http://post-mag.org/tag/potential-energy.

8 Climate change, public engagement, and integrated Environmental Humanities

Steven Hartman

In 2007 the Nordic Network for Interdisciplinary Environmental Studies (NIES) was formed by nine scholars from Sweden, Norway, and Denmark with a shared concern over accelerating social-ecological change in the twenty-first century. I was one of the founders of the network and have served as its chair since 2008. Roughly two dozen international symposia, workshops, and research training courses organized over the past five years have brought approximately 150 new scholars of all experience levels to the network from throughout the Nordic region and beyond. The global change agenda has increasingly engaged the attentions and energies of NIES members, as stand-alone projects devoted to different aspects of environmental change have grown out of the network's activities. Participating scholars in these initiatives come from the arts and humanities, the social sciences, the educational sciences, and increasingly the natural sciences. Such a mix of scholars engaging jointly in theoretical discussions, educational efforts and problem-driven, team-based research is one of the hallmarks that may distinguish NIES's particular approach to integrated environmental humanities (IEH) from the methodological logics of kindred networks grounded in distinct discourses or scholarly disciplines such as ecocriticism, environmental history or environmental philosophy (cf. Hartman 2015). Above and beyond its core activities promoting integrated scholarly exchange and capacity building across the major scientific domains from arts and humanities through the social and natural sciences, NIES has initiated longer-term initiatives focused more specifically on environmental change. One of these, *Project Bifrost*, is a public humanities initiative focused on climate change action involving close collaboration of Environmental Humanities scholars and visual media artists. The second of these projects, *Inscribing Environmental Memory in the Icelandic Sagas* (IEM), is a larger integrated initiative—essentially a scholarly community of practice (cf. Wenger 1998)—that explores historical environmental change through cross-cutting, team-driven studies spanning multiple knowledge communities and scientific domains effectively organized (or even self-organizing) around questions difficult to address satisfactorily within the confines of single disciplines.

Inscribing Environmental Memory in the Icelandic Sagas

Inscribing Environmental Memory in the Icelandic Sagas (IEM) is an unfolding experiment in integrated Environmental Humanities, drawing together scholars from literary studies (both ecocriticism and medieval saga studies), archaeology, anthropology, geography, environmental history, and historical ecology/climatology.[1] IEM collaborations seek to complete and refine our understanding of how past societies responded to environmental change by drawing upon the rich vein of medieval saga literature unique to Iceland, alongside equally rich material cultural and palaeoecological data from Iceland and the wider North Atlantic. A deeper historical focus informed by critical humanities scholarship has been underrepresented in previous research on global change. If we truly wish to come to terms with the implications, and potential complications, of human-environmental interactions in the future, we would do well to better understand those of the past at various temporal and geospatial scales.

The IEM initiative[2] is defined by a radical openness to disciplinary border crossing that seeks to align physical environmental studies with aesthetic, ethical, historical, and cultural modes of inquiry (Hartman 2016). By integrating analyses of historically-grounded literature with archaeological studies and environmental science, the project aims to offer new insights into how past societies understood and coped with environmental change. It adopts the long-term approach of historical ecology as developed especially in the work of scholars such as anthropologist Carole Crumley, which examines changing human-landscape-environment interactions through time at various scales, spanning periods of known change (cf. Crumley 2012). In this way, IEM examines an archive of human responses to socioecological challenges, completed experiments of the past (Dugmore et al. 2013, p. 436) that may help us navigate the challenges of the present and future in a time of accelerated global change.

The period from Iceland's first settlement around AD 870 to the end of the fifteenth century was a time characterized by substantial environmental change. Evidence for climatic variations in the northern hemisphere during these centuries is based on climate proxy data with additional support from various documentary records (see Ogilvie 1991). The fairly rapid establishment of a frontier society on an erstwhile pristine island in the North Atlantic by Norse and Celtic-derived peoples from the late ninth century makes Iceland a particularly interesting focus of study on historical processes of environmental change, cultural adaptation, and social-ecological resilience. It is a case especially well suited to contributions from the Environmental Humanities in light of the comparatively early development in Icelandic society of literary and historiographic narratives focused on identifiable Icelandic ancestral communities and the environs in which they lived and died, sometimes in conflict over natural resources.

Not all the outputs of the IEM collaborations are fully interdisciplinary. Some studies can be more accurately characterized as multidisciplinary, insofar as formulation of their driving research questions along with their execution and dissemination of outcomes may be defined in certain cases by the agendas, methods, and conventions of a particular field, such as archaeology (cf. Frei et al. 2015). But concerted efforts are also being made within the IEM collaborations to co-design and co-execute joint research studies according to more fully interdisciplinary principles of integrated research, defined not by the normative expectations of any particular discipline but by collectively defined research problems that lend themselves less readily to investigation from a single disciplinary perspective.

What do we want/need to know?

What expertise must be enlisted to achieve this knowledge?

Exploratory framing questions along these lines help multiple disciplinary communities define research problems and co-design studies in ways that can satisfy the epistemological, methodological, and disciplinary expectations of their respective scientific/scholarly communities (e.g. by ensuring questions and approaches are relevant to their own traditions of inquiry) while also bridging disciplinary divides and pooling data/expertise that might otherwise remain trapped in knowledge silos. Such a joint stake in co-defining the terms of inquiry from the earliest stages in the research design process is essential to integrated environmental study.

Can publication be carried out collectively in interdisciplinary research journals?

For the most part, such journals do not exist at present.

Or must joint publication take place in multiple iterations, adjusted to the readership and discourse conventions of different research communities?

Such an approach may entail different sets of authors taking the lead in framing a particular iteration of a co-produced study for dissemination in their respective scholarly discourses (e.g. parallel iterations of the study in the form of distinct articles reconstituted for different disciplinary journals or scientific readerships). This is far from easy work. There are high transaction costs not only in formulating the research question, but also in planning the execution of the study and then finally in addressing the outcomes to diverse end users. It's not surprising in light of these challenges that truly interdisciplinary work does not happen more often. Without time and opportunity for network meetings this kind of work is hard to carry out. The efforts involved in this kind of integrated interdisciplinary research can be considerable, but so too are the potential gains. This is the model that the IEM initiative is working to promote.

Project *Bifrost*—a research–arts intervention on climate change

NIES's project *Bifrost* is a research and media arts initiative that has aimed since 2011 to document an emerging environmental humanities community. It is now also serving as a multimodal platform for communicating environmental studies knowledge and case studies to academic and non-academic audiences alike, following a trajectory of increasing engagement in the public sphere outside of academia.

The earliest iterations of the project involved production and exhibition of multi-screen documentary installations that served as bridges between conferences and symposia organized by NIES. Study themes highlighted at early symposia served as focal points in the earliest documentary installations, and filmed interviews carried out with participating researchers at these meetings served as raw materials for the narratives elaborated artistically in the installations. Materials from those interviews are carefully edited and re-presented within the documentary installations shown at successive conferences. Effectively the aim has been to bridge the different symposia and connect their diverse themes in a metanarrative meant to reflect development and continuity of the scholarly conversations anchoring NIES's activities over an arc of several years.

For instance, at the NIES V Environmental Humanities conference in Sigtuna in 2011 a 40-minute spatial documentary was projected on three screens in the chapel of the Sigtuna Foundation throughout the week-long program.

This installation incorporated interviews filmed at the previous NIES symposium in Odense five months earlier devoted to the theme of "Anti-Landscapes." In May 2012 a new documentary installation was exhibited at the NIES VI symposium in Hornafjordur, Iceland, incorporating interview footage from both Sigtuna and Odense and adding new case studies reflecting themes addressed at the most recent meeting. The full triptych and single-channel versions of these installations have also been exhibited at other international conferences over the past three years (see Figure 8.1).

Many environmental studies researchers brought in from around the world to present their work at NIES workshops and symposia have been interviewed for this project in an evolving series of scientific ethnographies meant to help document the emerging field of Environmental Humanities (EH) slowly gaining force as an academic community internationally. All *Bifrost* interviewees are invited to discuss

Figure 8.1 Composite from Bifrost 1.0 (2011) and Bifrost 2.0 (2012) installation films featuring ecocritic Ursula Heise on what the Environmental Humanities bring to the study of nature and environment

their work, to reflect on what is at stake in their research and teaching, and to offer thoughts on a range of questions concerning the entanglement of environment, nature, culture and society as well as on challenges facing the planet today. Since the project's inception more than 60 hours of scientific ethnographies have been shot, foregrounding a wide range of projects and ideas central to the emerging EH field, and this body of materials is expected to double over the next few years. Only a small fraction of these materials ever make it into *Bifrost*'s research-arts documentary installations. The bulk of this growing corpus of interviews will be used to form an online archive of mini-essays and topically organized short narratives documenting the development of interdisciplinary environmental studies over roughly a decade as the EH community moves from an inchoate field to a more cohesive and unified research area (or so we anticipate). This planned archive is envisaged as its own distinct output of the *Bifrost* project, a resource we believe may have tremendous educational and documentary value for many years to come.

A new iteration of the *Bifrost* project was launched in 2015. Titled *Bifrost—This is the Beginning*, this new project phase is dedicated to climate change as one of the preeminent challenges of the early twenty-first century. The project's premise is fairly straightforward: We are not likely to witness effective amelioration of anthropogenic global warming or successful human adaptations to global changes already underway without a coalescence of top-down and grassroots efforts. Political and economic reforms are essential, but so too are cultural interventions. We need action from artists and educators as much as we need mobilization of religious and spiritual communities on local and international scales. *Project Bifrost* aims to mobilize environmental studies expertise and knowledge through a series of coordinated

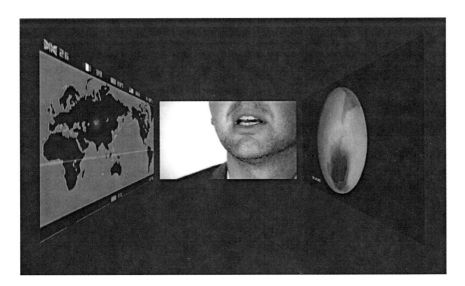

Figure 8.2 Segment from Bifrost 1.0 (2011) installation film featuring ecocritic Greg Garrard on contemporary challenges of representing environmental issues

public humanities interventions that can heighten awareness of the causes and effects of climate change. One aim of the project is to help counteract apathy and inertia by closing the distance between the denizens of city centers (initially in Western cities) and the distant environments and front-line communities exposed to the greatest risks of continued, significant climate change in the present century. In a more ambitious form than previously attempted in the project, *Bifrost—This is the Beginning* is attempting a coordinated multimodal public Environmental Humanities action comprising several distinct components.

The *Bifrost* action is event-specific and site-specific, utilizing different public niches and media actions simultaneously to present compelling stories, scenarios, and scripted scientific communications concerning climate change mitigation and the need for successful cultural and societal adaptive processes.

In part, the *Bifrost* action will attempt to achieve this end through a highly visible discussion-based public event organized with local partners, aiming for an audience of 500 – 1000 people over the course of a weekend. The *Bifrost* action will also engage the public through coordinated art installations built around specific climate change cases linked in various ways to a common thematic element—water. One of these installations will be a multi-screen spatial documentary presented in a large public space, based to some degree on the model of earlier *Bifrost* installations, though involving a wholly new presentation format and all new video content; another installation will consist of large-scale urban videos projected on nearby high-rise structures. Finally, all of these various elements will be tied together and reinforced through a well-coordinated media campaign that engages the press, local broadcast media, social media, schools, NGOs and other partnering public institutions (educational, scientific, and cultural). The *Bifrost* action is our in-house term for the large-scale, weekend-long event at which these various modalities are brought together in concert: communicative channels, art and media engagements, and the series of public talks and activities involving experts, activists, politicians, and common people living on the front lines of climate change.

The action also involves two additional components that are not site-specific and event-specific in the same way. These are the *Bifrost* website and the free #climatethought mobile subscription, which delivers short, thought-provoking text messages, memes, and podcasts of carefully scripted media outputs concerning climate change to subscribers daily during the month leading up to the *Bifrost* event.[3]

What's at stake? How can we move forward with effective humanities engagement?

The humanities remain conspicuously absent in top-down international efforts to address climate change and other pressing issues linked to today's global change developments. Calls for integrative approaches to global environmental change research are on the increase (Holm et al 2015; Castree et al. 2014). Holm et al. indicate "a crying need for experiment over and above the traditional university and its disciplinary divides" in ushering forth "developments that promote the integration of knowledge" (p. 192).

Education and learning are central to these aims and to the overriding environmental predicaments we now face. Our great challenge in the early twenty-first century is not merely to survive by adapting to increasing and ever more acute environmental constraints. Rather we must work to ensure that human societies can flourish in their totality, not merely the great and powerful at the expense of the fragile and marginalized. Moreover the welfare of the human species cannot be bought at the expense of the planet's rich biodiversity and resource base. Ultimately these challenges boil down to fundamental questions of justice and ethics, and to the knowledge, critical awareness and engagement of citizens and public institutions. The Environmental Humanities should be leading the way in global efforts to plan for and realize a sustainable future for the planet. Throughout human history, societies have shaped and legitimated relationships with their environments through arts, philosophy, literature, science, and religion. The rich repertoire of human experience embedded in these cultural traditions must be brought to bear in our quest for new paradigms of sustainable human endeavor. The great environmental predicament of the early-twenty-first century is not primarily an ecological crisis, though its ramifications are far reaching within ecological systems. Rather, it is a crisis of culture (Hartman 2015).

The educational potential of an initiative like *Bifrost* in this sense is considerable. The public action that is now being planned for the project's next and most ambitious iteration to date is being developed in cooperation with multiple partners in Sweden, not just academic institutions but also foundations and public institutions intended for the betterment of society and environment, human achievement and the production of knowledge, among them the Nobel Museum, Sigtunastiftelsen, Mid Sweden University, the Swedish International Centre of Education for Sustainable Development, and the Seed Box International Environmental Humanities Collaboratory at Linköping University. The highly visible open program intended for public participants from all ages and all walks of life will include not only prominent scientists, politicians, and public figures as speakers, but also ordinary people with compelling stories to tell about their lives and communities affected by climate change. The purpose-built website and #climatethought components of the project are intended to have a good deal of longevity and potential use long after the first *Bifrost* action takes place in 2016, with open source media components developed for the action made freely available for reuse in diverse educational contexts. Additional plans are confirmed as well with *Bifrost* partner the Nobel Museum in Stockholm for exhibits linked to the action at the museum, including a coordinated program with schools and youth groups devoted to climate questions: young people will visit the museum in excursions co-organized by their schools and the Nobel Museum during spring 2017 to meet and speak with researchers and knowledgeable public figures about environmental challenges and opportunities for societal engagement and renewal linked to climate change mitigation efforts. A contribution from these young people to the *Bifrost* action in fall 2017 is also a prominent goal; representatives of youth groups will be asked to share the stage and offer their perspectives alongside experts and political leaders. The art components of the *Bifrost* action can also have distinct educational connections and applications both during the public actions and beyond them, just as previous artistic works developed in earlier iterations of the project have continued to have a life as online documentaries after exhibition in their inaugural contexts.

As a specialized research endeavor IEM admittedly has more limited, though not less important, educational dimensions. Mostly these have been realized in doctoral education contexts. Experimental interdisciplinary summer field schools have been organized around the IEM project by NIES, NABO (North Atlantic Biocultural Organization), and the Svartarkot Culture-Nature project in Iceland during the summers of 2014 and 2015. These two-week intensive courses involve field visits to environmental sites in the contiguous northern Icelandic regions of Eyjafjörður and Þingeyjarsýsla, including active archaeological field sites, ecological research stations, and significant sites of literary production and environmental contestation as memorialized in native storytelling traditions. Environmental Humanities scholars, archaeologists, life sciences and geoscience researchers contributing to the IEM collaborations lecture in the courses, which have been attended by graduate students and postdocs from around the world, representing the fields of literary studies, history, anthropology, archaeology, geography, and medieval studies. The courses are interactive and intensively interdisciplinary. Lecturers and students live in the same housing facilities on the edge of the northern Icelandic interior wilderness. The courses are intended as embedded models of how capacity can be built at the doctoral training level in the kind of active interdisciplinary environmental studies approaches IEM is promoting in its research projects.

The two distinct NIES projects outlined in this chapter illustrate different models by which Environmental Humanities scholars can engage in integrated work that links education and research, arts and sciences, public humanities and integrated environmental study, all of which are not only relevant to climate change engagement, but necessary to our understanding of global change challenges of the past, present and future.

Notes

1   The initiative is a collaboration between NIES and the North Atlantic Biocultural Organization (NABO) anchoring the Circumpolar Networks program of the Integrated History and Future of People on Earth (IHOPE), a core project of Future Earth.

2   IEM is a confluence of research projects and scholarly collaborations that straddles the fence between a large project and a cohesive program, without being easily definable as either. It may be best characterized as a Scholarly Community of Practice (SCoP).

3   The first action in the next iteration of the *Bifrost* project is planned to take place in the center of Stockholm (at Kulturhuset, Sergels Torg, near Central Station) over the course of a full weekend in October/November 2017, near the two-year anniversary of the COP 21 climate meeting in Paris in 2015. Subsequent actions are now in the planning stages at other international sites, such as New York and Calgary in 2018-2019. More information on *Bifrost—This is the Beginning* will be updated periodically on www.projectbifrost.org.

References

Castree, Noel, et al. "Changing the intellectual climate." *Nature Climate Change,* 27 August 2014, 763–768.

Crumley, Carole. 2012. "A Heterarchy of Knowledges: Tools for the Study of Landscape Histories and Futures." In *Resilience and the Cultural Landscape: Understanding and Managing Change in Human-Shaped Environments.* T. Plieninger and C. Bieling (eds). Cambridge: Cambridge University Press, 303–314.

Dugmore, A, et al. 2013. "'Clumsy solutions' and 'elegant failures': lessons on climate change adaptation from the settlement of the North Atlantic islands." In *A Changing Environment for Human Security: Transformative approaches to research, policy and action.* Linda Sygna, Karen O'Brien and Johanna Wolf, (eds). Abingdon and New York: Routledge.

Frei, Karin M., et al. 2015. "Was it for walrus? Viking Age settlement and medieval walrus ivory trade in Iceland and Greenland". In *World Archaeology* 47:3, 439–466.

Hartman, Steven. 2015. "Unpacking the Black Box: the need for Integrated Environmental Humanities." *Future Earth Blog,* 3 June 2015.

Hartman, Steven. 2016. "Revealing Environmental Memory: what the study of medieval literature can tell us about long-term environmental change." *Biodiverse.* No. 2, 2016.

Holm, Poul, Dominic Scott & Arne Jarrick. 2015. *Humanities World Report 2015,* Palgrave Macmillan.

Ogilvie, A.E.J. 1991. "Climatic changes in Iceland AD c. 865 to 1598." In *The Norse of the North Atlantic, Acta Archaeologica 6,* Copenhagen: Munksgaard, 233–251.

Wenger, E. 1998. *Communities of Practice,* Cambridge University Press, Cambridge.

Part II

Teaching and learning climate change head-on

9 Thinking climate change like a planet

Notes from an environmental philosopher

J. Baird Callicott

Let's assume that these notes sketch out an elective course with no prerequisites and open to all students, not a required course in an environmental studies program centered on climate change.

Right off the bat: Global climate change is the most urgent environmental problem of the twenty-first century and will probably remain so for the following centuries. Not only does it eclipse all other environmental issues, it also entrains them. Biodiversity loss, to take but one example, is exacerbated by climate change because the habitats of many organisms may migrate northward more rapidly than they can—or disappear altogether. Desertification is another example.

Environmental philosophy has been heavily skewed toward environmental ethics and this is certainly true of the philosophical response to climate change— called "climate ethics." Most of the existing work in climate ethics, however, has been done less by those philosophers long invested in environmental ethics than by those steeped in mainstream twentieth-century Anglo-American moral philosophy.

Environmental ethicists have been slow to address climate change in large part because climate change has radically expanded the spatial and temporal scales that have framed the field from its inception. When academic environmental ethics emerged in the 1970s, it was scientifically informed primarily by evolutionary biology and ecology and has been scaled accordingly. Aldo Leopold, the most influential precursor of academic environmental ethics, famously urged us to "think like a mountain." In his day, that was thinking big. When he turned that phrase in the mid-1940s, Leopold was making a plea on behalf of big, fierce predators— which coevolved with their prey to the mutual benefit of such interrelated species. He notes that a buck pulled down by wolves can be replaced (through reproduction) in three years, but a range, over-eaten by deer, will take as many decades to recover (through ecological succession). The temporal difference between deer reproduction and range recovery is a neat order of magnitude. Now, however, we must think like a planet, and that requires us to think in temporal terms of at least another order of magnitude more. And the spatial scale of global climate change is, well, global. And how many mountains are there on the globe? Therefore, existing environmental ethics—such as the Aldo Leopold land ethic, focused on the integrity, stability, and beauty of biotic communities—cannot simply be scaled up to address climate change ethically. Further, the sciences informing climate ethics are biogeochemistry and Earth systems science. So environmental philosophers have to come up to speed in these sciences, as they once had to do in evolutionary biology and ecology. And that's no easy task.

Thus the first thing will be teaching the basics of climate science: greenhouse gases; rising average global temperature; heat-expansion of seawater + melting glaciers and Arctic and Antarctic sea ice = rising sea level; acidification (carbonic acid) of the oceans and the impact of a downward pH shift on shellfish; increase in the frequency and violence of storms, floods, droughts, northward migration of tropical pathogens. The most general characterization of the phenomenon is not "global warming" but a shift to a more energetic planet. This initial part of the course is not science—no advanced mathematics, no modeling software—but science literacy, a humanities.

Homing in on a fitting temporal scale for climate change is the second thing. Methane (CH_4), one of strongest greenhouse gases, is highly reactive (it's the "natural gas" that heats homes and generates electricity); and it is thus short-lived in the atmosphere. But carbon dioxide (CO_2) is an inert gas, removed from the atmosphere mainly by photosynthesis. The effects of its increase in the atmosphere, even up to just this point in time, will last centuries into the future. Thus the residence time of CO_2 in the atmosphere might be one way to specify the temporal scale of climate ethics. Obviously and unproblematically, the fitting spatial scale for climate ethics is the whole biosphere—the living Earth, Gaia.

According to Aldo Leopold, the fitting objects of concern for the land ethic are biotic communities. Is Gaia the fitting object of concern for climate ethics? The answer is Definitely not. And to many students of a warm heart and romantic disposition that may come as a shocking disappointment. But again the reason is temporal scale. That of climate change and that of Gaia's biography, in which climate change is the norm, are wildly different.

So the next thing to teach—as a lesson in intellectual sobriety—is a biosketch of Planet Earth with an emphasis on past climate change. Life on Earth is resilient and tenacious, having been around for some three and a half billion years. Over that time, Gaia has experienced a number of environmental cataclysms and rebounded to be more vigorous and biodiverse than ever. When life first emerged on Earth there was no free oxygen in the atmosphere. Oxygen is produced by cyanobacteria, the first photosynthetic organisms, and its accumulation in the atmosphere was a lethal poison for the older anaerobic organisms that evolved in its absence. (I say "is" produced by cyanobacteria, not "was" because it still is. The chloroplasts of all photosynthetic organisms are descendants of formerly free-living cyanobacteria, just as the mitochondria in our human cells are descendants of formerly free-living prokaryotic cells.) Anaerobic organisms survive today in oxygen-free environments, such as lake sediments and the guts of animals like ourselves. Talk about climate change: the oxygenation of Earth's atmosphere was a really big one. Subsequently, the Earth went through cycles of near total glaciation (whimsically called Snowball Earth) and melting. Those were big climate changes too. Carbon dioxide concentrations in the atmosphere have fluctuated greatly over geologic time. About 500 million years ago, CO_2 was up to about 5000 parts per million—an order of magnitude greater than what climatologists regard as a worst-case scenario in the coming centuries—and it was really hot. During the more recent Pleistocene glaciations, atmospheric CO_2 dropped to a low of 180 parts per million. (All these numbers should be referenced for comparison to the pre-industrial Holocene norm of 250 ppm.) On the geologic-temporal scale, the overall trend is down as carbon is buried underground and volcanic emissions of CO_2 peter out.

In short, Gaia is in absolutely no serious danger from us *Homo sapiens*. From Her unimaginatively long temporal perspective, we might indeed be prolonging Gaia's lifespan by digging up and rereleasing sequestered carbon. (Remember, atmospheric CO_2 is what green plants derive their carbon from to photosynthesize carbohydrates.) Gaia's secret name for us might be *Homo petroleumus*, her own sapient invention for "enriching" the atmosphere for plants—on which, of course, animals ultimately depend—and keeping that vital element, carbon, in circulation a good while longer than it otherwise might be.

The most general point of these considerations is that all ethics, including climate ethics, is scale-sensitive. Was the meteor strike that doomed the dinosaurs a bad thing? For the dinosaurs living then, it certainly was; but not for us, because it ushered in the age of mammals and paved the way for our own eventual evolutionary emergence. There do exist genuine objects of ethical concern associated with the current episode of global climate change. But one of them is not the biosphere in its temporal totality. Rather, it's the current state of the biosphere, which has enabled our species to flourish, that we need to be worried about. *Homo sapiens* evolved in the Pleistocene, but the Holocene enabled our species to domesticate plants and animals, thus to settle down, and build cities, and invent all the arts, both practical and fine—from agriculture and architecture to music and medicine to ziggurats and zoological gardens—that constitute human civilization. And it's the current state of the biosphere to which "our fellow voyagers in the odyssey of evolution" are adapted. If biodiversity has intrinsic value, as many conservation biologists contend, then the most fundamental axiom of biodiversity conservation is to preserve the Holocene climate.

In short, what global climate change threatens is the survival of human civilization and biodiversity. If Earth's past biography is any indication, biodiversity will recover—but not for several million years and not with the same species composition as when we humans inherited the Earth. So, on any temporal scale that is humanly meaningful, a sixth mass extinction would be tragic; and certainly biodiversity as we presently know it would be lost forever. Global climate change is not something that *might* happen, not just something that surely *will* happen, but something that *is* happening. Glaciers and Arctic and Antarctic sea ice *are* melting. Sea levels *are* rising. The oceans *are* acidifying. More frequent and violent storms, floods, and droughts *are* occurring. And we see the future of global human civilization in the rash of failed states—such as Libya, Chad, Somalia, Afghanistan, and Syria—precipitating mass migrations, which threaten the stability of the states absorbing the migrants. If we do nothing to slow, eventually to stop, and finally to reverse climate change, the world will be biologically impoverished for the next several million years and *Homo sapiens* will survive, if at all, in remnant populations living in a state of barbarism and in an interminable Dark Age.

Now that we have identified the objects of concern—two of them anyway— how do we address them ethically? Twentieth-century mainstream Anglo-American moral philosophy was dominated by two major paradigms and a minor third: utilitarianism, Kantian deontology, and virtue ethics.

All three, however, share two fundamental characteristics: (1) moral agents (those who act) and moral patients (those who are affected by the actions of agents) are individuals; and (2) the wellspring of moral action is reason. We may thus call the uber-paradigm of twentieth-century mainstream Anglo-American moral philosophy Rational Individualism. The utilitarian principle of equality or impartiality is an ethical application of logic. To treat equal interests unequally—say to relieve the suffering of a relative or friend but not that of a stranger—is to be inconsistent and irrationally partial to one's own kith and ken, utilitarians argue. And only individuals have interests. Groups (such as a nation, a race, a species) per se do not. Kant argues that his "categorical imperative"—Act only on those maxims that you can will to be a universal law—is an application of the logical law of non-contradiction. The antithesis of so-called "perfect duties," such as promise keeping, would be self-annihilating. For example, if it were a universal law that everyone always break their promises, no one's promise would be believed, and thus eventually promise making *and therefore promise breaking* would cease to exist. The antithesis of so-called "imperfect duties" involves a "contradiction of the will." I will, for example, that giving alms to the poor were a universal law, but do not give any myself. The poor would be poorer if my maxim—Give no alms to the poor—were a universal law, but non-alms-giving would not cease to exist.

Climate ethicist Dale Jamieson has nicely summarized the core assumption of the uber-paradigm of ethics in mainstream twentieth-century moral philosophy: "An individual acting intentionally harms another individual; both the individuals and the harm are identifiable; and the individuals and the harm are closely related in time and space." Jamieson illustrates this core assumption with a little ditty about Jack stealing Jill's bicycle. Then Jamieson "alters the case along various dimensions": Jack is one of several people, each of whom steal a part of Jill's bike; Jack buys a bike in Jamaica assembled from stolen bike parts including one of Jill's who lives in Jerusalem; and finally Jack and the other seven billion people of his generation on Earth use up all the resources necessary for manufacturing bikes, such that Jill, living several centuries after Jack, will never have a bike. As the case alters along all these dimensions, Jack's personal culpability diminishes to a vanishing point. The last two cases are analogous to climate change. Can we assign blame to Jamaican Jack for the theft of Jerusalem Jill's bike? A little maybe, but is he as blameworthy as the Jack who stole Jill's bike, lock, stock and barrel? Analogously, can we assign blame for the suffering of Micronesians who are now experiencing periodic flooding (and eventually will see their whole islands slip beneath the waves) to you, the reader of this chapter, who puts somewhere between 2000 to 5000 tons of carbon into the atmosphere each year out of about 600,000,000,000 tons per year total? Can we assign blame to Present Jack for Future Jill's bikelessness, just as we did when he and he alone stole her bike? Analogously, can we assign blame to people suffering from climate change in 2315 to any person living now who burns fossil fuels? If no individual can be blamed for climate change, no individual has a moral obligation to shrink their carbon footprint. As Jamieson puts it, in the face of global climate change the prevailing uber-paradigm of ethics "collapses."

That should send moral philosophers back to the drawing board to come up with a new paradigm, but Rational Individualism seems to be baked into mainstream Anglo-American philosophical DNA. Meanwhile, a completely different ethical paradigm has been gestating in evolutionary biology, since it was explored by Charles Darwin in *The Descent of Man*. We can call it Emotional Collectivism. Its philosophical pedigree goes back to the mid-eighteenth century and the moral philosophy of David Hume, who argued that the wellspring of ethics is a reservoir of emotions called the "moral sentiments"—such as sympathy, benevolence, loyalty, and care. Some of the moral sentiments—sympathy, for example—are oriented to individuals. But some—patriotism and some forms of loyalty—are oriented to collectives, such as our nations, our institutions, our professions, even our beloved sports teams (such as Manchester United or the Oakland Athletics).

Hume's original Emotional Collectivism was purely descriptive, but Darwin's was explanatory. The moral sentiments evolved because *Homo sapiens* is a quintessentially social species and, as Darwin pointed out: "No tribe could hold together if murder, robbery, treachery, etc. were common." And if the tribe could not hold together, its members would have to make it as solitaries and that's pretty impossible for humans to do. So those who were "well endowed" with the moral sentiments—and thus could live peaceably together with others and pursue life's struggle cooperatively and share the benefits thereof fairly—survived and passed their emotional profile on to their offspring. Those who could not, starved or got picked off by predators; and with them died their larcenous, murderous, and treacherous proclivities.

Make no mistake though, reason plays a crucial cognitive role in Emotional Collectivism. The objects of the moral sentiments are genetically underdetermined. To whom should one's sympathy be directed? To what corporate entity should one be loyal? On what social organization should one's self-sacrificing patriotism be lavished? The answers to these questions are a matter of cognitive learning. And some answers are good, and some are bad. Examples of bad answers follow: as to sympathy, only to members of one's ethnic group, religious sect, or race and not "alien" others; as to patriotism, not to the country of one's birth or naturalized citizenship, but to the Islamic State in Iraq and Syria (ISIS); as to loyalty, not to one's civil society, but to the mafia or a street gang.

Now apply Emotional Collectivism to the moral problem presented by global change. Depending on each individual to see the light and voluntarily reduce his or her use of fossil fuels will not work. Only if everyone is either compelled or incentivized to reduce their carbon footprint will climate change be mitigated. That requires collective action in the form of policies and laws—making coal burning illegal, instituting carbon taxes, cap and trade, public investment in alternative energy. The effective moral agents are not individuals but governments and international corporations.

Aldo Leopold understood that our responsibility to future generations crosses a temporal threshold several generations out in the future. He distinguishes between "immediate posterity" and "the Unknown Future."

Collective Emotivism is not about onerous duties, but such things as love and care. And practically everyone loves and cares for their own children and grandchildren. One can bequeath a trust fund to one's own children and grandchildren and not to those of others, but one cannot bequeath an optimal climate to one's own immediate posterity, but not to that of others. That takes cooperation and collective action. So appeals to support candidates for political office who will enact laws and implement policies that compel or incentive everyone to reduce their carbon footprint might be effective if pitched in terms of love and care for one's own immediate posterity. Because practically everyone has (or eventually will have) children and grandchildren that they love and care about, the nearest and dearest objects of the moral sentiments are thus collectivizable.

One cannot love and can hardly care about presently nonexistent (and moreover indeterminate) individual members of the Unknown Future, despite the arguments of Rational Individualists that we owe them equal consideration because they will be as interested as we in life, liberty, and the pursuit of happiness. Intergenerational justice has proved to be a hard sell, as mainstream Rational Individualists themselves lament. The duration of human civilization—emerging about 10,000 years ago and becoming robust about 5000 years ago unfolds on the same temporal scale as global climate change. And it is something that is present to our minds and senses and something that we can care about a lot. Consider the current orgy of destruction of the pre-Islamic antiquities of the Middle East by ISIS. Our sense of loss and moral outrage is palpable. Now imagine the destruction of the *all* the concert halls, art museums, architectural marvels, literature, philosophy, and religious diversity on a global scale. That's a distinct possibility if the great coastal cities of the world are inundated by a sea-level rise measured in meters and the chaos and collapse of law and governance that would ensue. Rational Individualists cannot conceive of global human civilization per se as a moral patient, but Emotional Collectivists certainly can because it is a fitting object of those of our moral sentiments directed to social wholes.

In conclusion, teaching climate change philosophically involves the following elements: science literacy; an appreciation of the relevance of spatial and temporal scale to ethics; how the spatial and temporal scales of climate change require a radical paradigm shift in ethics; what is at stake as we confront climate change (not the biosphere, not the human race, but human civilization and biodiversity); and finally positive (love and care), not negative (self-sacrifice and cold, rational duty) motivation for responding to the challenge of climate change via incentivized collective (not voluntary individual) action.

References

Callicott, J. Baird. *Thinking Like a Planet: The Land Ethic and the Earth Ethic*. New York: Oxford University Press, 2013.

Gardiner, Stephen M., Simon Caney, Dale Jamieson, and Henry Shue (eds). *Climate Ethics: Essential Readings*. New York: Oxford University Press, 2010.

Jamieson, Dale. *Reason in a Dark Time: Why the Struggle Against Climate Change Failed—And What It Means for Our Future*. New York: Oxford University Press, 2014.

10 Teaching about climate change and indigenous peoples

Decolonizing research and broadening knowledge

Mark Carey, Kathy Lynn, Kevin Hatfield, and Jennifer O'Neal

Introduction

Indigenous peoples are likely to suffer disproportionately from climate change because marginalized populations are often among the most heavily affected but have the fewest resources to respond to rapid environmental change. From the displacement of tribes due to rising sea levels and declining permafrost to melting sea ice crucial for livelihoods, indigenous peoples already confront the realities of climate change. Additionally, indigenous people's understandings of climate change, their perceptions of risk, and their knowledge and experiences that form the basis for their decisions are often distinct from non-indigenous peoples or government policies (Bennett et al.).

In an era when theories of coupled natural-human systems and social-ecological systems are abundant but generally not integrated into climate change research or policies, teaching about climate change and indigenous peoples shows how essential these more culturally oriented perspectives are for analyzing global environmental change. As Terri Plake, a geologist at Northwest Indian College, explains, "Traditional indigenous perspectives view Earth as the interrelationships and interdependence of all living and non-living things, including humans" (Plake). Teaching climate change with a focus on indigenous peoples thus shows students not only that climate change is deeply cultural but also, and more broadly, that nature and culture—and thus various university departments from the natural sciences to the humanities—cannot be bifurcated into separate categories. It also demonstrates that a humanities approach is critical to understand how people live with, engage, debate, respond to, become vulnerable, and adapt to (or don't) global climate change (Carey, James, and Fuller; Castree et al.).

Teaching about indigenous peoples and climate change is insightful because climate issues can engage classrooms in broader discussions about environmental epistemologies across diverse cultures, as well as race and class dynamics in environmental management. Courses focusing on climate change and indigenous peoples teach students about native histories and sovereignty, decolonizing research methodologies, distinct knowledge systems and cultural values, environmental justice, and notions of multicultural tolerance.

The courses

Three courses at the University of Oregon (UO) merged in fall 2014 to analyze indigenous peoples and climate change under the umbrella theme of "environment, culture, and indigenous sovereignty in the Americas." The four faculty collaborating in this initiative approached their courses through diverse perspectives. "Climate and Culture in the Americas" (Carey) was an interdisciplinary Honors College environmental history course that analyzed climate change through historical and cultural perspectives to underscore differential climate impacts and vulnerabilities alongside the cultural construction of climate through time and space, with case studies addressing the Andes and Arctic. "Climate Change and Indigenous Peoples" (Lynn) was an Environmental Studies course that examined both climate change impacts on indigenous ways of life, subsistence, lands rights, future growth, cultural survivability, spirituality, and financial resources as well as indigenous rights and tribal sovereignty in the United States. "Decolonizing Research: The Northern Paiute History Project" (Hatfield and O'Neal) was an Honors College history colloquium that emphasized the values of community-based, intercultural, decolonizing, multidisciplinary research among native and non-native students, historians, and scholars, with a specific focus on the Confederated Tribes of Warm Springs and the Burns Paiute Tribe.

These courses explored issues from distinct disciplinary and cross-disciplinary perspectives, but with related core themes that transcended all three courses. A decolonizing research methodology underpinned our courses, which led us to include indigenous perspectives regarding traditional knowledge, to share our research with indigenous communities, and to follow appropriate ethics protocols, such as those outlined by Linda Tuhiwai Smith, who explains that "Indigenous methodologies tend to approach cultural protocols, values and behaviors as an integral part of methodology. They are 'factors' to be built into research explicitly, to be thought about reflexively, to be declared openly as part of the research design, to be discussed as part of the final results of a study and to be disseminated back to the people in culturally appropriate ways and in a language that can be understood" (Smith 15).

These methodologies are crucial to examine because, while there is some recognition of the ways in which epistemologies of indigenous knowledge and the natural sciences vary markedly, indigenous knowledge is nonetheless often marginalized from climate change research, policies, and media attention (e.g. Ford, Vanderbilt and Berrang-Ford). Further, in the context of global environmental change, traditional knowledge can inform indigenous strategies in response to climate change (Bennett et al.). Decolonized research methods that rely on tribal leadership and indigenous knowledge based in particular places and cultures can help produce culturally relevant and respectful knowledge held sacred by tribes. Identifying vulnerabilities and assessing adaptation strategies in the face of global change can only occur when the cultural values that mediate behavior and perceptions are both recognized and respected. Moreover, cultural resources may be threatened by changes in temperature and precipitation, rising sea levels, thinning sea ice, shrinking glaciers, drought, and wildfire (Bennett et al.). Climate change can further erode cultures and indigenous sovereignty by reducing access to cultural resources and triggering yet another forced relocation of indigenous peoples from their lands.

Pedagogical strategies and approaches

Pedagogical justification for these three UO courses came not only from the need to focus on climate change and indigenous peoples, but also from insights into university teaching that focus on team teaching, active learning, experiential learning, student engagement, and public dissemination of research. For example, geographers Susan Hanson and Susanne Moser explain how courses on the human dimensions of global change that emerged in the 1990s were most successful when they went beyond lectures by developing "teaching and learning materials that invite active student participation, challenge students to think critically and discover principles on their own, and ask students to work cooperatively to solve problems" (Hanson and Moser 17). Other university professors stress the benefits of linking geology, environmental studies, and Native American Studies into a single course, such as the GeoJourney course at Bowling Green State University (Elkins, Elkins, and Hemmings); or by linking university coursework with civic engagement projects in which undergraduates do research for public consumption, such as with the Veterans History Project at the University of Nebraska at Kearney (Davis, Ellis, and van Ingen); or to involve students in all aspects of research, writing, and dissemination within the context of a single university course, such as through the "Book Project" at Virginia Tech (Stephens, Jones, and Barrow).

In our UO case, we substituted this Book Project for a public student conference, and students wrote substantive final papers shared as conference posters or oral presentations that were "published" on our course website (http://ccip.uoregon.edu). Overall, our courses were informed by increasing tendencies across universities for cross-disciplinary, collaborative, engaged learning that have professors learning alongside students in the active learning environment, thereby modeling intellectual growth and scholarship (Shibley; Vogler, and Long). By putting more than one professor—and especially professors from different disciplines—into the same classroom where they could learn alongside students, the students engaged topics, grappled with issues, and retained material, often teaching each other. They also gained exceptional professional development and research experience by presenting projects in the public conference.

Pedagogical innovation for our courses came primarily in three ways: simultaneous courses, community-engaged learning, and a collaborative student conference featuring student research and direct engagement with native students and tribal elders.

Simultaneous courses

Carey and Lynn taught separate courses with different disciplinary emphases, many distinct readings, and different geographical coverage (Carey on Latin America and the Arctic, Lynn on the United States), but with shared themes. They held joint meetings with the same readings every two weeks, putting students from both courses into the same classroom where the students could discuss perspectives and teach each other how their own class had been grappling with common themes. Combined course meetings focused on five principal topics ranging from indigenous knowledge and understandings of climate, drawing on indigenous perspectives from Daniel Wildcat and various international indigenous climate change declarations to explorations of climate science, justice, and the relationship between indigenous knowledge and the natural sciences (Whyte). The simultaneous courses also examined several case studies in their joint meetings, including a Latin America case examining the indigenous concept of *buen vivir* (living well) as an alternative ideology to neoliberal, capitalist worldviews, policies, and economies (Cunningham Kain; Cochrane) and cases on climate change impacts and indigenous responses in the Arctic from Kivalina, Newtok, and Shishmaref, Alaska (Bronen; Cochran et al.). A culmination of the joint classes focused on climate change solutions related to adaptation, migration, and indigenous-scientific partnerships (Wildcat).

Community-engaged learning

Visiting indigenous scholars and students presenting at our "Climate Change and Indigenous Peoples" conference resounded the maxim, "we don't care what you know, until we know that you care" when reflecting on their collaborations with researchers and academic institutions. Hatfield and O'Neal's "Decolonizing Research" course thus developed an overarching partnership with tribal elders and community members of the Confederated Tribes of Warm Springs and Burns Paiute Tribe in the Northern Great Basin of central and eastern Oregon. Through continuous interaction with community partners, students confronted the traditional dichotomy between the authorized "academic expert" and the "subordinated subject," and they explored how research universities generally, and non-native historical scholarship specifically, have often functioned as sites of oppression, assimilation, and ethnocide (Garroutte). Students worked closely with the community partners and received feedback and mentorship on each step of their research papers through field research trips to the Warm Springs Reservation, as well as course partner class visits on campus, conference calls, and written correspondence.

Within this context of collaboration, students participated in an "apprenticeship" in the historian's craft designed to offer an inquiry-based intellectual space encouraging discovery, curiosity, empathy, and reciprocity. The instructors and course partners co-constructed a body of research questions with particular meaning for the tribal communities, encompassing the broader themes of identity, indigeneity, sovereignty, self-determination, resistance, rights, and restoration. A two-day field research trip to the Confederated Tribes of Warm Springs Reservation embodied the transformative centerpiece for undergraduate learners and placed students in direct dialogue with tribal community partners. This community-engaged learning throughout the course helped students understand that, as Wilson Wewa, Warm Springs tribal elder and spiritual leader, told us, "most of the books and history that has been written that are in libraries ... is not our own history, it has been a diluted history based on writings from the military, from the federal government, from the state government, and the Indian agents. With dedicated researchers and students, they are the ones that want to know the truth, they are the ones that are unlocking those doors of change."

Student conference

Another pedagogical innovation in these courses was the student conference open to the public near the end of the term. This "2014 Climate Change and Indigenous Peoples Conference: Environment, Culture and Indigenous Sovereignty in the Americas" featured keynote speaker Patricia Cochran, Executive Director of the Alaska Native Science Commission, as well as presentations from four native students from universities around the United States and Canada. All students enrolled in the three courses either gave an oral presentation alongside visiting native students during a conference panel or presented a poster at a public session juried by a panel of UO faculty. The conference sessions focused on four themes: (1) "decolonizing research: traditional knowledge, history, and science"; (2) "climate impacts and culture"; (3) "sovereignty and environmental justice"; and (4) "case studies."

   The student conference and its interacting components generated several critical outcomes for students. For some, there was a practical aspect of seeing a major project through to the end with the added pressure of delivering the results to the general public. As one student explained in her course feedback, the conference "was productive in giving us practice in managing long-term research projects. ... I also greatly benefited from the practice of giving an academic presentation in preparation for my upcoming thesis defense." For others the conference aspect of these courses—and the fact that multiple courses came together to participate in it—stimulated engagement with course content. One student, for example, indicated: "I don't think if I've ever been part of an academic environment where people invest so heavily in grappling with and understanding the issues. The conference was a great opportunity to share what we've learned, and it also provided context to reflect on the importance of the issues." Another student reflected, "I think the conference served as a great culmination of what we learned, particularly because we got to hear from native scholars who live every day what we have been learning in the course, particularly on incorporating Western science into the knowledges of their tribes." Students also reported how the conference facilitated discussion across a great range of perspectives. One student concluded that "... the poster session gave me an opportunity to see the direction other students had taken what we learned in the course and applied it to their research." Overall, the pedagogical techniques of simultaneous courses, community-engaged learning, and the student conference significantly transcended the value of teaching a single course on climate change and indigenous peoples.

Outcomes and conclusions

Several noteworthy outcomes resulted from the faculty collaborations, student-faculty interactions, community-engaged learning, and culminating student conference. Two students from our courses won the UO's prestigious Undergraduate Research Award, while another won the UO's Martin Luther King, Jr. Essay Award. Three students presented their course papers at the Western Social Science Association Conference with tribal partners, while individual students presented at both the 2015 American Historical Association Annual Meeting and the 2015 National Conference on Undergraduate Research. A dozen more presented at the UO's Undergraduate Research Symposium. Two students published their papers in a peer-reviewed undergraduate journal (Dier; Peck). Research that two other undergraduate students began in this course subsequently turned into an article in *Nature Climate Change* (Carey, James, and Fuller). Finally, O'Neal and Hatfield recently highlighted their course in an American Historical Association publication (O'Neal and Hatfield).

Teaching climate change and indigenous peoples provides opportunities to explore innovative pedagogies and mentor students in climate change research and the public dissemination of results. These UO courses fostered public discussions of climate change through a lens of diverse knowledge systems, of differential vulnerabilities and responses to climate change, and of diverse human-focused (rather than solely scientific) ways of understanding climate knowledge, impacts, and adaptation. They emphasized decolonizing research methodologies in the analysis of indigenous voices, perspectives, and knowledges. In our current era when climate change discussions and policies continue to eclipse the humanities while overly privileging the natural sciences and Western worldviews, this focus on indigenous peoples and the critical analysis of epistemologies are urgently needed to make climate change adaptation more just.

Acknowledgments

This chapter is based on work supported by the National Science Foundation grant #1253779 and by the University of Oregon's Tom and Carol Williams Fund for Undergraduate Education.

References

Bennett, T. M. Bull et al. "Indigenous Peoples, Lands, and Resources." *Climate Change Impacts in the United States: The Third National Climate Assessment.* Eds Jerry Melillo, Terese Richmond, and Gary Yohe. Washington, DC: U.S. Global Change Research Program (2014): 297–317.

Bronen, Robin. "Forced Migration of Alaskan Indigenous Communities Due to Climate Change." *Environment, Forced Migration and Social Vulnerability.* Eds. Tamer Afifi and Jill Jäger. New York: Springer, (2010): 87–98.

Carey, Mark, Lincoln C. James, and Hannah A. Fuller. "A New Social Contract for the IPCC." *Nature Climate Change* 4 (2014): 1038–39.

Castree, Noel et al. "Changing the Intellectual Climate." *Nature Climate Change* 4 (2014): 763–68.

Cochran, Patricia et al. "Indigenous Frameworks for Observing and Responding to Climate Change in Alaska." *Climatic Change* 120.3 (2013): 1–11.

Cochrane, Regina. "Climate Change, *Buen Vivir*, and the Dialectic of Enlightenment: Toward a Feminist Critical Philosophy of Climate Justice." *Hypatia* 29.3 (2014): 576–98.

Cunningham Kain, Mirna. "Laman Laka: Our Indigenous Path to Self-Determined Development." *Towards an Alternative Development Paradigm. Indigenous Peoples' Self-Determined Development*. Philippines: Tebtebba Foundation, 2011: 89–116.

Davis, Roger, Mark R. Ellis, and Linda van Ingen. "Civic Engagement and Task Force Teaching: Integrating the Veterans History Project into the University Classroom." *The History Teacher* 42.3 (2009): 341–49.

Dier, Dean. "This Year the Birds Fly North: A Historical Short Story of Medicine Man Oytes and the Forced Removal of the Northern Paiute to Yakima." *Oregon Undergraduate Research Journal* 8.1 (2015): 71–87.

Elkins, Joe, Nichole M.L. Elkins, and Sarah N.J. Hemmings. "Geojourney: A Field-based, Interdisciplinary Approach to Teaching Geology, Native American Cultures, and Environmental Studies." *Journal of College Science Teaching* 37.3 (2008): 18–28.

Ford, James D., Will Vanderbilt, and Lea Berrang-Ford. "Authorship in IPCC and Its Implications for Content: Climate Change and Indigenous Populations in Wgii." *Climatic Change* 113.2 (2012): 201–13.

Garroute, Eva Marie. *Real Indians: Identity and the Survival of Native America*. Berkeley, CA: University of California Press, 2003.

Hanson, Susan, and Susanne Moser. "Reflections on a Discipline-Wide Project: Developing Active Learning Modules on the Human Dimensions of Global Change." *Journal of Geography in Higher Education* 27.1 (2003): 17–38.

O'Neal, Jennifer, and Kevin Hatfield. "Decolonizing Research: Engaging Undergraduates in Community-Based Inquiry with Tribal Partners." *AHA Today: A Blog of the American Historical Association* (2015): http://blog.historians.org/2015/02/decolonizing-research-engaging-undergraduates-community-based-inquiry-tribal-partners/ (accessed 8 Dec. 2015).

Peck, Mairin. "Ecuador's Yasuni-Itt Initiative: A Case Study on International Climate Change Mitigation Narratives." *Oregon Undergraduate Research Journal* 8.1 (2015): 17–26.

Plake, Terri. "'I Don't Know What I Don't Know.'" *In TeGrate: Interdisciplinary Teaching about Earth for a Sustainable Future* (2013): http://serc.carleton.edu/integrate/workshops/envirojustice2013/essays/71256.html (accessed 19 Nov. 2015).

Shibley, Ivan A., Jr. "Interdisciplinary Team Teaching: Negotiating Pedagogical Differences." *College Teaching* 54.3 (2006): 271–74.

Smith, Linda Tuhiwai. *Decolonizing Methodologies: Research and Indigenous Peoples*. New York: St. Martin's Press, 1999.

Stephens, Robert P., Kathleen W. Jones, and Mark V. Barrow, Jr. "The Book Project: Engaging History Majors in Undergraduate Research." *The History Teacher* 45.1 (2011): 65–80.

Tuck, Eve and K. Wayne Yang. "Decolonization is Not a Metaphor" *Decolonization: Indigeneity, Education and Society* 1 (2012): 1–40.

Vogler, Kenneth E., and Emily Long. "Team Teaching Two Sections of the Same Undergraduate Course: A Case Study." *College Teaching* 51.4 (2003): 122–26.

Wewa, Wilson and Myra Johnson Orange. "The Northern Paiute History Project." Oral History Interview Videos, 2014.

Whyte, Kyle Powys. "Indigenous Women, Climate Change Impacts, and Collective Action." *Hypatia* 29.3 (2014): 599–616.

Wildcat, Daniel R. *Red Alert! Saving the Planet with Indigenous Knowledge*. Golden, CO: Fulcrum Publishing, 2009.

11   Teaching teleconnection

Gillen D'Arcy Wood

The mainstream western news media, like Hollywood, are addicted to natural disaster scenarios. In the late summer of 2010 came an unprecedented boon of apocalyptic footage from vastly different geographic contexts and opposite ends of the spectrum of human misery: a biblical flood in north Pakistan, and hellish heat and fires in Russia. A monsoonal system of historic intensity, amplified by a prevailing La Niña, delivered sustained, extreme rainfall to Pakistan's main riverine artery, the Indus River Basin. The heaviest rains in 80 years overwhelmed Pakistan's degraded irrigation infrastructure, resulting in the worst natural disaster in the nation's history. With up to 20 million homes destroyed, the economic cost of the weeks-long deluge to struggling Pakistan was more than $40 billion (World Meteorological Organization 5). Meanwhile, at the other end of the Euro-Asian landmass, western Russia lay crippled by a multi-year drought. From mid-July, an unprecedented "mega-heatwave" saw temperatures rise 10°C above their seasonal mean. Operating on already moisture-depleted soils, the weeks-long heatwave sparked forest and peat fires across more than a million hectares of the vast grain-producing regions of Russia and the Ukraine. Woefully unadapted to such extreme wildfire danger, Russian emergency services floundered in the crisis. 25 percent of the nation's harvest was lost, the death toll topped 55,000, and economic losses from the disaster reached US$15 billion (Barriopedro et al. 220–24).[1]

Reporting in the 24-hour news cycle is strong on disaster imagery but weak on climatological analysis, including the vital principle of teleconnection, by which climate scientists trace the remote and complex linkages between weather events on hemispheric scales. The Russian fires and Pakistan floods, to all appearances unconnected weather crises, were, in fact, inextricably linked, as a subsequent body of climatological literature has shown (Lau and Kim 392). An "extraordinarily strong and prolonged extratropical atmospheric blocking event" over eastern Europe paralyzed the northern jet stream in July 2010, channeling heat from North Africa to Russia, while sucking monsoonal rains to the north over Pakistan. In climatic terms, urban European Muscovites, clutching handkerchiefs to their faces, suffered the same extreme meteorological event in summer 2010 as the impoverished peasants of Northern Pakistan swimming for their lives.

What are the implications of such events as the interlinked 2010 Pakistani floods and Russian wildfires —belonging to the larger narrative of a deteriorating climate in a teleconnected globe—to academic teaching in the humanities? In this short essay, I will make the case for "teleconnection" as a new principle of environmental pedagogy in the humanities, in which students are challenged to synthesize data and analyses from a variety of disciplines into narratives of climate change that exemplify the inteconnectedness of the global human-natural system.

As postcolonial environmental history teaches, the relative vulnerability of human communities to the rapid climate change now unfolding is to a significant degree historically determined. For half-a-millennium North Atlantic countries have displaced the biophysical impact of their rapid development through an "extractivist" agro-industrial regime imposed on the resource-rich South, with dire consequences for both the human populations and ecosystems of those regions. These overlapping, centuries-old histories of colonialism and economic globalization now shape the inequitable distribution of human costs of a deteriorating global climate whose uneven ripple effects will deliver the worst impacts of drought, flood, and rising sea levels first to the most historically impoverished regions of the world, such as South Asia, sub-Saharan Africa and the Pacific Islands. An essential characteristic of twenty-first century climate change is thus its tendency to reinforce the asymmetric economic relationship between the industrialized North and Global South.

In the coming decades, however, these historical borders and hemispheric inequities will become increasingly blurred as countries in all latitudes face critical disruptions to infrastructure, water resources, and food systems. In this sense, the increasing devastation of climate change, which has been called market capitalism's greatest failure, also represents the ironic end game of the postcolonial era: the North created climate change as a byproduct of its industrialization, but cannot meet the challenge of mitigating destructive warming absent close partnership with its rapidly developing former dominions in the Global South—such as India and Brazil—who are in turn suspicious of Western-imposed constraints on their carbon-driven growth.[2] The atmosphere is a unique planetary commons, less administrable even than the oceans. Who will regulate its runaway use as a carbon sink? Adding to the political paralysis, progressives in the developed world appear stricken by the "wicked," teleconnected character of the climate change problem, which sets two cherished liberal goals—economic development of the South and environmental protection—at seemingly irreconcilable odds. Carbon, after all, has been Earth's greatest gift to the poor.

There are other, good reasons why traditional historiographies and humanities curricula have rendered the complex processes of climate and environmental change, and their interaction with human societies, mostly invisible. Modern liberal historiography might be said to have originated as a counter-discourse to the climate determinism of the eighteenth century, with its reductive and racist tendencies. Under this post-Enlightenment discursive regime, any allowance for the influence of climate on human affairs has been automatically suspect. Second, both liberal and postcolonial histories emphasize the bi-lateral relation between European nation states and their colonial dominions, rather than the multivalent, transnational flows of capital and resources that crisscross and subsume these geographical entities. As with traditional liberal historiography, postcolonialism likewise deals mostly in politically proximate causes, that is, how the colonial state apparatus and its manifold organs of ideological dissemination shaped, distorted, or destroyed subject populations. These histories are vital and revealing, but almost entirely neglect environmental drivers and constraints.

In short, though the public rhetoric of the climate change debate is replete with snapshot historical references—to paleoclimatic eras and temperature datasets of the past—there is as yet very little genuine scholarly historicism or related pedagogy of climate change filtering through to undergraduate classrooms in North America. Instead, climate has been largely ignored by the academic humanities and abandoned to its sorry fate in the public sphere, as another fast-food item of partisan politics and the vulgar news cycle, a rhetorical sinkhole of hoaxes, half-truths, and multiplex apocalypse. Is this state of affairs sustainable? Given the truly bleak prospects for our global climatic future, and the urgency of our adapting to it, it is difficult to name a more vital task for the academic humanities than to bring climate change into the classroom. With crisis comes opportunity. The fractious and demoralized debate over global warming opens the horizon for a new ecological pedagogy, one that will play a vital role in producing actively-informed, climate-progressive students and citizens for the future.

The American Meteorological Society defines "teleconnection" as "a linkage between weather changes occurring in widely separated regions of the globe" (American Meteorological Society). I have cited the Pakistan floods and Russian wildfires of 2010 as a *physical* example: what of its potential as a working figure for climate pedagogy in the environmental humanities classroom? The work of the teleconnected imagination—and thus of the teleconnected classroom—is to trace and make visible the linkages between apparently separate events or phenomena. To do this work, the instructor, teaching on teleconnected principles, must create an interdisciplinary platform for "mapping" a global network of human production and consumption interlinked with scenes of ecological crisis. The central learning outcome here is methodological: students learn *how* to think and work teleconnectedly, that is, outside simple, normative models of causation and connection—to see the kinship in disparate things. The materially assessed learning outcome is to develop student skills in the digestion of complex information and data, which they then synthesize into a sequence of short, compelling environmental narratives or "eco-histories." To best learn this ecological method and produce these narratives, the classroom should be *flipped*; that is, the lecture/content component of the course should be packaged for the students to cover outside of the classroom (as "homework") while the majority of classroom time is given over to assignments, project research, group work, with the instructor acting as mobile mentor, advisor and consultant.

That said, fundamental content delivery should not be left solely to student reading outside of the classroom. A basic goal of teaching in the environmental humanities is *systems literacy*: helping students understand the vital physical and cultural co-dependencies of human and natural systems. Because we cannot ask students to simply take this co-dependency on faith, the instructor bears the responsibility of introducing ecological systems theory as it is framed through various disciplines in the physical sciences, social sciences, and humanities. This introduction includes bringing to the classroom an ecological vocabulary unfamiliar to the traditional student in the humanities, such as "chaos," "complexity," "emergence," and, of course, teleconnection itself. This preliminary instruction should also include the next-generation task of introducing humanities students to the language and protocols of peer-reviewed research in the sciences. Students should be required to study, absorb and reference key papers in the scientific literature relevant to their research projects. The importance of this course content cannot be overstated. Only with a baseline literacy in the physical sciences relevant to climate change—or the tools to develop that literacy—can a student emerge from their humanities course on climate change equipped to fully understand and engage with global warming discourse in the public sphere.

A climate change course that has "teleconnection" for both its subject matter and method might look something like this:

Take a semester of fifteen weeks divided into five three-week units. The first week of the unit conforms to a conventional classroom format where the instructor, building upon required reading for the unit, introduces students to principles of ecological systems thinking, and from thence to the complex systemic linkages, or teleconnections, between a geophysical example of climate change—such as Arctic melting and the displacement of northern indigenous peoples—and the social-industrial phenomenon that drives the crisis, namely the rapid rise in industrial carbon emissions and resultant global warming. This introduction is thorough and grounded in the scientific literature on the subject. Here, in this first week, the instructor is modeling for her students the style of analysis the students themselves will undertake in the ensuing two weeks of project-based, in-classroom work.

A strategy for the "flipped" classroom work of weeks 2 and 3 of the unit would be to create, collectively, a list of major elements of our global socio-economic infrastructure (List A), alongside a list of apparently unrelated climate-based issues and crises (List B). Here's an off-the-top-of-the-head example:

List A	List B
US farm subsidies	Collapse of Atlantic cod fishery
The Chinese stock market	Drought in California
Real estate prices in Miami	Air pollution levels in Beijing
OPEC oil pricing	Ocean acidification levels
Abandoned neigborhoods in Detroit	$ cost of extreme weather events in Asia
Trans-oceanic shipping	Inundation of low-lying Pacific Islands
Staple food prices (wheat, rice)	Rising global temperatures
Fracking	Mass extinction of non-human species

The first class of week two of the unit involves splitting the class into research groups of three or four, while the instructor holds two hats (Lists A and B, respectively). A representative of each group picks a topic from the List A and List B hats. The groups, armed with laptops, then spend the bulk of the class "speed-searching" their topics—say, "Real estate prices in Miami" and the "Inundation of low-lying Pacific islands"—with the goal of tracing possible teleconnections through synthesis of readily accessed news articles and reliable internet sources. A class presentation looms at the end of week 3, so each group will need to decide by the end of that first class whether it wishes to keep its teleconnected pairing, trade one of its items with another group, or take its chances on another draw from the hat. This "open," negotiable dimension of the assignment encourages real-world intellectual independence, creativity and collaboration among the groups, as well as being great fun. Obviously, this first class in week two is designed to be exciting and empowering for the students, and to help build camaraderie and project momentum within each group.

Once each group has its pairing at the beginning of week 2, the students spend the balance of the unit building a narrative of teleconnection between the two phenomena. The students combine hard data and relevant scientific literature with historical timelines and critical imagination to construct a story of how, for example, Miami's vulnerability to global sea level rise will inevitably impact the real estate market there, a scenario for which the impending evacuation of Pacific communities such as the Marshall Islands and Tuvalu offers a dramatic prelude and caution. A brief, rudimentary PowerPoint presentation from the groups crowns each unit, a class in which the responsibility for critique is shared between the instructor and fellow students. A successful presentation will demonstrate the students' grasp of teleconnected thinking, where simple chains of causation are enhanced and vitalized through an ecological vocabulary of non-linear change, tipping points, emergence, etc.

The emphasis in this vital session is not on judgment/assessment of each presentation, but on what questions have been answered, which unanswered, and how well the narrative of teleconnection holds up. Might the narrative be sufficiently robust and credible, for example, to form the basis of an "op-ed" style article or environmental media campaign? Might it serve as the outline for a longer, honors-style undergraduate thesis? What would be needed, through further research and revision, to effectively communicate the truth and importance of the teleconnection narrative, without compromising its inherent complexity? The sustaining pedagogical objective of the two-week mini-research project—repeated five times during the course of the semester—is to avoid, as much as possible, the customary top-down form of information delivery in favor of student-led inquiry. Students are instructed in ecological principles and methods, but must research and synthesize data related to climate change topics on their own and collaboratively with the goal of constructing compelling, evidence-based narratives that illuminate difficult-to-see aspects of our twenty-first century climate crisis.

The limits of this essay preclude a thorough modeling of climate change pedagogy in a next-generation climate class such as this, but what the foregoing does suggest are serious limits to the capacity of conventional postcolonial and globalization instructional frameworks to address the systemic complexity, novelty, and planetary scope of climate change as an accelerating historical phenomenon. To apply Dipesh Chakrabarty's suggestive term, global warming demands we rethink our idea of the human "disjunctively" (2). Postcolonialism has envisioned the peoples of the world endowed with the same basic rights, but as anthropologically distinct and historically differentiated over the last half millennium through the operations of a brutally hierarchized global economy.

The scientific literature of climate change, on the other hand, views humanity collectively, as a unique, high-impact species whose development of carbon-based infrastructure beginning two centuries ago, and accelerating exponentially since 1950, now threatens the essential planetary conditions for civilization itself, not to mention the mass extinction of other creatures. This great age of carbon-driven growth, the Anthropocene, introduces a concept of human agency beyond the terms of postcolonial theory. "We" are altering the physical character of the planet, and yet, as Chakrabarty writes, "we cannot ever experience ourselves as a geophysical force" (12). To be human in the twenty-first century thus means to exist on disjunctive planes, both as an anthropological subject imaginatively endowed with history and "rights," and as an in-human, non-ontological agent of biophysical change.

Just as European industrialization and colonial expansion redrew the map of the world between 1750 and 1950, so climate change, and its attendant natural resource crises, will shape planetary history in the twenty-first century and beyond. Governments will fall, social systems collapse, species and ice caps disappear, and environmental refugees stream across borders to populate the shrinking well-resourced regions of the planet. Postcolonialism, as a critical account of the 1750–1950 era, never represented a truly global paradigm, tied as it was to a Eurocentric core-periphery model based on the historical extension of North Atlantic trade, conquest, and settlement. The emerging map of global climate change in the twenty-first century, by contrast, exhibits a more dense, complex, and multivalent network of physical and political relations, governed by a principle of teleconnection linking remote places, peoples, and events.

Put another way, postmodern thought—as it has influenced classroom teaching in the humanities over the last three or four decades—instructs us to be wary of origins, periodizations, and teleological thinking. But the scientific literature of global warming suggests a divergent view. If, as anthropological subjects (and teachers), we are to embrace the non-ontological human, and acknowledge our outsized place in the material history of the Earth, the origins of our global carbon-based modernity lie in the late eighteenth century, and accelerate massively after 1950. This *fact*—and its demonstrable, deterministic, revisionist power—entails a new global, materialist timeline in literary, historical, and cultural studies, and with it a new pedagogy of climate. Postcolonialism, among others, inherited a constitutive prejudice against environmentalist accounts of social history. But "history" has a way of eroding all certainties, and so it is with the anti-climatic anthropocentrism of our dominant disciplinary model of teaching in the humanities. The challenge of a twenty-first century, humanistic pedagogy of climate climate is to adopt the non-linear, teleconnected character of the climate system itself as the model for a new global historiography, one attentive but not tethered to postmodern critique and to the discourse histories of European colonialism.

Teaching teleconnection cannot be easy because it requires truly interdisciplinary curiosity on the part of the instructor, who must pass along that curiosity to her students. But the climate change classroom should hold up a mirror to the world, not the disciplinary structure of the university we all are slave to. If this means instructors become co-learners in the classroom, all the better. In the teleconnected classroom, disciplinary mastery is a myth. In its place are the three Cs: competence, conversance, and communication. At the semester's end instructors should ask themselves (and the students themselves): did they demonstrate knowledge *competence* in multiple climate-related fields? Are they *conversant* with other fields, their methods and data? And can they *communicate*, through narrative examples, how teleconnection underlies and drives the co-dependency of human and natural systems in this era of climate crisis?

The Pakistani floods and Russian wildfires of 2010—byproducts of the same extreme weather system over the Asian continent—exemplify teleconnection both in their complex feedback relationship to each other and their influence on events farther afield (the Arab Spring!). This 2010 example, and its dramatic aftermath, shows how teleconnection characterizes global politics within an integrated twenty-first century world economy in ways both analogous to and materially dependent upon the physical operations of the newly unstable climate system. The challenge ahead for the environmental humanist is to make the tracing of such remote links, in all contexts, a vital classroom method and activity. To teach teleconnectedly is to deploy the ecological vocabulary of climate change—of chaotic systems, feedback loops, tipping points, and non-linear change—as a conceptual platform from which to elevate climate pedagogy above the numbing rodomontade of news cycle reporting on global warming, and to produce students who are themselves capable of toppling that discursive regime (and saving us all).

Notes

1   See also Stefan Rahmstorf and Dim Coumou, "Increase of Extreme Events in a Warming World," *Proceedings of the National Academy of Sciences [PNAS]* 108.44 (1 Nov. 2011): 17905–09.

2   The British government sponsored *Stern Report* (2006) on the economic impacts of climate change first made the "official" public case for global warming as a systemic "market failure," and as a fundamental challenge to the global economic order.

References

American Meteorological Society. "Teleconnection." Glossary of Meteorology, 2015.

Barriopedro, David et al. "The Hot Summer of 2010: Redrawing the Temperature Record Map of Europe." *Science* 332 (8 April 2011): 220–24.

Chakrabarty, Dipesh. "Postcolonial Studies and the Challenge of Climate Change." *New Literary History* 43.1 (2012): 1–18.

Lau, William K. M., and Kyu-Myong Kim. "The 2010 Pakistan Flood and Russian Heat Wave: Teleconnection of Hydrometeorological Extremes." *Journal of Hydrometeorology* 13 (2012): 392–403.

World Meteorological Organization. *Weather Extremes in a Changing Climate: Hindsight on Foresight.* Geneva, 2011.

12 Building paradise in the classroom

Janet Fiskio

Causing trouble

Early in Ian McEwan's novel *Solar*, Nobel Prize-winner Michael Beard is "the only scientist among a committed band of artists" traveling through the Arctic with the "Eighty Degrees North Seminar" (62). One evening, "not quite drunk," Beard describes the wind turbine to be installed at his research center, aware that "He was among scientific illiterates and could have said anything" (McEwan 76). A woman artist makes "an impassioned statement of support" in response, declaring "that Beard was the only one here doing something 'real,' at which the whole room warmed to him and applauded loudly" (McEwan 76). The particular irony in this scene is that, as the novel progresses, we learn Beard is in fact a morally and intellectually bankrupt anti-hero who steals his junior colleague's ideas for " 'artificial photosynthesis,'" seeking personal glory and money to fund his luxurious lifestyle (McEwan 155). While climate change is more a backdrop than a central event in the novel, the portrait of interdisciplinary dialogue at the Arctic seminar touches on plausible dynamics in these kinds of endeavors. Humanists and artists, insecure about our contribution to solving "real" problems, tend to fail at articulating why what we do is essential in thinking through climate change, and instead accept both the problems as defined by the natural sciences and the solutions—often technological, almost always within the status quo of neoliberal capitalism—that are proposed (see J. Foster).

I open my course on climate change by stating that, while environmental studies is usually described as a problem-solving discipline, this class is about not-solving the problem of climate change. Instead, we will be causing problems, asking questions, causing trouble—that is, redefining the problem itself rather than searching for solutions. On an affective level, what this means is that I hold students in the presence of the unbearable grief of climate change, and I resist their attempts to break out of this "unbearability" by turning to technological optimism or environmental education (J. Butler, *Precarious Life* 30). Students arrive on the first day in anguish about the magnitude of the climate crisis and their inability to do anything to change it as individuals. They are knowledgeable enough to realize that 'reduce, recycle, reuse' is a form of neoliberal, individualist consumer behavior (see Maniates). But unfortunately, few alternatives to this consumer model are offered within either academic or popular discourse: when I ask students to think of collective, non-consumer actions they can take to confront climate change, they struggle. This struggle becomes a focal point we return to throughout the course, which serves as a laboratory for imagining collective responses that carve out what Nicolas Bourriaud calls "micro-utopias," or temporary autonomous zones, within the status quo (31). The course opens a space where students articulate their desires for justice, solidarity, and social change, and begin to trust that desire can be a resource for social action.[1] Throughout the course we build a vocabulary to talk about these desires through a critical engagement with the concept of affect. The course culminates in an expressive project that engages with the question of aesthetics and politics through the mode of relational aesthetics. In the following pages I offer a notated syllabus with readings, assignment notes, and the narrative that binds the course together.

"Fear of a black planet"[2]

Potential readings and media:

- Jamieson, "Ethics, Public Policy, and Global Warming"
- Hardin, "Living on a Lifeboat"
- Kaplan, "The Coming Anarchy"
- Dunn, "Fear of a Black Planet"
- Davis, *Ecology of Fear*
- Butler, *Parable of the Sower*
- Film: *Climate Refugees*
- Potter, *Green is the New Red*
- Maira and Sze, "Dispatches from Pepper Spray University"

Guiding questions:

- How do the genres of utopia, dystopia, and apocalypse construct the discourse and experience of climate change?
- What concerns might be raised about the use of apocalyptic rhetoric? Is the genre of apocalypse a problem in itself?
- What beliefs about human nature undergird these narratives?
- What concepts of responsibility are adequate to respond to those displaced by climate change?

Assignment note: inviting students to contribute media examples and analyses though a course blog, formal presentation, or informal sharing at the beginning of class is an effective way to demonstrate the pervasive narrative of apocalypse in popular discourse of climate change, as well as racialized imagery and language that links this discourse to long-standing environmental fears about overpopulation.

At the center of debates around climate change—and environmental conflicts more widely—is the question of human nature. Students often articulate a feeling of powerlessness in the face of structural inequalities that drive climate change. In response to this feeling of helplessness, they sometimes say—as they have been taught by sociobiology and popular media—that people are 'fundamentally selfish,' and that therefore the only option is to work within the capitalist system by appealing to self-interest. This narrative of self-interest is perpetuated by the widespread use of Garrett Hardin's "parable" "The Tragedy of the Commons" in environmental studies (ENVS) courses at both the high school and college level (Nixon, "Neoliberalism" 593).

Hardin's Malthusian vision in "Living on a Lifeboat" sets the stage for the first unit of this course on dystopia and apocalypse. The proliferation of dystopian fiction and film in popular culture means that students are familiar with this genre as entertainment. I ask students to become aware of how utopian, dystopian, and apocalyptic narratives influence not only the discourse but also their *experience* of climate change. The key to linking Hardin's essays with contemporary racialized anxieties is a rhetorical examination of his language and an analysis of his argument, revealing that his logic is based on a certain view of human nature rather than on empirical evidence. Reading Hardin's "lifeboat ethics" helps to clarify the ways that climate change engages with and re-energizes fears of Paul Ehrlich's "population bomb" through depictions of climate migration (Hardin 1974, 561). This section culminates in an examination of the way climate change, and specifically climate refugees, are conceived in national security discourse. I close with Octavia Butler's speculative fiction novel *Parable of the Sower*, which describes a near-future when migrants from California are barred from entering the Pacific Northwest. Butler's dystopia traces the consequences of neoliberal privatization under a changing climate regime, including a border that shifts northward, and at the same time offers a compelling vision of the potential of coalitional politics (see Fiskio).

Affect

Suggested readings and media:

- Solnit, *A Paradise Built in Hell*
- Butler, *Precarious Life*

Guiding questions:

- Why is it so difficult to imagine collective responses to climate change? How can we deprivatize our imaginations? (Solnit 9).
- What affective responses to climate change are there beyond hope and despair?
- How can the climate justice movement articulate and form communities capable of responding to the ethical and social demands of the "slow violence" (Nixon, *Slow Violence*) of climate change?

The turning point of the course is reading Rebecca Solnit's radiant work on "disaster utopias," *A Paradise Built in Hell: The Extraordinary Communities that Arise in Disaster* (21). In the first part of the course, students are immersed in dystopian and apocalyptic rhetoric, critically analyzing the way that race and gender stereotypes are evoked in climate discourse and how current thinking about population, immigration, and security reinforce the status quo of economic inequality. These narratives seem to leave no alternative to the bleak future imagined in *Parable of the Sower*. Solnit offers a persuasive account of a different human nature revealed by disaster—one that is "resilient, resourceful, generous, empathic, and brave" (8). She argues that institutions, not human nature, prevent us from creating the world we wish we lived in; the cause of our daily "social disaster" is unjust structures and in particular the hegemony of neoliberal capitalism (3). Solnit makes the invaluable observation that the privatization of public goods depends upon an internalization of neoliberal ideology: "economic privatization is impossible without the privatization of desire and imagination [...] Disasters, in returning their sufferers to a public and collective life, undo some of this privatization, which is a slower, subtler disaster all its own" (9). Solnit's text gives students permission to begin articulating their deep desires for justice without having to argue against the straw man that radical change is not possible because people will only seek self-interest, or that it is not practical to imagine fundamental social change. Once Solnit helps us identify the privatization of the imagination under neoliberal capitalism, students understand why I block their proposals for technological and consumer solutions and advocacy for environmental education, since these kinds of 'solutions' avoid engaging with the central problems that climate change reveals. Climate change is not a problem of technology and will not be solved by technological solutions. It is, instead, an effect of the economic and political systems that create injustice and inequality. *Paradise* offers the possibility that climate change, rather than becoming a Malthusian nightmare of struggle over scarce resources, might instead offer an opportunity to restructure our public life and sharing of public goods.

As my chapter title indicates, *Paradise* is the touchstone for the course. In engaging with this text, we pivot from a more conventional classroom of reading and analyzing to a community engaged in thinking together. I teach this course every year, and I am always profoundly moved by the way students respond to one another with generosity, empathy, and support. The struggle in the first part of the class to articulate collective responses outside of a market economy suddenly makes sense: it is a consequence of how the doctrine of human selfishness and the privatization of public life have subjugated our minds and desires. As students experience this freedom to talk about their utopian political longings, I introduce the concept of affect as a resource for the work of social change. Solnit again offers a way to begin this conversation, describing "that sense of immersion in the moment and solidarity with others caused by the rupture in everyday life [...] We don't even have a language for this emotion, in which the wonderful comes wrapped in the terrible, joy in sorrow, courage in fear" (5). I ask students to think beyond the cliché dichotomy of hope/despair that dominates the usual discussions of climate change and to conjure their own words for the affective flows that run through their experiences. As we read Judith Butler's work on precarity and violence, I ask them to think about mourning, an affect and practice that gets little attention in mainstream media and society (see "Violence, Mourning, Politics," in J. Butler, *Precarious Life*). Together we build a vocabulary for talking about climate change: not the language of mitigation, adaptation, technology, and hope; but of mourning, solidarity, hospitality, and love.

"Welcome to Blockadia"[3]

Potential readings and media:

- Thoreau, "Civil Disobedience"
- King, "Letter from a Birmingham Jail"
- Foreman, *Confessions of an Eco-Warrior*
- Jensen and McMillan, *As the World Burns*
- Foster, "Choreographies of Protest"
- Butler, "Bodies in Alliance and the Politics of the Street"
- Klein, *This Changes Everything*
- Films: *Occupy Love*, *Do the Math*

Guiding questions:

- How do literature, art, new media, and performance function as forms of political intervention? How do politics and aesthetics come together in blockades, protests, encampments, occupations, and demonstrations?
- Where and how does white privilege and settler colonialism manifest in the climate justice movement? How can the climate justice movement interrogate white privilege within organizations and the movement as a whole?

Note: watching protest footage together in class is a valuable way to practice how to 'read' the body in protest. Inviting students to post examples to a class blog is one way to engage students in this kind of analysis.

In Spring 2010 I was teaching my first course on climate change when student activism at COP 15 and the rise of 350.org revitalized the practice of environmental protest, and students asked me to restructure the syllabus in response to these events. Many of my students are involved in activism, and this section of the class has become a space for students to reflect on their work and to place current activism in historical context. An important aspect of my class is that we integrate a specific discussion of the significance of cultural productions such as literature, art, performance, and protest. Interdisciplinary conversations often consign the humanities and arts to the role of "public relations"—ways to get the media's attention, communicate the urgency or scientific reality of climate change, or offer an emotional appeal to the public (Toadvine 2). In contrast, I ask my students to think of protests, demonstrations, blockades, encampments, and occupation as an extension of Solnit's disaster utopias: as ephemeral sites where we can "re-stitch the relational fabric" that has been distorted by neoliberal capitalism (Bourriaud 36). The Occupy movement is a good case study for thinking through the significance (and challenges) of protest communities.

Insights from performance studies are especially helpful in giving students ways to think about the arts and humanities as more than communication of scientific facts or emotional appeals but rather as sites of political and epistemological work. Susan Leigh Foster's "Choreographies of Protest" offers an introduction to think-ing about the body as "articulate matter" in protest (395). She asks "the kinds of questions that a dance scholar might ask: what are these bodies doing?; what and how do their motions signify? [...] what do they share that allows them to move with one another?; what kind of relationship do they establish with those who are watching their actions?; what kinds of connections can be traced between their daily routines and the special moments of their protest?" (397). Together in class we view media clips of protests, examining the bodies of protestors and also the bodies of police to see the meanings that emerge about power and social relations. This exercise facilitates a conversation that expands to events like Ferguson, Baltimore, and Elsipogtog, and allows conceptual links between decolonial and anti-racist activism and climate justice.

The projects

Suggested readings and media:

- Bourriaud, *Relational Aesthetics*
- Jackson, *Social Works*
- The Canary Project: http://canary-project.org

Project: in this project, you will create your own response to the political, ethical, and aesthetic questions raised in class. Collaborative projects are encouraged! The project has several components:

1   A proposal and annotated bibliography of four sources.
    - The proposal should articulate the question your project poses to the audience, provide a context (who else is talking about this question? are there other works that are comparable?), and explain its significance (how does it respond to the ethical, political, and imaginative problems posed by climate change?).
    - In addition, include some thinking about the form or genre of your proj-ect. How will you ask the audience to move from the position of spectator to participant/witness?
    - Your bibliography should include at least two academic sources. The other two can be installations, performances, social media, or other artis-tic projects that have influenced your thinking.
2   A product (this will depend on your project).
3   A class presentation of the project.

4 A reflection on the project that integrates discussion of works in the annotated bibliography and class readings.
- If you collaborate on a project, you will complete 1 and 4 individually and 2 and 3 with your partner/group.

As we think about bodies acting collectively, Shannon Jackson's work on "'socially engaged art'" offers a theoretical framework and also describes how the lines between research, art, and activism are blurred—and how this social practice engages in interdisciplinary and collaborative projects (17, 60, 68–70). Jackson lists some of the possible forms that relate to "'social practice'": "activist art, social work, protest performance, collaborative art, performance ethnography, community theatre, relational aesthetics, conversation pieces, action research" (17). The goal of student projects is to engage in critical and creative thinking about aesthetics and politics, extending the work we have done together through readings, class discussions, and more conventionally academic writing. I make clear to students from the beginning of class that these projects are not about communicating scientific data in an accessible format, but rather enact a different concept of interdisciplinarity, one in which the humanities are an epistemology, a way of knowing the world (J. Foster, Toadvine).

I especially encourage students to structure projects that are interactive (though not all students choose this format). Here we are informed by Bourriaud's work on "relational aesthetics," which is also a guiding concept for this class. Relational aesthetics describes a movement among contemporary artists that resists commodification (16). It turns the focus from the production of an object that can be bought and sold to the encounter—the "inter-subjective exchange" (Bourriaud 14–15; Jackson 15). In this shift there is also a turn from the individual experience of art to the creation of an ephemeral community among the participants—a movement away from the position of spectator and into a form of witness (Bourriaud 14–17). I emphasize that the conceptual development of the projects is crucial, rather than technical expertise. Many students do bring their talents in music, composition, and other art forms to the project, while others draw on skills in social media. In addition to interactive performances and sculpture installations, students document intersubjective exchanges through the creation of group collages and murals, both textual and visual. Through these projects, students imagine and create different modes of social relations (Bourriaud 9). Jackson warns that the danger of "'anti-state' or 'anti-institutional resistance'" is that it can create what Nancy Fraser calls "'weak publics [...] unable to imagine the forms'" of public engagement that are necessary to "'a democratic and egalitarian society'" (quoted in Jackson 9). This is where the course converges with utopian and dystopian literature and film, with Solnit's disaster utopias, and with the ephemeral utopias of protest actions: these projects are forms of political imagination, what Bourriaud calls "everyday micro-utopias," interstitial sites where we can learn to *"inhabit the world in a better way"* (Bourriard 31, 16–17, 13). During presentations of the projects at the end of the course, I witness paradise being built in the classroom.

Acknowledgements

My thanks to the students in ENVS 219 at Oberlin College, who have taught me how to teach about climate change. This class is truly a collaborative endeavor, and every year my students confirm Rebecca Solnit's radiant view of human nature. Thanks also to Oberlin College, especially the Environmental Studies program, which first invited me to design a course on climate change from a humanities perspective. I am grateful to colleagues Victoria Fortuna and Michelle Martin-Baron for their guidance on performance studies. Finally, my thanks to Anthony Lioi and Ted Toadvine for helpful comments on earlier drafts of this essay.

Notes

1   My thanks to Meredith Raimondo for this insight.
2   This section title refers to both Public Enemy and Dunn.
3   Martin and Fruhwirth.

References

Bourriaud, Nicolas. *Relational Aesthetics*. Trans. Simon Pleasance and Fronza Woods. Dijon, France: Les Presses du Réel, 2002.
Butler, Judith. "Bodies in Alliance and the Politics of the Street." *EIPCP* (September 2011), www.eipcp.net/transversal/1011/butler/en. Accessed 20 May 2016.
Butler, Judith. *Precarious Life: The Powers of Mourning and Violence*. London: Verso, 2004.
Butler, Octavia. *Parable of the Sower*. New York: Warner Books, 2000.
Canary Project. http://canary-project.org. Accessed 20 May 2016.
Davis, Mike. *Ecology of Fear: Los Angeles and the Imagination of Disaster*. New York: Metropolitan Books, 1998.
Dunn, Kevin. "Fear of a Black Planet: Anarchy Anxieties and Postcolonial Travel to Africa." *Third World Quarterly* 25.3 (2004): 483–99.
Ehrlich, Paul R. *The Population Bomb*. Cutchogue, New York: Buccaneer Books, 1995.
Fiskio, Janet. "Apocalypse and Ecotopia: Narratives in Global Climate Change Discourse." *Race, Gender, and Class*. 19.1–2 (Spring 2012): 12–36.
Foreman, Dave. *Confessions of an Eco-Warrior*. New York: Harmony Books, 1991.
Foster, John. "What Price Interdisciplinarity? Crossing the Curriculum in Environmental Higher Education." *Journal of Geography in Higher Education* 23.3 (1999): 358–66.
Foster, Susan Leigh. "Choreographies of Protest." *Theatre Journal* 55.3 (October 2003): 395–412.
Hardin, Garrett. "The Tragedy of the Commons." *Science*. 162.3859 (1968): 1243-48.
Hardin, Garrett. "Living on a Lifeboat." *Bioscience* 24.10 (1974): 561–68.
Jackson, Shannon. *Social Works: Performing Art, Supporting Publics*. New York: Routledge, 2011.
Jamieson, Dale. "Ethics, Public Policy, and Global Warming." *Science, Technology, and Human Values* 17.2 (Spring 1992): 139–53.
Jensen, Derrick and Stephanie McMillan. *As the World Burns: 50 Simple Things You Can Do to Stay in Denial*. New York: Seven Stories Press, 2007.
Kaplan, Robert. "The Coming Anarchy." *Atlantic Monthly* (February 1994), www.theatlantic.com/magazine/archive/1994/02/the-coming-anarchy/304670. Accessed 20 May 2016.

King, Dr. Martin Luther, Jr. "Letter from a Birmingham Jail." 1963. The Martin Luther King, Jr. Research and Education Institute. https://kinginstitute.stanford.edu/king-papers/documents/letter-birmingham-jail. Accessed 23 July 2016.

Klein, Naomi. *This Changes Everything: Capitalism vs. the Climate.* New York: Simon and Schuster, 2014.

Maira, Sunaina and Julie Sze. "Dispatches from Pepper Spray University: Privatization, Repression, and Revolts." *American Quarterly* (June 2012): 315–330.

Maniates, Michael. "Teaching for Turbulence." Worldwatch Institute State of the World 2013: Is Sustainability Still Possible? Project Directors, Erik Assadourian and Tom Prugh. Ed. Linda Starke. Washington: Island Press, 2013: 255–68.

Martin, Melanie Jae and Jesse Fruhwirth. "Welcome to Blockadia!" *Yes! Magazine.* (January 2013), www.yesmagazine.org/planet/welcome-to-blockadia-enbridge-transcanada-tarsands. Accessed 28 June 2016.

McEwan, Ian. *Solar.* New York: Nan A. Talese/Doubleday, 2010.

Nash, Michael P. (director). *Climate Refugees: The Global Human Impact of Climate Change.* Beverly Hills, CA: LA Think Tank, 2010.

Nixon, Rob. "Neoliberalism, Genre, and 'The Tragedy of the Commons'." *PMLA* 127.3 (2012): 593–599.

Nixon, Rob. *Slow Violence and the Environmentalism of the Poor*, Cambridge, MA: Harvard University Press, 2011.

Nynks, Kelly and Jared P. Scott, (directors). *Do the Math.* Brooklyn, NY: PF Pictures, 2013. https://youtu.be/KuCGVwJIRd0. Accessed 23 July 2016.

Potter, Will. *Green is the New Red: An Insider's Account of a Social Movement Under Siege.* San Francisco, CA: City Lights Books, 2011.

Public Enemy. *Fear of a Black Planet.* New York: Def Jam Recordings, 1990.

Ripper, Velcrow (director). *Occupy Love.* Canada: Fierce Love Films, 2013.

Solnit, Rebecca. *A Paradise Built in Hell: The Extraordinary Communities that Arise in Disaster.* New York: Viking 2009.

Thoreau, Henry David. "Resistance to Civil Government" *Reform Papers*, ed. Wendell Glick. Princeton, NJ: Princeton University Press, 1973. 63–90.

Toadvine, Ted. "Six Myths of Interdisciplinarity." *Thinking Nature Journal* 1.1 (2011), www.academia.edu/2440706/Six_Myths_of_Interdisciplinarity_2011_ Accessed 21 July 2016.

13 Learning in the Anthropocene

Environmental justice and climate pedagogy

Robert Melchior Figueroa

This chapter provides a discussion of climate change pedagogy from an environmental justice approach, specifically through consideration of what I call *bivalent environmental justice* (Figueroa 2001). This approach has evolved since my first environmental justice course in 2005. Over twenty years of combining research and pedagogy, always tracking the evolution of climate change discourses, my most recent arrangement of course material is explicitly designed to develop understandings of environmental justice that will later bear on the broader context of climate change. This chapter follows the trend of my current course, "Worldviews and Environmental Values," at Oregon State University. In Part I, I introduce the main features of bivalent environmental justice that carry through the course. Part II, explores these main features, specifically environmental identity and environmental heritage, with a focus on the pedagogy of climate change. Part III, shifts these discussions to Anthropocene discourse, considering pedagogical implications of environmental despair, along the way. This chapter progresses with environmental justice encompassing a vital thread through descriptions of course literature and topics.

Part I: Features of bivalent environmental justice

The class launches with Wangari Maathai's two essays from 2004: "Nobel Lecture" and "Cracked Mirror," in order discuss the relationship of overlapping social-environmental issues. Among the most pertinent of the issues that Maathai includes are environmental colonialism, women's vital contribution to addressing environmental crises, and the Green Belt Movement as a successful form of activism that recognizes the agency existing between humans and non-humans to transform social-environmental relations toward sustainable communities.

After some reflection on Maathai and further thought on environmental philosophy and environmental colonialism through Val Plumwood's earlier work, an extended discussion of environmental justice in South Africa, Australia, United States, Oceana, Latin America, and South East Asia, provides multiple perspectives on environmental justice theory and practice. By providing multiple perspectives from various sites around the world, students are able to see common threads among a number of scholars (Whyte 2013; Schlosberg 2007; Shrader-Frechette

2003). Although scholars may differ in approach and terminology, there is enough of an agreement that key dimensions of justice must be simultaneously considered. Distributive justice, especially in the context of climate change, focuses on disparities of environmental burdens across different populations; typically the most marginalized populations by histories of colonialism, racism, and contemporary development strategies. Distributive justice in climate change considers who has benefited most, the super-industrialized nations, and who is burdened without benefits and/or without compensation. Desertification, sea level rise, migration, resource depletion, and the continued practices producing the harms mark some of the issues of distributive justice. Recognition justice considers the collective values and identities that make up the environmental values of a collective—for instance the community's relation to place in understanding its identity in environmental discourses. Who makes what decisions in distribution and compensation is largely a recognition issue, but only the surface of cultural injustices is scratched by these "who/what" questions. Participation in environmental decision making is crucial, but even with certain procedures in place, there are numerous voices marginalized from these procedures, especially in climate change negotiations.

This chapter emphasizes recognition justice, but the bivalent environmental justice remains overarching—distribution and recognition are interdependent. They are co-imbricated but we cannot reduce one form of justice to the other. That is to say, attempting to resolve distributive justice without considering recognition justice would be a failure from the bivalent perspective because recognition cannot be reduced to the distributive dimension. Emphasizing recognition in environmental justice requires consideration of collective identities, collective lifeways, cultural sustenance, and the situated power conditions under which agents struggle for effective participatory involvement, sovereignty, and epistemological agency that can shape environmental relations (Figueroa 2006; Whyte 2013). I have extended the bivalent conversation to emphasize concepts I find useful for robust recognition; specifically, notions of environmental identity and environmental heritage (2006). Additionally, the class studies narratives of that can guide reconciliation efforts, or restorative justice. Lastly, the environmental justice approach emphasizing recognition justice presents students with the concepts of moral terrains and affective ontology in order to consider embodied agency and environmental justice.

The class covers material that articulates different situated knowledge of "environmental identity" and "environmental heritage" which I define as the following:

> Environmental identity is the amalgamation of cultural identities, ways of life, and self-perceptions that are connected to a given group's physical environment. And, my use of environmental heritage pertains to the meanings and, symbols of the past that frame values, practices, and places peoples wish to preserve as members of a community. Environmental heritage is the expression of an environmental identity in relation to the community viewed over time.
>
> (Figueroa 2006, 371–2)

Students receive several assignments to address these concepts, including one in which they are able to explore these concepts from their own situated location. Some of the students will anticipate future discussions of their place in the world's climate crisis, grasping ways in which their environmental identity and heritage are implicated.

Part II: Lessons on climate change: environmental identity and environmental heritage

The presumption that a particular arrangement of texts is *the* way to conceptualize climate change underestimates the extent to which an individual instructor can capture how much scholarship and how many angles are cut through the discourse. I am constantly realigning the course literature to my own exposure to contextual permutations, such as a campus event, a vital international meeting like the UNFCCC Conference of Parties (COP 21) in Paris and its aftereffects, a guest speaker, or a new documentary. Focusing environmental justice onto climate change, I currently rely upon Stephen Gardiner's "Climate Justice" (2011). He introduces several relevant conceptions of justice in light of three major challenges that climate justice must address: the global, intergenerational, and theoretical challenges pose nasty moral problems, or moral storms. Climate justice portends an overlapping of these challenges to generate the "perfect moral storm." The individual challenges converge in force and magnitude compounding the complexities and revealing the limitations of current institutional structures, breadth of intergenerational implications, and constrains our moral norms to meet the scale and collective agency of climate change. Gardiner responds with consideration of two mutually engaged avenues. 1) Reconsider if our current practices and parameters for addressing the existing storms demonstrate the potential to engage climate justice and develop a transitional ethics that draws from the better institutional and theoretical candidates for taking on the respective challenge. From existing insights we may expand our approach to match the scale and implications of climate change. 2) Engage as a witness to an epoch where humanity faces an ultimate threat. What an engaged witness to climate change means or entails is discussed by the class with varying affects: pessimism, optimism, collective, reactionary, passive, and what we call "environmental despair."

Gardiner admittedly narrows his analysis of climate justice to a distributive dimension. As a recognition justice counterweight, Kyle Powys Whyte (2013) offers a discussion of institutions between indigenous tribes and nation states (global storm); the scale of moral considerations that tribes take with regard to future generations, especially as regards the sufficiency of current institutional arrangements (intergenerational storm); and a joinder of intergenerational and relational moral consideration through a defense of cultural continuance, which echoes the concept of environmental heritage (moral storm). As Whyte states:

> Collective continuance is a community's capacity to be adaptive in ways sufficient for the livelihoods of its members to flourish into the future. Adaptation

refers to "adjustments that populations take in response to current or predicted change." The flourishing of livelihoods refers to both tribal conceptions of (1) how to contest colonial hardships, like cultural discrimination and disrespect for treaty rights, and (2) how to pursue comprehensive aims at robust living, like building cohesive societies, vibrant cultures, strong subsistence and commercial economies, and peaceful relations with a range of non-tribal neighbors, from small towns to nation states to the United Nations (UN). Given (1) and (2), tribal collective continuance can be seen as a community's aptitude for making adjustments to current or predicted change in ways that contest colonial hardships and embolden comprehensive aims at robust living.

(Whyte 2011, 120)

Thus, Whyte offers a conceptual tool of recognition justice—cultural continuance—in addition to an analysis of current institutional obstructions that need to be addressed in the forward-looking justice of climate adaptation. Cultural continuance blends the intention of considering environmental heritage by taking lifeways, political relations, and epistemic agency through a current value assessment to determine what vision of institutional arrangements will generate adaptive strategies for current and future generations. Similarly, collective continuance reifies the community and relational basis of environmental heritage by refusing the individualistic accounts of justice. The recognition dimension is inherently community and relationally bound; a collective identity approach is able to specify responsibility to parties related in climate adaptation strategies that respect or hinder tribal collective continuance.

The order of the readings is intended to bring back earlier insights and lessons of the term, and from Whyte's insights, we have environmental identity and heritage, collective continuance, and recognition returned to a central place in the discussion. Bivalent environmental justice continues to be a general parameter the class seeks to extend and test. In my own piece, "Indigenous Peoples and Cultural Losses," I concentrate the concepts of bivalent environmental justice to the environmental identity and heritage discourse directly concerning climate refugees; this analysis examines several indigenous coastal communities in both hemispheres, and further issues surrounding traditional ecological knowledge (2011). The chapter reasserts a relational ethics to ward off the tendencies that incorrectly presume ineffably human and non-human bifurcations in environmental justice approaches. As the class proceeds, the choice over whether or not non-human justice and/or interspecies justice is indeed an *ecological justice*, as distinct from *environmental justice*, is suggestive of a misdirection. Emphasizing relational ethics and environmental identity throughout the course offers an environmental justice approach inclusive of interspecies justice; especially, where indigenous people, local communities, and non-indigenous peoples alike are bound in collective interspecies justice. A broad sampling of collective (shared between human and non-human communities) interspecies justice is provided in "Indigenous Perspectives," by Laurie Ann Whitt, Mere Roberts, Waerete Norman, and Vicki Grieves (2001). Deborah McGregor's, "Honouring Our Relations: An Anishnaabe Perspective on Environmental Justice" addresses water issues effecting the tribe and she calls for a revision of environmental justice that expands into a collective interspecies justice where agency is recognized throughout creation (2009). "Indigenous Peoples and Cultural Losses" uses narratives of climate refugees, tsunami survivors, and consideration of environmental identity and environmental heritage to draw out a collective interspecies justice that can be described from a bivalent extension. What an ecological justice would provide apart from this environmental justice is unclear. Perhaps a reorientation of a perspective, or newly envisioned forms of living, reasoning, and social institutions that would consider *ecological* as distinct from environmental like non-Anthropocentric perspectives may be considered distinct from Anthropocentric perspectives. However, these terms fail to line up (i.e. ecological: non-Anthropocentric, environmental: Anthropocentric) if we already demonstrate non-Anthropocentric inclusion through the environmental justice approaches to collective interspecies justice.

Continuing this conversation to explore extensions in environmental justice for both human and non-human consideration, I adopt either of two articles by David Schlosberg, "Climate Justice and Capabilities: A Framework for Adaptation Policy" (2012) or his piece with David Carruthers, "Indigenous Struggles, Environmental Justice, and Community Capabilities (2010). In either case, the benefit of a capabilities approach assists students in considering the dynamics of distributive, recognition, and more options that address human flourishing and environmental justice. Utilizing the benefits and mutually inclusive implications between Amartya Sen and Marth Nussbaum's respective capabilities approach, Schlosberg's works aim to find opportunities where consideration of community or collective agents of justice might be consistent with the standard individualism of the capabilities approach. Between these two readings, the Schlosberg and Carruthers piece reaches slightly further into questions of interspecies justice, or ecological justice. Both works promote the collective capabilities approach by considering indigenous examples, and provide an opportunity to further consider relational human and non-human justice under conditions of climate change.

Part III: Teaching in the Anthropocene

Earlier in this chapter, I mentioned environmental despair by reference to nasty moral challenges that can misfire, paralyzing moral agency. Courses emphasizing environmental justice deliver numerous case studies of environmental discrimination intersecting race, class, gender, nationality, indigeneity, and colonialism. The extent of injustices and the need for theoretical perspectives to understand interlinking human and non-human impacts can weigh heavily on the social consciousness of many students who have unaware of the vast number of cases. Likewise the peoples impacted weighs heavily on the conscience of many students. Theories of justice, though abstract, provide a discourse to look more closely at the cases, injustices, and critical components for proposing transformative conditions to ameliorate injustices. Students have multiple theories, cases, and multiple scales to consider, including recognition of their own position in the scheme of things.

Thus, while students have honed numerous skills for approaching environmental justice at simultaneously global and local scales, the affect of environmental despair requires its own attention.

The sheer scope of the environmental despair extends to an aligning of both human and non-human conditions, at multi-scalar levels, across intergenerational values and practices. This is magnified by the problem of agency. Students acknowledge the realization that they are caught up in perpetuating something they would prefer to eliminate. At this scale, they are fundamentally a causal part of that which could be their own undoing. And, at least for the immediate horizon, there's nothing they can do about it. Enter the Anthropocene, a discourse describing an epoch of forces uncontrollable by humans despite their efficient creation. I use Jedadiah Purdy's essay, "Anthropocene Fever" to introduce one way the Anthropocene can be described (2015). For Purdy, the Anthropocene represents the end of nature as it has been conceived by Western traditions. Nature, always shot full of socially constructed values, is now supplanted of its Earthly force by an unbridled human force. Purdy still explores the notion of a "democratic Anthropocene" to encourage readers to push against misdirected fatalism of the "Darkness of the Anthropocene"—a catastrophic trajectory lacking human importance. Having numerous environmental justice cases and conscientiously studied across multiple scales, the students are equipped to fold the earlier climate change readings into Purdy's account of the Anthropocene, and we further discuss the symptomatic effects and implications of environmental despair. This affective exploration brings out earlier course study of environmental identity and environmental heritage as affectively producing moral terrains. Elements of moral terrains include embodied narratives about what behaviors are permissible, who belongs where, how we perceive the moral status of other bodies (human and non-human), and the ways in which we establish moral, social, and political identities in embodied relations to space and place. Environmental despair opens up affective territory that opens further moral gateways into the Anthropocene.

Finishing this section of the course (often the grand finale of the term), I rely upon Nancy Tuana's, "Being Affected by Climate Change: The Anthropocene and the Body of Ethics" (2016), as a means to redirect us to affective ontologies, and to better provide an approach within the bounds of New Materialism that bends the Anthropocene into an opportunity for optimism and transformation. The optimistic account is to shift scales of relations to those at the social-natural level. To capture the scope of Tuana's ethic she states:

> The ethos of the Anthropocene is not the disciplined study of values and principles. It rather calls for an appreciation of and ability to respond to the deep interconnectivity between near and distant others, between the now and the future, between the local and the global, and between humans and the world they are of and in. Simply put, a relational ontology effects an affective shift to embracing the *corporeal vulnerability* of things in the making and the concomitant *accountability* that accompanies this shift.
>
> (n.p.)

Tuana's work is rich with opportunity for students to interpret nuances and conditions for environmental justice within a world of climate change, a world of the Anthropocene, and a world where relational ethics has some traction against tendencies of getting overwhelmed by environmental despair. With credence to the environmental trauma that climate change has and will set off on many peoples and populations, the social imaginary Tuana offers includes shared material conditions between relational agents, both humans and non-humans, a deeper recognition and reconciliation between human and non-humans, which can be explored by environmental justice perspectives. New Materialist discourses in the Environmental Humanities, and that of the Anthropocene, specifically, eliminates the use-value of Anthropocentric vs. non-Anthropocentric tendencies; the environmental vs. ecological justice formulations are similarly compromised as the moral agents are contextualized under the same rubric of an epoch and a multi-scalar approach that resists defining human justice apart from interspecies justice.

Concluding thought

The responsibility to teach climate change is a moral and professional responsibility of every discipline, sub-discipline, area studies, and interdisciplinary venture. Perhaps this is unfair to many specializations of research inside and outside of the academy, but it is the subject matter of our human and non-human condition. This chapter provides a transdisciplinary philosophical thread of environmental justice that I am able to engage with my students. It is merely one thread that should be braided in with the many areas and examples of climate pedagogy found within this volume.

References

Figueroa, Robert Melchior. "Bivalent Environmental Justice and the Culture of Poverty." *Rutgers University Journal of Law and Urban Policy* 1.1 (2003): 27–43. Print.

Figueroa, Robert Melchior. "Evaluating Environmental Justice Claims." *Forging Environmentalism: Justice, Livelihood, and Contested Environments*, ed. Joanne Bauer, Armonk, NY: M.E. Sharpe, 2006, 360–376. Print.

Figueroa, Robert Melchior. "Indigenous Peoples and Cultural Losses." *The Oxford Handbook of Climate Change and Society*, ed. John S. Dryzek, Richard R. Norgaard, and David Schlosberg, New York: Oxford University Press, 2011, 232–247. Print.

Gardiner, Stephen M. "Climate Justice." *The Oxford Handbook of Climate Change and Society* ed. John S. Dryzek, Richard R. Norgaard, and David Schlosberg, New York: Oxford University Press, 2001, 309–322. Print.

Maathai, Wangari. "The Cracked Mirror." *Dialogue with Nature – Resurgence & Ecologist*, 227, web, (November/December 2004): 1–4, print and online. www.greenbeltmovement.org/wangari-maathai/key-speeches-and-articles/the-cracked-mirror.

Maathai, Wangari. "Nobel Lecture." *Nobelprize.org.* Nobel Media AB 2014, www.nobelprize.org/nobel_prizes/peace/laureates/2004/maathai-lecture-text.html, accessed 3 Jan 2015. (Speech originally given 2004). Web.

McGregor, Deborah. "Honouring Our Relations: An Anishnaabe Perspective on Environmental Justice." *Speaking for Ourselves: Environmental Justice in Canada*, eds Julian

Agyeman, Peter Cole, Randolph Haluza-Delay, Vancouver: UBC Press, 2009, 27–41. Print.

Plumwood, Val. "Paths Beyond Human-Centeredness: Lessons from Liberation Struggles." *An Invitation to Environmental Philosophy*, ed. Anthony Weston, New York: Oxford University Press, 1999, 69–106. Print.

Purdy, Jedidiah. "Anthropocene Fever." *Aeon Media* (2015), https://aeon.co/essays/should-we-be-suspicious-of-the-anthropocene-idea.Web

Shrader-Frechette, Kristin. *Environmental Justice: Creating Equality, Reclaiming Democracy*, New York: Oxford University Press, 2005. Print.

Schlosberg, David. "Climate Justice and Capabilities: A Framework for Adaptation Policy." *Ethics & International Affairs* 26.4 (2012): 445–461. Print.

Schlosberg, David. *Defining Environmental Justice: Theories, Movements, and Nature*, New York: Oxford University Press, 2007. Print.

Schlosberg, David and David Curruthers. "Indigenous Struggles, Environmental Justice, and Community Capabilities." *Global Environmental Poltics*. 10.4 (2010): 12–35. Print.

Tuana, Nancy. "Being Affected by Climate Change: The Anthropocene and the Body of Ethics." Forthcoming in *Ethics and the Anthropocene*, eds Kenneth Shockley and Andrew Light, Cambridge, MA: MIT Press, 2016. Print.

Whitt, Laurie Ann, Mere Roberts, Waerete Norman, and Vicki Grieves. "Indigenous Perspectives." *The Blackwell Companion to Environmental Philosophy*, ed. Dale Jamieson. Malden, MA: Blackwell Publishers Ltd, 2001. Print

Whyte, Kyle Powys. "Justice Forward: Tribes, Climate Adaptation and Responsibility." *Climatic Change*. 120. 3 (2013): 117–130. Print.

14 In-flight behaviour

Teaching climate change literature in first-year intro English

Greg Garrard

What I did and why I did it

The climate fiction course I taught at the University of British Columbia (UBC) Okanagan in 2014–15 was a first-year service course that would cater mainly to non-English majors. I wanted this most crucial of topics to reach the largest possible number of students, and I wanted to use the course to demonstrate the value and significance of humanities-based approaches to a subject that is overwhelmingly discussed in terms of science, engineering and governmental politics. I had a class of 35 students, which meant I gave only a few formal lectures and spent a lot of time practising close textual analysis. The next version of this course will be a large section of 150 students, so I will be giving a lot more formal lectures and allocating reading and writing practice to the Graduate Teaching Assistants.

My choice of literary and other texts could, I hoped, enrich students' knowledge and understanding of climate change, while teaching evaluation questionnaires (TEQs) could provide a rudimentary sense of whether or not the objectives of the class had been achieved. However, students normally complete TEQs in a rapid, unconsidered fashion, and some research suggests such questionnaires really only measure the likeability of the teacher and the students' estimate of their expected grade for the course (see Clayson, Frost and Sheffet; Clayson and Sheffet), so I also included an essay prompt that implicitly asked for reflection on the value of the course: "'Literature has little to contribute to progressive climate politics.' Do you agree?" Quotations from students below appear under their real names, are drawn verbatim from both TEQs and essays, and are used with permission. It is worth noting, though, that the addressee of these statements, qua pedagogical researcher, was also grading the students' essays, making them questionable as sources of reliable evaluation (Garrard, "Problems and Prospects in Ecocritical Pedagogy" 236) The responses gathered by means of a learning-focused essay question suggested that formal assessment is underused as a means of obtaining more reasoned and thoughtful pedagogical reflections from students than TEQs.

The 13-week course justified its 'service' designation by incorporating substantial elements of composition. The course texts included Al Gore's *An Inconvenient Truth*; selected stories from Helen Simpson's *In-Flight Entertainment*; Barbara Kingsolver's *Flight Behaviour* (the title of which we perennially confused with

Simpson's, as in my chapter heading above); Steve Waters's play, *The Contingency Plan*; and a small number of critical essays and extracts.

The objectives of the course had to be strictly limited from the outset. The requirement to spend a minimum proportion of 35% on the writing component had to be borne in mind, even if the stated figure is impossible to measure and in any case never checked. Additional objectives included introduction of basic narratological terminology, and reflective analysis of the ways various disciplines characterize, or 'frame', climate change. The commitment to spend a decent amount of time on each literary text meant that other attractive options relevant to the teaching of climate change fiction, notably Mitchell Thomashow's suggestions for enhancing 'biospheric perception', were not included (Garrard, "A Novel Idea: Slow Reading"). Nevertheless, Thomashow's characterization of the problem was a guiding insight throughout:

> A fine paradox emerges. Global environmental change is too elusive to grasp, yet too profound to ignore. Not yet the province of concentrated public attention, it appears more subtly, through its images and metaphors. Not easily understood, it leaves its marks and trails nevertheless, in the form of local signs and global reflections. International networks of commerce and communication may hide the ecological origins of your daily life, but they bring images of the planet to bear on your every move, whether it's the Netscape icon of a comet passing over the globe, or a Coca-Cola ad panning the world's cultures for coke drinkers.
>
> (Thomashow 37)

Thomashow's work includes numerous practical activities designed to train students to perceive change at different temporal and spatial scales. For example, he enjoins learners to develop a reflective relationship to the technologies that mediate their knowledge of the biosphere, notably transportation and information technologies. He argues for 'barefoot global change science', combining communal, participatory 'place-based perceptual ecology with advanced electronic communications' (Thomashow 135) and scientific instrumentation. In the next iteration of this course, students will read and debate Rebecca Solnit's essay "In the Day of the Postman" and an extract from Nicholas Carr's *The Shallows*, both of which warn of the fracturing of consciousness by digital technology.

Where Thomashow wants to *re-orientate* learners by alerting them to knowledge – primarily scientific – of other temporal and spatial scales, Timothy Clark stresses the necessary, instructive *disorientation* brought about by precisely the same kind of knowledge (Clark, "Some Climate Change Ironies"; Clark, "Scale"). For Clark, the problem with Barbara Kingsolver's *Flight Behaviour* – a popular required text on the course – is precisely that it concludes soothingly with the survival of the imperilled monarch butterflies, which coincides in turn with hopeful personal prospects for the protagonist Dellarobia (Clark, *Ecocriticism on the Edge* 176–7). Clark's argument about the novel was introduced into the course along with a simplified version of his central claim about the implications of living in the Anthropocene era (Garrard, "The Unbearable Lightness of Green: Air Travel, Climate Change and Literature"). A guiding principle of the course was the idea that narrative technique functions as a *cognitive technology* that shapes our comprehension of climate change.

What we learned, what students said

Our starting point was the failure of the U.N.-sponsored Intergovernmental Panel on Climate Change (IPCC)/Conference of the Parties (COP) process, which was originally designed to forge a science-based political consensus for global action to curb greenhouse gas emissions. A student named Jessy pointed out that "As global reports and documentaries have not been effective in reaching the general public so far, climate change literature may be our last hope in convincing many people that climate change is happening". Five successive reports, each of them better grounded and more confident than the last, have not, as yet, galvanized international action. As Mike Hulme points out, the supposed separation between the scientific work of the IPCC and the politics of the COP forums has proven difficult to sustain, leaving the scientists open to charges of 'politicization':

> Does the IPCC offer impartial science or does it shape policy? Does the IPCC reflect the views of participating scientists or the views of the government officials who have to approve its reports? Some disagreements about climate change can be traced to different interpretations of the authority of the IPCC.
> (Hulme 96)

The climate fictions chosen for discussion provided opportunities for two types of reflection on this problem. Since Kingsolver, Waters and one of Simpson's stories feature scientists as characters, discussion of the fictional dilemmas they face illuminated the fundamental problem with the hegemonic construction of scientific knowledge in Western societies: scientific authority is seen to depend not only on *methodological* impartiality (guaranteed procedurally by peer review and public funding), which is indeed essential, but also on *rhetorical* impartiality. For example in *Flight Behaviour*, Ovid Byron resists the suggestion of protagonist Dellarobia that he try to 'save' the imperilled monarch butterflies, saying: "I am not a zookeeper ... I'm not here to save monarchs. I'm trying to read what they are writing on our wall" (Kingsolver 320). Dr Byron believes that his reputation as a scientist depends on *sounding* unconcerned about the fate of the butterflies, although the two kinds of impartiality have no necessary relationship at all. In the event, goaded by a TV journalist desperate to avoid talking about climate change, Byron violates the disciplinary protocol, venting his passionate feelings in a tirade that is then posted on YouTube. Discussion of this point is especially useful for students intending to major in natural sciences, clearly. The next iteration will include Val Plumwood's critique of the hyper-separation of Reason and Nature, which will substantiate a challenge to the underlying dualism plaguing these scientists.

The other discussion one can initiate based on the failure of the IPCC/COP process is a more general one about the social utility of science and its limits. As Hulme explains, "climate" is a concept with deep-rooted meanings for different cultures and bioregions, so it cannot be revised overnight by scientific appropriation and redescription. *Flight Behaviour* conveys this complexity by means of the vivid symbol at the centre of its narrative: the monarch butterfly swarm. Dellarobia first encounters it without spectacles, on her way to an adulterous assignation, and so is forced, against her agnostic disposition, to think of the butterfly-clothed trees in Biblical terms:

> The burning trees were put here to save her. It was the strangest conviction she'd ever known, and still she felt sure of it. She had no use for superstition ... By no means was she important enough for God to conjure signs and wonders on her account. What had set her apart, briefly, was an outsize and hellish obsession. To stop a thing like that would require a burning bush, a fighting of fire with fire.
>
> (Kingsolver 16)

Her Appalachian neighbors publically proclaim the arrival of the monarchs as a miracle and a sign from God, although there is little agreement as to what precisely it means. Privately, they see the butterflies as either an economic opportunity – for tourist dollars – or a potential obstacle to their plans for land development. As the novel progresses, the symbolic meanings *accumulate*: Ovid Byron and his team add a scientific perspective, while environmentalists from California and England emphasize the beauty and fragility of the butterflies. Such is Kingsolver's conciliatory ambition for the novel, moreover, these symbolic meanings more often grow together than clash violently (Garrard, "Conciliation and Consilience"). Reacting perhaps to the obdurate incommensurability of cultures of nature in contemporary American political discourse, Kingsolver chooses in her fiction to imagine figures like Pastor Ogle, an evangelist preacher with remarkable environmental sensitivities. Siobhan explained this intermediating function in her essay:

> Literature is a cultural broker and like Dellarobia in *Flight Behavior*, literature connects us to ideas that could have happened years ago, in a far off country, or maybe both. Dellarobia connects two far off worlds, the world of scholars and scientists, and the world of low-income church-goers. She connects her community to the world around her, where tragedy is disguised as beauty.

The phrase "cultural broker," which had been coined by another student earlier in the course, came to be used frequently in class.

Much discussion throughout the course focused on the "knowledge/action gap," at both individual and international levels. A wide range of explanations for the gap was discussed: the limitations of our evolved psychological capacities; the organized resistance of fossil fuel-funded scepticism; the inertia of existing energy systems; the social norms that restrict conversations about weather; the power of international capital; and so on. I tried to dissuade the students from seeing the selected climate fictions as evidence for or against any of these explanations, but rather as *dramatizations* of the cultural processes by which climate change becomes cognitively and emotionally legible. By drawing attention repeatedly to the distinctiveness of Kingsolver's prose – her facility with memorable metaphors; her occasionally cloying descriptive passages – I sought to emphasize the artifice of the author's realism. In short, I wanted to encourage them to see the *text*, rather than the fictional *storyworld*, as the source of valid evidence for their essays.

Furthermore, the fictions were seen as making implicit or explicit *metanarrative* claims for literature itself in relation to climate change. For example, Simpson's title story incorporates several narrative levels that imbricate the reader in complex emotional responses: Alan, the focalizer, is an arrogant, sexist climate sceptic. His interlocutor is a former climate scientist, who reiterates the force of the scientific consensus, strengthening our suspicion of the narrator. However, the scientist has now retired and, having realized no one else is acting to prevent climate change, wants nothing more than to die in the first class cabin of an international flight. Alan's uneasy resistance to such heedless hedonism at once challenges his earlier scepticism and encourages the reader to question the relationship of knowledge and action in her own case. In this instance, it is the distinctive quality of narrativity that gives this story its significance.

In my experience, persuading students, English majors or no, to analyse the formal qualities of a narrative as well as to engage with the human dynamics of its storyworld is a Sisyphean challenge. Dellarobia, in particular, was judged to be highly "relatable" (top candidate for the neologism most hated by English profs), which meant her travails were considered beneficially emotive. Much as I wished students to observe *how* Kingsolver used focalization and idiolectal metaphor to encourage such identification, I agreed with their judgment. Several students claimed that climate fiction was needed because few people respond emotionally to data, as in Kate's suggestion that:

> Human beings respond to all different kinds of information. … I feel that to be able to visualize is an advantage that hopefully humans can look past the dramatized Hollywood idea of climate change and see that the effects are real and no matter if one responds to scientific data or fictional stories that it is occurring and connection must be made to change it.

In our discussion of methodological impartiality, I stressed that since the humanities also partake of the practices of anonymous peer review and public funding, they too institutionalize progressive forms of rationality. I also attempted to introduce Ursula Heise's reading practice, which treats literature *diagnostically* as a source of information about encultured notions of environmental risk, to little effect (Heise 138). As it turned out, demonstrating the utility of literature and criticism in advancing the rational understanding of climate change as a 'wicked' socio-ecological problem proved too demanding for this particular instructor/class confluence.

Kate's response was like several others who continued to map the science/literature distinction onto a similarly dualistic configuration of reason/emotion. Siobhan, for example, stressed the value of the immersive, empathic experience of reading a novel like *Flight Behaviour*:

> A common saying is "you are what you eat" but I have a radically different and definitely more reasonable twist. What about "you are what you read?" … Reading puts our brain into gear to think about the world around us.

Much as I want to honour the capacity of literature for realistic depiction and emotional involvement, I also feel the need to emphasize its distinctive forms of rationality and artificiality. I will see, as the course is refined in future, whether this objective exceeds the capacity of a single introductory course.

An intriguing extension of the idea that climate fiction renders cold, hard data emotive, in Thea's essay, emphasized the cognitive as well as affective benefits of the multiplicity of stories contained within a single novel of substance.

> When written effectively climate change literature has the ability to make the arguably [sic] most influential issue of our time accessible to society. … works of fiction offer multiple stories regarding climate change, proving to readers that there is an array of stories connecting climate science to emotion, giving readers a reason to care about the issue.

The emotional power of literature is its ethical warrant, as before, but that power is seen as deriving from its specifically dialogic narrative techniques rather than a single source in the author or narrator.

Implications

I envisaged the course as incorporating reflection of the place of science in contemporary culture, as well as justifying the humanities to those who will not continue to study them. I also talked a lot about narrative technique and the fictionality of fiction – its complex, ambiguous relationship to the nonfictional world we think we inhabit. Despite my efforts, many essays treated the fictions as unmediated sources of information about such extratextual realities as the relationship of gender and climate change. The abrasive, disruptive, unassimilable singularity of literature was not much in evidence – though Barbara Kingsolver, for one, was a poor choice to convey such otherness, and the fictionality of fiction is a complex topic that takes years of advanced literary study to convey.

The next, much larger, iteration of the course will also switch topic somewhat, dropping the play to focus on narratives only, and combining climate change and biodiversity loss under an "Anthropocene Culture" rubric. We will study Julia Leigh's *The Hunter*, that depicts the extinction of the Tasmanian thylacine in a masculine narrative idiom of terrifying beauty, as a deliberate counterpoint to the honeyed prose and redemptive plot of Kingsolver's *Flight Behaviour*. I have added

Gerald Graff and Cathy Birkenstein's popular *They Say/I Say* to shape the composition element away from the correct employment of semicolons and toward the use of evidence to develop reasoned argument. Over further iterations, I plan to explore the ways that the assessment regime for this and other courses constitutes a "hidden curriculum" that may convey values at odds with those overtly endorsed (Sambell and McDowell). I will also try to incorporate some of Thomashow's smart perceptual exercises to look for constructive means of redirecting students' irrepressible obsession with smartphones and laptops towards genuine, deep learning. My learning curve in the next few years will be every bit as steep as theirs.

Acknowledgments

I gratefully acknowledge the insights of the editors and the perceptive comments of voluntary reviewers on academia.edu in redrafting this essay.

References

Clark, Timothy. *Ecocriticism on the Edge: The Anthropocene as a Threshold Concept*. London: Bloomsbury, 2015.

Clark, Timothy. "Scale." *Telemorphosis: Theory in the Era of Climate Change*. ed. Cohen, Tom. Ann Arbor, Michigan: Open Humanities Press, 2012 of *Critical Climate Change*.

Clark, Timothy. "Some Climate Change Ironies: Deconstruction, Environmental Politics and the Closure of Ecocriticism." *Oxford Literary Review* 32, 1 (2010): 131–49.

Clayson, Dennis E., Taggart F. Frost, and Mary Jane Sheffet. "Grades and the Student Evaluation of Instruction: A Test of the Reciprocity Effect." *Academy of Management Learning & Education* 5, 1 (2006): 52–65.

Clayson, Dennis E., and Mary Jane Sheffet. "Personality and the Student Evaluation of Teaching." *Journal of Marketing Education* 28, 2 (2006): 149–60.

Garrard, Greg. "Conciliation and Consilience: Climate Change in Barbara Kingsolver's 'Flight Behaviour'." *De Gruyter Handbook of Ecocriticism and Cultural Ecology*. ed. Zapf, Hubert. Berlin: De Gruyter, forthcoming.

Garrard, Greg. "A Novel Idea: Slow Reading". Times Higher Education, 2010. Accessed 20 July 2015. www.timeshighereducation.co.uk/news/a-novel-idea-slow-reading/412075.article%3E.

Garrard, Greg. "Problems and Prospects in Ecocritical Pedagogy." *Environmental Education Research* 16, 2 (2010): 233–45.

Garrard, Greg. "The Unbearable Lightness of Green: Air Travel, Climate Change and Literature." *Green Letters* 17, 2 (2013): 175–88.

Gibbs, Graham. *Using Assessment to Support Student Learning*. Leeds: Leeds Metropolitan University 2010.

Heise, Ursula K. *Sense of Place and Sense of Planet: The Environmental Imagination of the Global*. Oxford, New York: Oxford University Press, 2008.

Hulme, M. *Why We Disagree About Climate Change : Understanding Controversy, Inaction and Opportunity*. Cambridge, New York: Cambridge University Press, 2009.

Kingsolver, Barbara. *Flight Behaviour*. London: Faber & Faber, 2012.

Plumwood, Val. *Feminism and the Mastery of Nature*. London, New York: Routledge, 1993.

Sambell, Kay, and Liz McDowell. "The Construction of the Hidden Curriculum: Messages and Meanings in the Assessment of Student Learning." *Assessment & Evaluation in Higher Education* 23, 4 (1998): 391–402.

Thomashow, Mitchell. *Bringing the Biosphere Home: Learning to Perceive Global Environmental Change*. Cambridge, MA: MIT Press, 2002.

15 Learning from the past – teaching past climate change and catastrophes as windows onto vulnerability and resilience

Felix Riede, Annette Højen Sørensen, Jan Dietrich, Mogens S. Høgsberg, Mathias V. Nordvig, and Esben B. Niels

Climate, culture, catastrophe – can we learn from the past?

Increasingly across the humanities, climate change has moved to the forefront of the agenda. This movement has been formalized under the label Environmental Humanities, which covers and contains a wide range of innovative approaches within history and literary and cultural studies concerned with re-centering the environment within the humanities. Here we report on a particular teaching effort that, although it can broadly be seen as part of this environmental humanism, also differs from it by its systematic focus on the temporal dimension of human-environment relations. At Aarhus University in Denmark, second-year undergraduate students are given the opportunity to broaden their disciplinary horizons by enrolling in so-called elective subjects worth ten European Transfer Credits. These "humanities electives are interdisciplinary courses of relevance to all humanities BA students at Arts" ("Humanities Electives"); their aim is to foster and promote competencies in interdisciplinarity (see Table 15.1).

In 2013/2014, the opportunity to design such an elective was seized by a group of humanities scholars from across several disciplines: archaeology,[1] classical studies, theology, comparative and Nordic literature. In the spirit of providing research-led teaching, this initiative grew out of past and on-going projects such as the Laboratory for Past Disaster Science and the Climate|Culture|Catastrophe Network (C³NET). The foundational rationale for this course has been outlined by Mike Hulme, professor of climate and culture at King's College, London (Hulme, "Climate Change" and "Conquering").

To us, Hulme highlights several important issues. First, he notes that the discourse about climate and climate change is also a discourse about catastrophe, about collapse, about apocalypse (cf. Nielsen). Second, he argues that in order to better understand human–climate/environment relations we need to investigate the many complex relationships between these multi-facetted factors across time and space. Thirdly and finally, Hulme argues that such investigations can be genuinely useful in preparing for the future.

Table 15.1 According to the Aarhus University study regulations, students are expected to acquire the knowledge, skills and competencies listed here by completing the humanities elective

Knowledge	Pedagogical method(s)
The student is expected to acquire:	
Knowledge of central concepts, theories, methodologies and empirical research of relevance to the subject covered by the humanities elective	Lectures/reading
Knowledge of central issues relating to the subject covered by the humanities elective	Lectures/reading
Insight into how the perspectives provided by different fields in the humanities illuminate the subject covered by the humanities elective	Lectures/reading/group exercises
Skills	
The student is expected to be able to:	
Independently formulate and analyze a scholarly issue or argument within the framework of the humanities elective	Project exam
Assess the relevance of different theories and methodologies in relation to this issue, which includes an assessment of the scope and limitations of the student's own primary field of study in relation to the issue	Focus on interdisciplinarity in teaching and assessment/mixed-disciplines group composition
Communicate the issue clearly	Oral exam component
Competences	
The student is expected to achieve:	
The ability to participate in academic collaboration with students from other fields of study.	Group work/jointly produced pre-oral synopsis
The intellectual independence required to discuss and reflect on an interdisciplinary issue of relevance to the humanities elective	Individual oral exam

The course, *Catastrophes | Cultures: Integrated humanistic perspectives on natural hazards from prehistory to present*, thus focused on climatic and environmental extremes, catastrophes, rather than "regular" climate or climate change because the human disasters these create have been argued to be "totalizing events", but their effects on human communities always underdetermined by their geological or meteorological parameters (Oliver-Smith). Risk, and hence its instantiation in disaster scenarios, is always socially rooted. Very much in the original meaning of the term "catastrophe" as denoting a turning point in a drama, of the term "disaster" as denoting the revelation of a "bad star", and of the term "apocalypse" meaning "to reveal," historians of disaster have argued that such events at once can trigger and reveal social change (García-Acosta). Albeit often plagued by issues of data resolution, investigations of past catastrophes offer the critical advantage of allowing us to investigate the long-term constellations of vulnerability and resilience *before* as well as *after* a given event. Historical disaster research thus in principle offers unique opportunities for learning from the past as suggested by historians (Pfister; van Bavel and Curtis), geographers (Mitchell), sociologists (Clarke *Worst Cases. Terror and Catastrophe in the Popular Imagination*), archaeologists (Riede "Towards a Science of Past Disasters"), and media/literature scholars (Horn).

Integrated humanistic perspectives on natural hazards from prehistory to present

The course we report and reflect on here ran for the first time in the autumn semester of 2014, over a total of 13 weeks. Twenty-one students were enrolled with diverse disciplinary backgrounds from across the Arts Faculty. This background diversity led us to begin the course with a reading and comprehension exercise on multivocality and interdisciplinarity in climate and catastrophe research, where groups composed of students from different disciplines were asked to read and subsequently summarize selected introductory texts written from perspectives important for the subsequent course (Table 15.2). In this exercise we highlighted the identified need for integration between the natural sciences, the social sciences and the arts and a definition of inter- or transdisciplinarity that relates to the reciprocal epistemic effects of collaborating disciplines.

Following an introduction to the course content, aims and structure and the initial round table on interdisciplinarity, the course unfolded in a case-based manner along reverse chronological lines, i.e. from the now into the deep past.

Table 15.2 Round-table exercise: The different voices of the humanities. Selected review-style texts outlining some of the humanities perspectives on climate change and catastrophe. The journal *Wiley Interdisciplinary Reviews: Climate Change* in particular offers a rich repertoire of such texts.

Discipline	Text
Introduction	Hulme, M. 2011. Meet the humanities. *Nature Climate Change* 1, 177–179.
Archaeology	Hudson, M.J., Aoyama, M., Hoover, K.C., Uchiyama, J. 2012. Prospects and challenges for an archaeology of global climate change, *Wiley Interdisciplinary Reviews: Climate Change* 3, 313–328.
History	Schenk, G.J. 2007. Historical Disaster Research. State of Research, Concepts, Methods and Case Studies, *Historical Social Research* 32, 9–31.
Anthropology	Oliver-Smith, A. 1996. Anthropological Research on Hazards and Disasters. *Annual Review of Anthropology* 25, 303–328.
Rhetoric	Dörries, M. 2010. Climate catastrophes and fear, *Wiley Interdisciplinary Reviews: Climate Change* 1, 885–890.
Theology	Chester, D.K. 2005. Theology and disaster studies: The need for dialogue, *Journal of Volcanology and Geothermal Research* 146, 319–328.

Beginning with critical analyses of current discourse on climate and catastrophe in contemporary literature and media (with a focus on the Intergovermental Panel on Climate Change (IPCC) and Hurricane Katrina), we moved to a similar consideration of historical periods with focus on the classic case studies of the Greenland Norse and on the portrayal of the end of the world (Ragnarok) in Nordic mythology. The former is relevant because it figures prominently in popular accounts of more or less deterministic or reductionist self- and/or climatically – induced societal collapse. The latter accounts have received much attention recently owing to new thoughts on the so-called "AD 536 event" – a widespread meteorological anomaly possible caused by the eruption of Vúlcan Ilopango in present-day El Salvador (see Dull, Southon and Sheets; Sigl et al.) – that posit not only dramatic effects on nearby Maya communities but also extensive indirect effects from China to northern Europe (Gunn; Sheets; Tvauri). Particularly in Scandinavia, this event may not only be traceable in the archaeological record of changing land-use and ritual, but also in the oral and subsequently written-down mythologies of this pre-Viking period (Price and Gräslund). The relevance of this case study lies in the consistent influence of this mythology on contemporary Scandinavian identity and its role as a blueprint for potential effects of similarly distant volcanic eruptions in the future (Self). Re-casting these culturally important narratives as (also) environmental narratives can potentially be used for levering increased environmental awareness in the present (Nordvig).

Moving further back into proto- and prehistory, additional case studies considered the effects of natural hazards and their knock-on effects on societies of the Ancient Near Eastern and Biblical World. Here, the political use and implications of calamity stand clear, both in the sense that rulers have been recorded to have lost their religious and thereby political mandate due to climatic irregularities, and in the sense that calamities have evidently been used as political, i.e. rhetorical, devices in these distant – but in cultural terms influential – societies. The influence of environmental change not only on politics but also on worldviews and religious change were debated (Dietrich; Kruger) and linked to ritual and trauma studies on the one hand and to contemporary theological concerns on the other (Chester, Duncan and Sangster; Skrimshire). Finally, true deep time case studies were presented. These discussed the role of environmental events in human evolution and prehistory, and highlighted that for large-scale events that occur but rarely (high-magnitude/low-frequency), the archaeological record may be the only direct evidence at hand. One excellent and iconic case study is the eruption of the Thera volcano in the Mediterranean. This event fully destroyed all settlement on the island and had a major and long-lasting impact on the geo-politics of Bronze Age societies in the wider region (Driessen and MacDonald; Knappett, Rivers and Evans). Moreover, this eruption has been linked to the myth of Atlantis that continues to capture the imagination of people today and which itself has undergone a transformation from dystopian to utopian (Friedrich; Schenk et al.). Particular attention was also given to the highly explosive eruption of the Laacher See in present-day western Germany (Schmincke, Park and Harms) and its societal effects (Riede *Splendid Isolation. The Eruption of the Laacher See Volcano and Southern*

Scandinavian Late Glacial Hunter-Gatherers). For this case study, the resolution of the societal data may be coarse, but it is complemented with rather detailed knowledge of the eruption's effects on weather, vegetation and animal life. The currently dormant but by no means extinct volcano's location close to multiple national borders in the heart of Europe – dotted as it is with critical infrastructure facilities – and very near one of Europe's major trade corridors (the River Rhine) allows this case study to be linked with considerations of possible future impacts. The occasional appearance of this eruption in popular media and the press as well as in fiction (e.g. Schreiber) were evaluated. Indeed, critical screenings of cinematic interpretations of the events in question were used often to underline their echoes in the present (Table 15.3), but also to show how little these often rather trivial pornographic "collapse" imaginations (*sensu* McKibben) are informed by robust humanities research.

Minding the gap – making deep history relevant

The various case studies presented in this course have served to underline how echoes of past climate change and catastrophe find their way into contemporary imaginations and debates about present and future impacts of climate change. In order to further formalize the links between each case study and to highlight the potential contribution of a historically informed, evidence-based approach to teaching climate and climate catastrophe in the humanities, we designed a final exercise asking students to engage in a form of counterfactual reasoning. Counterfactual thinking has been shown to increase general logical reasoning capacity, and the exploration of counterfactual scenarios has been promoted both as a thinking and planning tool in adaptation research as well as a tool in the teaching of specific analytical skills such as the interpretation of maps, in history teaching, and – following Staley – in thinking historically about the future (Buchsbaum et al.; Clarke, "Possibilistic Thinking: A New Conceptual Tool for Thinking About Extreme Events"; Lillquist; Roberts; Jensen; Huijgen and

Table 15.3 Selected screenings presented in the course *Catastrophes | Cultures: Integrated humanistic perspectives on natural hazards from prehistory to present*

Film/footage	Focus area
An Inconvenient Truth	Modern medialization of climate catastrophe, the role of the natural and cultural sciences
The Day After Tomorrow	Ice-age cooling and its effects in contemporary imagination
Mega Disasters – Atlantis Apocalypse & The Biblical Plagues, Episode 2: Darkness in Egypt	Transformations of the Atlantis myth and apocalyptic biblical narratives
The Last Days of Pompeii	Imaginations of iconic volcanic catastrophe

Holthuis). We urged the students to draw eclectically and creatively on the different components of the course when putting together their narratives of potential futures. Climate and science fiction here provide the imaginative resources for thinking about future societies, whereas the historical, archaeological and anthropological data presented in this course provide the scaffold constraining that imagination. Teaching has been case-based and the cases are selected to provide a suite of 'portable analytics' or rather 'trans-temporal hinges', i.e. not analogies but platform for thinking laterally and creatively about other – future, hypothetical, possible – cases (Howe and Boyer; Pedersen and Nielsen).

This exercise brought us full circles to a consideration of fictive narratives of *future climates and societies* in relation to narratives of *past climates and societies*. Fictive narratives serve useful purposes for exploring the societal dimensions of climate, catastrophe, and human impact, but scenarios that explicitly draw on historical data on how human communities did (rather than may) adapt to climate change or fail to do so, on how they were (rather than may be) affected by particular kinds of natural hazards and extreme environmental or climatic changes, are less fictive, their speculative components constrained or disciplined by the historical and archaeological records. Projects took, for instance, their starting points in renewed volcanic activity at Thera and its potentially destabilizing impacts, in the effects of Little Ice Age-like cooling on Europe, especially in relation to religious responses and the role of scientists in communicating and mediating risks.

Throughout the course and the exams, issues of historical substance were uncovered, but we also returned many times to discussions of ethical and political considerations, where our focus on past calamities and their long-term sociocultural effects touches upon debates of environmental ethics in disaster sociology (Browne and Peek), the geosciences (Wyss and Peppoloni) and the Environmental Humanities (Rigby; Hulme, "Climate"). The Environmental Humanities are strongly linked to an explicit ethical stance and forms of scholarly activism. Interestingly, some geoscientists are now beginning to suggest that those studying human-environment relations should take an oath akin to the Hippocratic one: a "Geoethical Promise" that would require them to take professional stance on, for instance, issues of anthropogenic climate change and resource exploitation (Matteucci et al.). Furthermore, some geologists are beginning to argue that more efficacious storytelling is needed to bolster such public environmental conscience (Bohle). In archaeology, similar debates about the usefulness of the past and the hard-won insights about societal sustainability and collapse are being held, although a profession-wide ethical engagement with these issues is not foregrounded (Stump; Dawdy; Van de Noort). The entrenched terminologies and frames of reference of these various disciplines remain to be fully reconciled. Perhaps shared ethical concerns about the future we want and do not want – in light of the past we see – will bring all the disciplines concerned with the environment closer together.

The foundational argument of the Environmental Humanities vis-à-vis the relevance of climate and the environment in culture and culture history urges us also to reconsider the role of these factors in dissemination arenas such as museums.

Such efforts are underway (e.g. Cameron and Neilson; Harvey and Perry) but remain largely confined to science museums rather than museums of, for instance, cultural and national history. In our view, it is those latter museums that in fact offer the greatest pedagogical potential for raising visitors' awareness of the past and present influence of climate, climate change and the environment on culture and vice versa. In this arena, the Environmental Humanities can be made to work.

In our teaching as in our research, we have attempted to develop an Environmental Humanities approach that stresses the importance of the temporal dimension – a palaeoenvironmental humanities – in producing and re-producing constellations of vulnerability and resilience. These in turn structure people's ability to face climatic changes and climate catastrophes. Throughout, we attempted to stress that different datasets come with their challenges but also their advantages. Initially, our goal was to move towards a great degree of integration between the different subjects, but – not least in light of student feedback – it may be more productive to aim for a disciplinary and epistemological pluralism that accepts the diversity of approaches (cf. Miller et al.), at least at the undergraduate level.

Looking ahead, we will include a greater number disciplines working with the contemporary (literature/media studies focused on popular culture), the history of climate research per se, as well as anthropology. Our course has tackled the dual challenge of teaching climate and of teaching interdisciplinarity head on. The students rose to the challenge producing, on the whole, creative and innovative project exams that drew widely and diversely on the taught resources, but in many instances also went well beyond them. We look forward to teaching the course again.

Note

1   Archaeology is in Europe most commonly placed in Arts and Humanities faculties.

References

Bohle, Martin. "Simple Geoethics: An Essay on Daily Earth Science." *Geological Society, London, Special Publications* 419.1 (2015): 5–12. Print.

Browne, Katherine E., and Lori Peek. "Beyond the Irb: An Ethical Toolkit for Long-Term Disaster Research." *International Journal of Mass Emergencies and Disasters* 32.1 (2014): 82–120. Print.

Buchsbaum, Daphna et al., "The Power of Possibility: Causal Learning, Counterfactual Reasoning, and Pretend Play." *Philosophical Transactions of the Royal Society B: Biological Sciences* 367.1599 (2012): 2202–12. Print.

Cameron, Fiona, and Brett Neilson, eds. *Climate Change and Museum Futures.* London: Routledge (2015). Print.

Chester, David K., Angus M. Duncan, and Heather Sangster. "Religious Interpretations of Disaster." *The Routledge Handbook of Hazards and Disaster Risk Reduction.* Eds. Wisner, Ben, J. C. Gaillard and Ilan Kelman. Abington: Routledge (2012): 109–20. Print.

Clarke, Lee. "Possibilistic Thinking: A New Conceptual Tool for Thinking About Extreme Events." *Social Research* 75.3 (2008): 669–90, 1033. Print.

Clarke, Lee. *Worst Cases. Terror and Catastrophe in the Popular Imagination.* Vol. Chicago, IL: The University of Chicago Press (2006). Print.

Dawdy, Shannon Lee. "Millennial Archaeology. Locating the Discipline in the Age of Insecurity." *Archaeological Dialogues* 16.02 (2009): 131–42. Print.

Dietrich, Jan. "Coping with Disasters in Antiquity and the Bible: Practical and Mental Strategies." *Past Vulnerability. Volcanic Eruptions and Human Vulnerability in Traditional Societies Past and Present.* Ed. Riede, Felix. Aarhus: Aarhus University Press. Print.

Driessen, Jan, and Colin F. MacDonald. *The Troubled Island: Minoan Crete before and after the Santorini Eruption.* Aegaeum, Vol. 17. Liege: Universite de Liege (1997). Print.

Dull, Robert A., John R. Southon, and Payson Sheets. "Volcanism, Ecology and Culture: A Reassessment of the Volcán Ilopango Tbj Eruption in the Southern Maya Realm." *Latin American Antiquity* 12.1 (2001): 25–44. Print.

Friedrich, Walter L. *Fire in the Sea: Natural History and the Legend of Atlantis.* Cambridge: Cambridge University Press (2000). Print.

García-Acosta, Virginia. "Historical Disaster Research." *Catastrophe & Culture: The Anthropology of Disaster.* Eds. Hoffman, Susanna M. and Anthony Oliver-Smith. School of American Research Advanced Seminar Series. Santa Fe, NM: School of American Research Press (2002): 49–66. Print.

Gunn, J.D., ed. *The Years without Summer. Tracing Ad 536 and Its Aftermath.* Oxford: Archaepress (2000). Print.

Harvey, David C., and Jim Perry, eds. *The Future of Heritage as Climate Change: Loss, Adaptation and Creativity.* London: Routledge (2015). Print.

Horn, Eva. *Zukunft Als Katastrophe.* Frankfurt a.M.: S. Fischer (2014). Print.

Howe, Cymene, and Dominic Boyer. "Portable Analytics and Lateral Theory." *Theory Can Be More Than It Used to Be.* Eds. Boyer, Dominic, James Faubion and George Marcus. Ithaca, NY: Cornell University Press (in press). Print.

Humanities Electives. Aarhus University, 20 June 2016. Web. 7 July 2016.

Huijgen, Tim, and Paul Holthuis. "Towards Bad History? A Call for the Use of Counterfactual Historical Reasoning in History Education." *Historical Encounters: A Journal of Historical Consciousness, Historical Cultures, and History Education* 1.1 (2014): 103–10. Print.

Hulme, Mike. "Climate Change and Virtue: An Apologetic." *Humanities* 3.3 (2014): 299–312. Print.

Hulme, Mike. "The Conquering of Climate: Discourses of Fear and Their Dissolution." *Geographical Journal* 174.1 (2008): 5–16. Print.

Jensen, Bernard E. "Counterfactual History and Its Educational Potential." *History in Education: Proceedings from the Conference History in Education Held at the Danish University of Education 24–25 March 2004.* Ed. Kemp, Peter. Copenhagen: Danmarks Pædagogiske Universitets Forlag (2005): 151–58. Print.

Knappett, Carl, Ray Rivers, and Tim Evans. "The Theran Eruption and Minoan Palatial Collapse: New Interpretations Gained from Modelling the Maritime Network." *Antiquity* 85.329 (2011): 1008–23. Print.

Kruger, P.A. "Disaster and the Topos of the World Upside Down: Selected Cases from the Ancient near Eastern World." *Disaster and Relief Management. Katastrophen Und Ihre Bewältigung.* Ed. Berlejung, A. Forschungen Zum Alten Testament 81. Tübingen: Mohr Siebeck (2012): 391–424. Print.

Lillquist, Karl. "Teaching with Catastrophe: Topographic Map Interpretation and the Physical Geography of the 1949 Mann Gulch, Montana Wildfire." *Journal of Geoscience Education* 54.5 (2006): 561–71. Print.

Matteucci, R. et al., "The Geoethical Promise: A Proposal." *Episodes* 37.3 (2014): 190–91. Print.

McKibben, Bill. *Eaarth: Making a Life on a Tough New Planet.* New York: Times Books (2010). Print.

Miller, T. R. et al., "Epistemological Pluralism: Reorganizing Interdisciplinary Research." *Ecology and Society* 13.2 (2008): article 46. Print.

Mitchell, James K. "Looking Backward to See Forward: Historical Changes of Public Knowledge About Climate Hazards in Ireland." *Irish Geography* 44.1 (2011): 7–26. Print.

Nielsen, Esben Bjerggaard. "Klima, Apokalypse Og En Topos Om Sted." *Rhetorica Scandinavica* 63.4 (2013): 39–53. Print.

Nordvig, Mathias Valentin. "What Happens When 'Hider' and 'Screamer' Go Sailing with 'Noisy'? Geo-Mythological Traces in Old Icelandic Mythology." *Past Vulnerability. Volcanic Eruptions and Human Vulnerability in Traditional Societies Past and Present.* Ed. Riede, Felix. Aarhus: Aarhus University Press. Print.

Oliver-Smith, Anthony. "Global Changes and the Definition of Disaster." *What Is a Disaster?* Ed. Quarantelli, Enrico L. London: Routledge, (1998): 178–94. Print.

Pedersen, Morten Axel, and Morten Nielsen. "Trans-Temporal Hinges: Reflections on an Ethnographic Study of Chinese Infrastructural Projects in Mozambique and Mongolia." *Social Analysis* 57.1 (2013): 122–42. Print.

Pfister, Christian. "Learning from Nature-Induced Disasters: Theoretical Considerations and Case Studies from Western Europe." *Natural Disasters, Cultural Responses: Case Studies toward a Global Environmental History.* Eds. Mauch, Christof and Cristian Pfister. Lanham, MD: Lexington Books (2009): 17–40. Print.

Price, Neil, and Bo Gräslund. "Excavating the Fimbulwinter? Archaeology, Geomythology and the Climate Event(S) of Ad 536." *Past Vulnerability. Volcanic Eruptions and Human Vulnerability in Traditional Societies Past and Present.* Ed. Riede, Felix. Aarhus: Aarhus University Press. Print.

Riede, Felix. *Splendid Isolation. The Eruption of the Laacher See Volcano and Southern Scandinavian Late Glacial Hunter-Gatherers.* Aarhus: Aarhus University Press. Print.

Riede, Felix. "Towards a Science of Past Disasters." *Natural Hazards* 71.1 (2014): 335–62. Print.

Rigby, Kate. *Dancing with Disaster: Environmental Histories, Narratives, and Ethics for Perilous Times.* Under the Sign of Nature: Explorations in Ecocriticism. Charlottesville: University of Virginia Press, 2015. Print.

Roberts, Scott L. "Using Counterfactual History to Enhance Students' Historical Understanding." *The Social Studies* 102.3 (2011): 117–23. Print.

Schenk, Gerrit J. et al., eds. *Von Atlantis Bis Heute – Mensch. Natur. Katastrophe.* Schnell und Steiner: Regensburg (2014). Print.

Schmincke, Hans-Ulrich, Cornelia Park, and E. Harms. "Evolution and Environmental Impacts of the Eruption of Laacher See Volcano (Germany) 12,900 a Bp." *Quaternary International* 61 (1999): 61–72. Print.

Schreiber, Ulrich C. *Die Flucht Der Ameisen.* München/Zürich: Piper (2006). Print.

Self, Stephen. "The Effects and Consequences of Very Large Explosive Volcanic Eruptions." *Philosophical Transactions of the Royal Society A: Mathematical, Physical and Engineering Sciences* 364.1845 (2006): 2073–97. Print.

Sheets, Payson D. "Armageddon to the Garden of Eden: Explosive Volcanic Eruptions and Societal Resilience in Ancient Middle America." *El Niño, Catastrophism, and Culture Change in Ancient America.* Eds. Sandweiss, Dan and Jeffrey Quilter. Cambridge, MA: Harvard University Press (2008): 167–86. Print.

Sigl, M. et al., "Timing and Climate Forcing of Volcanic Eruptions for the Past 2,500 Years." *Nature*. Print.

Skrimshire, Stefan. "Climate Change and Apocalyptic Faith." *Wiley Interdisciplinary Reviews: Climate Change* 5.2 (2014): 233–46. Print.

Staley, David J. "A History of the Future." *History and Theory* 41.4 (2002): 72–89. Print.

Stump, Daryl. "On Applied Archaeology, Indigenous Knowledge, and the Usable Past." *Current Anthropology* 54.3 (2013): 268–98. Print.

Tvauri, Andres. "The Impact of the Climate Catastrophe of 536–537 Ad in Estonia and Neighbouring Areas." *Estonian Journal of Archaeology* 18.1 (2014): 30–56. Print.

van Bavel, Bas, and Daniel R. Curtis. "Better Understanding Disasters by Better Using History: Systematically Using the Historical Record as One Way to Advance Research into Disasters." *International Journal of Mass Emergencies and Disasters*. Print.

Van de Noort, Robert. *Climate Change Archaeology: Building Resilience from Research in the World's Coastal Wetlands*. Oxford: Oxford University Press (2013). Print.

Wyss, Max, and Silvia Peppoloni, eds. *Geoethics. Ethical Challenges and Case Studies in Earth Sciences*. Oxford: Elsevier (2015). Print.

16 Climate visualizations as cultural objects

Heather Houser

In 2012 Bill McKibben aimed to jumpstart climate activism with "[t]hree simple numbers that add up to global catastrophe." Sharing the cover of *Rolling Stone* with teen idol Justin Bieber, he offers a set of statistics that add up to "Global Warming's Terrifying New Math": 2° Celsius (threshold for atmospheric temperature increase), 565 gigatons (allowable pre-2050 carbon dioxide emissions to avoid crossing this threshold), 2795 gigatons (coal currently in hydrocarbon corporation reserves). From these calculations McKibben proposes a worldwide campaign to pressure institutions to divest from fossil fuel companies and keep those 2795 gigatons underground.

Our students likely possess the cultural literacy to situate Bieber on a cultural map but lack the numerical literacy to comprehend the "simple numbers" McKibben cites to goad climate action. Yet, as environmental teachers and scholars are well aware, numbers are at the heart of environmental debates, climate change especially. Data referencing CO_2 emissions, temperature and sea level rise, and deforestation communicate urgency but present at least two problems: they are rarely understood and don't hit the gut as photographs or narratives can. To communicate information to audiences and address this affective gap, scientists, artists, and designers have increasingly turned to data visualization, which ranges from basic line graphs, to the multimodal visualizations of climate research, to explicitly artistic visualizations that appear in actual and virtual galleries. In the ranks of the latter, artist Chris Jordan exemplifies visualizers' position when he announces his mission "to take these numbers, these statistics [about pollution and waste] from the raw language of data, and to translate them into a more universal visual language, that can be felt" (Jordan). The visual is universal, the idea goes, and it's a vector for both knowledge and emotion-laden concern.

Rather than resolve problems of numeracy,[1] however, visualizations couple it with a need for greater visual literacy. Because these objects engage multiple literacies, we do our students well to guide them in interpreting visualization rather than propagate the notion that they are self-evident or dismissible; this is true for artistic visualizations as well as those from scientific bodies.Organizing a climate change humanities course around visualizations, or weaving these works into a broader course on climate culture, we can teach students the tools of ecocultural analysis—close reading, inquiry-based critical thinking, and verbal and visual expression—alongside numeracy and visual comprehension. These interpretive skills carry beyond the classroom and into our roles as public citizens.

A course with a strong visualization component brings the interpretative humanities—that is, those disciplines like media and literary studies that attend closely to the formal structures and meanings of cultural objects—to bear on scientific modes of understanding environmental processes. Three main objectives are: building tools to interpret visual culture and works' authority and impact, understanding positions on constructivism and realism, and establishing the role of heuristics in environmental debates. With these objectives, a visualization course invites multimedia, collaborative, and community-based projects in addition to the essays and other writing humanities classes often require.

Building vocabularies

Studying climate visualizations engages the overlapping fields of eco-media and visual studies. The latter especially has a body of scholarship too vast to cover thoroughly, but a fine place to start is with John Berger's enduring *Ways of Seeing* and Nicolas Mirzoeff's introduction to his *The Visual Culture Reader*.[2] These pieces provide a lexicon for studying images while denaturalizing seeing and vision and demonstrating how power and contests over authority manifest in visual media. They pair well with the pronouncements of visualization practitioners and critics of this cultural form. While practitioners (notably, Card et al.; Corby; Jordan; Koblin; Klanten et al.) tout the transparency, immediacy, and consumability of their works, critics (Butterworth; Larsen) question not only whether any artifact achieves these values but also whether they're desirable.

With terms and debates established, the syllabus can proceed to apply the visual studies toolkit to climate change culture with essays by Birgit Schneider and Mirzoeff. Schneider interprets visualizations germinal to climate science and policy debate: the so-called "hockey-stick graph" by Michael Mann et al. (see Figure 16.1), which is also featured in Davis Guggenheim's *An Inconvenient Truth* (see Figure 16.2). She argues that "even a matter-of-fact graph ... can be embedded into the metanarratives of climate change, i.e. The plot of threat, realization, morality and possible salvation through timely action" (Schneider, "Climate Model Simulation" 206). To assess how students' interpretive skills develop over the semester, the teacher can retain a record of this initial discussion and return to the same artifacts at course's end. This fruitful exercise demonstrates a lesson of the course: that our understandings of visualizations depend on the contextual knowledge, vocabularies, and sociocultural positionings we bring to them. Mirzoeff's take on climate change images is more polemical than Schneider's and challenges the predominance of an iconic metonym for climate disruption: the polar bear stranded on dwindling ice. He proposes that visuality is "a strategy of authority" for political regimes and calls for an "Anthropocene visuality" that would bring climate injustice out of the shadows (Mirzoeff, "The Clash of Visualizations" 1194, 1204).

Defamiliarizing practices of seeing while inflecting visuality with political and

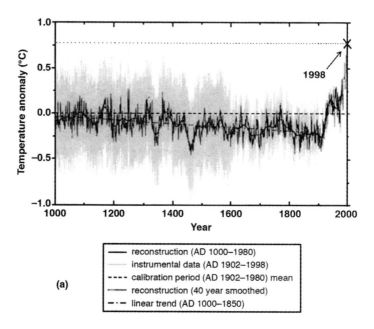

Figure 16.1 Hockey-stick graph. Mean temperatures in the northern hemisphere during the last 1,000 years

Source: Michael E. Mann, Raymond S. Bradley and Malcolm K. Hughes, 'Northern hemisphere temperatures during the past millennium: Inferences, uncertainties, and limitations' in *Geophysical Research Letters*, 1999, Fig. 3. Courtesy of John Wiley and Sons.

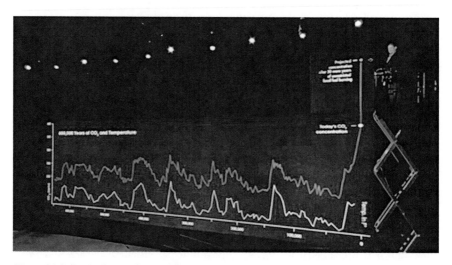

Figure 16.2 Davis Guggenheim. Al Gore with chart correlating CO_2 and temperature increases from ice core data

Source: Film still from *An Inconvenient Truth*, 2006.

epistemological implications are learning objectives of eco-media studies as well. Several new anthologies offer a menu of short essays from which an instructor may draw to orient students in this field (Rust, Monani, and Cubitt; Starosielski and Walker). Additionally, selections from Ursula Heise's "From the Blue Planet to Google Earth" in *Sense of Place and Sense of Planet*, models critical analysis of varied visualizations: the famous "Blue Marble" photograph of earth taken on NASA's 1972 Apollo 17 space mission; John Klima's 2002 digital installation, *EARTH*; and Google Earth navigation software. The chapter contextualizes these objects within the modern environmentalist movement and identifies in them a tension between the local and the global. Read early in the course, it provides historical and conceptual background and promotes discussion of the effects of representing climate change at different scales and through diverse media.

Reading visualizations

The theoretical readings make it clear that the term "visualization" encompasses everything from magazine covers to charts and graphs in peer-reviewed scientific articles. When students recognize this variety, it's important to emphasize that even artifacts without explicit artistic ambitions are rhetorical objects whose formal features are meaning-laden and shape how we comprehend them and incorporate them into our personal and political lives. Two artifacts—the hockey-stick graph and climate model visualizations—solidify this claim and introduce key course concerns: how authority accrues to a work, constructivism vs realism, and the functions of heuristics. Mann et al.'s graph provides an opportunity to "teach the controversy" of climate change; in this case, this means disabusing students of the existence *of* a controversy over scientific consensus. The so-called controversy is a problem of representation and reception[3] and an ideological contest between free marketeer and business-as-usual politicians and environmental and social justice groups willing to disrupt the economy to mitigate climate damage. A 2006 article from *The Chronicle of Higher Education* concisely presents the controversy for lay audiences and effectively complements the 1999 *Geophysical Research Letters* (*GRL*) article in which the graph originally appeared. A highly specialized piece like this might intimidate teachers and students, but it instructs that visualizations detach from their original contexts, rove, and reach varied audiences; their representational conventions therefore bear a great burden of signification.

Crucial to all visualizations' meaning are the chromatic choices creators make. The course can address the importance of color in graphs by comparing the black and white chart that appears in the *GRL* article to the vivid versions in Intergovernmental Panel on Climate Change (IPCC) reports and other venues. The colors for temperature and other environmental phenomena seem like givens (naturally, red = hot, blue = cold), but they too have a history and politics. Color isn't just a practical device for differentiating temperatures; along with features such as scale, animation, and temporality, it makes the data experiential by provoking affective and psychological responses in viewers. An instructor can emphasize this point by introducing the controversial "burning embers diagram" that was censored from the 2009 IPCC assessment report for being too incendiary (Mahony and Hulme).

Guggenheim's *An Inconvenient Truth* follows logically from a unit on climatological graphs because the latter figure so prominently in Al Gore's performance. This documentary grounds discussion of the historical separation of number from narrative and interpretation. Mary Poovey explains the isolation of these domains in her history of the "modern fact," and the legacy of this separation endures in climate discourse. Scientists generate numbers and humanists craft narratives, the story goes. The course already reverses this tendency by placing artifacts based in the mathematical sciences within the purview of the interpretative humanities. Because it oscillates between climate charts and Gore's life narrative and demonstrates the performativity of numbers, Guggenheim's film emphasizes that both numbers and their representations are rhetorical objects couched in figural language and imagery.

Climate model visualizations muddle the lines separating number and figuration and are at the heart of climatology and policy making. In addressing these points, the instructor must not suggest that climate science is a "mere fiction"; to say models stray from reality into representation does not mean they are wild guesses or culturally constructed fantasies. The constructivism–realism debate, which also structures feminist and critical race theory, is challenging for undergraduates who tend to dismiss constructivism or embrace a misinterpretation of it, the extreme relativism of "anything goes." Philosopher Kate Soper's indispensable, albeit dry, *What Is Nature?* details these positions; if time is scarce, her essay, "Nature/'Nature,'" will suffice. Soper delineates historical conceptions of nature: "that which we are not"; the totality of being; and an essence or set of determined responses, which humans frequently adduce to separate ourselves from nonhuman animals (*What Is Nature* 22–29). With these understandings of nature in mind, she charts a path between constructivism and realism that acknowledges how ideas of nature are culturally and politically inflected without denying the facticity of environmental phenomena. Selections from Paul Edwards magisterial history of modeling, *A Vast Machine*, moves the challenges of realism into the field of climate science and provides essential context for examining model visualizations. Edwards's work also brings focus to the epistemological authority of visualizations and the historical shifts in that authority. Crucial to the construction of authority is the free circulation of models and visualizations. As climatologist Mike Hulme writes, "[t]o earn their social authority climate models ... need to inhabit public venues, displaying to all their epistemic claims of offering credible climate predictions" (Hulme 33), but they also enter charged sociocultural, political, and economic discursive spaces where audiences may lack cultivated expertise.

Despite the epistemological and representational complexity of model visualizations, they are largely "looked *through*," rather than at, because "they are thought to be ... self-evident" (Schneider, "Image Politics" 191–92). These two visualizations: NOAA's "Surface Air Temperature Anomalies" (see Figure 16.3) and NASA's "A Year in the Life of Earth's CO_2," (see Figure 16.4) promote slow looking and reading because they make climate data experiential. Cultural analysis of them establishes that viewers aren't vessels into which information is poured; rather, they

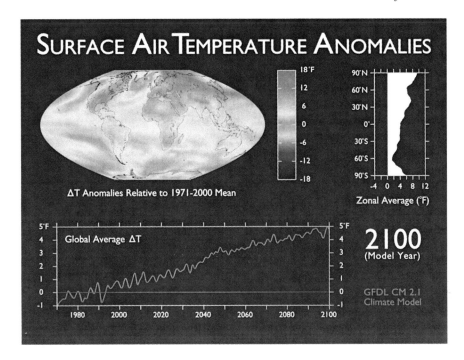

Figure 16.3 Keith Dixon, "Surface Air Temperature Anomalies," NOAA/Geophysical
    Fluid Dynamics Laboratory, October 2005

Source: www.gfdl.noaa.gov/visualizations-climate-prediction

Figure 16.4 "A Year in the Life of CO_2," NASA/Goddard Space Flight Center, November
    2014

Source: http://svs.gsfc.nasa.gov/cgi-bin/details.cgi?aid=11719

are social and psychological beings in whom a visualization's formal features produce varied responses. Crucial to their aesthetics are the multiple temporal scales they depict; their sophistication; and their use of color and cartography. Most climate modelers hold that models don't establish axiomatic facts; rather they simulate climate sensitivity to address specific questions and spur new research trajectories. It's on this point that the instructor should emphasize the heuristic function of modeling and visualization, how they make knowledge move rather than fix immoveable facts about the climate system's present and future states. They are not strictly predictive or mimetic. The maps in the vivid *Atlas of Climate Change* carry these concerns about visualizing climate data into the realm of cartography and productively complement the research models.

Thus far I've focused on scientific visualizations because they are integral to climate discourse and students may hesitate to read them as cultural artifacts. However, there is a rich archive of climate art that energizes related lines of inquiry. The Cape Farewell expeditions are valuable resources to mine. The foundation sends artists of all stripes to regions facing extreme climate disturbance in hopes of inspiring informed cultural production around global warming. Architect Sunand Prasad's visualization of CO_2 emissions through balloons and Sharon Switzer's *#crazyweather*, which aggregates tweets about the weather, raise questions of what counts as climate data and how the media that transmit data affect their meaning. Sherry Wiggins's *Carbon Portraits* combines photographic portraiture, narrative, and quantitative personal and climate data to visualize how individuals understand themselves as participants in climate destabilization; it suggests we primarily apprehend carbon impacts through comparison rather than in absolute terms.

Creative assessments

With its compelling variety of primary works, a course or unit on visualizations is ripe for inventive assignments that either supplement traditional argument-based essays or swerve from them. Given the vast number of visualizations available in print and online, an instructor cannot gain mastery over the archive. Therefore, asking students to select a striking piece and briefly report on it either on a blog, in a response paper, or in a presentation will expand awareness of this body of work. While this assignment could productively cap the course and foster discussion of what interpretive skills they now bring to bear on environmental representation, it could also be the first task for a research project (interview, essay, wiki page, etc.).

In a productive activity that queries the sources for visualizations, students choose a popular visualization from books such as David McCandless's *The Visual Miscellaneum* or Gareth Cook's annual *The Best American Infographics*, track down the original datasets, and evaluate the selection principles and design decisions the visualizer made to produce the object. Pairing this exercise with a selection from the introduction to Lisa Gitelman's *"Raw Data" Is An Oxymoron* reinforces the idea that data always emerge from specific historical moments, institutions, and socio-cultural positions.

These assignments keep students in the roles of consumers and interpreters;

those that ask students to design their own visualizations make them producers. In a challenging group assignment, students envision other forms a scientific visualization might take, translating it from, say, a map into a graph, or a dot plot into a time series. This teaches the drawbacks and benefits of different forms and employs visual studies concepts. Delving further into the visualization process, students might also select a current news or scientific report and interpret it visually. Johanna Drucker's "Humanities Approaches to Graphical Display" brings theoretical depth and formal possibilities to the assignment.

These assignments are excellent opportunities to encourage collaborative work. Team projects tend to be less familiar to humanities majors, especially those in literature and languages, but experience proves that, once the grumbling and anxiety wane, students retain more about course content through team projects. They make discoveries about their thinking and work styles and establish an intellectual community within their class and on campus. To extend the course's intellectual work into the community, the instructor might seek out a partnership with a government office or nonprofit needing visualization services.

***

"[F]or better or worse, [visual storytellers] are the new meaning-makers, the priests of shorthand synthesis." So declaims novelist Reif Larsen with an amalgam of feelings he dubs "infogasm": a "slightly nauseating feeling of delight." "Infogasm" succinctly captures the challenge and satisfaction of a course engaging climate visualizations. Students typically take to the visual and share practitioners' belief that they are a transparent lingua franca. Our task is to denaturalize what seems too easily digestible, to bring qualitative analysis to bear on quantitative representational forms, and to remind students of what extends off the charts: the biotic systems, species, and communities that climate change irrevocably disturbs.

Notes

1   For more on numeracy in climate change communication, see Hart.
2   For critiques of visual culture studies, see Bal and Mitchell.
3   For a précis of how the social sciences have framed this problem and a compelling alternative to those approaches, see Howe and Smith.

References

Bal, Mieke. "Visual Essentialism and the Object of Visual Culture." *Journal of Visual Culture* 2.1 (2003): 5–32. Print.
Berger, John. *Ways of Seeing.* New York: Penguin, 1977. Print.
Butterworth, Trevor. "Goodbye, Anecdotes! The Age of Big Data Demands Real Criticism." *The Awl.* 15 Jan. 2013. Web, accessed 9 May 2015.
Card, Stuart K., Jock D. Mackinlay, and Ben Shneiderman. *Readings in Information Visualization: Using Vision to Think.* San Diego, CA: Academic Press, 1999. Print.
Corby, Tom. "Landscapes of Feeling, Arenas of Action: Information Visualization as Art Practice." *Leonardo* 41.5 (2008): 460–67. Print.
Dow, Kristin, and Thomas E. Downing. *The Atlas of Climate Change: Mapping the World's*

Greatest Challenge, 3rd edn. Berkeley, CA: University of California Press, 2011. Print.

Drucker, Johanna. "Humanities Approaches to Graphical Display." *DHQ: Digital Humanities Quarterly* 5.1 (2011): no page. Web, accessed 20 May 2015.

Edwards, Paul N. *A Vast Machine: Computer Models, Climate Data, and the Politics of Global Warming*. Cambridge, MA: MIT Press, 2010. Print.

Gitelman, Lisa, ed. *"Raw Data" Is an Oxymoron*. Cambridge, MA: MIT Press, 2013. Print.

Hart, P. Sol. "The Role of Numeracy in Moderating the Influence of Statistics in Climate Change Messages." *Public Understanding of Science* 22.7 (2013): 785–93. Print.

Heise, Ursula K. *Sense of Place and Sense of Planet: The Environmental Imagination of the Global*. New York: Oxford University Press, 2008. Print.

Howe, Nicolas, and Philip Smith. *Climate Change as Social Drama: Global Warming in the Public Sphere*. New York: Cambridge University Press, 2015. Print.

Hulme, Mike. "How Climate Models Gain and Exercise Authority." *The Social Life of Climate Change Models: Anticipating Nature*. Eds Kristen Hastrup and Martin Skrydstrup. New York: Routledge, 2013. 30–44. Print.

Jordan, Chris. "Chris Jordan: Turning Powerful Stats into Art." TED Talks, Feb. 2008. Web, accessed 18 May 2015.

Klanten, Robert, Sven Ehmann, and Floyd Schulze, eds. *Visual Storytelling: Inspiring a New Visual Language*. Berlin: Gestalten, 2011. Print.

Koblin, Aaron. "Visualizing Ourselves … with Crowd-sourced Data." TED Talk, Mar. 2011. Web, accessed 20 May 2015.

Larsen, Reif. "This Chart Is a Lonely Hunter: The Narrative Eros of the Infographic." *The Millions*. 7 Feb. 2012. Web, accessed 20 May 2015.

Mahony, Martin, and Mike Hulme. "The Colour of Risk: An Exploration of the IPCC's 'Burning Embers' Diagram." *Spontaneous Generations* 6.1 (2012): 75–89. Print.

Mann, Michael E., Raymond S. Bradley, and Malcolm K. Hughes. "Northern Hemisphere Temperatures During the Past Millennium: Inferences, Uncertainties, and Limitations." *Geophysical Research Letters* 26 (1999): 759–62. Print.

McCandless, David. *Visual Miscellaneum: A Colorful Guide to the World's Most Consequential Trivia*. New York: Harper Design, 2012. Print.

McKibben, Bill. "Global Warming's Terrifying New Math." *Rolling Stone*. July 2012: no page. Web, accessed 1 May 2015.

Mirzoeff, Nicholas. "The Clash of Visualizations: Counterinsurgency and Climate Change." *Social Research* 78.4 (2011): 1185–210. Print.

Mirzoeff, Nicholas. "Introduction: For Critical Visuality Studies." *The Visual Culture Reader*. Ed. Nicholas Mirzoeff, 3rd edn. New York: Routledge, 2013, xxix-xxxviii. Print.

Mitchell, W.J.T. "There Are No Visual Media." *The Visual Culture Reader*. Ed. Nicholas Mirzoeff. 3rd edn. New York: Routledge, 2013, 7–14. Print.

Monastersky, Richard. "Climate Science on Trial." *The Chronicle of Higher Education*, 8 Sept. 2006: A10. Print.

Poovey, Mary. *A History of the Modern Fact: Problems of Knowledge in the Sciences of Wealth and Society*. Chicago, IL: University of Chicago Press, 1998. Print.

Rust, Stephen, Salma Monani, and Sean Cubitt, eds. *Ecomedia: Key Issues*. New York: Routledge, 2016. Print.

Schneider, Birgit. "Climate Model Simulation Visualization from a Visual Studies Perspective." *Wiley Interdisciplinary Reviews: Climate Change* 2 (2012): 185–93. Print.

Schneider, Birgit. "Image Politics: Picturing Uncertainty. The Role of Images in Climatology and Climate Policy." *Climate Change and Policy: The Calculability of Climate Change and the Challenge of Uncertainty*. Eds. Gabriele Gramelsberger and Johann Feichter.

Berlin: Springer-Verlag, 2011, 191–209. Print.

Soper, Kate. "Nature/'Nature'." *Futurenatural: Nature, Science, Culture.* Ed. George Robertson et al. New York: Routledge, 1996, 21–34. Print.

Soper, Kate. *What Is Nature?: Culture, Politics and the Non-Human.* Malden, MA: Blackwell, 1995. Print.

Starosielski, Nicole, and Janet Walker, eds. *Sustainable Media: Critical Approaches to Media and Environment.* New York: Routledge, 2016. Print.

17 Engaging the 'Eaarth'

Teaching and making climate change cultures in an art and design context

Nicole Merola

A handmade rag rug, stuffed in the middle to produce a perch for writing, and an accompanying handmade journal call forth a sense of community around creating and sharing climate change stories (Margaret Kearney). A series of landscape prints, produced by inking found aluminum cans and running them through a French etching press, underscores consumption and energy use (Jessica Biletch). A digital drawing of the Statue of Liberty bound by a gasoline pump hose and wreathed with ribbons of oil critiques the entrenchment of U.S. petro-capitalism (Cara Lowe). An artist's book, loaded with charcoal that dirties the fingers of the reader, uses the topic of smog in Beijing to explore links between privilege, manufacture, consumption, and pollution (Cathy Lee). An "apocalypse pack," underwritten by satire and filled with items that coddle the user and quickly lose all value, mocks inaction on preparedness for climate disasters (Paige Silverman). These examples mark the range of objects students have created for my undergraduate course, "Representing 'Unrepresentable' Environments: Climate Change."

My course is designed to help students at the Rhode Island School of Design (RISD) negotiate written, visual, and material climate change cultures by introducing them to a variety of Anglo-American climate change texts, topics, and genres; helping them become more sophisticated and attentive readers with respect to the formal, rhetorical, and affective strategies that shape climate change texts; and, whether or not their art and design work ultimately engages explicitly with climate change, aiding them in situating their professional practice within the context of a climate-changed planet. Three primary assumptions anchor "Representing 'Unrepresentable' Environments." First, as many environmental humanities scholars argue, climate change confronts us with both material and representational challenges.[1] Second, as a descriptor of planetary circumstances, climate change names not only future socioecological milieux, but also many socioecological presents. In other words, as Bill McKibben notes, we already live in uncanny circumstances, on an "earth*like*" planet we should think of not as the Earth, but rather as the "Eaarth" (McKibben 2–3). Third, as Rob Nixon avers, writer-activists, and, by extension, artist-activists, are uniquely positioned to intervene in how we conceptualize and respond to the multidimensional socioecological disasters that constitute slow violence, climate change among them. Taken together, these three assumptions add urgency to a mode of teaching climate change cultures attentive to students' intellectual *and* emotional trajectories. In my classes, the phrase climate change cultures means both works of literature, visual art, and performance art that engage with causes, effects, discourses, and affects of climate change and the process of creating community through discussion of climate change.

In an attempt to help students "navigate between hope and horror", my course moves from texts that foreground forms of climate change disavowal, for instance skepticism or denialism, to those that present forms of climate change affect— resilience, fortitude, apathy, resignation, melancholy, anxiety, fear, sadness, anger—tempered by what Clive Hamilton calls "the new reality" (Lioi 14).[2] In sketching this arc, both here and in class, I purposefully avoid the overly simplistic pessimism/optimism binary that marks much climate change discourse.[3] This binary conceals three important things I foreground and work through with students. First, as Stephanie LeMenager reminds us, "feeling ecological need not be pleasant" (LeManager 105). Second, unpleasant ecological feelings are myriad. Third, to different varieties of ecological feeling accrue different stakes and forms of agency. To track how different climate change discourses and affects show up in contemporary culture, we consider topics such as Arctic ecologies, biodiversity and extinction, climate denialism, climate change-induced migration, energy systems, environmental toxicity, industrial agriculture, resource scarcity, and visual and performance art responses to climate change. Our discussions of climate change genres, forms, and modes include short stories, poems, novels, films, and nonfiction texts that employ the conventions of apocalypse, comedy, documentary, eco-thriller, elegy, jeremiad, irony, melodrama, satire, speculative fiction, and tragedy.[4]

To evaluate how students engage with individual texts they write two short analytical papers. To cover a range of visual and performance artworks, students give one in-class group presentation on climate change visual culture. For the culminating project, students produce either a final analytical paper or a final art/design object accompanied by a contextual statement that situates their object in relation to climate change cultures.[5] The option to write a paper or produce an object offers students the chance to play to their strengths. Most choose the object option, engaging in a practice of critical making that functions, simultaneously, as a location for inter-animating the different tools and methods of the liberal arts, fine arts, and design arts; as an active response to the ongoing slow violence of climate change; as a space in which to experiment with the range of affects that accrue to our new reality; and as an example of what Donna Haraway and Anna Tsing call telling stories on, and for, a damaged planet.

One of the keys to the success of this course is giving students ownership over the contours of the final project. In keeping with the problem-based inquiry model that suffuses studio disciplines, the final project prompt is open-ended, requiring only that the object respond in some way to climate change and that, in the process of making conceptual, material, and design decisions, students consider our discussions about affect, audience, genre, mood, tone, and the rhetorical strategies of logos, ethos, and pathos. The accompanying contextual statement asks students to articulate the reasons behind their conceptual, material, and design decisions, the relationship of their object to specific texts or ideas from the course, and the particular climate change intervention they aim to make. The range of texts, modes, strategies, and affects we discuss provides students with a "climate change cultures" smorgasbord from which they can choose the topics, texts, or affects they find most compelling as catalysts for their own work. Repeated practice at developing and defending answers to questions about how a specific moment, motif, strategy, or text positions them to understand or feel something about climate change and the consideration of how certain texts work for certain audiences, eventually helps to soften students' initial assertions that either nonfiction or fiction are generally "better" at apprehending climate change and its consequences. Genre and mode are important analytic categories for us, but ultimately I want students to be able to parse how strategies and affects operate across genres, to focus on how a text functions rather than on what it is. While one overarching goal of the course is to help students develop as literary and cultural critics of climate change texts, another is to use environmental humanities, literary studies, and cultural studies questions and methods, and the transit of course concepts and ideas into studio work, to help students develop their own sense of ecological identity and articulate the relationship between it and their professional identity as artist/designer.[6]

To this end, all semester we foreground the question of how artists can intervene in climate change cultures. Rob Nixon's theorization of slow violence and the conceptual and representational challenges posed by long-term socioecological disasters (1–17) and his arguments about the importance of literature and writer-activists in shaping discursive and material socioecological circumstances frames this inquiry (Nixon 22–35, 42–44). In particular, we discuss Nixon's account of the specific interventions writer-activists can make in climate change and other discourses of slow violence: materializing "the outsourcing of environmental crisis", for instance, or "giv[ing] life and dimension to the strategies—oppositional, affirmative, and yes, often desperate and fractured—that emerge from those who bear the brunt of the planet's ecological crises", or "speak[ing] in defense of socioenvironmental memory" (22, 23, 24). Nixon derives this list—which includes more items that I can offer here—from an archive of postcolonial texts and contexts that may seem distant from my course materials. However, students find juxtaposing Nixon's list and our course texts productive. In some cases they excavate unexpected resonances. In other cases, Nixon's list helps them identify blind spots or deficits in our course materials. It also provides students a starting point for delineating the potential stakes of their final projects.

Our first class meeting ends with conversation about how to extend Nixon's arguments about literature and writers to encompass visual and material culture and its makers. I ask students to respond in writing to Nixon's provocative, and central, question—"How can we convert into image and narrative the disasters that are slow moving and long in the making?"—with an initial reflection on the limits and possibilities of their own studio practice as an intervention into climate change cultures (Nixon 3). We regularly return to this sort of reflective activity so students can map how exposure to different texts and class discussions impacts both their sense of their studio discipline in general and their sense of themselves as participants in making climate change cultures. For instance, I might ask them to imagine how particular conventions of speculative fiction might be rendered through architecture, video, or printmaking. We might discuss how the use of satire would play out on a poster, how an elegiac mood might be registered through painting or sculpture, how a photograph might align with the aim of a jeremiad, or how a piece of jewelry might engage with mourning biodiversity loss. While the writing and discussion prompts change based on our readings and conversations, this exercise helps me see how students are processing the course materials. The exercise also gets students to translate course concepts across written, visual, and material mediums and to concretize the notion of making new climate change cultures.

As the list of student projects with which I opened indicates, individual students found very different entry points for engaging with climate change cultures. In general, the topics and texts that most animated students were the Arctic ecologies materials; our discussions about material consumption, food and resource scarcity, and energy systems; and our discussions of climate skepticism/denialism. For the unit on Arctic ecologies, students read excerpts from Barry Lopez's *Arctic Dreams* ("Ice" and "Lancaster") and from the collection *Arctic Voices: Resistance at the Tipping Point*, edited by Subhankar Banerjee. They found the pieces from *Arctic Voices* (Cone, James, Shearer, and Thompson) especially powerful. Although, prior to class, most students understood that the Arctic functions as a barometer for climate change, most had only considered the Arctic abstractly. That is, they had not made connections between climate change and the cultural changes, already underway, to subsistence forms of life in indigenous communities in the Arctic. The *Arctic Voices* excerpts provided one location where students could see the outsourcing of socioecological disaster—the uneven distribution of the effects of climate change and the bioaccumulation of toxic chemicals in the bodies of the marine mammals and the humans who rely on their flesh for survival. In response to the texts from *Arctic Voices*, Shannon Crawford explored rhetorical and visual strategies for reaching different stakeholders to produce a pair of propaganda posters representing opposing sides in debates about drilling for oil in the Arctic. Thomas Arena, motivated by Barry Lopez's "Ice," created a large-scale info-graphic about the loss of Arctic sea ice. As a meditation on consumption, materialism, and personal complicity in carbon emissions, Alec Stewart filmed everything he consumed during a single day and manipulated the code of the image files to create a glitch art video loop that emphasizes consumption as a relentless process. The climate skepticism/denialism materials galvanized particular inventiveness. Nina Hartman conceived the "Enviro-Shield," a fake product that enables the wearer to hide from reality and disavow all environmental problems, as a parodic vehicle for exposing and ridiculing climate denialism. Brigid Rau, who patterned her delicate machine-knit textile by watching CSPAN debates about climate change and performing specific actions when particular "denialist" words or phrases were spoken or particular speakers appeared, engaged how right-wing pundits and politicians sow doubt.

Teaching climate change cultures in a liberal arts class in an art and design context is an extraordinary privilege, one that allows me and my students to inhabit what Joni Adamson calls "something of a middle place or door between landscapes where students move back and forth, honing the tools and critical theories they will need to work for a more socially and environmentally livable world" (113). As artists and designers, my students are makers of present and future worlds. They shape our material and conceptual landscapes in myriad ways. They create illustrations and visualizations that communicate complex ideas. They make films and paintings and sculptures that facilitate encounter with elusive concepts. They document environmental devastation. They design the products with which we live and the processes by which those products are manufactured and distributed. They plan for and build spaces, buildings, and communities adaptable to future conditions. I try to train my students to make targeted use of their critical thinking and making skills to agitate for the socioecological changes they want to produce. I ask them to refine their skills of discernment, to survey a range of climate change affects, and to test the creation of powerful narratives, things, and moods. Like climate change itself, this training produces results both immediate and deferred.

Acknowledgments

Many thanks to my "Representing 'Unrepresentable' Environments" students for their willingness to make with me new ways to compose the environmental humanities and art and design education.

Notes

1   See, for instance, Garrard, Kerridge, Latour, Nixon, Potter, and Yusoff and Gabrys.
2   Hamilton 132. See x–xiv and 128–133 for Hamilton's discussions about the dangers of unthinking, or unrealistic, optimism. Bill McKibben echoes Hamilton on the need for realistic forms of optimism commensurate with current socioecological circumstances in *Eaarth*.
3   For a recent essay that charts how pessimism and optimism function in two climate change novels see Murphy.
4   See References for selected course texts.
5   I designed this course in Summer 2011 and initially taught it in Spring 2012, when my teaching unit was partially supported by National Science Foundation grant #1004057 to Rhode Island Experimental Program to Stimulate Competitive Research EPSCoR. For information on EPSCoR, see "Experimental."
6   I borrow the notion of ecological identity from Mitchell Thomashow (*Ecological*). For discussion of the emphasis on ecological identity in my Narragansett Bay course, see Merola. Thomashow has also written specifically about pedagogy and climate change (*Bringing*).

References

Adamson, Joni. *American Indian Literature, Environmental Justice, and Ecocriticism: The Middle Place.* Tucson: University of Arizona Press, 2001. Print.
Banerjee, Subhankar, ed. *Arctic Voices: Resistance at the Tipping Point.* New York: Seven Stories Press, 2012. Print.
Cone, Marla. "From Silent Snow: The Slow Poisoning of the Arctic." *Arctic Voices: Resistance*

at the Tipping Point. Ed. Subhankar Banerjee. New York: Seven Stories Press, 2012, 125–41. Print.

"Experimental Program to Stimulate Competitive Research (EPSCoR). *National Science Foundation*, n.p., n.d. Web, accessed 1 June 2015, https://www.nsf.gov/od/iia/programs/epscor/index.jsp.

Garrard, Greg. "Ecocriticism and Education for Sustainability." *Pedagogy* 7.3 (2007): 359–83. Print.

Hamilton, Clive. *Requiem for a Species: Why We Resist the Truth About Climate Change*. Washington, DC: Earthscan, 2010. Print.

Haraway, Donna. "Anthropocene, Capitalocene, Plantationocene, Chthulucene: Making Kin." *Environmental Humanities* 6 (2015): 159–65. Print.

James, Sarah. "We are the Ones Who Have Everything to Lose." *Arctic Voices: Resistance at the Tipping Point*. Ed. Subhankar Banerjee. New York: Seven Stories Press, 2012, 260–64. Print.

Kerridge, Richard. Introduction. *Writing the Environment: Ecocriticism and Literature*. Ed. Richard Kerridge and Neil Sammells. London: Zed Books, 1998, 1–9 Print.

Latour, Bruno. "Agency at the Time of the Anthropocene." *New Literary History* 45.1 (2014): 1–18. Print.

LeMenager, Stephanie. *Living Oil: Petroleum Culture in the American Century*. Oxford: Oxford University Press, 2014. Print.

Lioi, Anthony. "Introduction: Teaching Earth." *Transformations: The Journal of Inclusive Scholarship and Pedagogy* 21.1 (2010): 14–22. Print.

Lopez, Barry. "Ice and Light." *Arctic Dreams*. New York: Vintage, 1986, 204–51. Print.

Lopez, Barry. "Lancaster Sound: *Monodon monoceros*." *Arctic Dreams*. New York: Vintage, 1986, 119–51. Print.

McKibben, Bill. *Eaarth: Making Life on a Tough New Planet*. New York: Henry Holt, 2010. Print.

Merola, Nicole M. "Connecting to Narragansett Bay: Fostering Ecological Citizenship Through Environmental Humanities and Arts and Design." *Transformations: The Journal of Inclusive Scholarship and Pedagogy* 21.1 (2010): 60–78. Print.

Murphy, Patrick D. "Pessimism, Optimism, Human Inertia, and Anthropogenic Climate Change." *ISLE: Interdisciplinary Studies in Literature and Environment* 21.1 (2014): 149–63. Print.

Nixon, Rob. *Slow Violence and the Environmentalism of the Poor*. Cambridge, MA: Harvard University Press, 2011. Print.

Potter, Emily. "Climate Change and the Problem of Representation." *Australian Humanities Review* 46 (2009): 69–79. Print.

Shearer, Christine. "Kivalina: A Climate Change Story." *Arctic Voices: Resistance at the Tipping Point*. Ed. Subhankar Banerjee. New York: Seven Stories Press, 2012, 207–19. Print.

Thomashow, Mitchell. *Bringing the Biosphere Home: Learning to Perceive Global Environmental Change*. Cambridge, MA: MIT Press, 2002. Print.

Thomashow, Mitchell. *Ecological Identity: Becoming a Reflective Environmentalist*. Cambridge: MIT Press, 1995. Print.

Thompson, Robert. "Why Can't We Get Answers to Our Questions?" *Arctic Voices: Resistance at the Tipping Point*. Ed. Subhankar Banerjee. New York: Seven Stories Press, 2012, 302–11. Print.

Tsing, Anna and Donna Haraway. "Tunneling in the Chthulucene: Stories for Resurgence on a Damaged Planet"; "Notes from Underground: The Depths of Environmental Arts, Culture, and Justice." The Eleventh Biennial Conference of the Association for the Study of Literature and the Environment, University of Idaho, Moscow, Idaho, 25 June 2015. Keynote address.

Yusoff, Kathryn and Jennifer Gabrys. "Climate Change and the Imagination." *Wiley Interdisciplinary Reviews: Climate Change* 2.4 (2011): 516–34. Print.

Selected course texts

Abeles, Kim. *Presidential Commemorative Smog Plates* (1991), n.p., n.d. Web, accessed 29 August 2015, www.kimabeles.com/artPages/smog.html.

The Age of Stupid. Director Franny Armstrong. Planet Green, 2009. DVD.

Bacigalupi, Paolo. "The Calorie Man." *Pump Six and Other Stories.* San Francisco, CA: Night Shade Books, 2010, 93–121. Print.

Buckland, David. *Ice Texts* (2005–2009), n.p., n.d. Web, accessed 29 August 2015, www.bucklandart.com/art/ice-texts.

Gee, Maggie. *The Ice People.* London: Telegram Books, 2008. Print.

Hersko, Judit. *Shifting Baselines: Seven Days of Dissolution* (2006), n.p., n.d. Web, accessed 29 August 2015, www.judithersko.com/jhindex0.html.

An Inconvenient Truth. Director Davis Guggenheim. Paramount Home Entertainment, 2006. DVD.

Kolbert, Elizabeth. "The Sixth Extinction?" *The New Yorker,* 25 May 2009, 53–63. Print.

McEwan, Ian. *Solar.* New York: Anchor Books, 2011. Print.

Shiva, Vandana. "Climate Change and Agriculture." *GWR: The Global Warming Reader.* Ed. Bill McKibben. New York: OR Books, 2011, 365–70. Print.

Simpson, Helen. "In-Flight Entertainment." *In-Flight Entertainment.* London: Vintage, 2011, 6–21. Print.

Spahr, Juliana. "Unnamed Dragonfly Species." *well then there now.* Jaffery, NH: Black Sparrow Books, 2011, 75–93. Print.

Wiggins, Sherry. *Carbon Portraits: Suzie and Wangari, 2007,* n.p., n.d. Web, accessed 29 August 2015, http://sherrywiggins.com/carbon5.html.

18 Signs, images, and narratives

Climate change across languages and cultures

Uwe Küchler

In late spring of 2015, the German weekly *DIE ZEIT* published an essay on climate change and built its argument around the claim that this topic was everything but new (Henk & Uchatius 2015, p. 15). By way of proof, the article is illustrated with cover shots of numerous international magazines ranging from the present all the way back to 1988.[1] To their astonishment, the authors find a rather limited number of climate change motifs in those illustrations: polar bear on melting ice, the globe in flames, storms, floods and the havoc they play (Henk & Uchatius 2015, p. 16). Considering the immenseness of climate change issues and the far reach of their impacts, this shortage of a visual language and the limitations of bold, alarmist headlines are particularly striking.

Others' signs, images, and narratives: principles of foreign language teaching

According to its mission and principles, particularly as a subfield to the newly formed Environmental Humanities, foreign language teaching should not so much guide its efforts toward scientific knowledge or political implications. What is particular to foreign language education is the linguistic, (inter)cultural or medial representation of topics across boundaries, that has the potential to also inspire climate change teaching and bring it forward.

Learners engage with a foreign language on the basis of their mother tongue. To make sense of utterances in the other language, they need to notice and explore, yet also relativize and decenter their native language with its complex network of (regional, national, transnational) designations, semantic fields, and perceptual habits. In addition to the functional linguistic components (such as grammar, lexicon or communicative routines), therefore, the learning of another language compellingly demands knowing the literature and culture of the target language in addition to one's own. Although language is a perceptible element of culture, it also gives clear indications of cultural or social characteristics not directly observable, such as the concepts behind (the formation or usage of) a word. Hence, the concepts of language awareness (Breidbach et al. 2011; James & Garret 1992; Fairclough 2014 [1989]) as well as that of differentiating and changing perspectives, or coordinating one's own and others' views on the world (Bredella 2012,

Nünning 1997) have been enthusiastically adopted into educational theory and (German) foreign language curricula.

Language(s) and the conceptualization of knowledge

The economic, political, cultural, as well as academic thrust of the English-speaking world, notably the U.S. and Canada, is creating a global demand for educational programs that teach English as a foreign language. At the same time, North America sees plummeting desire for and political interest in foreign language education. From an economic perspective, the dominance of English as the academic lingua franca appears to be a rational and cost-effective strategy to navigate the knowledge economy. From the perspective of language ecology, the Environmental Humanities and climate change, the situation is a lot more ambiguous. Especially because climate change is conceived of as a global phenomenon, the language(s) of climate change should be called into question. While I have just advocated concentrating on the core of the discipline in teaching efforts, for reasons of argumentation and illustration, I need to reconceptualize language learning as a somewhat larger issue: that is the (comparative and contrastive) conceptualization of knowledge.

Giving more attention to the role of foreign languages and cultures within the conceptualization of knowledge promises insights into the effect of language diversity on the choice of research questions, theoretical pervasiveness as well as methodological diversity. I propose considering monolingualism as a possible distortion of the underlying question of how humans relate to the non-human environment. Monolingualism limits our ecological understanding by creating the illusion of a one-to-one relationship between ways of perceiving and categorizing the world around us, finding words for it (e.g. pet, animal, pest or beast) and, subsequently, reacting toward or against this world. Particularly with education (and climate change) in mind, the following questions can provoke new thoughts, observations and insights:

- why is there such a shortage of public images, imaginings and visions of environmental issues?
- with specific regard to climate change: what can foreign language education offer for the perception of climate change and the creation of knowledge about it, including its symbolic, iconographic, linguistic and sociocultural specifics as well as regional, intercultural or transnational differentiation and variability?

In our recent article "Claiming the Language Ecotone," Natalie Eppelsheimer, Charlotte Melin and I have explicated our understanding of foreign language education in the context of the ecological debate in greater detail (2014). We have argued that the Environmental Humanities – hence also the teaching of climate change in the foreign language classroom – would gain immensely from multilingualism, in terms of international or intercultural diversity. Being able to perform such an argument, however, requires not an economical but a semiotic understanding of language. Ecolinguist Michael A. K. Halliday explains this conceptualization:

> Language [...] is not a superstructure on a base; it is a production of the conscious and the material impacting each on the other – the contradiction between our material being and our conscious being as antithetic realms of experience. Hence language has the power to shape our consciousness; and it does so for each human child, by providing the theory that he or she uses to interpret and to manipulate their environment.
>
> (2001, pp. 179–180)

Language cannot be considered a neutral instrument of communication and exchange. A shared or hegemonic language evokes inadvertent agreement on values, norms and orientations in the conceptualization of knowledge. By relying on a lingua franca, so it must be assumed, the disparities between national communities are harmonized due to the sociocultural implication of the shared language.

The learning of a foreign language and the engagement with different and possibly diverse ways of seeing the world, of making sense and expressing one's associations or explanations linguistically, broaden the awareness of how language shapes cultural expectations:

> Matters of language, then, including its foreignness, become central to understanding context. The comparatist or anthropologist learning of a target language and culture from the perspective of someone else's first language or mother tongue gains unique insights into the similarities and differences of alternate worldviews. We learn about ways of perceiving, experiencing, and, most importantly, encoding human and nonhuman environments.
>
> (Eppelsheimer, Küchler, Melin, 2014)

The process of comparing and contrasting symbols and language codes provides ample opportunities for creativity, serendipity or critique. Learners realize that things have not always been as they are today or as their language makes them believe.

(Climate) change and the knowledge-behavior fallacy

For any teaching context, it is quite crucial to decide upon a goal and a specific knowledge base. Not surprisingly, knowledge is considered a relevant factor for changing habits or behaviors. More often than not, it is hypothesized that people would change their ways if only they knew more about consequences of their daily actions. With greater awareness and more insight into all matters of climate change, so it is assumed, the general public could alter behavioral patterns and influence, if not prevent, the severe disruption that rampant climate change is likely to set in motion. The here-described assumption is known as the knowledge-gap hypothesis:

"Simply put, one cannot assume that increased knowledge about nature leads to a favorable attitude toward nature which in turn motivates action on behalf of nature" (Kretz, 2012, p. 14; cf. also Goralnik & Nelson, 2011). To inculcate factual knowledge about climate change, therefore, will hardly do the trick. The knowledge-behavior-dilemma requires each discipline to scrutinize its language, principles, methods and epistemic purpose in order to ascertain its contribution to current plights and possible solutions. From that vantage point, interdisciplinary inspiration and cooperation can occur. So how can foreign language education contribute to this?

With its emphasis on the power of language in the conceptualization of knowledge, foreign language education thrives on narratives, which often enough establish a sense of community and relationship between (foreign) narrator and readers. Quite comprehensibly, Kretz argues from a psychological perspective that those characteristics − a sense of belonging or of community as created in storytelling − have more force in inspiring care or empathy than moralistic obligations or didacticism (cf. 2012, p. 15). Likewise, other beneficial factors lie in the "forward looking, positive way" in which environmental teaching or research can be conceptualized (Kretz, 2012, p. 17), in a discourse governed by motivation rather than sacrifice (Kretz, 2012, p. 20) and in a closer scrutiny of the technical language in which disciplinary ideas are framed (Kretz, 2012, p. 21).

The global disposition of climate change and its abstract characteristics, Manfred Lenzen and Joy Murray argue, augment the difficulties in finding solutions to it (2001, p. 2). They suggest that educators find a closer connection between "students' personal spheres, in other words, their lifestyles" (Lenzen & Murray, 2001, p. 32) and those climate change issues that seem so abstract, difficult to grasp and globally far-removed.

The fact that the knowledge-gap hypothesis is vehemently disputed does not so much undermine the role of knowledge in education. Rather, the uses to which knowledge is put and the role that is attributed to knowledge may be an issue here. For the field of foreign language learning it needs to be asked, *what kinds of* knowledge should be taught. Like most mainstream media, many current foreign language textbooks and learning materials favor scientific knowledges and exercises as most important kinds. Yet, are they?

As climate change knowledge is greatly specialized, people can hardly use their own senses to verify the trustworthiness of claims about it, as Debra Davidson has found (2012, p. 625). Therefore, they need to rely on policy-makers and academics to judge those claims. The 'lay population' must base their decisions on believing those institutions and emotionally trusting them (Davidson, 2012, p. 631). Therefore, it seems that decision-making boils down to convincing narratives, compelling images, or culturally coherent symbols about climate change and its future impacts.

Environmental literacy

Although many academic disciplines have encompassed ecological concerns and have developed their own environmental subfields, foreign language education has been reluctant to keep up. Some researchers, such as Leo van Lier (2004) and Claire Kramsch (2008), devote their efforts to this topic by asking "what an ecological perspective on foreign language education [...] would look like" (Kramsch, 2008, p. 389). Yet, ecology is used as a metaphor here for the sociocultural, interactive and increasingly multilingual characteristics of contemporary foreign language learning. Kramsch uses the term "ecological" to speak about complexity theory and to illustrate the relationships between speakers, the languages they use and their multilingual settings as a complex interweave (2008, p. 391).

Since the communicative turn in foreign language education during the 1970s, any topic – including the environment or climate change – has become a possible choice for the language classroom. While many teaching materials still rely on facts and figures of global issues, albeit formulated in a foreign language, it seems more promising – with regards to the conceptualization of knowledge – to engage in comparatist, interlingual and intercultural teaching approaches. Such a choice would tie foreign language teaching back to the core tasks of the humanities.

- What sort of knowledge is used or promoted in the foreign language classroom?
- Which ecological scenarios do chosen materials foreground? How are they embedded in social, cultural and linguistic knowledge?

At the University of Bath, a model of environmental literacy (Stables, 2006; Bishop, et al. 2000) has been developed for the native speaker context that might prove productive in a foreign language setting as well. The three-step model interweaves (foreign) language learning and environmental literacy and offers a convincing progression for the development of a knowledge base from a basic, scientific or ecological stage via cultural constructions and contexts all the way to critical engagement. It has to be assumed that human and non-human environments can be categorized – for a more rapid perception – along the lines of perceptual patterns and metaphors. By being named, animals, plants or phenomena are categorized and, henceforth, constitute the linguistic representation of the environment within the culture of a speaker's community. Those cultural patterns are passed on from one generation to the next as cultural tradition (Stables, 2006, p. 145). Furthermore, if we can perceive our environment by means of arbitrary linguistic signs, metaphors or cultural narratives, it must also be possible to "read" the environment and verbally interpret those signs and perceptual conventions (Stables, 2006, pp. 149–55). Three different phases build different kinds of environmental knowledge and make it useful in the learning of languages, cultures, and literatures:

Functional environmental literacy

During the first stage, students learn language referring to general, scientific, ecological knowledge. This helps them to identify and differentiate non-human environments, such as one's surroundings, its flora and fauna as well as the most crucial phenomena that frequently occur in those environs (cf. Stables, 2006, p. 155).

What do I know about the climate that is prevalent in an area?

Which climatic specifics does a region have? How are they particular in the larger scheme of things? Are there rivers, forests, or mountains?

Explorations of "facts and figures" of the target language, culture or society are part of the foreign language classroom. Thus functional environmental literacy easily fits into foreign language teaching. Learners practice their pragmatic communicative skills by naming and describing phenomena, noticing the similarities and differences between their homes and otherwise unknown environments.

Cultural environmental literacy

In a second stage, learners acquaint themselves with dominant cultural practices of their own as well as the target culture(s). They grapple with traditions, perspectives and worldviews, with attitudes and perceptual patterns. Learners begin to reflect on cultural constructedness as well as on encoding or decoding mechanisms (cf. Stables, 2006, p. 156). They notice the historicity of images, metaphors, or mitigation strategies.

Which images are (over)used with regards to climate change?

Which narratives are retold and how do they contribute to our daily behavior?

Which heroes and villains can be made out with regards to climate change? How do the heroes influence their society's narratives and what influence do we as individuals have?

The identifying and differentiating of different cultural perspectives or (perceptual) traditions, their constructedness and historical development, are crucial aspects of foreign language education and the above-mentioned changing of perspectives.

Critical environmental literacy

During the third stage, learners begin to cognizantly and consciously engage in public discourse. Now, they are ready to explore how discourse functions, and which kinds of agency it offers individuals (cf. Stables, 2006, p. 156). Activities during this stage comprise analyzing texts, films or interactive situations, understanding the effects of media, its products and the way they influence or are made to influence the broader societal discourse.

How is the environmental debate linguistically, symbolically or iconographically constructed? Which images, metaphors, phrasal expressions or perspectives on climate change are very frequent, and which are quite rare?

How do those expressions in (another) language, in imagery, or (textual, iconographic, audiovisual) genre interact with or influence our perceptual conventions?

In the third stage, learners begin to coordinate the different perspectives they have begun to notice, describe, identify and contextualize.

The apparent dearth or one-sidedness of climate change imagery puts education and the Environmental Humanities at the center of attention. It can be observed that textbooks often choose scientific or mass media, therewith alarmist, lurid topics and articles for examples in the teaching of climate change. As a consequence, not only the covers of news magazines, but also foreign language textbooks, are rather limited in their selection of imagery. The emotional effect of such predictable and sensational imagery wears off quickly and may possibly incite frustration, depression, or more denial. By allowing learners to walk through three stages of environmental literacy, they are given time and space to develop general knowledge about facts, yet also about cultural differences and historicity. Such an approach facilitates working on emotional, communal, cooperative aspects of climate change and provides a broader spectrum of imagery and cultural viewpoints. Because of the core of what foreign language education accounts for – its focus on diversity in perspectives, on the emotional, narrative rendering of human experience, on the visible as well as opaque, interpretive aspects of human cultures, foreign language education in all its multilingual complexity becomes such a necessary, interdisciplinary and multinational element in the climate change era.

Note

1   The cover shots depicted are taken from the following magazines: *Newsweek, Time, The Nation, Business Week, Wildlife, The Economist, National Geographic, Audubon*, yet also *Spiegel, Stern, Greenpeace Magazine*, and many others.

References

Bishop, Keith, Alan Reid, Andrew Stables, Marina Lencastre, Steven Stoer, and Ronald Soetaert. 2000. Developing Environmental Awareness through Literature and Media Education: Curriculum Development in the Context of Teachers' Practice. *Canadian Journal of Environmental Education* 5 (Spring): 268–286.

Bredella, Lothar. 2012. *Narratives und interkulturelles Verstehen: Zur Entwicklung von Empathie-, Urteils- und Kooperationsfähigkeit.* Tübingen: Narr Verlag.

Breidbach, Stephan, Daniela Elsner, and Andrea Young. 2011. *Language Awareness in Teacher Education: Cultural-Political and Socio-Educational Perspectives.* Frankfurt am Main: Peter Lang.

Davidson, Debra. 2012. Analysing Responses to Climate Change Through the Lens of Reflexivity. *The British Journal of Sociology* 63 (4): 616–640.

Eppelsheimer, Natalie, Uwe Küchler, and Charlotte Melin. 2014. Claiming the Language Ecotone: Translinguality, Resilience, and the Environmental Humanities. *Resilience* 1 (3). [Web] www.jstor.org/stable/10.5250/resilience.1.3.005. Accessed 30 January 2015.

Fairclough, Norman. 1989. *Language and Power.* London, New York: Longman.

Fortner, Rosanne W. 2001. Climate Change in School: Where Does It Fit and How Ready Are We? *Canadian Journal of Environmental Education* 6 (Spring 2001): 18–31.

Goralnik, Lissy, and Michael Nelson. 2011. Forming a Philosophy of Environmental Action: Aldo Leopold, John Muir, and the Importance of Community. *The Journal of Environmental Education* 42 (3): 181–192.

Grünzweig, Walter. 1996. *Kulturelle Narrative und Dekonstruktion: Von den American Studies zu den Cultural Studies*. Edited by P. Freese, *Paderborner Universitätsreden: PUR 53*. Paderborn: Hausdruckerei Universität-Gesamthochschule-Paderborn.

Halliday, Michael A. K. 2001. New Ways of Meaning: The Challenge to Applied Linguistics. In *The Ecolinguistics Reader: Language, Ecology, and Environment*, ed. by A. Fill and P. Mühlhäusler. London, New York: Continuum, 175–202.

Henk, Malte, and Wolfgang Uchatius. 2015. Die Grenzen der menschlichen Natur: Morgen vielleicht. *DIE ZEIT* 23 (3 June 2015): 15–17.

James, Carl, and Peter Garrett. 1992. *Language Awareness in the Classroom*. London, New York: Longman.

Kramsch, Claire. 2008. Ecological Perspectives in Foreign Language Education. *Language Teaching* 41 (3): 389–408.

Kretz, Lisa. 2012. Climate Change: Bridging the Theory-Action Gap. *Ethics and the Environment* 17 (2: Fall 2012): 9–27. [Web] www.jstor.org/stable/10.2979/ethicsenviro.17.2.9. Accessed 14 May 2015.

Lenzen, Manfred, and Joy Murray. 2001. The Role of Equity and Lifestyles in Education about Climate Change: Experiences from a Largescale Teacher Development Program. *Canadian Journal of Environmental Education* 6 (Spring 2001): 32–51.

Lier, Leo van. 2004. *Ecology and the Semiotics of Language Learning: A Sociocultural Perspective*. Dordrecht: Springer Science & Business Media.

Mühlhäuser, Peter. 2001. Talking About Environmental Issues. In *The Ecolinguistics Reader: Language, Ecology, and Environment*, ed. by A. Fill and P. Mühlhäusler. London, New York: Continuum, 31–42.

Nünning, Ansgar. 1997. Perspektivenübernahme und Perspektivenkoordination: Prozeßorientierte Schulung des Textverstehens und der Textproduktion bei der Behandlung von John Fowles' The Collector. In *Literaturdidaktik – Konkret: Theorie und Praxis des fremdsprachlichen Literaturunterrichts*, ed. by G. Jarfe. Heidelberg: Universitätsverlag C. Winter, 137–161.

Stables, Andrew. 2006. On Teaching and Learning the Book of the World. In *Ecodidactic Perspectives on English Language, Literatures and Cultures*, ed. by S. Mayer and G. Wilson. Münster: Rodopi, 145–162.

Part III

Teaching and learning climate change sideways

19 The elephant in the room

Acknowledging global climate change in courses not focused on climate

Scott Slovic

Man cannot afford to be a naturalist, to look at Nature directly, but only with the side of his eye. He must look through and beyond her. To look at her is as fatal as to look at the head of Medusa. It turns the man of science to stone.

(Henry David Thoreau, *Journal*, 1841, p. 45)

Not until we are completely lost, or turned round,—for a man needs only to be turned round once with his eyes shut in this world to be lost,—do we appreciate the vastness and strangeness of Nature. Every man has to learn the points of compass again as often as he awakes, whether from sleep or any abstraction.

(Henry David Thoreau, *Walden*, 1854, p. 171)

The Earth's climate is changing. We hear this message loud and clear from the vast chorus of scientists around the world. Bill McKibben's *The End of Nature* (1989) sounded the clarion cry long before this issue was on the radar of the general public, even before many environmental scholars (at least in the humanities) were attuned to this most fundamental of concerns. And then the Intergovernmental Panel on Climate Change (IPCC) began issuing its periodic assessment reports in 1990, affirming the reality and significance of anthropogenic climate change and unleashing a firestorm of controversy ... and attracting an ever-broader constituency.

Why should a physical, environmental phenomenon such as climate change require "a constituency," a community of believers or supporters? The phenomenon is happening, whether human beings support it or not, and whether or not people even believe it exists. Many would argue that climate change represents perhaps the gravest threat to the future of our species on this planet and that, as Kathleen Dean Moore and Michael Nelson assert in the 2011 volume *Moral Ground*, it is simply our ethical responsibility, having belonged to generations contributing heavily to climate change, to do what we can to mitigate biospheric changes and leave an inhabitable planet for future generations. Thus we have organizations such as 350.org coordinating lectures and holding rallies, mobilizing the American public to think about individual lifestyle changes and broader policy reform in the interest of reducing the atmosphere's carbon dioxide levels from approximately 400 parts per million (ppm) to at most 350 ppm, which could pull us back from the current tipping point.

But all of this is dauntingly grim and numbingly abstract, not really the kind of topic likely to draw average university students into the classroom at a time when academic administrators are counting empty seats.

★★★

Climate change is as much a psychological phenomenon as it is a geophysical one. Or, at least, for teachers and scholars in the humanities, it is important to recognize that our ability to engage with this topic may be chiefly on the level of perception and representation (or communication). In his 2014 work, *Don't Even Think About It: Why Our Brains Are Wired to Ignore Climate Change*, activist and author George Marshall outlines in forty-two brief chapters an array of psychological reasons for the inability of the human mind to apprehend not only the gravity but the mere reality of climate change. Marshall's explanations range from the tendency to use uncertainty as rationale for inaction to the complicated emotional reactions people have to the topic of death (and even extinction of the species), something we tend to push to the margins of consciousness as scary and unimaginable.

In *Numbers and Nerves: Information, Emotion, and Meaning in a World of Data* (2015), my father (psychologist Paul Slovic) and I discuss, in a somewhat more circumscribed and focused way than Marshall, a set of core psychological conditions and tendencies that complicate human sensitivity to a host of social and environmental concerns, ranging from genocide to climate change. In particular, we focus on psychic numbing, pseudoinefficacy, the prominence effect, and the asymmetry of trust.

At the core of the *Numbers and Nerves* project is what we call "the psychophysics of brightness": the simple fact that the human mind is tragically insensitive to large-scale phenomena. The change from one to two is more salient to us than the difference between thirty and thirty-one. By the time we're talking about 350 or 400 ppm of carbon dioxide in the atmosphere, the numbers wash right past us, causing virtually no affective response. Social scientists have identified and attached names to these various mental processes, but writers and artists have also intuited such cognitive limitations and have invented communication strategies (usually involving multidimensional combinations of abstract, quantitative overviews and salient, individualized narratives or "trans-scalar" movements between individual and collective representations of information) designed to strike home with audiences. This is where, for me, the prospect of effective teaching of climate change literature comes into play.

★★★

I began this chapter with two epigraphs from Henry David Thoreau, the patron saint of American nature writing but perhaps an unlikely voice to present at the beginning of a discussion of climate change pedagogy in the twenty-first century. These two passages, though, represent psychological insights that have resonated with me for the past thirty years and serve as foundations, at least on an unconscious level, for my teaching of environmental literature and ecocriticism. The first passage, lifted from Thoreau's 1841 journal, suggests to me the importance of indirection. When we stare at nature directly, the writer states, we turn to stone—we become insensitive to its subtleties. For various reasons (including those I mentioned above in my discussion of psychology and climate change), something similar happens if we teach topics like climate change "directly," especially in a literature class. I prefer to sidle up to this topic gradually or to talk about it without quite talking about it—and to allow students to raise the issue themselves without feeling as if I have trapped them in their seats and will now force them to confront this fearful and overwhelming subject.

The second epigraph comes from the chapter in *Walden* called "The Village," in which Thoreau writes about how easily we can become disoriented in the world. For him, disorientation was, I would argue, a very good thing, a way of waking up to reality. I try in much of my teaching to foster small and large moments of disorientation and realization, and I prefer to have these moments simply happen, when the students are ready. Sometimes this occurs for an entire class at one moment, such as the occasion last year when a pack of wolves began howling just outside of our camp in the central Idaho mountains at precisely the moment when we were discussing the idea of iconoclastic activists howling their literary voices toward the powers that be. More often, individual students achieve small awakenings when specific books—or even singular passages—strike a poignant chord with them. When students linger after class to say, "I just realized something about my life"; or when they come shyly to office hours for the first time to say, "I needed to talk with you about this line in today's readings"—at these moments, I understand that something akin to Thoreau's "man … turned round once with his eyes shut in this world" has occurred. These are the moments I live for as a teacher.

★★★

I have been teaching environmental writing and environmental literature for more than thirty years, dating back to my days as a graduate student. Nearly always, in contexts ranging from freshman writing to graduate seminars, I've had my own goals for the classes that I have not explicitly shared with my students, hoping that seemingly marginal topics would emerge as core foci or that delayed approaches to particular authors or works would enable these encounters to resonate more deeply because of the month or two of preparation we've experienced. I do not call my classes "Literature and 'Elephants'." I wait for the moment when one of my students will say, "Has anyone noticed there's an elephant sitting in the corner? Let's talk about that." My approach to controversial and difficult topics as a teacher tends to be far less direct than my approach as a scholar and editor.

I would like to mention three specific courses in which the climate "elephant" has been subtly present but not foregrounded:

In 2006, I taught a graduate seminar at the University of Nevada, Reno, called "The Literature of Energy." The course description did not mention climate change, but this idea was a subcurrent throughout the syllabus. The explicit goal of the seminar—and the textbook, *Currents of the Universal Being: Explorations in the Literature of Energy* (2015), that emerged from the class—was to broaden the scope of the energy conversation and take this ubiquitous and fundamental topic beyond the headline debates of the popular media, beyond questions of fossil fuels and alternative/renewable sources of energy. Of the eight books we studied together, only three—McKibben's *The End of Nature*, Ross Gelbspan's *Boiling Point: How*

Politicians, Big Oil and Coal, Journalists, and Activists have Fueled the Climate Crisis— and What We Can Do to Avert Disaster, and Susan Gaines's *Carbon Dreams*—explicitly engage with climate change. And these appeared in weeks six (McKibben), seven (Gelbspan), and ten (Gaines) of the fifteen-week semester. Climate change was the elephant in the seminar room, but the purpose of the class was essentially to situate the topic of climate change in much broader personal, social, and environmental contexts. As energy scholar Vaclav Smil writes in *Energy at the Crossroads*, "Tug at any human use of energy and you will find its effects cascading throughout society, spilling into the environment and coming back to us" (Smil 373). In other words, tug on the topic of energy, and you may find it connected to an elephant's trunk—the elephant of climate change.

The detailed syllabus for this class was published in *Currents of the Universal Being*, along with other sample syllabi prepared by my co-editors, Jim Bishop and Kyhl Lyndgaard, who were doctoral students in the 2006 seminar and are now professors. In addition to the explicitly climate-focused readings mentioned above, we read and discussed diverse publications such as Kenneth Brower's *The Starship and the Canoe* (1978) and Alan Weisman's *Gaviotas: A Village to Reinvent the World* (1998), which explore alternative ideas about energy use without directly mentioning the connection with climate change. The essential challenge of this course, though, was to offer a coherent curriculum in a field (energy literature) that, as some might have argued at the time, did not even exist. Our class sought to cover a topic and *define* that topic at the same time. In order to bring my students on board as active learners, I enlisted them to help create the field of energy literature. Students developed individual and group projects that helped to clarify the nature and scope of energy literature: interviews with someone knowledgeable in the field of energy, reviews of recent books relevant to energy, final Powerpoint presentations on energy literature, a group bibliography of energy-related texts, and the collaboratively written proposal for our book project (i.e., for the anthology of energy literature that was quickly granted an advance contract and eventually published in 2015).

Between 2008 and 2012, I offered four different versions of a course on the literature of sustainability at Nevada, team-teaching with atmospheric chemist and University of Nevada (UNR) environmental affairs manager John Sagebiel. A longtime specialist in air pollution and climate science at Reno's Desert Research Institute, John obviously had deep knowledge of global climate change. We made the most of this knowledge, weaving climate texts and tasks throughout our classes, but we made a conscious decision not to bludgeon our students with this topic, which we expected to be overwhelming to some students and contentious for others. The fundamental objectives of the two major versions of the course—one a broad survey of sustainability topics (food, water, transporation, architecture, and ecosystem health) and the other a more focused treatment of sustainable food practices and American culture—were to help undergraduates appreciate the relevance of literature and the relevance of broad environmental discussions to their individual lives and to invite non-humanities majors (most students were not English majors) into the study of literature by showing how profoundly these texts could explore the human meaning of environmental issues. For the broader course on sustainability literature, our texts included, among others, Michael Pollan's *The Omnivore's Dilemma* (food), Ellen Meloy's *Raven's Exile* (water), Jack Kerouac's *On the Road* (transportation), Sarah Susanka's *The Not So Big House* (architecture), and Sandra Steingraber's *Living Downstream* (ecosystem contamination and public health). The only book that explicitly addressed climate change was Al Gore's *An Inconvenient Truth*, but we asked our students to write (and talk about) the book's rhetorical strategies, not only its content and argument, and in focusing students' attention on *form*, we managed to ease the challenging content into the classroom rather than pushing students directly into a discussion of the monstrous climate elephant that had been in the background of other discussions throughout the term.

Since 2013, I have been teaching environmental writing as one of five courses offered to a group of approximately a dozen undergraduates who participate each fall in the University of Idaho's Semester in the Wild Program, which takes place at the Taylor Wilderness Research Station in the central Idaho wilderness (the Frank Church—River of No Return Wilderness is part of the largest roadless area in the lower forty-eight states). Students hike to the research station early in the fall semester and remain for two and a half months, studying river ecology and wilderness area management, cooking for themselves, and spending free time flyfishing and mountain climbing. Much of my writing class focuses on the nuts and bolts of writing personal essays about environmental experience and philosophical essays about wildlife and wild places. But toward the end of the class, we turn our attention to using our literary voices in crafting "personal testimonies" that can be used as letters to the editor or statements to be presented at public hearings. Two of our readings late in the semester from the anthology *Literature and the Environment*, Derrick Jensen's essay "Forget Shorter Showers" and Michael Pollan's "Why Bother?," function implicitly as a debate about the importance of militating for systemic changes in public policy versus the value of small-scale changes of individual lifestyles in response to such problems as climate change. By the time we get to the Jensen and Pollan readings, about ten weeks into the term, the students have been primed to engage in the intense and irresolvable self-reflection required by these essays on such provocative topics.

Timing is everything in course design, especially when the unspoken goal is to allow students to wake up to the presence of the elephant in the room—or the elephant in the Idaho wilderness. Although Semester in the Wild students tend to fret about the fact that their off-the-grid lives require weekly food deliveries on small bush planes, bringing essential supplies from distant farms, they tend not to say much about this until we get to the Jensen and Pollan articles. I find that some of our best class discussions—and the best student writing—occur at this point, when their prose skills have been sharpened and they're ready to address intractable questions of personal values and lifestyle inconsistencies. After the students have wrestled for a few hours with Jensen and Pollan, I ask them to read Donella Meadows's "Living Lightly and Inconsistently on the Land," also from our anthology, as a way of letting them off the hook for their own eco-hypocrisy (of which all of us are guilty to some degree) and also showing how we can be mindful of our environmental impact and struggle meaningfully with the inconsistency between our values and our behavior. One Semester in the Wild student was so moved by the ethical questions arising from the readings mentioned above and by the unique paradox of living an off-the-grid life in the wilderness and relying upon bush planes to deliver food each week that she wrote an essay addressed specifically to college undergraduates for the Winter 2014 global warming issue of *ISLE: Interdisciplinary Studies in Literature and Environment*.

★★★

Over many years of teaching, I have found that when I want students to think about potentially abrasive or abstract topics I'm better off—that is, more likely to spark student engagement and lively conversation—when I approach these subjects as Thoreau recommended approaching nature itself: in a sideways manner. For instance, even by asking students to focus on the literary form of Gore's *An Inconvenient Truth* rather than the subject matter—until the students themselves, after talking about visual imagery and numerical data and family stories, suddenly bring up the fact that the book is about climate change. "Oh, yeah," I say. "What do you think about that?" By approaching climate change gradually and indirectly through the lens of sustainability and energy (and, in a sense, the secondary lenses of food, water, transportation, and architecture), the topic becomes somewhat disentangled from the all-too-familiar entrenched positions of talking heads in the media. Climate change comes to be recognizable, as an extension of our daily lives.

What's more, by bringing the subject of climate change down to earth, so to speak, the smaller aspects of this huge topic start to seem approachable, even correctable. Much of Mitchell Thomashow's powerful 2003 study *Bringing the Biosphere Home: Learning to Perceive Global Environmental Change* addresses (without ever using this phrase) what ecocritics have come to call "slow violence," thanks to Rob Nixon's *Slow Violence and the Environmentalism of the Poor*, meaning the vast, slow, systemic problems, from poverty to extinction to global warming, that we can hardly apprehend. But Thomashow's purpose, in offering various cognitive and sensory suggestions that enable perception of global change on the individual human scale, is to deliver a sense of modest hopefulness to readers. Early in the book, he says, "you don't have to be optimistic to be hopeful" (Thomashow 18). This, too, is the linchpin of my own approach to the indirect teaching of climate change literature. Yes, in the long run, things don't look too good. But that doesn't mean we—and our students—can't live idealistic, engaged, and, indeed, *hopeful* lives, taking on problems like climate change one small idea at a time.

References

Anderson, Lorraine, Scott Slovic, and John P. O'Grady, eds. *Literature and the Environment: A Reader on Nature and Culture*. Second edition. Upper Saddle River, NJ: Pearson, 2013.

Gaines, Susan. *Carbon Dreams*. Berkeley, CA: The Creative Arts Book Company, 2001.

Gelbspan, Ross. *Boiling Point: How Politicians, Big Oil and Coal, Journalists, and Activists Have Fueled the Climate Crisis—and What We Can Do to Avert Disaster*. 2005 (2004). New York: Basic Books.

Gore, Al. *An Inconvenient Truth*. Emmaus, PA: Rodale, 2006.

ISLE: Interdisciplinary Studies in Literature and Environment 21.1. Special issue on global warming. Winter 2014.

Kerouac, Jack. *On the Road*. New York: Viking, 1997 (1957).

Marshall, George. *Don't Even Think About It: Why Our Brains Are Wired to Ignore Climage Change*. New York: Bloomsbury, 2014.

McKibben, Bill. *The End of Nature*. 1989. New York: Anchor, 1997.

Meloy, Ellen. *Raven's Exile: A Season on the Green River*. 1994. Tucson, AZ: University of Arizona Press, 2003.

Moore, Kathleen Dean, and Michael P. Nelson, eds. *Moral Ground: Ethical Action for a Planet in Peril*. San Antonio, TX: Trinity UP, 2011.

Nixon, Rob. *Slow Violence and the Environmentalism of the Poor*. Cambridge, MA: Harvard University Press, 2011.

Pollan, Michael. *The Omnivore's Dilemma: A Natural History of Four Meals*. 2006. New York: Penguin, 2007.

Slovic, Scott, James E. Bishop, and Kyhl Lyndgaard, eds. *Currents of the Universal Being: Explorations in the Literature of Energy*. Lubbock, TX: Texas Tech University Press, 2015.

Slovic, Scott, and Paul Slovic, eds. *Numbers and Nerves: Information, Emotion, and Meaning in a World of Data*. Corvallis, OR: Oregon State University Press, 2015.

Smil, Vaclav. *Energy at the Crossroads: Global Perspectives and Uncertainties*. Cambridge, MA: MIT Press, 2005.

Steingraber, Sandra. *Living Downstream: A Scientist's Personal Investigation of Cancer and the Environment*. New York: Vintage, 1998 (1997).

Susanka, Sarah. *The Not So Big House: A Blueprint for the Way We Really Live*. Newtown, CT: Taunton, 2001.

Thomashow, Mitchell. *Bringing the Biosphere Home: Learning to Perceive Global Environmental Change*. Cambridge, MA: MIT Press, 2003.

Thoreau, Henry David. *The Journal of Henry David Thoreau*. Ed. Bradford Torrey. Volume 6. Boston: Houghton Mifflin, 1906.

Thoreau, Henry David. *Walden*. Princeton, NJ: Princeton University Press, 1971 (1854).

20 Teaching climate change otherwise

Swayam Bagaria and Naveeda Khan

Attunement to being acted upon

The recent May 24, 2015 encyclical by Pope Francis on climate change provides an opportune moment to consider what climate pedagogy might look like for those of us who teach in the Social Sciences and the Humanities. The most significant contribution of the encyclical, as we see it, is that it provides a pathway for thought, a means for us to cross scales to be able to implicate individual lives and actions within a phenomenon that has been largely perceived as a scientific construction, distant, abstract, and far in the future. The pathway that Pope Francis proposes not surprisingly is grounded in spirituality and takes the words of God as spurs to relate individual lives to human suffering. We are urged to anticipate the large scale of suffering already underway, now much intensified because of climate change, through the means of our personal capacity for suffering. Pope Francis terms this mode of anticipation 'ecological conversion.' We might understand this in the following way: we can imagine how hunger, thirst, weariness must feel like for the wider community through the fact that our bodies know these experiences. We have to renew these experiences, further intensify them, to be able to grasp the dimension that climate change introduces to them. Climate change is nothing new. It is already in our experiences. We have to learn to be attuned to it to produce change in ourselves.

Dale Jamieson, in his 2014 book, *Reason in a Dark Time*, provides another pathway for thought, comparable in some ways to that of Pope Francis. Showing how the United Nations Framework Convention on Climate Change-sponsored conversation on climate change has by and large failed to arrive at any meaningful global plan, he urges us to avoid the threat of nihilism that this critical insight might bring. To succumb to nihilism is to assume that a single global model was the only way forward. Rather he suggests that evolving an individual climate ethics is as necessary to produce urgency in one's actions as learning to continue living in a flagging global process. The virtues he foregrounds towards this ethics are those of humility, temperance, mindfulness, simplicity, and so on. He writes: "The virtues do not provide an algorithm for solving the problems of the Anthropocene, but they can provide guidance for living gracefully while helping to restore in us a sense of agency" (Jamieson 8).

These are very modest proposals, even somewhat conservative and apolitical, to undergo ecological conversion by means of one's experiences of suffering, and to inculcate virtues that enable a sense of grace and agency. In the course we planned and taught at Johns Hopkins University in Spring 2015, titled, *Ethnographies: Everyday Religion and Ethics,* we wanted to bring such a modesty to our climate pedagogy. We did not wish to directly teach on the phenomenon called climate change as we risked either an anthropological tendency towards deconstructionism or an activist tendency towards didacticism. We wanted to see how a sense or even an intimation of climate change, as already present in our experiences and shaping our future horizons, could bubble up from within a larger discussion on the evolution and mobilization of the concepts of religion, ethics and political theology within the anthropological canon. And we had a minimal understanding of what the sense of climate change could be, such as, the sense of being caught in a system with its own momentum, the sense of being buffeted by micro-forces; or, the sense of loss of one's familiar world. You will quickly realize that all of these are about attunement to being acted upon rather than acting, much like the experience of suffering and the threat of nihilism. Our idea was to see how we could both view this mode of being – that is, of being acted upon – as problematic and in need of changing in some circumstances but also as positive and animating or even simply productive in other circumstances in indicating a line of connection across our separate bodies. Our interest was also to excavate gestures and postures that one might call religious or ethical with respect to this mode of being, that could add to those provided by Pope Francis and Jamieson, specifically ecological conversion and the cultivation of virtues, to orient us better towards climate change.

The unfolding of the course

The three sections were organized sequentially to: consider ways in which religion endures within the social as more than just a practice; return to an earlier historical moment in which the crisis and demise of religion (specifically in its Christian mode) served as a springboard to rethink ethical relations without recourse to a transcendent category; consider several ethnographic contexts in which ruptures in the social, whether in the form of witchcraft accusations or as cultural devastation, prompted questions of how the social is both precarious and durable; and move to contemporary discussions of political theology that returns to the conceptual inseparability of the religious from the ethico-political to enable intellectual and practical responses to issues of our globalized present.

For the first part we returned to canonical understandings of religion in anthropology, notably by Emile Durkheim (1965 [1915]) and Max Weber (2002 [1904]). While both remarked on the fact that religion was a constitutive part of various social undertakings, they underlined that it was far from being something to which one voluntarily submitted. This detachment of religion from individual choices and practices is what ensured it enduring. Durkheim, writing in the context of the First World War and the fragmentation of Europe into different nation states, considered religion as producing the adherence of individuals to their respective collectives. The distinction between the sacred and the profane which Durkheim considered the elemental factum of religion and which he traced to totemism, the most elementary form of religion, not only survived the transformation of totemism into our more contemporary religions of the book, but also became more sweeping by the co-alignment of the social with the nation. This force that binds a person to the collective is the force of the religious that impinges upon the individual from the outside through the form of the social and the nation, while also arising as it were from within the individual as something that the individual binds oneself to.

Weber, who was also interested in considering how religion survives the transformation into modernity, shifted emphasis from the language of force with which religion binds us into a collective whole to the language of spirit with which religion remains a more silent presence within the lives of individual people in capitalist modernity. Noting the simultaneous overarching historical processes of the disenchantment of the world and the asymmetrical development of capitalism between the US and European nations, Weber sought to understand this uneven development as a symptom of the unequal significance placed on worldly life in Protestantism and Catholicism. The notion of calling and its development into the doctrine of predestination engendered a continual commitment to the worldly affairs of work within Protestantism whereas it was seen as a distraction from more spiritual matters in Catholicism. Thus, the 'spirit of capitalism' had as its basis not purely an economic motive but also bore an elective affinity to the 'Protestant Ethic.'

This agential nature of religion, working from within and without individuals by means of 'force' and 'spirit,' was brought within a more organized rationality by Clifford Geertz (1973) and Talal Asad (1993). For Geertz, religion served to bind community by its symbolic and ritualistic function but also to generate a cosmological order within which the world could be meaningfully explained. In contrast, Asad precisely sought to question this naturalization of meaning that Geertz assumed and asked what were the authorizing processes of power that render religion meaningful in the first instance. For Asad, the emphasis was not so much on who authorizes what but the necessity of such authorization. In contrast to force and spirit, religion now operated through 'order' and 'authority.'

For Asad, the commonsensical distinction maintained between the religious and the secular is very specific to the history of secularism in which the former was made the exclusive domain of the private as opposed to the latter that would form the know-how of public deliberation. This distinction between the religious and the secular and the containment of the former within acceptable limits was strikingly illustrated by Winifred Sullivan's 2007 ethnography, next on the reading list, of a legal case around the burial practices of a particular community in Florida where the point of contention revolved around the placement of religious artifacts, such as crosses and Stars of David, in cremation grounds owned by the city. For Sullivan, the fact that the community members were constantly called upon to say what had authorized their burial practices meant that religion never belonged properly to the domain of the private but was always in the realm of public authority.

What was most striking in Sullivan was her exploration of 'death' as a fraught event never to be exhausted by authorized religious injunctions and the diversity of individual practices. This perspective on death as soliciting a religious response not only drew our attention to the shadow of death upon the collective-making but also life-giving forms that religion took in Durkheim, Weber, and Geertz, but was a fruitful occasion to return to the historical moment in which the demise of religion was asserted through the announcement of the death of God. These themes were further engaged through a viewing of Robert Gardner's ethnographic film *Forest of Bliss* (1986) in which the event of death saturated everyday life in Benares, India, not feared and dreaded but invited into the various domains of life – ritual, economic and social.

Consequently, our next reading was one of Nietzsche's pithy later text, *The Anti-Christ* (2013 [1895]), in which he provides a vitriolic assessment of Christianity. By making life in this world contingent on an afterlife, Christianity emptied life of all meaning in and of itself. Here religion functioned as a form of 'nihilism' parasitic on life. And the overcoming of this nihilism was a necessary step towards a recognition of 'life in its plenitude,' which was also a logical step in Alan Badiou's ethics, but with the added disposition he had towards affirming the human subject through that which we precisely don't share with animals, the capacity for an ascent into the infinite rather than through a shared communion of death. For Badiou, the possibility of ethics after the death of God has to be maintained not within our make-up as finite subjects but in our potential to be infinite or divine-like. It is through this potential that we are able to suspend the predicates of our existence, giving up ourselves to an encounter that fractures our existing ways of comprehending the world. This encounter, what Badiou calls the 'event,' befalls the individual but to which the individual has to be truthful in order to find a new way to be. We consider this to be a radicalization of the virtue ethics espoused by Jamieson (2014).

These philosophical readings were given to the students to encourage them to struggle with the changes of tonality in the readings – from the systems-building nature of Durkheim's writings or the critical analytics of Asad's to the passionate polemics of Nietzsche – to make them realize that intellectual insights not only emerge from turbulence but also to retrospectively sense uneasy consciences and uncertainties within the earlier anthropological accounts of religion. For instance, at the end of *The Protestant Ethic*, Weber makes the now almost prophetic observation that having been set on its course the capitalist system would not run down until all fuel was exhausted. However, while Nietzschean affirmation and Badiou's embracing of the future in its utter strangeness may be added to our ongoing list of religious/philosophical dispositions towards crisis, they leave us unclear as to what the social contours this picture of ethics might bear. Hence, in our next section, we brought our previous emphasis on the social and its ethical undertones to particular instances of crisis and catastrophe in which what was precisely at stake was the viability and durability of the social. Here we read the three ethnographic monographs by Jeanne Favret-Saada (1981), Jonathan Lear (2008), and Lisa Stevenson (2014) and watched the 2014 film *Beasts of the Southern Wild*.

Favret-Saada, in her ethnography of witchcraft accusations in rural Bocage, France, speaks about her inability to maintain her role as a detached observer in conditions in which the only way to remain a part of the social was to be involved in the elaborately imbricated network of witchcraft accusations. Even though the relations between the bewitched, the witch, and the enunciator who made the diagnosis of bewitchment were nothing but antagonistic and hostile, the only way in which one could persist within them was as Favret-Saada puts it "by being caught" in them; efforts to separate and extricate oneself often leading, as Favret-Saada shows through striking ethnographic instances, to a form of social and possibly even biological death. Lear, in his account of the Crow Indians, speaks about the impossible choice that the Crow Indians had to make between suffering the physical annihilation of their tribe in the hands of the neighboring tribe or an ontological destruction assured by their aligning with the U.S. army in which their entire order of values and way of life would be erased in lieu of something new. The indomitable task that the Crow Indians faced was to re-learn and recreate the very sediment of their world from the ashes of their traditional way of living that had served them for centuries before the unprecedented possibility of its destruction arose. This radical reconstruction of life is only possible if one is able to embrace what Lear calls 'radical hope.' Stevenson, in her book, contrasts the biopolitical efforts of the Canadian state to keep the Inuit people alive after two historical epidemics, that of tuberculosis in 1940s and of suicides in 1980s, by displacing them onto sanatoriums, and the ethical efforts of the people left behind to maintain relationships between themselves and the loved ones who are now dead. What comes into stark relief is the strain between the state's management of the biological lives of people while rendering them lifeless in all other capacities and the attentive ways in which those who are left behind find shared forms of life with those who are dead that allow the latter to continue living. In all the three texts, one notes the crumbling of the certainty and sanctity that Durkheim placed at the heart of social relations in a time of crisis when achieving the continuity of the social can entail an abandonment of everything that one had thus far valued. Following upon the three ethnographies, the film *Beasts of the Southern Wild,* seen through the eyes of the six-year-old Hushpuppy, well illuminated the antagonisms entailed in the management of biological life by the state at the expense of distinct forms of life.

It is at this juncture of thinking about the arrival of the new and the unprecedented, and how the social is rendered precarious, that we turned to the section on political theology not as a return to the theological in its purity but as a conceptual resource yet to be mined. In this context we read an essay by Bhrigupati Singh (2013) and Naveeda Khan (2014) each to bring our peregrinations on the notion of ethics to bear on the question of the non-human and of climate change. Singh provides us with an ethnographic analysis of how the occasion for the arrival of a neighborly god elicits a conversion of the Sahariyas, a former tribe of bonded labors, into vegetarianism and teetotalism. The Sahariyas themselves are marked with extreme poverty and the region in which they live is characterized by continually dwindling resources, but they don't see their conversion to vegetarianism as a means of managing thrift. Instead, the occasion for the arrival of god, whose name is Tejaji, is also an occasion for a shift in moral values in which vegetarian-ism and tee-totalitarianism are not considered virtues of frugality that one is forced to adopt but rather are signs of a more vital form of life that one embraces. Khan in her essay shows how Muslim farmers living on the continually eroding and accreting silt islands of Bangladesh express disbelief at the imported discourse of climate change from the West, while finding readings within the narratives of creation in Islamic thought to continually expand the periphery of their social bounds. In particular she shows how the otherwise repulsive figure of the dog finds a way of becoming incorporated into the life world of the Muslim farmers by the simple contingency of the dogs being placed on the same eroding silt lands as them. This unbeknownst coming together of two beings tied by their mutual fate of being present on the same piece of erratically vanishing land, and the responsive gestures that this 'mutual-fatedness' demands, congeals in a singular instant the conceptual apparatus through which the course aimed to shift from a discussion of religion and ethics to that of climate change. Announcements of the death of God, eruptions of ways of life, and the steady approach of climate change as becoming an increasingly urgent predicament not only entails stretching the bounds of who we incorporate into our social spaces but also amounts to rethinking, as we saw throughout the course readings, the manifest form of these social relations them-selves. A persistent thread of this course, was thus to consider how any invitation that brings the non-human into the folds of our lives will always involve returning to our more fundamental presuppositions of what it means to keep beings together. This disposition towards 'mutual-fatedness' felt to us an attunement and positive transvaluation of being acted upon and acting on others.

In conclusion

At the tail end of our course, Freddie Gray's homicide in the hands of the police brought on riots followed by peaceful demonstrations in Baltimore, the home of the university. The university closed down for several days, leading us to lose some class time but also injecting a new urgency into our conversations. Even as we brought to the foreground the necessity to orient ourselves towards climate change in a Nietzschean mode, that is, not to embrace the nihilistic view of life on this earth as 'done for' or death as a means of escape to the after-life but to face it as a condition of our own making, for climate change to be rendered real, fragile and embraceable, we sought to do the same for the violence in the city. The riots reminded us that concerns over climate change cannot be allowed to eclipse ongo-ing struggles for social justice, and where possible they had to be thought together.

One way to think the togetherness of this event of violence in Baltimore and climate change is to think back to Pope Francis's suggestion as to what allows us to jump scales, to go from our thirst, our hunger, our weariness, to that of wider collec-tives. What Freddie Gray's fate points to is not just the violence of racism actualized in policing but also the experience of toxicity, specifically lead poisoning, as racial-ized. Here we might heed Mel Chen (2012), specifically her contention that toxicity is animate and that following its animacies allows us to follow the physical tracks of racism. Perhaps we need to think beyond our felt experiences to those that make silent tracks through us and position us differentially within the world. After all, even though climate change affects everyone, some will rebound from it much better than others. Some senses of hunger may be overcome while others are so embedded, say in malnutrition, as to make hunger here in this body not the same as the hunger there in that body, suggesting the incommensurability across distinct selves and social milieus. Freddie Gray's fate points to the possible limits of sympathy and scaling up to political urgency from one's attunement to the world acting on one. These are contradictions that this course raised rather than dealt with. But as is in the nature of coming to appreciate how one is acted upon, this awareness may be slow in the coming. We hope we have given ourselves further pathways for thought towards change through the animation of such concepts as 'force,' 'spirit,' 'power,' 'life in its plenitude,' 'event,' 'being caught,' 'radical hope,' and 'mutual-fatedness.'

This paper is gratefully dedicated to the students of AS070.273 *Ethnographies: Everyday Religion and Ethics* (Spring 2015).

References

Asad, Talal. "The Construction of Religion as an Anthropological Category." *The Genealogies of Religion*. Baltimore, MD: Johns Hopkins University Press, 1993.

Badiou, Alan. *Ethics: An Essay on the Understanding of Evil*. New York: Verso, 2013.

Durkheim, Emile. *Elementary Forms of Religious Life*. New York: The Free Press, 1965 (1915).

Favret-Saada, Jeanne. *Deadly Words: Witchcraft in the Bocage*. Cambridge: Cambridge University Press, 1981.

Geertz, Clifford. "Religion as a Cultural System." *The Interpretation of Cultures*. New York: Basic Books, 1973, 87–125.

Chen, Mel. *Animacies: Biopolitics, Racial Mattering, and Queer Affect*. Durham: Duke University Press, 2012.

Jamieson, Dale. *Reason in a Dark Time: Why the Struggle Against Climate Change Failed*. Oxford: Oxford Univerity Press, 2014.

Khan, Naveeda. "Dogs and Humans and What Earth Can Be: Filaments of Muslim Ecological Thought." *Hau* 4(3), 2014: 245–264.

Lear, Jonathan. *Radical Hope: Ethics in the Face of Cultural Devastation*. Cambridge, MA: Harvard University Press, 2008.

Nietzsche, Friedrich. *The Anti-Christ*. New York: Soho Books, 2013 (1895).

Pope Francis. "Laudato si' (Praise be to you – On Care for Our Common Home)", Encyclical, May 24, 2015. http://w2.vatican.va/content/francesco/en/encyclicals/documents/papa-francesco_20150524_enciclica-laudato-si.html, accessed August 12, 2015.

Singh, Bhrigupati. "Agonistic Intimacy and Moral Aspiration in Popular Hinduism: A Study in the Political Theology of the Neighbor." *American Ethnologist*, 38(3), 2011: 430–450.

Stevenson, Lisa. *Life Besides Itself: Imagining Care in the Canadian Artic*. Berkeley, CA: University of California Press, 2014.

Sullivan, Winnifred Fallers. *The Impossibility of Religious Freedom*. Princeton, NJ: Princeton University Press, 2007.

Weber, Max. *Protestant Ethic and the Spirit of Capitalism*. New York: Penguin Classics, 2002 (1904).

21 Teaching ecological restoration in the climate change century

Cheryll Glotfelty

> Restoration is like adding a birthing room to a hospital that had only a trauma center.
>
> (Peter Berg)

I have been teaching eco-related courses for twenty five years. For much of the time my work has been propelled by a sense of impending crisis, to the point where I now suffer from crisis fatigue. So I have begun to move toward more utopian topics. Bioregionalism and the work of Peter Berg are centrally motivating for me as they offer a vision and action plan for a future in which human culture harmonizes with natural systems. Influenced by Berg's three-fold mandate to restore and maintain natural systems, meet basic human needs sustainably, and support the work of reinhabitation, I developed a graduate seminar on the literature and theory of ecological restoration. The seminar presents climate change amidst a network of interlinked environmental problems, such as invasive species, loss of biodiversity, habitat degradation, toxic waste, unsustainable cities, and a habit of mind that regards nature as separate from culture. The class engages with the science of restoration ecology while analyzing literary texts that feature people who are restoring damaged ecosystems and renewing human communities. Mitigating and adapting to climate change will require imagination and cultural change. Narratives of ecological restoration offer a creative path of hope that can inspire effective action from the grassroots and provide an antidote to crippling despair.

One of the implications that climate change has for teaching is boded in the word "change" itself. For educators to become actors in arguably the most serious issue of our time requires that we teach new material, straddle fields, and try new approaches. While the prospect of teaching outside our area of expertise—especially at the graduate level—can be intimidating, I have found that my best seminars are the ones where the students and I explore new territory together. An approach that works well is to require "cogitations" and to delegate roles. Cogitations are directed, informal writing due every week on the assigned readings. Roles include providing background information on the primary text; parsing the supplemental articles; and reviewing a book related to the course topic. For the first few classes I orchestrate the flow of these moving parts—cogitations, background, critical articles, book review, and a changing menu of in-class activities. After about the third week, orchestrating class is performed by students. When I first tried the experiment of having students orchestrate, I was anxious about giving up control. But the approach has worked brilliantly.

Turning now to a discussion of texts, I will highlight those works with explicit ties to climate change. It is helpful to begin the semester by assigning history and theory, providing students the context, vocabulary, and conceptual lenses to become critical readers of the primary texts that follow. William K. Stevens's *Miracle Under the Oaks: The Revival of Nature in America* offers an engaging introduction to ecological restoration. A journalist, Stevens explains that in writing an article for *The New York Times* in late 1990 he learned about "a movement afoot to restore damaged, degraded, and destroyed ecosystems" and that "the restorationists even had their own newly formed society," the Society for Ecological Restoration (Stevens vii). That article planted the seed for *Miracle Under the Oaks*, which focuses on a project begun in 1977 in the suburbs north of Chicago to restore an oak savanna known as Vestal Grove. Stevens likens ecological restoration to reassembling Humpty Dumpty and describes the enterprise as a "healing art" in which "restorationists intervene to repair the damage caused by other humans so that the natural evolutionary processes that generate biodiversity can resume" (7–8). Vestal Grove is a success story and symbol of hope, a weedy, garbage-strewn thicket transformed by "green-thumbed" volunteers into a place "'almost holy,... rich, healthy, and ancient—and young at the same time'" (Stevens, quoting Packard 310). Moreover, doing the work of restoration—clearing brush, identifying plants, collecting seeds, planting, and weeding—helps people reconnect with nature. As one volunteer put it, restoration work "'has filled a very deep need in me to give myself a sense of place and a better understanding of just how complex the natural world really is. ... I've restored myself, in a sense, to the natural world'" (Stevens 198). When Stevens visits Vestal Grove, some fifteen years after restoration efforts began, he finds that the savanna has "gloriously, fulsomely, returned from the edge of oblivion, a resurgent enclave of life populated by a number of rare and endangered species" (Stevens 10).

But the future of Vestal Grove is uncertain, Stevens writes. If prevailing scientific opinion is correct, there will come a day when Vestal Grove will be buried under a half a mile of ice, "and all the works of humans in and around what is today called Chicago... will be ground to dust" (Stevens 310–11). Or, aware of a "much more immediate possibility," Stevens prognosticates that "carbon dioxide poured into the air by humans' burning of fossil fuels created out of the plants of another epoch will warm the atmosphere and create conditions too hot and dry, too quickly, for Vestal Grove's finely tuned ecology to survive" (311). Nevertheless, lessons learned at Vestal Grove and other restoration sites may prove essential to preserving biodiversity—"the raw material of evolution"—as well as to "reviving damaged and destroyed ecosystems and re-creating others in new and more hospitable places if future climatic change makes it necessary" (Stevens 311).

Cogitation instructions for this first book ask students to pose one or two questions that might serve as touchstones for the rest of the semester. I compile and we discuss the students' questions, which reflect the class's diverse interests and in some cases propel their final paper. For example, Laura Ofstad's question, "Can ecological restoration be combined with a posthumanist or deep ecologist perspective?" led to a final paper on human rewilding in Margaret Atwood's *MaddAddam* trilogy. Landon Lutrick's question, "Does the man-imposing-his-will character (restorationist as hero) problematize environmental efforts, or could restoration be a redemptive way to use a familiar recurring character?" culminated in a final paper on "The Man Who Knows: Restoring the Environment and the Myth of the Frontier." Patrick Russell's question about ecological restoration in an urban context led to his final paper, "Ecological Restoration & Human Restoration: Reimagining the City" and ultimately led him to pursue graduate studies in Community and Regional Planning. And Sarah Neri's question, "What narratives can be used to explore the process of restoration on a global scale?" became linked to her interest in climate change, resulting in a final paper that explored climate-induced migration and scattered identities in emerging climate change fiction.

The more one learns about ecological restoration the more complicated the picture becomes. The Society for Ecological Restoration provides this seemingly simple definition: "Ecological restoration is the process of assisting the recovery of an ecosystem that has been degraded, damaged, or destroyed" (qtd in Allison 4). However, many of the questions that students raise at the beginning of the semester persist unanswered. For example, what historical condition should be the goal of restoration efforts? Is the goal to restore a place to its condition before humans? before European contact? before large-scale human settlement? or before industrialization? Once we choose a place in time as the target goal, how do we know what that place was like then? Does it do any good to restore an area to a pristine condition if the land around it is filled with invasive species? How does the project of ecological restoration privilege some epistemologies over others? Metaphorically, are restorationists gardeners, doctors, managers, stewards, engineers, or something else? What cultural change is necessary for ecological restoration to succeed over the long term?

Within the field of ecological restoration itself, questions multiply and debates flare. Today it is widely accepted that there is no stable, climax state that has ever existed or could ever occur in a world of unremitting change. Some practitioners envision ecological restoration as returning land to a healthy state within its historical range of variability so that evolution can resume with a minimum of human interference. Others believe that human intervention will always be needed. Some prize biological diversity for its own sake, regardless of its value to humans. Others prioritize restoring ecosystem function and services—"natural capital"—such as flood control, water filtration, soil fertility, nutrient cycling, and decomposition. In this view, returning a degraded area to ecological functionality takes precedence over and may be more feasible than bringing back the complete spectrum of biological diversity that once existed at a particular site. More recently, some scientists argue that large-scale anthropogenic changes, such as climate change, land degradation, and alien invasive species, have created "novel ecosystems," which have no historic analog. They argue that it will not be possible to return land to a state prior to these massive disturbances, which means that a new suite of goals should be considered, perhaps accepting and accommodating non-native species. At this point, some people question whether "restoration" is even the correct term for this project of "intervention ecology" that engineers "designer ecosystems."[1]

Fully cognizant of these debates, Stuart K. Allison's *Ecological Restoration and Environmental Change: Renewing Damaged Ecosystems*, the second book of the seminar, is an accessible textbook on the science and practice of restoration ecology in an age of climate change. A biology professor, Allison is a restoration insider who insists that "You can't not choose," explaining, "[A]t this stage in human cultural and ecological history the future of all habitats will depend upon human choice, whether our choice is to preserve, restore or continue to develop habitat" (Allison 1, 8). His research suggests that the goals for restoration efforts vary in different regions of the world, with the U.S. and Australia often aiming to recreate the pristine conditions of pre-settlement, wild or natural landscapes. However, as he observes, notions of "pristine," "wild," and "natural" must be reconciled with the fact of the continuous residence and active land management of indigenous peoples in North America and Australia for thousands of years prior to European settlement. In Europe, where almost no wild landscapes remain, restoration goals strongly favor biodiversity, while in Asia the preferred goal is to restore ecosystem function (such as photosynthesis, energy flow, and nutrient and hydrological cycles) and ecosystem services (e.g. pollination, pest control, and flood prevention).

Allison's chapter on climate change reviews different model predictions of future climate change, that forecast new ecological domains that have no current analog in North America in that "they represent combinations of temperature, precipitation and humidity that do not currently exist there" (85). No-analog conditions force restorationists to reconceive appropriate goals and actions for restoration in the twenty-first century, such as assisting the migration of species to climate zones where they can survive, managing "novel" and "hybrid" ecosystems, and employing ecological restoration proactively to mitigate the effects of global environmental change—by planting trees, for example, that remove carbon dioxide from the atmosphere.

Ultimately, Allison proposes that we need to move toward what he calls *renewed restoration*—projects that maintain as much historical fidelity as possible while "utilizing the reality of rapidly changing, no-analogue, hybrid and novel ecosystems in order to promote biodiversity, ecosystem services and human connection to the environment" (120).[2] My class responded very positively to Allison's informed and reflective treatment, which takes account of cultural values, explores the philosophical aspects of restoration, and even includes a section on environmental art and ritual.

Concluding the introductory unit on the history, theory, and practice of ecological restoration, we read Aldo Leopold's *A Sand County Almanac* and learn about his pioneering experiments to restore ecological communities at the University of Wisconsin Arboretum in the 1930s and his family's ambitious reforestation project (they planted approximately 40,000 trees) on some degraded farmland in Sand County, Wisconsin. Curiously, although Leopold is widely recognized as the father of ecological restoration, his classic work, *A Sand County Almanac*, has almost nothing to say on the matter. Nevertheless, the book made a profound impact on my students. Jonathan Katalenic, for example, writes, "Leopold's message is not that nature should be kept behind glass and only viewed in the detached manner of a passer by; rather, that our understanding of the beauty, the soul, and the power of the land comes from actually experiencing it, learning what makes it tick, and adjusting how we treat the land accordingly."

Leopold's example is instructive and his ideas of the "land ethic" and "biotic community" are important, but it is the beauty of his prose that leaves the deepest imprint on me and my students, once again convincing me—not that we in literary studies need convincing—that beauty restores the soul and must be part of an environmental and specifically climate change curriculum. *A Sand County Almanac* is a book that you might want to read every year; favorite passages will become rooted in the mind and spring up seasonally like flowers:

> When dandelions have set the mark of May on Wisconsin pastures, it is time to listen for the final proof of spring. Sit down on a tussock, cock your ears at the sky, dial out the bedlam of meadowlarks and redwings, and soon you may hear it: the flight-song of the upland plover, just now back from the Argentine.
> (Leopold 37)

To date, the principal literary genres to explore ecological restoration themes are journalism and memoir. Hence, with only one exception—T.C. Boyle's novel *When the Killing's Done*—the readings in my seminar are nonfiction. Units include memoirs of restoring key species (beaver, buffalo, and salmon); interventions into current controversies (removing invasive species, dismantling dams, and respecting traditional ecological knowledge); and narrative treatments of urban, post-mining, and postcolonial sites.[3]

In the context of this volume's focus on teaching climate change, I highly recommend Emma Marris's book on novel ecosystems, *Rambunctious Garden: Saving Nature in a Post-Wild World*, which we read in the unit on current controversies. Marris, who holds a Master's degree in science writing from Johns Hopkins University, writes on ecology and conservation biology. Adrian Zytkoskee, a student in my seminar, sums up the book well:

> For Marris, any and every space has the potential for restoration, including apartment decks, toxic mine sites, and even gas station parking lots. "Rewilding, assisted migration, and embracing some exotic species and novel ecosystems may seem like disparate strategies, but they are all at some level about making the most out of every scrap of land and water, no matter its condition" (Marris 135). Perhaps it is an odd analogy, but when contemplating this approach, I often think of a pair of patchwork pants that create a functioning whole out of bits and pieces of scraps discarded from previous work. The result is colorful, functional, and a far cry from traditional attire.

Rhetoric of hope

When it comes to motivating people, climate change discourse has as at least three problems. First, it tends to cast people as the problem, as defilers of the planet. Many people resist being typecast as villains and sinners. They would rather play the good guy in the drama of life. Second, climate change discourse forecasts gloom and doom, conjuring terrifying images of a burning planet, cities drowning, monster storms, widespread famine, and even the end of civilization. Some people don't go to horror movies; for their mental health they need a cognitive diet of positive images and hopeful stories. Third, climate change discourse sends the message to sacrifice and be small—turn off those lights! reduce your carbon footprint! But most people do not want to minimize their impact; they want to *have* an impact, *be* the light.

Ecological restoration avoids the motivational pitfalls of climate change messaging while inspiring actions that will nevertheless help us to mitigate climate change and improve ecological function. Instead of being cast as the problem, people become part of the solution. Instead of being seen as the enemy of nature, people are envisioned as part of and partners with nature. Instead of focusing on calamities that might happen, restorationists tend to imagine places positively transformed. And instead of thinking in terms of sacrifice, people involved in ecological restoration find their lives *enriched* by their connection to nature. While both projects aim to address environmental crises, climate change discourse engenders fear, whereas ecological restoration discourse inspires hope.

As we grapple with the enormous challenge of educating students for the climate change century, I am reminded of Emily Dickinson, reaching out to us from the nineteenth century, who advised, "Tell all the Truth but tell it slant – /Success in Circuit lies." Facing climate change head-on as the topic of a course may "blind" us. But presenting climate change circuitously—in a course on ecological restoration, for example—offers a way to see climate change as a feature of a much larger panorama, "eased with explanation kind" of inspiring people and dazzling stories of environmental and cultural renewal.

Notes

1   Woodworth's *Our Once and Future Planet* helpfully delineates the differences of opinion among experts in ecological restoration (see 396–406).
2   This overview of Allison's book is drawn from my published review in *PULSE*.
3   The books for the seminar are listed in the bibliography. For a list of the assigned supplemental essays and an annotated bibliography of ecological restoration readings, compiled by the students in the seminar, email the author at glotfelt@unr.edu.

References

Allison, Stuart K. *Ecological Restoration and Environmental Change: Renewing Damaged Ecosystems.* New York: Routledge, 2012. Print.
Berg, Peter. *The Biosphere and the Bioregion: Essential Writings of Peter Berg.* Eds. Cheryll

Glotfelty and Eve Quesnel. London: Routledge, 2015. Print.

Boyle, T.C. *When the Killing's Done*. New York: Penguin Books, 2011. Print.

Brower, Kenneth. *Hetch Hetchy: Undoing a Great American Mistake*. Berkeley, CA: Heyday, 2013. Print.

Carpenter, Novella. *Farm City: The Education of an Urban Farmer*. New York: Penguin, 2009. Print.

Collier, Eric. *Three Against the Wilderness*. New York: Dutton, 1959. Print.

Glotfelty, Cheryll. Review of *Ecological Restoration and Environmental Change: Renewing Damaged Ecosystems* by Stuart K. Allison. *PULSE* 14 (Spring 2014): 14.

Goin, Peter, and C. Elizabeth Raymond. *Changing Mines in America*. Santa Fe, NM: Center for American Places, 2004. Print.

House, Freeman. *Totem Salmon: Life Lessons from Another Species*. Boston, MA: Beacon, 1999. Print.

Katalenic, Jonathan. "Re: Leopold." Message to Cheryll Glotfelty, 30 July 2015. By email.

Leopold, Aldo. *A Sand County Almanac*. New York: Ballantine Books, 1970 (1949). Print.

Maathai, Wangari. *Unbowed: A Memoir*. New York: Anchor, 2006. Print.

Marris, Emma. *Rambunctious Garden: Saving Nature in a Post-Wild World*. New York: Bloomsbury, 2011. Print.

Nelson, Melissa K., ed. *Original Instructions: Indigenous Teachings for a Sustainable Future*. Rochester, VT: Bear & Company, 2008. Print.

O'Brien, Dan. *Buffalo for the Broken Heart: Restoring Life to a Black Hills Ranch*. New York: Random House, 2002. Print.

Stevens, William K. *Miracle Under the Oaks: The Revival of Nature in America*. New York: Pocket Books, 1995. Print.

Woodworth, Paddy. *Our Once and Future Planet: Restoring the World in the Climate Change Century*. Chicago, IL: University of Chicago Press, 2013. Print.

Zytkoskee, Adrian, VI. "A Rhetoric of Hope: Ecological Restoration for a Troubled Planet." Unpublished essay, 2014. Print.

22 Exploratory concepts, case studies, and keywords for teaching environmental justice and climate change in a lower-level humanities classroom

Julie Sze

Introduction

I must confess that I haven't taught climate change in my classroom, at least not explicitly. The primary reason I haven't taught it is because the context and field in which I teach and research is American Studies, and within American Studies, environmental justice. Climate change has not been a core topic in American Studies. Although my primary research area is environmental justice activism, dominant scholarship on climate change has not explicitly focused on race and class. Thus, my chapter is focused on how I have taught exploratory concepts, case studies, and keywords to a generalist undergraduate audience (and particularly first year students, from across the disciplinary spectrum) as a way of indirectly teaching environmental justice and climate change.

The primary concepts I teach are *ideology, hegemony*, and as a particular example, *neoliberalism*. Second, I teach through the case study of Hurricane Katrina. The last part of this essay is, at this point, purely tentative, in which I discuss how I will teach climate justice in the future. In this speculative section, I examine how to teach through a keyword: scale, with a particular case study of an Arctic Native community named Kivalina that is facing imminent relocation from flooding related to climate change.

Key concepts

In my "Introduction to American Studies" course I have 150 students. The vast majority are first year students, as the course satisfies General Education requirements. A significant percentage are international students, overwhelmingly from East Asia (my estimate is about 15–20 percent). There are many challenges and opportunities in this class. My overarching pedagogical goal is to teach skills and concepts that they can take with them throughout their educational career, in whatever major they ultimately decide upon (very few are humanities majors, and even fewer are in American Studies). In this context, I focus on core concepts in the humanities and social sciences, specifically, ideology and hegemony. To teach ideology, I use Paul Robbins's *Lawn People: How Grasses, Weeds, and Chemicals Make Us Who We Are*. In it, he explores how lawns came to dominate in U.S. society, using Gramsci's notion of hegemony as a process in which multiple institutions and processes work together to garner consent. Robbins also explores the possibilities for transformation. Gramsci's notion of hegemony shows change over time, and how what is "common sense," becomes naturalized, and is actually a product of institutional and historical forces that are complex, and contradictory. The lawn is an effective case study because it reaches many of the science-oriented majors. Lawns are also a very live issue and an effective case study in California and the contemporary Western U.S. as a result of the multi-year mega drought, thus showing how policies, cultures and normative values around the lawn can change in a very short span of time.

Moving from *Lawn People*, I then turn to the predominant ideology in the lives of our students: neoliberalism. As David Harvey describes, neoliberalism is "the doctrine that market exchange is an ethic in itself, capable of acting as a guide for all human action" (3). Scholars across social science and humanities fields have used neoliberalism as their predominant analytic framework in the last two decades, as the impact of neoliberal policies after 1970 has become increasingly clear. The valorization of privatization, finance, and market processes, and the retrenchment of the state and public sectors is, in many areas, nearly complete (or at least, hegemonic). To further concretize the rise of neoliberalism, and to give this ideology meaning, I focus on the decline in state support in public higher education, and its impacts on student fees, using the example of the University of California system. Neoliberalism and market fundamentalism are useful anchor concepts in teaching climate change for two primary reasons. First is the prevalence of cap-and-trade in policy discussions around climate change. The second is the intensification of transnational corporate capitalism and its extension, consumption, in our lives and the experiences of our students. By consumption, I mean not only of things, but of what was formerly considered a public good, such as affordable higher education. Our students self-identify as consumers, of things, and, crucially, of their education. Without idealizing some perfect past, my point here is that the intensification of consumption—of things, experience, knowledge and education—is suffocating in its seeming totality. The ability of our students to learn is shaped very much by ideological choices, and in the shift from seeing students and education in a public frame, to an individualized and personal identity as paying customers and in producing good consumer citizen behaviors.

My goal in the classroom in teaching these concepts to a lower-division generalist audience is to *de-naturalize* common-sense ideologies, whether the examples are the prevalence of lawn in the United States, the seeming inevitability of the neoliberal university, or of consumption itself.

Case study: Hurricane Katrina

One of the ideologies I focus on in my "Introduction to American Studies" class is the American Dream, or the fundamentally optimistic narrative around economic mobility, hard work and national identity in the U.S. Near the end of the course, I close with a unit on Hurricane Katrina (2005). For current and future students, Hurricane Katrina is but a distant memory, in sharp contrast to its impact for those of us who watched it in real time. On August 29, 2005, Hurricane Katrina was a Category three hurricane when it hit the Gulf Coast. Bringing massive winds, and covering a large landmass (over 400 miles), the true devastation was in its aftermath, when the levees broke, which led to massive flooding. Almost 2000 people died, hundreds of thousands of people were displaced, and there was over 100 billion dollars in property damage. Race and class were key factors that shaped the failures in evacuation planning, and in its aftermath.

Even before Hurricane Katrina, environmental justice activists were anticipating the racially disproportionate effects of climate change, in coastal flooding and the health effects of heat waves, through the Environmental Justice and Climate Change Initiative (EJCC). The EJCC is a coalition of 28 U.S. environmental justice, climate justice, religious, policy, and advocacy groups, which formed to call for action from the Bush Administration and Congress on climate change. According to a 2002 fact sheet (since taken down): "People of color are concentrated in urban centers in the South, coastal regions, and areas with substandard air quality. New Orleans, which is 62 percent African-American and two feet below sea level, exemplifies the severe and disproportionate impacts of climate change in the U.S." It continues (and eerily predicts Katrina's effects): "Global warming will hit the uninsured hardest.... Global warming will increase the number of flood, drought and fire occurrences worldwide. Wealthy homeowners are able to move, whereas low-income people (who usually rent) cannot. Also, low-income people typically lack insurance to replace possessions lost in storms and floods. Only 25 percent of renters have renters insurance."

According to an engineering professor at Louisiana State University who served as a consultant on the state's evacuation plan before the hurricane: "little attention was paid to moving out New Orleans's 'low-mobility' population – the elderly, the infirm and the poor without cars or other means of fleeing the city, about 100,000 people" (these were the exact populations that were stranded in the Superdome in terrible conditions after the levees broke). In an article in the aftermath of Katrina called "Government Saw Flood Risk but Not Levee Failure," reporters document that when explicitly asked about what to do with those populations at disaster planning meetings, "the answer [of government officials and disaster planners] was often silence."

My interest, as both a scholar of environmental justice, and as a scholar based in the humanities, is to teach topics like Hurricane Katrina and climate change in ways that take different experiences and ways of knowing into account. The "silence" of technocrat and disaster planners is a result, I've argued elsewhere, of a problem of recognition of extreme social, class and racial difference (Sze, 2015). Political philosopher David Schlosberg, in *Defining Environmental Justice*, expanded the definition of justice beyond the traditional understanding of justice as distribution and procedural. In this definition, there are reasons why some people get more goods (and bads) than others (the distributive model) or the procedural (how politically and culturally disenfranchised people or communities can or cannot take part in governance). Schlosberg adds a third dimension, arguing that "recognition" of diverse cultural identities in a critical pluralism is a pre-condition for entry into the distributional system. The problems of lack of distribution and participation are linked to lack of recognition. Part of the problem of environmental injustice, and part of the reason for unjust pollution distribution, is a lack of recognition of group difference.

To counter the hegemonic silence that preceded and followed Hurricane Katrina, I show students the 2009 Oscar-nominated documentary, *Trouble the Water*. The protagonists, Kim Rivers Roberts and her husband Scott, were among the 100,000 (the "low-mobility population") left behind during the hurricane. The film includes 20 minutes of footage Roberts shot during the storm, as well as her journey afterwards – literal (leaving Louisiana after the hurricane, and her return soon after), bureaucratic (struggles with FEMA), and metaphoric. Roberts is an incredibly compelling narrator who commands the screen. A performer-rapper, her song "Amazing" focuses on her pain and her strength as two sides of a coin, building up to a powerful aural climax.

Roberts literally embodies those unseen by bureaucrats and disaster planners, based on her race and class, but she is much more than the sum of these social "factors" (you learn in the film about her mother's drug addiction and AIDS death and her brother's incarceration and his frightening abandonment during the storm while imprisoned). She makes real and concrete the lived impacts of bad public policy around climate change, in which analysts and scholars have argued that those who are in *most need* of climate change mitigation and adaption receive the *least protection*, a classic definition of an environmental injustice.

By focusing Hurricane Katrina from a humanistic perspective, and specifically, through Kim's eyes (literally, through first, her video footage, and then, her post-Katrina travels and travails), the film succeeds in centralizing her perspective and experiences. The film grounds the natural disaster with social and racial factors, and it is an excellent overview for an American Studies class (the tag-line for the film is: "It's not about a hurricane. It's about America"). In the context of Hurricane Katrina, the failure of disaster planning and the disastrous aftermath of the levee break, this centralization of the perspective of a "low-mobility" and politically and culturally disenfranchised black woman are key components of environmental and climate justice analysis.

Keyword: scale and case study: Kivalina

This last section is speculative, based on my plans to add a climate justice section to an existing environmental justice seminar. This upper division seminar is very small (15 students) and self-selected in terms of interest in the topic. I will begin with an overview of the Bali Principles of Climate Justice and its links to the Principle of Environmental Justice (www.ejcc.org/resources). Then, I will focus on a particular case study of climate injustice, focusing on the keyword of scale.

Environmental problems often "cross" or jump scales, and there is a "spatial mismatch" that can occur in discussing an environmental problem (i.e. between the scales of environmental pollution and its political regulation). Thus, environmental and other social movements (labor) also organize and network across scales, using communication technologies and sophisticated understandings of local, regional, national and global relationships.

Scalar analysis is spatially and temporally complex, and thus offers useful analytic lenses to approach climate change. Scale as an increasingly prominent analytic tool is intimately connected to intensifying conditions of globalization, specifically capitalist economic development and related ideologies of neoliberalism, privatization and deregulation. Scale and globalization are linked in part because of how the increasing movement of pollution and peoples and the concomitant weakness of environmental regulation (at multiple scales) are connected. The failures to address climate change are linked to analytic problems related to scale. For example, a significant percentage of industrial pollution in China is a result of production for consumers in the U.S., Europe and Australia, but this pollution crosses the Pacific, landing in the Western United States. How can this pollution be measured? In national terms? Global? Pacific Rim? Geographer Nathan Sayre argues that the difficulties of confronting global warming are a function of the unique scalar qualities of climate change, including the temporal. Nations such as China and India use historical and temporal dimensions in their political arguments against international treaties. In effect, countries in the West have historically contributed greater carbon emissions and have had a head start on economic development.

To explore issues of scale and its intersections with dimensions of climate change from a humanistic perspective, I will focus on the case study of Kivalina, and in particular, the Re-Locate project (www.relocate-ak.org). Kivalina is an Iñupiaq village of 400 people that may be destroyed in Northwest Alaska, as sea ice melts and rates of coastal erosion increase. Re-Locate is a transdisciplinary global collective working with a group of delegates from Kivalina to initiate a community-led and culturally specific relocation, using social arts methods and online media, that (according to their website), "intend to make the social, political, and environmental issues related to relocation visible to global audiences; support community discussion and consensus building; locate, connect and educate new relocation partners; create spaces where people in Kivalina can share original media and ideas about local identities and ways of life; and develop an infrastructure for managing global support and pursuing relocation planning opportunities." The Re-Locate project is founded on "solidarity and engagement" and a long-term dialogue, where a group of transdisciplinary global partners travel to the village on a recurrent basis to develop shared priorities and activities.

Kivalina garnered global attention to their situation and the relocation process they had initiated through their lawsuit on climate change, *Kivalina v. ExxonMobil Corporation, et al.*, filed on February 26, 2008, in the Northern District of California. Kivalina was represented on the case by the Center for Race, Poverty and the Environment and the Native American Rights Fund, along with a number of major law firms. The lawsuit, filed against the twenty-four largest oil and electric companies in the United States, alleged that these corporations are substantially contributing to global warming and are liable to Kivalina for the resulting damage. The lawsuit also alleged that a small number of defendants led by ExxonMobil have engaged in a conspiracy to mislead the public about the causes and effects of climate change (see "Climate Justice"). The suit, based on the federal common law theory of nuisance, claimed up to $400 million in monetary damages to pay for the relocation of the village. The District Court dismissed the case, on the grounds that regulating greenhouse gas emissions was a *political,* rather than a legal issue. This distinction between political, legal and cultural in regards to climate change is a view rejected by climate justice activists, and in particular, by indigenous and small island communities.

Re-Locate has written about their guiding principles, and the website itself is a way to make concrete issues of climate injustice in a particular time and space (Gerace, Griffin, and Marlow). As I have not yet taught this material, I cannot speak as to its efficacy, but concretizing large political issues through particular stories is one effective way to teach in the environmental and public humanities. To teach issues of scale and climate justice in Kivalina, I would start with a video of a local tribal leader named Colleen Swan, before moving to the Re-Locate Website. I would take care to ensure that racial and tribal justice issues with respect to climate change are not conflated, in that indigenous sovereignty is unique historically and legally. That would entail offering a primer of additional readings on the broader issues of indigenous sovereignty and of the Arctic North (ed. Banerjee). I would require reading on Kivalina itself, both its larger social movement struggles (Shearer) and in the legal and media realm (law review articles and journalistic accounts) (Shearer). The diversity of approaches in Kivalina shows the complex relationships across scale (individual, Arctic Northern, Global) and institutional/ structural factors (tribal, corporate). Taking a multi-scalar approach highlights, rather than buries, the difficult and core questions of power, development, colonialism/sovereignty, and consumer capitalism (production/ consumption) that are both the roots and obstacles of climate change problems, narratives, and policy remedies.

Conclusion

As a humanities-based scholar who teaches a wide range of undergraduate students from all backgrounds, I attempt to use tools that have applicability across topic areas. This piece highlights the implicit ways to teach environmental and climate justice in that context, using exploratory concepts, case studies, and keywords geared to a generalist undergraduate audience.

With a usable and working grasp of ideology, hegemony, and neoliberalism, combined with case studies (Hurricane Katrina and Kivalina), I believe that students from all backgrounds will be able to understand core concepts and conflicts that undergird political disputes around climate change, from an environmental and public humanities perspective. It is crucial to teach beyond the students already interested and engaged by climate change, or climate justice. The broader public is comprised of those people who are unaware of their own ideological and hegemonic belief systems and their entanglements with existing political and environmental systems that perpetuate deep social, spatial and racial injustices. My contention here is that teaching with diverse voices, media, and perspectives can be leveraged in potentially powerful and unanticipated ways.

References

Banerjee, Subhankar. *Arctic Voices: Resistance at the Tipping Point.* New York: Seven Stories Press, 2013.

"Climate Justice." Center for Race, Poverty and the Environment. Accessed May 30, 2014, www.crpe-ej.org/crpe/index.php/campaigns/climate-justice.

Gerace, Michael, Joshua P. Griffin, and Jen Marlow. "Re-Locate Response." *Resilience: A Journal of the Environmental Humanities* 2.2 (2015).

Harvey, David. *A Brief History of Neoliberalism.* Oxford: Oxford University Press, 2007.

Robbins, Paul. *Lawn People: How Grasses, Weeds, and Chemicals Make Us Who We Are.* Philadelphia, PA: Temple University Press, 2007.

Sayre, Nathan. "Climate Change, Scale, and Devaluation: The Challenge of Our Built Environment." *Washington and Lee Journal of Climate, Energy and the Environment* 1.1 (2010): 93–105.

Shane, Scott and Eric Lipton. "Government Saw Flood Risk but Not Levee Failure." *The New York Times,* 2 September 2005. Accessed 30 May 2014, www.nytimes.com/2005/09/02/national/nationalspecial/02response.html?pagewanted=all

Shearer, Christine. *Kivalina: A Climate Change Story.* San Francisco, CA: Haymarket Books, 2011.

Schlosberg, David. *Defining Environmental Justice: Theories, Movements and Nature.* Oxford: Oxford University Press, 2009.

Sze, Julie. "Environmental Justice and Anthropocene Narratives: Recognition and Representation in Kivalina." *Resilience: A Journal of Environmental Humanities* 2.2 (2015).

Trouble the Water. Directors Tia Lessin and Carl Deal. Zeitgeist Films, 2009.

23 Garbage and literature

Generating narrative from a culture of waste

Stephanie Foote

Over the last few years I have offered a handful of undergraduate courses in the Environmental Humanities in the English Department at the University of Illinois at Urbana-Champaign. As is the case with many of my colleagues, teaching is one of the most powerful ways I think through the broad questions and assumptions guiding my writing projects. It is the most immediate, satisfying, and surprising way of thinking with others, which is, after all, the goal of our writing and research. Especially in the case of topics in the Environmental Humanities, teaching affords an opportunity to calibrate our assumptions about our audiences. I can, for example, make no assumptions about my students' commitment to environmentalism because more obviously than the other keywords that form the ground of my classes – keywords like literature, print culture, realism, or nineteenth century – the terms of the Environmental Humanities are still emerging in relationship to debates in the academy, the media, the political arena, and the corporate world.

That is, while in a more traditional course it may well become clear that certain terms like "literature," once thought to be fixed, are actually always under debate, it is already the case that the terms "environment," "nature," and "climate change" are under pressure in an Environmental Humanities class. Indeed, that's part of the intellectual energy of the field. But it also means that I do not know how my students define those terms, how they arrived at their definitions, or even whether they are especially attached to them. Among the most interesting things I've learned as I organize classes in the Environmental Humanities is which terms students who are committed in some way to environmental politics – anything from conservation and animal welfare to freeganism – don't care at all about. One of those terms is, oddly enough, "climate change," which strikes students as too abstract. They are indifferent to the warning that seems curled in the word "change," and they much prefer the contested, now-superseded term "global warming."

Certainly the question of scale is at work here – framing problems in different temporal registers, from the geologic to the immediate, is among the challenges of teaching literature about climate change. The act of reading a novel, after all, occurs in a familiar and a soothing temporality, no matter how extravagant the novel's own experiments with time. Rather, the preference for "global warming" over climate change is linked to tactility of the word "warming." Despite the menace of the phrase, warming has a sensory component that localizes it, anchors it in the body, in touch, in the present. Tactility and materiality is, then, the final piece of how I've evolved with my students a class in narrative, garbage, and climate change. Garbage and waste seem democratically available for analysis, but they are also words that let us think about scale – the immediacy of consumer desire, for example, in relationship to the slow accumulation of toxins in the human body. And they let us think, quite obviously, about materiality – not just about what an object *is* when it becomes garbage, but how an object embodies values that are in the midst of changing.

When scholars discuss pedagogy, it's easy to speak abstractly about the kinds of knowledge we hope to convey, to invoke principles of good teaching, to describe the interactions between an ideal instructor and an ideal student, but we also know that no matter how meaningful those pedagogical abstractions are, all teaching is local. And it too is embodied, material, shot through with half understood knowledges that come from sensory input other than what is audible in discussion. Real teaching unfolds as a particular, embodied group of students evolves into a class with its own personality, a personality that in turn begins to direct the shape and the speed of conversation, the specific way a text yields under pressure, the intellectual intimacies that spring up when ideas become more than academic.

Indeed, teaching is even more local than that: a given class depends on the time of day, the arrangement of chairs, the room itself. It is a strangely contingent exercise, and yet it is deeply materially grounded. The classroom is its own ecology, and part of how I have strategized the design of my classes on garbage and literature is by connecting the lived, local expertise that students have about their environments to the environment of the classroom, in which material concerns are connected to longer histories and patterns of representations. But if the classroom is its own ecology, it is also paradoxically positioned to let students see the ascending scale of material problems. The design of the class is also intended to enable students to work from the local to think about how ideas about scale structure how we know and experience narrative. The most obvious illustration of the scale of imagining and narrating garbage? It's everything from an irritating candy wrapper on a city street to a huge global industry connected to resource extraction, human exploitation, material recovery, and toxic dumping. The trick of the class is how to coordinate scale, how to identify and relate different discourses about garbage and begin to theorize how those discourses emerge from deep fantasies about the significance of objects, especially at the end of their lives.

It's here that literary studies has a privileged vantage point; it's the bread and butter of the field to be able to think about how discourse and narrative structure representations of historical problems. And it is the bread and butter of the field to hold open those representations so that we can look closely at how narrative itself tries to propose solutions to deep historical problems. Garbage, the end result of a process of production or consumption intended to make something wonderfully new and pristine, is thus, like Marx's commodity, a very queer thing indeed. And for that reason, it is a fascinating category through which to focus attention on objects, commodities, gifts, and fetishes because it seems to be outside the systems of exchange. Garbage looks all used up, as though its story has already been fully told. Once used up or discarded, any object – a broken radio, a popsicle stick, a torn shirt – is just trash. Drained of value, it seems to be the end of once-complex, once luxuriantly proliferating narratives of pleasure or necessity.

Practically speaking, a literature class on garbage can come together in a lot of ways. You can, for instance, take a book history approach and look at what happens in the making of books – the role of the paper industry, the ecological impact of the shipping and circulation of books, the recycling and the disposal of books (a surprisingly lucrative niche industry), and the emergence of e-waste. You can organize a class on the how the metaphor of garbage has historically structured representations of devalued people and places, or how trash figures a degraded literary taste, a degraded literary text, and even the degraded subjects who read those texts. After a some tinkering with how to most broadly conceive of the heart of the course – what is the relationship between metaphor and materiality, a question that is, as literary scholars know, the stubborn and unresolvable problem of representation itself – I decided to approach garbage and waste by focusing on the category of objects whose value is compromised. Garbage, to paraphrase Mary Douglass, is "matter out of place," and it therefore directs our attention to how we come to value things, how we experience the work of things in our psychic lives, how their disappearance or inevitable decay helps us see the shape of a particular individual or cultural desire.

This is why we begin with objects – what we might call cynically "pre-garbage." We begin by surveying theories about the value of objects: Freud's "Mourning and Melancholia"; Marx's theory of exchange and use; Bill Brown's work on things and thing theory; Marcel Mauss's work on the gift; studies of garbology and the excavation of dumps and midden heaps; and recent studies of the waste and recycling industries. Those studies inform our analysis of a selection of novels that pay particular attention to objects whose value is somehow compromised, objects that teeter between categories of useful and useless, priceless and worthless, working or damaged. The class – nominally categorized as contemporary U.S. literature – thus includes Frank Norris's *McTeague*, Don DeLillo's *White Noise*, E.L. Doctorow's *Homer and Langley*. We read a memoir of a woman who was raised by a mother who was a clinical hoarder, and then we look at episodes of *Hoarders* and *Antiques Roadshow*. The long twentieth century is not short of novels about what it means to love objects – to collect them or hoard them, to value them or imbue them with fetishistic meaning. How, we ask as we read them, do different narrative genres from specific historical periods figure the relationship between human desire and objects? How do they tell the story of objects and compromised value, and how do they assume that objects themselves can tell a story about human desires and needs?

And finally, in the last part of the class, we turn our attention to compromised objects in the world around us, researching them and building narratives around them. The final assignment is a group project in which students find an example of garbage they see everywhere around them and research it. What's it made of? Where is it made? How much does it cost to make, ship, and purchase? Where is it sold? How is it advertised? Most importantly, the end goal of the assignment is for the students to analyze how these facts are variously coordinated in common-sensical narratives or conventional discourses about the objects in question. How, for example, is an object produced through narrative as "good quality" or "useful" or "fun" or "loveable"? Is it pleasurable? Does it or can it cause pain? Must it be dusted? Will it chip? Must it be replaced when it is broken? Can you fix it yourself? How does its compromised status – its demotion to garbage – work against or within those narratives?

To accomplish this, students work in groups. Their first order of business is to agree on their test case: one mass-produced object they saw around campus and categorized as garbage. I should say that if you ever try this exercise, you'll discover, as I did, that deciding on an object that has been drained of value, or the value of which is compromised, is extremely difficult. Often students would choose an object that had far too many constituent parts. One group decided to do a cell phone, which they quite rightly argued becomes garbage all the time, at the corporation's whim, as a result of planned obsolescence. But it was a nearly impossible task for them to even get an accurate breakdown of every one of a phone's components, much less complete the assignment, the second step of which was to research the entire life cycle of the object. This includes where and by which company an object is made, how its material is sourced, how and by whom the object is distributed, how it is advertised, where it is purchased, how it is consumed, and how it is discarded. But of course, this is one of the most interesting parts of figuring out what hidden histories of objects are; most objects, it turns out, are made of many components, and in the case of the cell phone, some of the central elements have been at the heart of Africa's most violent civil wars.

In this step, students need first to learn to research corporate history, to learn at least the outlines of the occulted means by which corporations and subsidiaries work together to corner sectors of the supply chain. That required them to learn to use the business library, and it introduced them to an entirely different set of databases – including Hoover's Online, the best place to begin an economic and corporate investigation. The students also look at the official corporate websites, research and excavate representative advertisements for their object, and last, try to find out what happens to the object when it is discarded. Can it be recycled? How is trash and recycling handled in central Illinois and the university anyway?

One of the most successful of these projects was organized around one of the most ubiquitous pieces of garbage on a Big Ten campus: the iconic red 'Solo® cup'. Solo® cups are quite interesting for this exercise because they are designed to be disposable. As single-use convenience products, they are as close to garbage as a product can get while still being new and untouched. Though they can be found at suburban birthday parties, summer picnics, and office Christmas parties, Solo® cups have a privileged place at universities. They are the obvious choice for students holding keg parties, and on certain parts of campus – around the fraternity houses, for example – Monday mornings are paradoxically festive because the sidewalks and green spaces are littered with dozens of cups, most of them still reeking of beer.

From the initial set of basic questions, the students generated a series of increasingly wide-ranging queries: What cultural conditions allow consumers to need or believe we need a red plastic Solo® cup? How did plastic enter mainstream life? There are a lot of data that can be generated around a red Solo® cup – you can discover how many of them are made in a year, how much they weigh, how they're shipped, how much they cost to make vs how much they cost to buy. You can find out about the company that makes them, and the companies that distribute and sell them. But if you want to do anything with that information, the students discovered, you have to think of the object as if it were, as one of them said in class, a character in a novel.

The Solo® cup turned out to be an interesting choice for another reason, though the students did not know it until they began doing research. They discovered that there is a Solo® cup plant in Urbana, about three-and-a-half miles from the classroom in which we met. Indeed, it has been an important source of employment in Champaign Urbana, where if you are not affiliated with the hospitals, the university, or the ever-expanding service economy, there aren't many other employment opportunities. The fact that the plant served a part of Urbana that the students usually never know exists became an important factor in the overall narratives that emerged from their research. In fact, it allowed an entirely different version of the local, one of the analytic touchstones of the project, to haunt the university party scene that had first inspired the choice.

The students inevitably give compelling presentations when they discuss the objects, and this case was no different. One discussed the rise of plastics in the U.S., referencing the military industrial complex as well as a history of advertising plastic products. Another located the rise of the Solo® cup in a narrative about gender politics, demonstrating how the rise of convenience foods and single-use products have been linked to debates about the effects of women joining the workforce; another discussed the global traffic in recyclables, offering a narrative in which she argued that though the plastic cup is advertised for the single hand of a fun-loving student, it is in fact really destined for the hardworking hands of underpaid workers in the recycling industry. The students argued that they could have easily had another five people in their group – the stories the Solo® cup bore within itself at various stages of its life cycle seemed barely touched by the presentations as they had imagined them. Their dissatisfaction, a refusal to achieve what we would call narrative closure, struck me then, and still strikes me, as a net win. Part of the aim of a project like this is not just to demonstrate to students that there is so much information about a given object that it takes a group to even begin to gather it, but to reveal how the consuming habits of individual bodies are the most obvious and in some ways least important elements of understanding garbage. Though the feel of an object when new, or the disgust the category of garbage provokes are experienced as deeply individual, known and felt in the body's preferences and desires, it's important to counter that sense of individualism in a class like this. Garbage is too often experienced as the rejectamenta of a consuming subject, rather than the material that will constellate bodies into groupings: consumer demographics; polluted bodies; workers.

I began this essay by saying that one of the interesting things about teaching a class in Environmental Humanities where I am is that I do not know my students' commitments to environmental matters. My university has plenty of committed environmentalists, but in general, it is not an especially activist or politicized campus. But in the process of a 16 week semester in which we studied the historically specific, affectively charged, and culturally schizophrenic relationship between objects and narratives, I hope that the students were able to make a richer, more populated mental map on which to chart their relationship to the key terms of debate about environmental ideas in the media, in political debates, and in popular culture. But more than this: I hope that the class gave them a way to get a handle, quite literally, on the stuff of climate change, to feel as well as know the stories embedded in the life cycle of the objects we no longer wish to see.

24 Teaching literature as climate changes

Ecological presence, a globalized world, and Helon Habila's *Oil on Water*

Anthony Vital

I prepare courses recalling what John McNeill's study of twentieth-century environments reveals, a globalizing industrialism's damage to planetary life. Even if climate change were not reality, we would still need to address issues of pollution—of air, soil, water and organisms, issues of human population and food and water provision, the sixth extinction spasm, etc.—issues ecological and social that climate change amplifies and augments. Doing so would require acknowledging how different regions of the world, in the North and South, attempt to benefit from modernity's promise while, from different historical positions, they try to disentangle from legacies left by European expansion and colonialism, with their accompanying dispossessions, enslavements, exploitation. Needing acknowledgment, too, would be how current attitudes toward living—toward self and other, toward nature—emerged in this long past of twinned promise and nightmare. This past, after all, looks to continue, in different guises, into the foreseeable future.

So, the problem: how to help students navigate between modernity's promise and its nightmare in the presence of climate change?

First, I offer a few words on my teaching situation. I work with undergraduates in Kentucky, contributing English courses to a multidisciplinary environmental studies minor, courses that supply, as well, general education credit. Few of the students are English majors. Some have gone on to environmental work in government, in the corporate sector, or in law. Most have not. My assumption is that I work with future citizens more than with future scholars or environmental professionals. Climate change becomes a topic in these courses, which, since the 1980s, have explored representations of the nature-human relation in US environmentalist writing, mostly. The courses circle about a haunting question: What role can literature and film play in edging a hi-tech industrial society, capital-driven and requiring high levels of commodity consumption, toward a more ecologically sound relation among people and planet?

Of course, I do not expect undergraduates to give an answer—or to know much about "global modernity" and its colonial pasts (Dirlik). I maintain minimum course requirements and then what happens semester-to-semester depends, largely, on those I work with. Each term, though, my goal is to help students grasp that when thinking of nature, both language/discourse and social inequities matter.

While informing students of the scale and dimensions of environmental problems, my focus is on texts and the language we use daily and how these might affect our society's relation to nature. There are no neat ways to think about any of this. My students live in times of extraordinary social and ecological change—propelled by investments in new technologies, including robotics, informatics, nanotechnology, genetic engineering. They will live to hear voices of urgency naming global warming's consequences, offering schemes for mitigation and adaptation. The suffering that climate change causes will track their lives.

Confronted by phenomena so dauntingly beyond straightforward understanding or remedy, I seek to supply an interpretive frame for both texts and daily life, one to contextualize future experience. This frame will (I hope) offer a compass in the quest to live well under changing conditions, enabling a spirit of transformative agency and, in some, spurring an informed activism. To build it, I encourage a new self-understanding to influence daily choices, one that combines ecological and social terms. The work is pragmatic. These are young people excited by the transition into independence, so I aim, beyond skill-development and information-building, to help us, myself included, find an ethical imagination adequate to our challenging, disquieting predicament. What students learn of global modernity (and its colonial pasts) they learn gradually through the term. I start with self-understanding and move outward into their complex, fast-changing world—back and forth—slowly uncovering the self's entanglements.

The first step has students, in journals, translating self-understanding into "basic ecology," something they find entirely new. Despite modernity's reliance on biological knowledge, there is nothing in the general culture to encourage any sustained imagining of one's being in ecological terms, little to counterbalance the steady focus on social identity. The fact that, from a biological perspective, humans are a species of organism and have a continuous ecological presence tends, if thought about, to be compartmentalized as "science," separate from daily activities and not drawn into personal narrative. So, I ask students to write a diary entry, recording a day's activities, avoiding any reference to their usual sense of identity or feelings or moods, using only the terms found in the supplied textbook/encyclopedic material introducing ecology as science. They are to observe themselves (with good detail and accuracy) as organisms-in-interaction and, as such, dependent in complex, multiple ways on the planet's elemental cycles (such as the carbon cycle) and on energy forms that have their eventual source in the sun's radiant energy.

While the cognitive dissonance can feel intense, students can be fascinated by apprehending their daily lives this way. They discover how, with attention absorbed by social concerns, they participate in the material processes enabling all life—their own, a blue whale's, a chigger's, a staghorn fern's... This rethinking of bodily existence—in ecological terms, this recognition that bodies (including "mine") live interwoven with the biosphere's flows of energy and matter—gives "love of nature" a conceptual content. Such informed wonder can offer an emotional counterweight to whatever upset might be spurred by the difficulties, social and ecological, that the courses expose.

With the ecology journal behind us, grasping how "nature" and "society" inter-sect comes easily, since thinking about ecological presence makes obvious the extent to which each of us satisfies basic material needs through social mediation. Noting how social mediation supplies organic need allows introduction of the idea that human life is ecosocial, emerging from social processes in interaction with natural processes (Harvey). This idea, in turn, opens the way to contrasting basic kinds of social organization (from gatherer-hunter to contemporary industrial) and then to contrasting different kinds of access to material goods within the contem-porary USA (a contrast many students become aware of when they explore ecological presence: money sustains consumption). From here, it is a short step to considering social position and identity and how we experience living that social identity, subjectively. Here, students are on familiar ground: They tap into contem-porary thinking about diversity, about race / ethnicity, gender / sexuality and economic inequality.

Exploring ecosocial being takes us quickly beyond national boundaries. It underscores how our lives participate in built environments integrated into an industrialized global order—and how this makes any accounting of an individual's consumption quite impossible. What we can and do note is how our dependence, as consumers, on such industrial infrastructure and its use of materials, including but not limited to its fuels, signals our connection to the marks that this infra-structure leaves across the planet, to damage observable on land and in oceans and atmosphere. We add this: Our life-project is to keep learning, to not take this infra-structure or the damage it causes for granted. Our project, too, is to keep our eyes on how the planet's people are affected likewise. Inequities in the built environ-ments of Kentucky's cities and the state overall provide an entry into thinking about inequities in global modernity, though, transnationally, the inequities can be extreme, both within countries and between those "developed" and "least devel-oped."

If the distribution of industrial civilization's benefits is highly uneven, so, too, are its harms. As climate changes, the poorest regions of the planet are least able to cope, just as they are least able to withstand exploitation by the North. This point opens discussion of environmental justice—and climate justice. African and south Asian countries—dealing with histories that connect current inequities to Europe's fossil-fueled expansionism—will suffer the impacts of climate change dispropor-tionately (Whiting).

With this new ecosocial self-understanding and ability to see the relevance of social identity to nature, students can analyze the course texts and begin to think critically about the different attitudes toward nature that they embody—and then transfer that thinking to questioning attitudes they notice in their communities (for example, the reduction of nature to desirable commodity on the realty market or to some pretty place that urban people need to drive to). Moreover, they can begin to interpret not only attitudes but also the geography of material opportunity, making sense of why inner-city "food deserts" exist and why community gardens have developed as a response or why, as William Cronon notes, the US wilderness preservation movement gained momentum among males of the then social elite (white and urban). Thinking about a globalized world adds further room for criticism, as doing so makes visible how much US environmental thought has been silent about global entanglements.

As mentioned above, our work in these courses is pragmatic. Aware of industrialism's benefits (for us) and the harms it inflicts on people and planet, what to do? Three sources ground a sense of agency: 1) the intelligence embodied in the texts, 2) our exploration of ecosocial being and 3) our sense of current social movements. Students do have choice as consumers, able in small ways to affect both material infrastructure and social practices, both locally and globally, purchasing local and organic food, for example, and, in relation to commodities in general, identifying which brands to avoid. Moreover, reflecting on ecological presence and daily activities throws into relief the socially induced need driving choice and gives substance to the question of what to consume and how much (Durning).

Yet, no matter how diligently we (who have that privilege) pursue best consumer choices, consumer pressure will not alone reduce harms, social and environmental. Social policy has to transform built environments, globally, making routine daily activities less damaging both to people and natural systems. So, another key dimension of choice involves political intervention, agitating for new technologies and redesigned material infrastructure along with improved social policies—again, both locally and globally. Moreover, observing how we live, how our built environment designs daily life for us, allows us to take initiative; we do not need to wait for existing movements to prompt us ("transition towns" offer example of grassroots initiatives).

In this way, I hope, the predicament we find ourselves in can be confronted—with a sense of self that connects us to biosphere-society and with an understanding that, within the built environment that mediates the nature-human relation for us, we can make good choices.

The careful reading of literature, moreover, helps us further develop this ethical imagination, by illuminating the strengths we can cultivate when faced by hazards we cannot avoid. In one course, to focus discussion of climate change, we read Helon Habila's *Oil on Water*, for how it depicts Nigeria's Delta region shattered by oil extraction and in the grip of a foreign-dominated oil economy.[1] The novel presents Rufus, a young journalist in the company of his mentor, searching through the Delta for the wife of a British oil engineer, kidnapped and held for ransom by local militants. While "about oil," the novel does not mention climate change. So why this novel?

I select it for how its critical response to the Delta's situation opens discussion of global modernity, its past, and the constraints it places on individuals' choices, constraints that make the struggle for a good future difficult.

Modernity's past: the course is on US literary representations of nature but Habila's novel fits well, reinforcing the postcolonial perspective that writers such as Eric Reece, Linda Hogan, Barry Lopez, and bell hooks have enabled in their references to American histories of colonizing. Indeed, the central metaphor of Lopez's *Rediscovery of North America*—that the dominant culture still has its citizens aboard Columbus' ships, reenacting attitudes toward "landfall" that need replacing—allows me to propose a frame for thinking that "American nature" is inextricably global, from the start, and that we may, in multiple ways, be living colonialism's continuities here in Kentucky, not least in our participation in American racism, legacy of conquest and slavery.

Moreover, the novel allows recognition of fossil fuel's role in building and maintaining Europe's global expansion—and its role in the West's historical dominance (Mitchell)—while keeping alive discussion of oil's role in our built environment (Manning supplies a useful supplement).

In this context, the novel allows a crucial point to be made regarding its representation of oil extraction's terrible damage to the Delta's people and environment. Industrial civilization requires a generalized extraction on industrial scale which has, historically, inflicted damage on regions away from and unnoticed by the metropole (Africa has suffered badly this way).

As we confront climate change, fuel substitutions must be struggled for, but fuel substitutions should not block out wider concerns. The geopolitical history of North and South, inflected in ecosocial terms, matters. Our choices, personal and political, need somehow to reflect awareness of such history. We in the US cannot simply work to protect *our* experience of civilization against climate change, an impulse related to NIMBY-ism.

Constraints on choice: The novel supplies in its narrator, Rufus, a character with a fragile hold on middle-class status in his Nigerian world. While he struggles in circumstances very different from those my students live through, still they (we) all know the pressures to maintain and improve middle-class positions. Thinking of Rufus' choices, behavioral and linguistic, allows for richer discussion of "what to do?"

Rufus' narration reveals him powerfully aware of the damage done to the world that gave him life. People emerge continuously as subject to "petro-capitalism"— including the British expats. Few characters important to the story-line are not chasing "petrodollars" (of these few some appear as heroically resisting—Chief Ibiram and his followers, the spiritual community on Irikefe Island). All appear caught in a world profoundly harmful, to morality as well as to the social and environmental fabric that a traditional fishing and agriculture economy sustained. Juxtaposed with images of abandoned villages are images of urban demoralization—and of unemployed youth drawn, for the money, into violent illegality. Rufus' depiction sets up a contrast between two kinds of economy, one familiar to my students, one not—and it is the familiar, capitalist economy that keeps people marginal and subservient, if it includes them at all.

The novel leaves us with an important question, crucial for discussion of choice. Early in his account, Rufus's mentor asks him what they seek on their perilous trip up the river. Rufus replies "the woman" and is corrected. "What we really seek is... a greater meaning" (Habila 5). Rufus, though, by account's end, has forgotten *that* quest. Why?

First, economic survival. With his awareness of the cut-throat, competitive character of a modern economy, he cannot produce the sort of incisive critique that would implicate people he needs to rely on for the petro-dollars that will cement his class position.

Second, and related, the language that Rufus *does* use: what he exposes he leaves either sensationalist (like his photographs of violent death at Irekefe—which sell) or morally ambiguous (all the "villains" have justifying back stories). But, to suggest what Rufus omits, Habila, in this postmodern novel, has him draw on three inter-texts for his account, Conrad's *Heart of Darkness* and two genres in popular fiction (crime and post-apocalyptic narrative), with the popular fiction discourses rein-forcing Conrad's vision of colonial corruption. Rufus' up-river quest, recalling Marlow's, recalls as well the questing of a private eye or journalist for the story of a specific crime, a questing that uncovers pervasive criminality reaching into the highest, capitalist class (Raymond Chandler, with his own Marlowe, offers exam-ple); and the post-apocalyptic, too, reworks Conrad, enriching the sense of local disruption with images expressing horror at industrialism's ruinous social and envi-ronmental consequences.

But Rufus does not tease out the implications in the language that he uses—nor does he struggle to find a new language adequate to what he experiences. What Rufus's narrative suggests are the socio-economic pressures that enforce conformity. Oil pollutes more than the landscape and it is safer not to be too clear about how. Rufus' linguistic and behavioral choices seem of a piece, a postmodern version of "survivor agency," his narrative revealing much but still allowing survival in a world without apparent remedy. If Rufus' response is inadequate to the situa-tion, so too are the novel's two other versions of "survivor agency"—isolating oneself in a postmodern spirituality, like the people of Irekefe, or surviving in modernity's interstices with as little participation as possible, like Chief Ibiram and his followers.

So, we note how Rufus avoids articulating a "greater meaning" and reflect on why. But then we turn the gaze on our own participation in modernity. We are not immune to such avoidance—or to avoiding confrontation with the "bad actors" that emerge when we *do* start piecing together the "greater meaning" enfolding daily activities. Even while noting difference, we can glimpse our own lives in Rufus, noting social roles, the capitalist economy and, not least, the power of language. We all use inherited language to make sense of the world we are cast into—mostly reflexively, because, mostly, it works. Yet, in these times (and here I leave the students), we surely need new language, spurred by ecosocial awareness, for our self-understanding, for our grasp of how to live in this globalized world.

Note

1   This reading of Habila's novel draws from a paper presented at the American Comparative Literature Association conference, March 2014. LeMenager and Caminero-Santangelo both note the novel's postmodern narration (but with differing evaluations) and LeMenager notes the novel's debt to crime fiction.

References

Caminero-Santangelo, Byron. "Witnessing the Nature of Violence: Resource Extraction and Political Ecologies in the Contemporary African Novel." *Postcolonial Ecologies and the*

Environmental Humanities: Postcolonial Approaches. Eds Elizabeth DeLoughrey, Jill Didur and Anthony Carrigan. New York: Oxford University Press, 2015, 226–41.

Cronon, William. "The Trouble with Wilderness; or, Getting Back to the Wrong Nature." *Uncommon Ground: Rethinking the Human Place in Nature.* Ed. William Cronon. New York: W.W. Norton, 1996 (1995), 69–90.

Dirlik, Arif. *Global Modernity: Modernity in the Age of Global Capitalism.* Boulder, CO: Paradigm, 2007.

Durning, Alan Thein. *How Much is Enough? The Consumer Society and the Future of the Earth.* New York: W.W. Norton, 1992.

Habila, Helon. *Oil on Water.* New York: W.W. Norton, 2010.

Harvey, David. *Justice, Nature and the Geography of Difference.* Cambridge, MA: Blackwell, 1996.

LeManager, Stephanie. *Living Oil: Petroleum Culture in the American Century.* Oxford: Oxford University Press, 2014.

Manning, Richard. "The Oil We Eat: Following the Food Chain Back to Iraq." *Harper's Magazine* 308.1845 February 2004: 37–45.

McNeill, John Robert. *Something New Under the Sun: An Environmental History of the Twentieth-Century World.* New York: W.W.Norton, 2000.

Mitchell, Timothy. *Carbon Democracy: Political Power in the Age of Oil.* London: Verso, 2011.

Whiting, Jonathan. *Countries Most Likely to Survive Climate Change.* 6 January 2015. Web. Accessed 14 March 2015.

25 Looking back to look ahead

Climate change and US literary history

William Gleason

How do we incorporate climate change into literature courses that are not explicitly focused on ecocriticism or the environment, but on literary and cultural history more broadly? And what if those courses are set not in the present but in the past? This essay describes the challenges and opportunities for integrating ideas about climate change into a "regular" late nineteenth-/early twentieth-century American literature survey course—into a course, in other words, that is not marked as "environmental." Doing so successfully, I believe, has two important benefits: first, it can help make climate change, broadly conceived, part of our "normal" discourse of US literary history rather than a special topic to which only ecocritics pay attention; and second, it can help show students how literary history can be brought to bear on the world in which we live today, or how we might look back in order to look ahead.

I base these remarks on a course I taught last spring, "American Literature: 1865–1930." One of four American literature period survey courses offered by my department, this course is taken predominantly by English majors and is offered every other year. It typically enrolls 50–70 students and is taught in a lecture/discussion section format. Although some courses in our department are cross-listed with the Program in Environmental Studies, including "Literature and Environment" (a course I have also taught), "American Literature: 1865–1930" carries no such cross-listing and thus does not advertise itself as an "environmental" course. But this time I experimented with a new approach to the syllabus, highlighting the ways in which the turn from the nineteenth to the twentieth century brought Americans face to face with many of the same questions that preoccupy us today, including anthropogenic climate change. In what follows I will describe how I adjusted the syllabus, the lectures, and the course assignments to bring the ecocritical concerns of the course—and the period—into relief.

My main goal in organizing the syllabus was to insert a "bright green thread" into the readings so that it would be possible for me to highlight the engagement of turn-of-the-century American literary texts with what we have come to call, in a broad sense, climate change. I did this in two ways. First, in one unit of the course I arranged a cluster of texts that have already been marked out by ecocritics for analysis. This cluster—which I placed at the beginning of the Progressive Era unit of the course, roughly at the semester's midpoint—included writing by Sarah Orne

Jewett ("A White Heron"), John Muir ("A Wind-storm in the Forests"), Jack London ("To Build a Fire"), and Charles Chesnutt ("The Goophered Grapevine").[1] Having these texts in the syllabus not only let me draw in my lectures on the rich variety of ecocritical interpretation they have engendered; it also permitted me to talk directly about the role of culture in the rise of new forms of environmental consciousness in the late nineteenth and early twentieth centuries.

Second, throughout the rest of the syllabus I sprinkled texts that could be brought productively into conversations about environmental concerns, even if those texts weren't already identified as "ecocritical." They might include, for example, depictions of extreme weather, environmental manipulation or degradation, or at the least a strong sense of place. I tried to make sure that these selections came from different regions of the US and that they represented a range of both "natural" and "human-made" environments (itself an artificial distinction). These texts included, for example, Mark Twain's *Adventures of Huckleberry Finn* (for its detailed descriptions not only of the Mississippi River but also the geographies of slavery); José Martí's essay, "Coney Island" (for its dazzling account of the garish transformation of a "barren heap of dirt" into a floodlit seaside resort); and F. Scott Fitzgerald's *The Great Gatsby* (for its haunting scenes of urban detritus and damaged dreams). None of these texts, I should note, would be out of place in a traditional "American Literature: 1865–1930" course, and that is very much the point: my goal was to populate the syllabus with works that could participate, when prodded, in fruitful discussions of the literary and cultural history of global climate change.

This also means that I prepared my twice-weekly lectures with an eye, where appropriate, toward bringing this green thread to the surface. It does not mean that every lecture was organized around climate change; that would have been a very different course. But it does mean that I frequently lingered over scenes and passages that I thought might resonate particularly well with that topic. At the same time, I did not necessarily identify these moments as being "about" climate change, particularly in the weeks before we reached the Progressive Era cluster described above. Once we reached that cluster, however, I could not only bring certain striking passages from earlier in the course back into view, offering students fresh ways to consider them in light of the ecocritical foregrounding the cluster provided; I could also refer back to the thematic concerns and formal strategies of the works within the cluster as we moved ahead into the second half of the course once the green thread had become more explicit. I should note that I was simultaneously doing this—pulling on different course threads—with several other topics regarding which I wanted the students to make connections between the texts of the past and the concerns of the present, including race relations and economic disparity. I made this rationale explicit in the introductory course lecture, encouraging students to look for these threads even in texts that didn't necessarily foreground them.

Take, for example, the case of *Huckleberry Finn*. Appearing at the end of our unit on Reconstruction, Twain's text spoke most emphatically to questions of race relations, and I spent a good deal of time in one of my lectures (as have many critics) discussing the novel's controversial ending, particularly Jim's farcical re-enslavement, in light of the failures of Reconstruction and its legacy for black civil rights struggles today. But I also made the point, in an earlier lecture, of highlighting this passage from chapter nine, a detailed description of "one of those regular summer storms":

> It would get so dark that it looked all blue-black outside, and lovely; and the rain would thrash along by so thick that the trees off a little ways looked dim and spider-webby; and here would come a blast of wind that would bend the trees down and turn up the pale under-side of the leaves; and then a perfect ripper of a gust would follow along and set the branches to tossing their arms as if they was just wild; and next, when it was just about the bluest and blackest—*fst!* it was as bright as glory, and you'd have a little glimpse of tree-tops a-plunging about away off yonder in the storm, hundreds of yards further than you could see before; dark as sin again in a second, and now you'd hear the thunder let go with an awful crash, and then go rumbling, grumbling, tumbling, down the sky towards the underside of the world, like rolling empty barrels down stairs—where it's long stairs and they bounce a good deal, you know.
>
> (Twain 56)

This long, tumbling sentence showcases Huck's distinctive voice as well as his talent not just for accretive observation but also evocative metaphor. Pausing to show students further how the stop-and-start repetition of semi-colons mimics the flow of the storm itself offered a glimpse into Twain's formal construction of Huck's narrative and even aesthetic sensibility. I didn't say anything—at the moment—about extreme weather or climate change. But a few weeks later, when we encountered the ecstatic description of Muir's "A Wind-storm in the Forests," I called Twain's passage back and reminded students that we had seen something like Muir's response before, encouraging them to ask what it would mean, in light of Muir, to reimagine Huck as a kind of naturalist, or even conservationist. One could even further ask: how might the naturalist aesthetics of Twain's text advance—or perhaps trouble—the questions of racial justice that operate so prominently on the surface of the novel?

Other texts on the syllabus, particularly in the second half of the course, helped me engage students more directly with the matter of global climate change. Upton Sinclair's *The Jungle*, for example, which closed the Progressive Era unit, was one such text. By this point, just a week or so after we had read Jewett, Muir, London, and Chesnutt, the students had been explicitly introduced to ecocritical analysis and were thus equipped to think about Sinclair's bleak description of turn-of-the-century Chicago—with its dingy streets and filthy creeks—as a conscious account of a physical environment profoundly altered by human activity. The most powerful sequence comes partway through chapter two, as Jurgis and his immigrant family journey to the infamous stockyards. At first they are mesmerized by the monotony of the landscape, the "same endless vista of ugly and dirty little wooden buildings." But soon the very environment around them begins to transform:

> A full hour before the party reached the city they had begun to note the
> perplexing changes in the atmosphere. It grew darker all the time, and upon
> the earth the grass seemed to grow less green. Every minute, as the train sped
> on, the colors of things became dingier; the fields were grown parched and
> yellow, the landscape hideous and bare.
>
> (Sinclair 31)

My students were quick to pick up here not only on the ominous de-greening of
the landscape but also on the bewilderment of the immigrants, newly arrived from
rural Lithuania. Their perplexity is amplified in the following paragraph, when
they are abruptly unloaded in front of the stockyards themselves:

> They were left standing upon the corner, staring; down a side street there were
> two rows of brick houses, and between them a vista: half a dozen chimneys,
> tall as the tallest of buildings, touching the very sky—and leaping from them
> half a dozen columns of smoke, thick, oily, and black as night. It might have
> come from the center of the world, this smoke, where the fires of the ages still
> smolder. It came as if self-impelled, driving all before it, a perpetual explosion.
> It was inexhaustible; one stared, waiting to see it stop, but still the great streams
> rolled out. They spread in vast clouds overhead, writhing, curling; then, unit-
> ing in one giant river, they streamed away down the sky, stretching a black pall
> as far as the eye could reach.
>
> (Sinclair 31–32)

The care Sinclair takes to position the reader here is critical. It's clear that Jurgis
and the others have no idea what they are seeing, where it is coming from, or why.
They stare, and we stare with them. Is it is earth's inferno, they wonder ("it might
have come from the center of the world")? Unfamiliar with the industrial West, the
newcomers postulate agentless origins ("it came as if self-impelled") rather than
human activity, naturalizing the "leaping" columns into "great streams" that writhe
and curl like snakes, intuiting a menace they can see but not explain. All too soon,
however, Jurgis and his family will come to understand what most of Sinclair's
readers (and my students) already knew: that this "inexhaustible" pall is a wholly
unnatural byproduct of industrial degradation. The rest of the novel, in an important sense, is about replacing their perplexed stares with a more clear-eyed view.

   Passages like this, I proposed to the class, suggest that writers like Sinclair were
keenly aware of the dramatic environmental changes happening around them,
"atmospheric" changes that threatened to alter the physical landscape itself. Such
writers might not use the phrase "climate change," but they nonetheless appear
powerfully attuned to—and deeply anxious about—the rate and magnitude of
anthropogenic change introduced by a fossil fuel-based industrial economy. (Jurgis's
gradual radicalization in *The Jungle* suggests the possible importance of political
intervention as well; one could imagine a future Jurgis, for example, as an activist
for environmental as well as economic justice.) On my syllabus, it was then a short
step from the smoldering stockyards to the "Valley of Ashes" that haunts Fitzgerald's

The Great Gatsby, the text with which I concluded the course a few weeks later and which helped me bring many of the central course concerns—including the matter of climate change—into focus one last time.

While the syllabus and lectures enabled me to tug on what I've called the "bright green thread," the writing assignments offered students opportunities to explore environmental questions on their own. In some cases the assignment directed them specifically toward ecocritical concerns; in others students could decide to pursue such concerns themselves. The first assignment, for example, simply asked them to select a brief passage from one of our Reconstruction texts and develop a short close reading (two to three pages). As it turns out, many students were drawn to descriptive passages of the river in Twain's text, their analyses frequently zeroing in on the tensions between the novel's "natural" and "social" spaces. The second assignment, which fell roughly at the course midpoint but before we had reached the cluster of ecocritical readings, asked students to develop a longer analysis (five to six pages) of a single text in response to one of several question prompts. These prompts included one question focused explicitly on urban space, giving interested students the chance to develop their own ideas about textual representations of the impact of human activity on the physical environment (and vice versa) in late nineteenth-century American literature. The third assignment—which came in the second half of the course, after students had already encountered the ecocritical cluster and the "climate change" passages in *The Jungle*—asked students to respond to a critical claim either made about a specific text on our syllabus or directed toward a thematic or formal concern taken up in any number of texts. For this paper (six to seven pages), we made sure to include several claims with an explicitly ecocritical focus, as well as other claims that might be productively turned toward questions of environmental representation.

The fourth assignment was a short exercise (two to three pages) that sent students into the campus art museum. It asked them to identify a work of American art produced between (roughly) 1865 and 1930 that they felt offered a "meaningful point of contact with a specific moment" from one of the texts on our syllabus, and to write an account of that contact. ("What does this juxtaposition make visible? How does the artwork speak to the particular textual moment you have in mind?") Here our goal was to encourage rigorous observation and intellectual creativity while amplifying the course's implicit proposition that literary texts are not isolated artifacts but works of culture that can engage profoundly with the pressing questions that preoccupy the eras in which they are produced— and that can continue to resonate long after. Although we did not guide the selection of art objects other than the restriction on the time period, I was pleased to receive several excellent papers that foregrounded "environmental" juxtapositions, as students were drawn, for example, to late nineteenth-century landscape paintings and portraits by such artists as Robert S. Duncanson, George Inness, and Winslow Homer, to early twentieth-century depictions of urban space by artists like Childe Hassam, as well as to the decorative arts, such as one of Frank Lloyd Wright's "Tree of Life" stained-glass windows. We also gave students a chance to explore ecocritical concerns on the final exam, where the culminating essay question included one option focused directly on the course's green thread. Although students were not required to write on this option, its presence reinforced the importance of that thread to the course's overall concerns.

In their anonymous term-end course evaluations many students reported that being asked to think about the interplay between imaginative literature and broader contextual matters enriched the materials they read. What's not quite clear is whether the students were also as engaged by the specific project of "looking back to look ahead," and thus whether they felt that the texts of the past could offer perspective on the world of today. (What we might need is a survey question that asks students to comment on the relevance of the course to their own lives.) For my part, I found that the process of redesigning this course to highlight select "threads" with contemporary resonance not only gave me a fresh awareness of the capacities of the historical survey—which I came to embrace less as a time capsule than as a laboratory of ideas—but that it also profoundly expanded my sense of the role the environmental humanities can play in the "regular" courses of a departmental curriculum. Instead of assuming (as perhaps our students assume) that only specially designated "eco" courses—such as classes on "cli-fi" or "literature and environment," for example—can provide insight into the cultural dimensions of climate change, we would serve ourselves well by bringing to the foreground—wherever we can—those texts and writers that, in different periods and genres, have engaged with the unsettling effects of environmental change. After all, the more ways we can help our students develop a surer sense of the power of cultural forms to engage "real world" challenges, the better prepared we will make them to grapple with the future of climate change, which is already as pressing a *cultural* question as it is a scientific one. Of all the ways we might hope that the environmental humanities will revolutionize our curricula, this modest revision may prove one of the most effective gestures of all.

Note

1   I organized the course into four major literary-historical units: Reconstruction, the Gilded Age, the Progressive Era, and the Roaring '20s.

References

Sinclair, Upton. *The Jungle*. New York: Penguin, 1985 (1906). Print.
Twain, Mark. *Adventures of Huckleberry Finn*. New York: Penguin, 2014 (1885). Print.

26 Atlas's shifting shoulders

Teaching climate change and classics

Darragh Martin

Carbon dioxide makes a very late appearance in "Literature Humanities," Columbia University's "Great Books" course. Emerging in the final section of Virginia Woolf's *To the Lighthouse*, one of the final texts in the year-long course, the greenhouse gas appears as part of a "great scroll of smoke" from a steamer, "curving and circling decoratively, as if the air were a fine gauze which held things and kept them softly in its mesh" (Woolf 182). Two chapters later, this smoke from the fossil fuel powered steamer is granted a capacity to persist that is denied humans and the steamer itself. As the boats and characters that Lily Briscoe is watching from the shore disappear into the horizon, the "great scroll of smoke still hung in the air and drooped like a flag mournfully in valediction" (Woolf 1188). It is tempting to read this mournful valediction as an elegy for the epic values that Great Books courses explore: in the Age of the Anthropocene, epic heroes have vanished from view while pollution lingers in the air. However, though carbon dioxide makes an attractive surprise villain (in the end, humanity's nemesis is neither god nor demon, but a hitherto invisible greenhouse gas!), it is difficult to advocate teaching this section of a book written in 1927 as a statement on anthropogenic climate change. What then is the value of thinking about this moment in the context of climate change? If greenhouse gases, anthropogenic or otherwise, remain largely invisible in the Western canon, how can teaching these classics contribute to students' understanding about climate change?

One contribution that classics can make is providing access to an environmental history that is deeper than the industrial revolution. In "'The Climate of History: Four Theses,'" Dipesh Chakrabarty argues for histories of climate change that begin earlier than Watt's steam engine or Smith's invisible hand, contending that "while there is no denying that climate change has profoundly to do with the history of capital, a critique that is only a critique of capital is not sufficient for addressing questions relating to human history once the crisis of climate change has been acknowledged and the Anthropocene has begun to loom on the horizon of our present" (Chakrabarty 212). Chakrabarty advocates putting global histories of capital into conversation with "deep history," reaching beyond the ten thousand years since the emergence of agriculture to engage with the species history of humans (212). While the texts considered here are necessarily part of a recorded history that is much shallower than the deep history that Chakrabarty plumbs, they offer students valuable insight into the classical roots of contemporary attitudes towards the environment in the West, with myth helping to provide a deeper history for the moral context of climate change.

A central contention of Great Books courses is that by examining classics, students can reflect upon their own moral lives; Columbia's Core Curriculum, which literature humanities is part of, promises that the courses will "cultivate a critical and creative intellectual capacity that students employ long after college, in the pursuit and the fulfillment of meaningful lives" (Core Curriculum). The quotation that I use to introduce my syllabus – from Margaret Atwood's *Negotiating with the Dead* – stresses the importance of reading classics in relation to contemporary issues. Imagining the contemporary writer as a traveller descending to a literary underworld stuffed with treasures of meaning, Atwood claims that "it's useless treasure unless it can be brought back into the land of the living and allowed to enter time once more – which means to enter the realm of the audience, the realm of the readers, the realm of change" (Atwood 178–9). Asking students to consider what "treasure" classical texts offer in relation to environmental attitudes can be valuable. This treasure can seem rather rusty, with toxins accumulating over millennia, so that traces of contemporary practices of environmental degradation can perhaps be found in the dominion established by humans over their surroundings in both Greco-Roman and Judeo-Christian traditions. Many of the classics I teach present the non-human world as something to be named and tamed by humans, through scythe or simile: rivers are anthropomorphized; animals are named by Adam; trees are felled to provide boats, weapons, or poetic parallels to dead heroes. Yet, to only focus on the separation between humanity and nature in classical texts clearly belies the complex ecosystems they present and my goal is to help students come to their own understanding of the relationship between humans and their surroundings in the texts we read and to use these findings as a way to reflect upon their own moral attitudes towards their environment. Drawing from my experience as an instructor of literature humanities between 2011–2015, this chapter focuses on case studies of teaching Ovid's *Metamorphoses* and *Genesis*.

Fabulous shoulders and gouged flesh: *Metamorphoses* and climate justice

> Both Poles are glowing. Once they go
> Your whole realm flies off its axle,
> Your palace is rubbish in space.
> And look at Atlas. He is in trouble.
> His shoulders are fabulous, but who can carry
> The incineration of a Universe?
>
> (Ted Hughes 41)

Earth's description of an environmental catastrophe heralded by warming poles can ring eerily true for twenty-first century students. A summary of the myth of Phaeton reveals further climate change connections. Phaeton, an Icarus with a better vehicle for air-travel, insists on cruising around the world in his father Apollo's chariot, the sun. When Phaeton proves unable to control the chariot, the Sun scorches the Earth, leading to enormous environmental degradation. A singed Earth goddess emerges to complain of her fate, prompting Jupiter to launch a thunderbolt towards Phaeton, who proves as aerodynamic as Icarus once expelled from the chariot. Unlike many of Ovid's other hubristic young heroes, Phaeton does not undergo any metamorphosis. Instead, his grieving sisters are turned into trees and the story ends with Apollo whipping the horses that Phaeton has already brutalized, "cursing and blaming *them* for his son's misfortune" (Ovid 66, original emphasis). As a parable about climate change, this myth is almost too neat: reckless use of vehicles leads to global warming and a catastrophe where marginalized characters with no responsibility for the catastrophe suffer disproportionately.

When exploring these connections in the classroom, I focus most of our discussion on Earth's appeal to Jupiter. Working in pairs, students are asked to contrast two translations of this speech, those of Hughes and David Raeburn. The ultimate aim is not to come to a definitive reading of Ovid's Earth (Raeburn's is certainly the more faithful translation) but rather to explore the subtly different representations of an anthropomorphized Earth.

In this extraordinary speech, Ovid presents an Earth who talks back to humanity, indicting not just the exceptional exploits of Phaeton, but quotidian agricultural practices, which injure Earth's body, leaving her with "flesh gouged and attacked and ground to a tilth" (Hughes 41). To further focus their discussions, I ask students to compare terms that define the interactions between Earth and humans. By prompting students to consider the difference between the "compensation" that Hughes' Earth receives with the "reward" that Raeburn's Earth claims, I hope to cultivate a fruitful discussion about the imagined obligation that each Earth has to humanity (Hughes 41; Ovid 60). I often present the argument of an excellent essay by Anjelica Neslin, one of my former students, which built on our class conversation to write a comparative close reading of these translations and indeed, partially inspired this pedagogic focus on translation. Neslin's essay argues that while Raeburn's translation presents an Earth indifferent to human activities, Hughes' Earth is more active and nurturing, and thus "merits reciprocal treatment on our part" (Neslin 3). I am particularly interested in probing the stakes of this argument with my current students, asking them whether or not they think that the image of a nurturing Earth *inspires* better environmental practices by humans.

To push this question further in our larger class discussion, I foreground the role of gender in imagining an anthropomorphized Earth, shifting the question from "what does it mean to present an anthropomorphized Earth?" to "what does it mean for Earth to be female?" At this point, I introduce some of Vandana Shiva's ideas and basic tenets of eco-feminism. Shiva helpfully describes eco-feminism as a form of resistance to patriarchal power rather than an innate connection between women and the Earth: "I have never seen eco-feminism as an issue of essentialism in biology. I do not say that women are genetically wired to be closer to nature but we are culturally wired because the patriarchal system pushed us out" (Jahanbegloo 58). This reading of kinship between women and the environment that is a result of patriarchal oppression is valuable in situating the role of a female Earth within the wider ecosystem of *Metamorphoses*. The ways in which Earth demonstrates power – nurture, eloquence – are familiar strategies for marginalized mothers within Greco-Roman literature and students are often keen to contrast the limited powers of Atlas, here a gorgeous lunk whose fabulous shoulders strain with the burden he carries, and Earth's rhetorical success. I have also found students to be attentive to the parallels between Phaeton's assault upon Earth and other instances of rape and sexual violence throughout *Metamorphoses*. This connection mobilizes readings of Earth's speech that emphasize her resistance to all forms of masculine control and violence.

The final stage of this conversation is to ask students to consider the role of gender in relation to climate change. Inviting students to explore gender more broadly in this story, I ask students to consider the role of Phaeton's sisters, who, like other women in *Metamorphoses*, find themselves transformed into trees. Although this arboreal transformation can often be ambivalent, with trees offering escape for Daphne and Myrrha, *this* metamorphosis often strikes students as profoundly unfair. After all, it is Phaeton who has caused the trouble; his sisters' only crime is to lament their brother's death. At this point, I ask students to consider how this myth functions as a parable of climate justice. As Shiva succinctly puts it "those least responsible for climate change are worst affected by it" and climate change has a disproportionate effect on poor women of color (Shiva 3). My aim here is not to present this story as a perfect account of contemporary climate change but rather to expose how it constructs certain environmental actions as masculine and feminine and to encourage students to consider the degree to which discourses around automobiles, fossil fuel extraction, and an anthropomorphized Earth are similarly gendered.

Joseph's dream–statute: *Genesis* and disaster capitalism

Unsurprisingly, *Genesis* has been used as a sort of moral alphabet, critical in helping to spell out Western environmental attitudes. Responding to the environmental movement of the 1960s, Lynn White Jr. used examples from *Genesis* to argue that Christianity had helped to inculcate an "exploitative attitude" towards the natural world and must bear "a huge burden of guilt" for contemporary environmental problems (White Jr. 1205–6). The more recent *Green Bible* offers an alternative reading focused on ecological care rather than dominion, with the Bible's messages accumulating urgency over the years so that "it is almost as if it were waiting for this moment to speak to us" (*Green Bible Gen.* 1:15). Genesis offers many opportunities to discuss environmentalism, from Eden to Noah's Ark; here, I will focus on teaching the Egyptian famine.

To frame the treatment of famine in *Genesis*, I introduce Naomi Klein's ideas about disaster capitalism. In *The Shock Doctrine: The Rise of Disaster Capitalism*, Klein argues that governments and corporations exploit disasters as opportunities, using "moments of collective trauma to engage in radical social and economic engineering" (Klein 8). Citing the examples of Sri Lanka after the 2004 tsunami

and New Orleans after 2005's Hurricane Katrina, Klein details the neoliberal
building blocks used in reconstruction: in Sri Lanka, poor families were displaced
from their beachside homes to make way for luxury condos for tourists; in post-
Katrina New Orleans, public school teachers were fired to pave the way for a
charter school system. I present Klein's ideas as a provocatively anachronistic lens,
inviting students to consider the presentation of a disaster in the following passage:

> So Joseph bought all the land of Egypt for Pharaoh; for all the Egyptians sold
> their fields, because the famine was severe upon them. The land became
> Pharaoh's; and as for the people, he made slaves of them from one end of Egypt
> to the other. Only the land of the priests he did not buy; for the priests had a
> fixed allowance from Pharaoh and lived on the allowance which Pharaoh gave
> them; therefore they did not sell their land. Then Joseph said to the people,
> "Behold, I have this day bought you and your land for Pharaoh. Now here is
> seed for you, and you shall sow the land. And at the harvests you shall give a
> fifth to Pharaoh, and four fifths shall be your own, as seed for the field and as
> food for yourselves and your households, and as food for your little ones." And
> they said, "You have saved our lives; may it please my lord, we will be slaves to
> Pharaoh." So Joseph made it a statute concerning the land of Egypt, and it
> stands to this day, that Pharaoh should have the fifth; the land of the priests
> alone did not become Pharaoh's.
>
> (*The Holy Bible* Gen. 47:21–6)

This exercise certainly has several problems, not least the dangers of mapping
Klein's critique of neoliberal policies onto a text from a much deeper stream of
history. My students are also often reluctant to read Joseph in a critical light; in
Genesis's murky moral universe, Joseph emerges as a hero, more benevolent than
manipulative. To complicate this reading, I try to push our class conversation
beyond a discussion of Joseph's character to an interpretation of the broader pattern
of post-disaster covenants between God and humans in *Genesis*. In this passage,
God is strikingly absent, with Joseph and the Pharaoh associated with the language
of salvation. Klein is helpful in illuminating the manner in which the shock of
disaster allows for exploitative policies that might not otherwise be possible, with
the statute determining the Pharaoh's right to a fifth of crop yields continuing to
the 'this day' of Genesis' composition. Typically, I ask students to consider whether
or not the tone of this passage endorses this statute and how this response to disaster relates to post-catastrophe policies across the rest of the text. Although the
Egyptians here are not presented as "wicked," language used to justify God's use of
flood and brimstone at earlier moments, it is difficult to read any narrative judgment into the presentation of this statute (*The Holy Bible* Gen. 6:5; 18:23). This
absence of moral language is also valuable in situating this episode in relation to
earlier disasters. Across the rest of *Genesis*, disasters are one of God's strategies to
curb human wickedness, an opportunity to reset; with each blank slate, fresh
legislative possibilities arise as covenants and rules are established. Within this
pattern, this episode stands out as a moment where humans use disaster to estab-

lish legislation that perpetuates exploitation rather than enshrining protection, despite the absence of moral language in the depiction of the famine. Having mapped out this pattern with students, I then steer conversation to a brief discussion of the climate change politics that Naomi Klein describes in Sri Lanka and the United States. As with my treatment of Ovid, the aim is less to provide a precise parallel between climate change and classical texts but rather to use close readings of classical texts to spark a conversation about contemporary environmental ethics.

Conclusion: outside classics

Plato's dictum from *The Apology*, "the unexamined life is not worth living" is a quotation sometimes used to introduce the literature humanities curriculum to students (Plato 41). In working on fossil fuel divestment, I have adapted this quotation to argue for ethical investing, claiming that "an unexamined endowment is not worth funding." While this tweak may be somewhat glib, it raises serious questions about teaching about climate change in a university environment. What is the point of talking about morality and climate change in a university which is invested in a fossil fuel industry that all but ensures climate chaos if left unchecked? As a member of Columbia Divest for Climate Justice, a coalition of students, faculty and alumni petitioning Columbia University to divest from fossil fuels, I helped to organize an event called Earth University on April 22 2014. Designed to return the celebration of Earth Day to its radical roots, the event called on members of the Columbia community to host one-off classes or workshops engaging with environmental justice and to bring regular classes outside in solidarity with the fossil fuel divestment movement. I facilitated a conversation on literature, humanities, and climate change, which helped me understand the importance of *where* conversations between classics and climate change are staged.

Sitting outside, participants were both in the shadow of Butler Library, with the names of classical authors etched into its stone, and resting on grass frequently rustled by student protest. Other parts of Earth University were visible to participants: a table with food; a music workshop conducted simultaneously, an enormous petition unfurled on the lawn; a climate justice art show which showed photographs of resistance to the fossil fuel companies Columbia had investments in, in countries outside of the breadth of the literature humanities syllabus, including The Democratic Republic of the Congo and Bangladesh. Part of the conversation touched upon the depiction of the environment beyond Western literature, with an excerpt from a Louise Erdrich essay framing our discussion: "Unlike the Tewa and other Native American groups who inhabited a place until it became deeply and particularly known in each detail, Western culture is based on progressive movement" (Erdrich 1). Putting classics from Western literature into dialogue with both contemporary university politics and texts from outside the Western canon is a important piece in staging conversations between climate change and classics and hopefully more spaces, in and out of classrooms, will continue this dialogue.

References

Atwood, Margaret. *Negotiating with the Dead: A Writer on Writing*. Cambridge: Cambridge University Press, 2002. Print.

"Core Curriculum." Columbia University. www.college.columbia.edu/core. Accessed 20 June 2015. Web.

Chakrabarty, Dipesh. "The Climate of History: Four Theses." *Critical Inquiry* 35 (Winter 2009): 197–222. Print.

Erdrich, Louise. "Where I Ought to Be: A Writer's Sense of Place." *The New York Times*. 28 July 1985. Print.

Hughes, Ted. *Tales from Ovid*. London: Faber and Faber, 1997. Print.

Klein, Naomi. *The Shock Doctrine: The Rise of Disaster Capitalism*. New York: Henry Holt, 2007. Print.

Plato. *Five Dialogues*. Trans: G.M.A. Grube. Cambridge: Hackett Publishing, 1981. Print.

Jahanbegloo, Ramin. *Talking Environment: Vandana Shiva in Conversation with Ramin Jahanbegloo*. Oxford: Oxford University Press, 2013. Print.

Neslin, Anjelica. "Ovid's Earth: Invested or Indifferent?" Unpublished MS. 2012. Print.

Ovid. *Metamorphoses: A New Verse Translation*. Trans: David Raeburn. London: Penguin, 2004. Print.

Shiva, Vandana. *Soil not Oil: Environmental Justice in an Age of Climate Crisis*. Cambridge, MA: South End Press, 2008. Print.

The Green Bible: New Revised Standard Version. San Francisco, Harper, 2008. Print.

The Holy Bible: Revised Standard Version. London: Meridian, 1974. Print.

Trexler, Adam. *Anthropocene Fictions: The Novel in a Time of Climate Change*. Charlottesville and London: University of Virginia Press, 2015. Print.

White, Lynn Jr. "The Historical Roots of our Ecologic Crisis." *Science 155* (1967): 1203–1207. Accessed 19 June 2015. Web.

Woolf, Virginia. *To the Lighthouse*. London: Harcourt, 1927. Print.

27 Stealing the apocalypse

Myths of resistance in contemporary popular culture

Anthony Lioi

"Care for nothing, hope for nothing," Darkseid commands (Fawkes 6). The supervillain targets John Constantine, the punk enchanter of DC Comics, but his words caught my attention because students seem to hear them in the literature and cinema of climate change. Apocalyptic environmental narratives haunt the most secular of students these days, and Constantine knows that despair is the right hand of apocalypse. In *Constantine #23*, he floats in orbit, blocking the god of destruction as his hand reaches for Earth. *Care for nothing, hope for nothing* echoes in the sky, and everyone hears it. Constantine responds with a fiction aimed at the mad god: *the world is already dead, there is no need to kill it.* Constantine's trick is fueled by his memories of joy: love, loyalty, resistance, victory. He binds these memories in a spell, the "Rings of Dolus," that sets "loose a great pulsing wave of light made of pure lies" (10). Dolus is a Greek god of trickery: it is his light that blinds Darkseid to the life of our world, making it possible to rescue souls already lost to despair. Darkseid retreats, and the world is saved. Constantine reflects: "I remember pulling some of the lost souls out of Darkseid's grasp and sending them to Earth. Laughing at the notion of picking the pockets of the apocalypse. Actually laughing" (9). There should be such laughter in all of our classrooms.

I begin here because Darkseid rules a planet, "Apokolips," that consumes other worlds as raw material.[1] He represents the corporate personhood behind extractive industries that generate despair at halting anthropogenic climate change. In his essay "Global Warming's Terrifying New Math," Bill McKibben cites the scientific consensus that we can only burn 565 gigatons more fossil fuel and stay below 2 degrees Celsius of warming (McKibben). In May 2015, however, the *Guardian* reported that Royal Dutch Shell is forecasting extractive activity consistent with a four to six degree average rise in global temperatures, risking catastrophic climate change (Macalister). The contradiction between these realities generates public despair about the end of the world. Teaching inhabitants of a petroculture to imagine the epic movement to zero carbon constitutes the affective labor of the environmental humanities at this time. We must help the public steal the apocalypse because we are subject to "an unresolvable grieving of modernity itself," a grief for the breakdown of oil-based societies as the end of civilization (LeMenager 27). Doom seems to have the facts on its side.

American environmental discourse lives by jeremiad, exhortation, and other modes of doom-saying, so it may not occur to us that trickery can also protect the world. This is where anti-heroes like Constantine—and comics as a genre—can assist us. In his analysis of environmental injustice, Rob Nixon defines "slow violence" as violence that occurs "gradually and out of sight," so environmental justice movements want to make violence visible (Nixon 2). But stealth should not be forgotten. In sites of environmental injustice—New Orleans, Alberta, the Amazon, Chernobyl, Ogoniland—we must remember Dolus, the god of guile, as the apprentice of Prometheus the fire-thief. Through this memory we enter the territory of myth. Bruce Lincoln, a historian of religion, offers three basic meanings of *myth* in the contemporary world: "a primordial truth" to be respected; a "lie" or "outmoded worldview" to be scorned; and a "pleasant diversion" or "story for children" (Lincoln ix). *Constantine* holds all three meanings together: the sacred story is also a scruffy fiction mediated by a comic book. This is myth as a coincidence of opposites, a lie that tells a truth, bundled in an illegitimate genre; this coincidence is a device for sneaking past the archons of academe. It is possible to reconstruct the narratives of apocalypse using powerful materials drawn from antiquity and transmitted by popular culture.

In its biblical form, apocalypse is a visionary genre that radicalized prophecy, a protest against injustice in Judah, Israel, and their Near Eastern neighbors. When independent Jewish states were conquered by Assyria, Babylon, Greece, and Rome, the prophets concluded that something was wrong with Creation itself: certain angelic lords, known to Gnostic traditions as *archons*, had become demonic spirits of empire.[2] Elisabeth Schüssler Fiorenza understands empire as the central rhetorical category of Revelation: Christians are "locked into a struggle with Babylon/Rome, whose imperial powers are the agents of the demonic and destructive power of Satan," which "corrupts and devastates the land" (Schüssler Fiorenza, *Revelation* 119). Apocalyptic writers despaired of a solution within history: God would have to re-create the world to overcome the archons. In *Revelation*, apocalypse unfolds as political disasters that herald cosmological destruction before the descent of the New Jerusalem. But Revelation is a comedy: its pattern consists of crisis, destruction, and salvation, not just Armageddon. Moreover, the plot is driven by divine rather than human agency. Once it begins, there is nothing humans can do to alter its course. The destruction of empire and the renewal of Creation are guaranteed by divine power. When apocalypse is secularized in the rhetoric of environmental disaster, the divine agent becomes human, removing the guarantor of the ending. Apocalyptic rhetoric preserves the sense of doom without the bulwark of God's power. Secular apocalypse never reaches the New Jerusalem, losing its way in an unending middle of destruction. Apocalypse itself nears collapse as a discourse.

Stealing apocalypse today means taking back the hope for a just end without sacrificing human agency. This kind of theft has been staged before by writers, activists, and scholars facing another world-historical force. For several centuries, feminists of the Atlantic world have confronted an intractable power of divinely-mandated domination—*kyriarchy*, "the rule of the lords." Schüssler Fiorenza coined the term "to redefine the analytic category of patriarchy in terms of multiplicative intersecting structures of domination" (Schüssler Fiorenza, *Wisdom Ways* 211). By combining the Greek words for "lord" (*kyrios*) and "ruler" (*arkhē*), kyriarchy promotes an intersectional reading of unjust political power, emphasizing the ways in which gender combines with race, class, and other social hierarchies to produce different patterns of domination under varying historical conditions. Though Schüssler Fiorenza does not include species in her analysis, it is simple enough to extend kyriarchy in an ecofeminist direction to point to the modern project of the mastery of nature.[3] Because it encourages us to investigate the complex social patterns that literature, film, and other media represent, kyriarchy is especially helpful as a category of semiotic, tropological, and narrative analysis. As anti-kyriarchal activity, stealing apocalypse constitutes a theft of canonical narratives and the elements of language itself, a venerable strategy of women writers (Ostriker). Theft is not the opposite of poiesis, but a strategy to transform patrimony without having to create *ex nihilo*. Such an immanent critique is particularly suited to the problem of teaching climate change, because we already inhabit stories of world-destruction. If Val Plumwood is right that the "ecological crisis requires a new kind of culture," we should invade the spaces where our meanings of profit and industry are stored to steal the apocalypse from petroculture (Plumwood 4). This requires what Catherine Keller calls a "counter-apocalypse," which "recognizes itself as a kind of apocalypse; but then it will try to interrupt the habit. It suggests an *apo/calypse* ["un/veiling"]: a broken, distorted text, turned to abusive purposes, only revelatory as it enters a mode of repentance for Constantinian Christendom and its colonial aftermath" (Keller 19). The formation of a counter-apocalypse to guide environmental culture is the treasure, and there is evidence that American popular culture struggles now to reveal it. Suzanne Collins's *The Hunger Games*, first a book and then a blockbuster film series, provides a popular example of a carbon counter-apocalypse.

If we understand *The Hunger Games* as a revision of Sophocles' *Antigone*, the rituals of grief appear as a blow to the archons of coal. *The Hunger Games* is the story of Katniss Everdeen, a resident of District 12 in Panem, a fascist state that arises in North America after a climate disaster that has been erased from historical memory. District 12 lies somewhere in the Appalachians, and Katniss's people are the coal miners whose suffering has been depicted in a distinguished literary lineage.[4] The people of the districts, who provide fuel, food, and raw materials for the Capitol, are kept in line by the Hunger Games, gladiatorial matches founded as a punishment for the last rebellion against the state. Katniss volunteers as a "tribute" in the games as a proxy for her younger sister, and she embodies the coal of District 12 in the spectacle that precedes the games. Before the games, her primary identity is that of sister, and her role as a new Antigone arises from sisterhood. In *Antigone, Interrupted*, Bonnie Honig argues that Antigone stands, in recent political theory, for a "mortalist humanism" that would ground the universal human subject in vulnerability and the capacity for suffering rather than reason (Honig 17). Honig objects to this on the grounds that grief is political "all the way down," so Antigone's grief for her unburied brother cannot be reduced to the essence of humanity. Antigone does not symbolize "grief for ungrievable life" but a "sororal solidarity": a praxis, not an essence (19). As an aristocrat trying to honor her brother with proper burial, Antigone must defy the will of the polis, represented by the tyrant Creon. She is not a figure of feminist democracy in the contemporary sense. She is an excellent model for Katniss, who defies President Snow by honoring a fallen tribute, Rue of District 11, during the games. The bodies of dead tributes belong to the state, but Katniss, who thinks of Rue as a younger sister, surrounds her corpse with flowers "to show the Capitol that whatever they do or force us to do there is a part of every tribute they can't own" (Collins 237). Her ritual takes place on national television, so all of Panem witnesses Katniss's defiance. This is the beginning of the revolution that topples the government of Panem, and it is rooted in the sororal solidarity of an Antigone who refuses to leave the body of Ismene to the state. In this myth of grieving against the state, there is a model of feminist solidarity rooted in burial that is also a revolt against slave labor.

Thor, God of Thunder: The Last Days of Midgard presents the opposite problem. Can a prince of Asgard, a model of warrior-masculinity, generate pathos in his confrontation with extractive industries in the present, connecting them to Norse mythology and the narratives of world-destruction endemic to Marvel Comics? What *The Hunger Games* treats as historical background, *Thor* figures as a conflict with superhuman powers, both corporate and cosmic, in the present. This series collected into a graphic novel asks a question sidestepped by the idea of the Anthropocene: what happens when humans become a planetary power, only to find other powers waiting for us? In this case, these powers include Asgardia, the home of the Norse gods, and Roxxon, an oil company whose name is a thinly-disguised version of a real corporate name. Roxxon's CEO is not merely a rapacious industrialist, he is also the vessel of an ancient Minotaur deity driven to dominate the Earth. As the story begins, Agent Roz Solomon of S.H.I.E.L.D. opposes Roxxon's drilling operations in the Southern Ocean.[5] Thor, her ally, decides to use the direct approach, destroying Roxxon facilities from orbit through lightning attacks. This strategy fails. Neither S.H.I.E.L.D nor the Avengers can destroy structural violence by physical attack. This failure necessitates a revision of the classic superhero strategy of punching your way to justice.

The second plot of *Thor* reveals that mythic self-revision is required to defend Earth. In a far future, Thor is king of Asgard and the last defender of a barren Midgard. Galactus, the devourer of worlds, arrives to extract Earth's energy. He argues that there is nothing left for Thor to defend, but Thor refuses to concede out of love for Midgard. His granddaughters stand by him: Atli, Ellisiv, and Frig, each a goddess of thunder. Their presence "flips the script" of gender relative to the first plot. Roz Solomon would be overwhelmed by Roxxon without Thor's help, but Thor could not drive away Galactus without his granddaughters. Roxxon and Galactus represent forces of extraction that cannot change of their own accord, personifications of the profit motive and amoral hunger. Thor, on the other hand, gives up his role as god-knight, traveling to a land of death to become a force of darkness while his granddaughters wield the lightning. The goddesses constitute a double-revision: the god of thunder transgendered and multiplied, and the human hero, Roz, empowered. Character revision triggers revision of plot: rather than a twilight of the gods, there is a second Creation that makes Earth verdant again. Galactus sheds Thor's blood, which falls to the ground, causing red flowers to bloom. Having been Orpheus, Thor becomes Hyacinthus and Christ, an inversion of his career as warrior. This ending suggests that defense of the world becomes possible through radical self-transformation through ecological-feminist action. The last days of Midgard deflect the Norse apocalypse in favor of a planetary restoration.

The counter-apocalypses traced here restore hope by allying human agency with transhuman creatures, generating stories of political solidarity, visionary resistance, and gender re-signification. But the ultimate success of myth depends on relating the figurative world of the text to the material world of action. A meta-narrative, in Lyotard's sense, is defined by its ability to motivate communities at the scale of the cosmopolis, the world-city. If this is the case, the introduction of these narratives into the classroom serves several purposes. Students of climate change should become aware of these narratives as a matter of contemporary culture. By doing so, they may question the ethos and efficacy of such myths and thereby refine them in their next iterations. Students should be encouraged not only to consume or critique popular myths, but also to participate in their creation and application to the work of climate justice. Critical mythologizing is difficult: there is always a risk in self-awareness, like watching your feet as you dance. But there is a greater risk in falling prey to self-delusion, to pretend that we are not part of petroculture, not part-time minions of Darkseid ourselves. If we proceed by telling better lies to save the world, we must also assess the trickster's complicity, lest we descend into an ideological prison of our own design. This complicity extends to the teaching of popular culture itself, long derided in an academy descended from the German model of academe, which understood *Massenkultur* (the culture of the masses) pejoratively, as the opposite of true cultivation, an industrial product imposed on the poor and uneducated classes who could not resist its siren song (Gans 3). Even cultural studies understands popular culture sociologically, as an instrument of hegemony, rather than as a legitimate source of meaning. The comic books, Young Adult novels, Hollywood films, and graphic novels offered here throw down a gauntlet of sorts. Though I believe that digital media and contemporary fan cultures have revealed as outdated the traditional objections to popular culture, I do not seek thereby to justify my recommendations.[6] Instead, I ask whether we have the luxury of dismissing popular works of counter-apocalypse while the glaciers melt in real time and centers of high culture flood and burn. We should admit that there are other purposes for literary pedagogy than the transmission of national canons, and that ephemera have their uses.[7] Precisely because it is profitable, popular culture reacts much faster to the concerns of its audiences.

While we wait for the climatological equivalents of *Gravity's Rainbow* and *To the Lighthouse*, we are ethically obligated to use all the instruments at our disposal to help our students combat their sense that the present hurtles uncontrollably toward catastrophe. For this reason, the environmental humanities should resist the Enlightenment myth of myth-as-mere-superstition.[8] As Kimberly Ruffin observes, we should not advocate for science to the exclusion of myth, because "myth often resides at the scientific limits of human understanding about nature, allowing people to address what they do not fully understand but still deem valuable. Myth gives us an aesthetic toolbox by which we attach ourselves to place" (Ruffin 112). Myths of resistance to petroculture give us the tools to attach ourselves to a planet that has not yet been consumed. It can provide our students with the power to locate their own place in the story of how we survived our most foolish mistakes. Like John Constantine after Darkseid, we must fall back to Earth, to the dirt of culture, to teach our way through the end of the world.

Notes

1   In 2015, the DC Comics title *Earth 2* ended its run when Apokolips consumed that version of Earth. The son of Darkseid consumed the oceans, the air, the "Green" or vegetal powers, the "Red" or animal powers, and finally the power of decay itself. Darkseid is a power of planetary destruction, and in the last decade DC Comics has emphasized his connection to climate catastrophe and ecocide. The relationship is explicit, not subtextual.

2   See "The Reality of the Rulers" in *The Gnostic Bible: Gnostic Texts of Mystical Wisdom from the Ancient and Medieval Worlds.* Edited by Willis Barnstone and Marvin Meyer, Boston: New Seeds, 2006. 168–178.

3   See Val Plumwood, *Feminism and the Mastery of Nature*, New York: Routledge, 1994.

4   The lineage includes Emile Zola's *Germinal,* Muriel Rukeyser's "The Book of the Dead," Robert Coover's *The Origin of the Brunists*, and Ann Pancake's *Strange as the Weather Has Been.*

5   S.H.I.E.L.D. is Marvel Comics' global defense force, patterned after Cold War spy organizations, but divorced from nation-states.

6   The work of media scholar Henry Jenkins demonstrates that contemporary audiences are no longer the passive consumers of mass culture so feared by mid-century critiques of film and television. See, for instance, Henry Jenkins, *Textual Poachers: Television Fans and Participatory Culture*, 2nd edition, New York: Routledge, 2012.

7   Indeed, it is impossible to tell from the perspective of the present which works will be valuable to the future. It is possible that graphic novels and Young Adult fiction will become canonical in due time, if we succeed in preserving a future in which it is possible to care about such things.

8   The critique of the myths of Enlightenment is now over half a century old. See Max Horkheimer and Theodor W. Adorno, *Dialectic of Enlightenment*, Palo Alto: Stanford UP, 2007.

References

Aaron, Jason (writer). *Thor, God of Thunder: The Last Days of Midgard.* Art by Esad Ribic. New York: Marvel, 2014.

Collins, Suzanne. *The Hunger Games.* New York: Scholastic Press, 2008.

Fawkes, Ray and Jeremy Haun, "The End." *Constantine* #23 (May 2015): DC Comics.

Gans, Herbert. *Popular Culture & High Culture: An Analysis and Evaluation of Taste.* Revised and updated edition. New York: Basic Books, 1999.

Honig, Bonnie. *Antigone, Interrupted.* New York: Cambridge Univeristy Press, 2013.

Keller, Catherine. *Apocalypse Now and Then: A Feminist Guide to the End of the World.* Boston, MA: Beacon Press, 1996.

LeMenager, Stephanie. "Petro-Melancholia: The BP Blowout and the Arts of Grief." *Qui Parle: Critical Humanities and Social Sciences* 19(2): Spring/Summer 2011, 25–56.

Lincoln, Bruce. *Theorizing Myth: Narrative, Ideology, and Scholarship.* Chicago, IL: University of Chicago Press, 1999.

Lyotard, Jean-François. *The Postmodern Condition: A Report on Knowledge.* Minneapolis, MN: University of Minnesota Press, 1984.

Macalister, Terry. "The Real Story Behind Shell's Climate Change Rhetoric." *The Guardian,* online, accessed 21 May 2015.

McKibben, Bill. "Global Warming's Terrifying New Math." *Rolling Stone,* online, accessed 21 May 2015.

Nixon, Rob. *Slow Violence and the Environmentalism of the Poor.* Cambridge, MA: Harvard University Press, 2011.

Ostriker, Alicia Suskin. *Stealing the Language: The Emergence of Women's Poetry in America.* Boston, MA: Beacon Press, 1987.

Plumwood, Val. *Environmental Culture: The Ecological Crisis of Reason.* New York: Routledge Press, 2002.

Ruffin, Kimberly. *Black on Earth: African American Ecoliterary Traditions.* Athens, GA: University of Georgia Press, 2010.

Schüssler Fiorenza, Elisabeth. *Revelation: Vision of a Just World.* Minneapolis, MN: Fortress Press, 1991.

Schüssler Fiorenza, Elisabeth. *Wisdom Ways: Introducing Feminist Biblical Interpretation.* Maryknoll, NY: Orbis Press, 2001.

28 Teaching climate change and film

Stephen Rust

In the humanities classroom, it is not uncommon for those of us who teach ideologically-motivated topics (e.g. race, class, gender, environment) to struggle to reach those students who feel we are overreaching when we conduct close readings of texts that do not overtly represent such topics. When it comes to the ideologically complex topic of climate change, I have found speculative (or science fiction) films particularly useful for reaching students because this genre lends itself readily to ideological interpretation and the ecological motifs and subtexts in such films force students to reconsider their understandings of the relationship between fictional representations of the world and the world itself. As I will discuss in this chapter, I devote considerable time to helping students understand how key concepts like landscape and setting operate in these films because I have found that for film majors and non-majors alike it is only when students have a clear understanding of the language of film studies that they are then able to progress to the more complex move of grounding their readings of texts within ideological (i.e. ecocritical) concepts. For film students and scholars, key vocabulary terms like *mise en scène*, cinematography, and editing are crucial to understanding how and why filmmakers choose to represent climate change cinematically. By grounding the teaching of speculative texts in the concrete language of landscape and setting, students can become less resistant to ecocriticism because they can more easily see and hear what might not at first be apparent in these films, particularly in fictional films.

While I do teach documentary films in my ecocinema courses, I have found that since climate change education is generally associated with documentary films I have a vested interest as a film studies instructor in helping students navigate the representations of this global sociopolitical topic in fictional narrative films. In a recent essay, Alexa Weik von Mossner demonstrates how documentary films and fictional films portraying environmental issues employ similar techniques to engage viewers but ultimately differ in the degree to which they appeal emotionally and intellectually to viewers (von Mossner 2014b, 42–45). When students make the intellectual move of recovering or discovering aspects of real-world concerns within fiction, they are doing the kind of intellectual heavy lifting central to ecocriticism. The increasing popularity of "cli-fi" (i.e. climate change fiction), a term coined by the journalist Dan Bloom in 2008 to describe the emerging genre of literature and film that overtly represents climate change, has also given me a

reason to help students learn to see and hear climate change in more covert representations as well (Holmes 2014). Proponents of cli-fi are right to assert the need
for direct representations of global warming but, as I have often seen on the Cli-
Fi Central Facebook group page, a strict adherence to the supposed "rules" of the
genre has led some to be too dismissive of films and novels that represent the issue
indirectly. Of the two films I discuss in this chapter, *Beasts of the Southern Wild*
(2012) presents a fairly overt representation of the issue while *Blade Runner* (1982)
addresses it more subtly. By spreading these films out across the term and using
setting and landscape to create a common conceptual ground between them, I am
actively working to help students analyze how climate change has infiltrated our
cultural artifacts in ways that are deeper and arguably more complex than one
might consider if looking only at climate change documentaries and cli-fi.

Part 1: Teaching ecocinema

While scholarly research on the intersections of media and environment has grown
at an accelerating pace since the late 1990s (Rust, Monani, and Cubitt 2013), pedagogical work in this area remains scant. While the number of course offerings is
also growing (see the resources page on the website EcomediaStudies.org for a list
of sample syllabi), ecocriticism has yet to fully crack into the curricula of most film
studies programs. As a graduate student and now adjunct instructor, I have faced
additional difficulties in that I have rarely had a say in the courses I have been
assigned and have thus had to "sneak" ecocriticism into the traditional curriculum
rather than being in a position in which I could help my institutions reshape their
curricula at a programmatic level. For these reasons, it is important for those of us
wishing to teach film ecocritically, not to mention to teach film and climate
change, to demonstrate our ability to navigate this new terrain from within the
field of film and media studies rather than positioning ourselves as infiltrators or
outsiders.

There are three articles in Greg Garrard's 2012 edited collection *Teaching
Ecocriticism and Green Cultural Studies* that are particularly useful starting points for
developing an eco-media pedagogy. In "Teaching Green Cultural Studies and New
Media," Anthony Lioi provides a defense for teaching visual media alongside
canonical literary texts in environmental literature courses; in "Teaching
Ecocriticism and Film" Adrian Ivahkiv explains how he introduces advanced
philosophical and eco-cultural concepts in his film courses; and in "Reading and
Writing Climate Change," Hayden Gabriel and Greg Garrard effectively apply
Steve Prachett's tri-part model for sustainability education – awareness,
analysis/evaluation, and participation – to the teaching of climate change through
combinations of literary, historical, scientific, and media texts. Andrew Hageman's
2012 Society for Cinema and Media Studies presentation, "EcoMedia and
iPadeology" motivated me to further develop my own pedagogy in relationship to
my research in this field. Yet more work remains to be done on helping students
learn to develop their discipline-specific knowledge while taking the next step of
interweaving their disciplinary skillsets with ecocritical toolkits.

Part 2: Setting and *Blade Runner*

In the first eco-film course I ever taught, a senior-level women's and gender studies course, I assumed that since students were already attuned to analyzing issues of gender, race, and power, this experience would translate quite smoothly to analyzing ecocritical issues in film texts. So in setting up our discussion of *Blade Runner*, I asked them to read Pat Brereton's ecofeminist analysis of the film in his book *Hollywood Utopia* along with Donna Haraway's seminal essay "Manifesto for Cyborgs." In class, I expected them to be able to immediately apply these philosophically dense readings to a deep understanding of *Blade Runner* as a precursor to contemporary climate change cinema. The students had to remind me that although they were seniors, they simply didn't have the necessary film studies vocabulary to articulate how the film was engaging the arguments raised by Brereton and Haraway. As a result of my thrusting too many ideas at once onto students, they ended up latching onto the most obvious connection between the film and the work of Haraway and Brereton: the cyborg. While we had a very productive discussion of the gendered nature of the cyborg figure, the students balked at my attempts to shift the conversation to the film's gendering of nature and the sophisticated figurations of global environmental change. By failing to provide students with the necessary vocabulary to connect the film's characters and plot with its *mise en scène*, I could not do justice to Brereton's astute observation that "[w]hile not explicitly revealed, it is clear that [in *Blade Runner*] ecocide has resulted from global warfare and the ultra-utilitarianism and exploitation of late capitalist production techniques" (Brereton 2005: 211). Reflecting on Steve Pratchett's awareness/analysis/participation model of sustainability education (see Gabriel and Garrard's article mentioned above for a more detailed description), in this initial effort to engage students in reading climate change (albeit through a specifically gendered perspective), I had overlooked the necessary steps in providing students with a basic awareness of film vocabulary, thus stunting their ability to analyze the film and fully participate in the discussion I struggled to direct. So several years later, when I had the chance to teach the lower-division course called "Films for the Future," I made the conscious decision tp focus more directly on setting in *Blade Runner* under the umbrella of science fiction before transitioning to a focus on landscape in *Beasts of the Southern Wild* later in the term under the umbrella of environmental film in order to help students see the differences between covert and overt approaches to representing climate change.

In this more recent course, I taught *Blade Runner* during the fourth week of our ten-week term, which meant that students had already become familiar with the key traits of the speculative fiction genre and been immersed in film-specific vocabulary like editing, cinematography, *mise en scène*, and sound design. I kept Haraway's essay on the cyborg in the syllabus because it is a foundational text of contemporary cultural studies. However, I left Brereton off so that I would not overwhelm the students as I had done previously. As a result, we were able to spend half of that class period discussing the cyborg figure by comparing Haraway's figuration of the posthuman and feminist aspects of the cyborg in relation to the film's cyborg characters. We then turned our attention to the film's setting. While I did not use Brereton directly, his work helped me craft a few leading discussion questions (e.g. "Why would the filmmakers emphasize the fact that many animals represented in the film are genetic clones or cyborgs rather than wild? What is the relationship between the film's noir setting in LA and its posthuman cyborg characters?", etc.). In general this felt like a more successful discussion than in the class described above because students were better able to explain how the film's use of camera angles, lighting, and set design contributed to the connections I was asking them to look for between the characters and the setting. Those students who were really on the ball began to help me consider that one of the reasons why the actual LA of 2015 does not (yet?) resemble the LA of 2019 portrayed in the film is that climate change manifests in ways that are less obvious on the surface than Ridley Scott could show in a narrative film that must grab the viewer's attention. One of the difficulties in public and political efforts to address climate change is the fact that its atmospheric and oceanic manifestations occur more slowly and covertly than its representation in blockbuster films like *The Day After Tomorrow* (2004).

To build on our conversations about setting in speculative fiction films like *Blade Runner*, I assigned weekly reading and film response assignments and a group project for which students design their own film concept. The group project asks students to create a tagline, a plot summary, two character sketches, a description of two settings, storyboard art for one short sequence, an analysis of how the film's plots, characters, and settings resonate with the history of science fiction cinema, and a discussion of the science on which the film is (however loosely) based. The last two items require students to cite the course materials and relevant scientific literature. The written description of the setting and the storyboard art give students two different ways to engage with the setting while the discussions of sci-fi elements and science offer opportunities to reflect further on elements of setting. While I wondered at first if college students would consider this project too "high school," most of them were very enthusiastic and spent considerable time on it. By participating in a group and then presenting their projects to the class, students also engaged in the third part of Pratchett's model in ways then went beyond our typical classroom discussions.

Part 3: From setting to landscape in *Beasts of the Southern Wild*

As an ecocritic, one of the first concepts that really sold me on the importance of our field (from the perspective of a textual scholar) was the pathetic fallacy. As an elementary, secondary, an undergraduate student, I was consistently taught to read literary (and cinematic) settings as reflections of the psychological state of the characters. One of the first lessons of ecocriticism, however, is to consider the agency and affect of settings in and of themselves. The pathetic fallacy reminds us that the nonhuman in literary and cinematic texts does not simply serve the anthropocentric motivations of the human characters. In my most recent ecocinema course, I chose the narrative film *Beasts of the Southern Wild* – which figures climate change as both a real event (occurring within and beyond the film's narrative world) and a psychological event (occurring within the mind of the film's protagonist, Hushpuppy) – because it presents an especially rich text to engage students in discussions of setting, landscape, and climate change.

To my surprise, several of my students did not initially see *Beasts of the Southern Wild* as an ecological film. For them, this seemed to be a film about race, gender, and class – not climate change. Yet while those themes are certainly central to the film, I try to show students that its heavy reliance on environmental motifs – the calving glacier, the aurochs, the hurricane, etc. – demonstrate the ways in which race, gender, and class are inextricably bound up with environment. In fact it is because the film interweaves these connections into its plot, characters, and themes that it may be the most compelling narrative feature film about climate change to date.

To prepare students for the film, I asked them to read a short article by Weik von Mossner entitled "Cinematic Landscapes," in which she uses the film to introduce readers to the basic differences between setting and landscape in cinema. Articulating the very connections between climate change and gender, race, and power that I am training my students to see, Weik von Mossner demonstrates how the film's portrayal of the Louisiana bayou and the characters that inhabit it as both setting and real-world landscape (a landscape in flux due to human industrial activities on both a local and global scale), represents "a form of what the American literary scholar Rob Nixon has called slow violence – a process of delayed environmental destruction that is dispersed across space and time" (von Mossner 2014a: 66). To help the class better understand her claims, I wrote the terms landscape and setting on the board and asked the class to list aspects of each term. Using their prior knowledge, the students quickly came up with a list of definitions for each term. I pushed them to consider how these terms apply specifically to film by lecturing briefly on film scholar Martin Lefebvre's definitions of each term. For Lefebvre, film viewers can understand representations of cinematic space "as the location for some unfolding action (setting); as a space of aesthetic contemplation and spectacle (landscape); and as a *lived* space that we possess – or would like to possess (territory)" (Lefebvre 2006: xviii). By defining these common cinematic terms as a group, I discovered that the class was able to better understand the ecocritical analysis provided by Weik von Mossner. Toward the end of the discussion, I circled us back to *Blade Runner*. While some of the students were still hesitant, most of the class agreed that our discussion of landscape helped them to see that there were deeper levels of meaning at work in *Blade Runner* as well, especially when comparing its entirely constructed landscapes with the actual built urban environments of modern cities like Los Angeles.

Conclusion: assessment

In designing assessments to give students the opportunity to demonstrate their skills in analysis and evaluation and to participate in shared learning activities, I combine an annotated keywords project with the reading response assignments discussed above and a traditional take-home final exam. Inspired by texts that combine visual and written communication strategies, such as Douglas Gayeton and Laura Howard-Gayton's multi-platform project *The Lexicon of Sustainability* (lexiconofsustainability.com), the annotated keyword project requires students to use the course readings, lectures, and their own imaginations to identify keywords important to ecocinema studies and to annotate them with written and visual analysis. The instructions are fairly straightforward:

> For this assignment you will generate a list of <u>six</u> annotated keywords that any student new to the study of ecocinema should have in their scholarly toolkit and design a visually appealing document incorporating these keywords and visual examples. Keywords are terms and phrases that academics use to represent important concepts, theories, and movements within a particular field of study. You may invent your own keywords or identify them from the course lectures and readings or other introductory texts in ecocriticism. Use the bibliography on the "Resources" page at EcomediaStudies.com to assist your research. You will present this project to the class.

For each annotation you will provide:

- A concise but complete definition of approximately 20 words;
- A 150-word description providing important background information about the term and/or how the term applies to the study of film/media texts;
- Two-three visual examples that represent the keyword;
- A 150-word analysis of how/why the visual images are useful for making sense of how the term applies to the study of film/media texts;
- Citations for the source of the term and two-three sources for further information.

The first time I assigned this project in my "Ecocinema" course, the results were mixed. While the description and analysis sections were strong, many of the projects were not visually appealing and failed to fully integrate the visual and written components. However, a few students created outstanding projects and agreed to let me share their work with future classes (examples of their work can be viewed at www.asle.org/features/key-words-ecocinema-studies). I have also transitioned from making this an individual project to a group project to build in more participation. As a result of these changes, the projects have become more dynamic each time I require this assignment. Since I do not assign specific keywords to the students, only a handful of students have focused specifically on terms like "cli-fi" and "setting versus landscape" but nearly all of the students include keywords that reference global environmental change in some way. I also assign a take-home final rather than a research paper in my ecocinema courses because I want students to engage with the specific concepts that we have spent considerable time discussing during the term. In this way, these exams also provide me with more direct feedback on my teaching than would research papers for which students choose their own topics. Building on the discussion of setting and landscape discussed in this chapter, in my most recent course, I asked the following question for students to answer in a 1200–1500 word essay:

> Understanding the differences between landscape and setting is crucial to our interpretation of both wildlife cinema and narrative feature films. Choose three of the following films – *Beasts of the Southern Wild, Even the Rain, March of the Penguins,* and *Grizzly Man* – and compare the ways they illustrate the tension between landscape and setting. How does this tension find its way into the themes and aesthetic techniques of each film? How do the course readings and our discussions enhance your understanding of landscape and setting? Use the essays assigned with each film to inform your response.

In general, my students impressed me with their ability to apply the ideas that we had discussed in class and read in Weik von Mossner's article. They built on our early discussions of terms like camera angles and shot distance to articulate how the filmmakers frame landscapes and how the settings of these films worked not only as settings for the action of the films but emerged as landscapes of real places impacted by global environmental change and the human and nonhuman agency of the subjects represented (and even absent from) each film. Of course, not every student "got" the broader connection to climate change that I was hoping for them to make in their essays, but that gives me something to work on the next time I have the opportunity to teach such a class. The next time around, for example, I plan to change the wording of the final exam question on landscape and setting to more directly reflect the comparison between *Blade Runner* and *Beasts of the Southern Wild* that I have discussed in this chapter. My particular method of teaching climate change and film is only one among many others, which instructors around the world are beginning to explore. It is my hope that the volume you are currently reading will inspire a much wider conversation about these topics.

References

Brereton, Pat. 2005. *Hollywood Utopia: Ecology in Contemporary American Cinema*. Bristol, UK and Portland, OR: Intellect Books.

Gabriel, Hayden and Greg Garrard. 2012. "Reading and Writing Climate Change." *Teaching Ecocriticism and Green Cultural Studies*. Ed. Greg Garrard. London: Palgrave Macmillan, 117–129.

Hageman, Andrew. 2012. "EcoMedia and iPadeology." Conference Presentation. Society for Cinema and Media Studies Conference, Boston.

Holmes, David. 2014. "'Cli-fi': Could a Literary Genre Help Save the Planet?" *The Conversation.* Blog, 20 February 2015, accessed 25 May, 2015. http://theconversation.com/cli-fi-could-a-literary-genre-help-save-the-planet-23478

Ivakhiv, Adrian. 2012. "Teaching Ecocriticism and Cinema." *Teaching Ecocriticism and Green Cultural Studies*. Ed. Greg Garrard. London: Palgrave Macmillan, 144–155.

Lefebvre, Martin. 2006. "Introduction." *Landscape and Film*. Ed. Martin Lefebvre. American Film Institute and Routledge Press, xi–xxx.

Lioi, Anthony. 2012. "Teaching Green Cultural Studies and New Media." *Teaching*

Ecocriticism and Green Cultural Studies. Ed. Greg Garrard. London: Palgrave Macmillan, 133–143.

Rust, Stephen, Salma Monani, and Sean Cubitt, Eds. 2013. *Ecocinema Theory and Practice.* New York: American Film Institute and Routledge.

Weik von Mossner, Alexa. 2014a. "Cinematic Landscapes." *TOPOS: The International Review of Landscape and Architecture and Urban Design* 88, 64–67.

Weik von Mossner, Alexa. 2014b. "Emotions of Consequence? Viewing Eco-documentaries from a Cognitive Perspective." *Moving Environments: Affect, Emotion, Ecology, and Film.* Waterloo, ON: Wilfrid Laurier University Press, 41–60.

Part IV

Archives and contexts for teaching and learning climate change

29 The persuasive force of the right supplementary materials for climate change humanities courses

Patrick D. Murphy

Climate change fiction is, after all, "fiction," whether textual or visual, no matter how realistic or science-based it may be. Also, a considerable amount of such novels are set in the future and marketed as the genre of science fiction. As a result, skeptical or previously uninformed students might dismiss the informational aspects and even the themes of mitigation and adaptation of such novels, even when they are based on existing data and already occurring practices. Climate change films tend to build in a justification for skepticism and denial because too often they rely on exaggerated paces of change and catastrophic events that are not scientifically justifiable. Supplementary materials can play a significant persuasive role in climate change humanities courses. The first and more important task for such texts consists of combatting complete denialism and unjustified skepticism about the scientific consensus on anthropogenic climate change (ACC). The second task, and one more appropriate for some courses than others, would be to provide recommendations for action and to consider the merits of competing narratives with an emphasis on mitigation or adaptation. But what materials will be most effective to achieve such goals, and how should they be made available to students?

In this chapter, I will present and discuss a variety of supplementary materials—from religious organizational statements, both of the churches themselves and groups within various denominations, to Defense Department and other military analyses of the security threats posed by ACC, to reinsurance websites, such as that of SwissRe, that analyze the economic implications of ACC, to popular science books and websites. In particular, I will encourage teachers to avoid assigning hot-button—easily dismissed as liberal propaganda—sources, such as *An Inconvenient Truth* or publications of left-leaning presses, such as New Society Publishers, and instead to look at materials that approach the issue of climate change from diverse perspectives and political orientations. Al Gore is unlikely to persuade many veterans to take the literature assigned in any course seriously, but the retired admirals and generals who signed off on the Center for Naval Analyses (CNA) report, *National Security and the Accelerating Risks of Climate Change*, are much more likely to do so. Similarly, anyone familiar with religious organizations would expect the Unitarians to be concerned about climate change, but may be shocked to read that a group of leaders in the Southern Baptist Church issued a statement that human beings bear responsibility for it and need to take mitigating action out of an obligation to be good stewards of creation.

In some ways academic supplementary materials may prove the least useful and effective source of information and opinion for many students. Scientific articles are often too technical and filled with formulas, numbers, charts, and graphs that make humanities students' eyes glaze over. The rhetorical structure of such essays also works against facile assimilation, since it often relies on the hedging subjunctive language common to scientific theories, extrapolations, and tentative conclusions. Popular science books and essays, many written by academic scientists or science writers for the general public, often work better because they tend to have a strong narrative structure and nontechnical language, yet are often quite well documented. That aspect of nontechnical languages is crucial because, after all, the general public continues to misunderstand the scientific definitions of such terms as "theory" and "correlation," not to mention having difficulty comprehending scientific syntactic structures. If one wishes to use these, however, summary booklets and panel papers are available. For instance, The American Association for the Advancement of Science has a twenty-eight page pamphlet uploaded in 2014 as a PDF written in clear, accessible English: *What We Know: The Reality, Risks and Response to Climate Change.* There is also *Climate Change: Evidence and Causes,* produced by the Royal Society and the US National Academy of Sciences and just over thirty pages in length, published in early 2014.

Religion is often presumed to be the belief system farthest from science because it relies on matters of faith, doctrine, and sacred texts. Yet, given the high percentage of people who define themselves as religious to some extent and the large number of adherents to the world's major religions, religious orientations toward climate change should not be ignored. Students, however, are unlikely to realize just how many religious organizations have taken positions accepting the basic science of ACC and calling for action to mitigate its effects and to adapt to its most immediate threats. The range of such positions is also significant, from approaches that emphasize the plight of the poor to a movement labeled "creation care," to the unanimity between the Roman Catholic Pope and the Greek Orthodox Patriarch. The Greek Orthodox Bishops of America took their position back in 2007, as evidenced by the "SCOBA Statement on Global Climate Change: A Moral and Spiritual Challenge." Recently the Roman Catholic Church has become quite outspoken on the subject as witnessed by the 2014 Cafod Lecture. As *The Tablet* report of that talk states, "Climate change and poverty were the focus of the 2014 lecture. ... The speaker was Argentinian Bishop Marcelo Sánchez Sorondo, who is Chancellor of the Pontifical Academy of Sciences and Social Sciences and a close friend of Pope Francis."

One can start with the forum on Religion and Ecology at Yale, the resources of the Religion and Nature program at the University of Florida, or the Interfaith Power and Light network, which claims the affiliation of 15,000 churches and synagogues nationwide. The Yale site provides statements on climate change from more than fourteen world religions. Not only have some Southern Baptists issued a call for climate stewardship, but also there has developed a movement among

Christian evangelicals. The Reverend Richard Cizik, President of the New Evangelical Partnership for the Common Good, has a pithy interview available on the web and students can see the same perspective at the National Religious Coalition on Creation Care.

Other sources include organizations outside of North America, such as the Australian Religious Response to Climate Change or the Earth Charter Religion and Spirituality Task Force. Articles are too numerous to mention, but Katharine Hayhoe, who identifies herself as an evangelical climate scientist, has a cogent presentation available on YouTube. A valuable survey of religious beliefs and attitudes about climate change has been conducted by the Public Religion Research Institute and the American Academy of Religion. A summary and the full report are available on the web at publicreligion.org. There are also organizations within religions that are lacking a position on the subject that try to move their religious leadership to establish a position or to promote work among the religion's members even without hierarchical authorization, such as the Mormon Environmental Stewardship Alliance (www.mesastewardship.org). While the Southern Baptist Convention of 2007 (www.sbc.net/resolutions/1171) took a wait-and-see approach to climate change expressing more doubts about the effectiveness of mitigation strategies than the warming of the planet in the approved resolution, a group within that religion, including prominent past presidents, responded the following year by endorsing the concept of creation care and promoting a Southern Baptist Environment and Climate Initiative (see cnn.com/2008/US/03/10/baptist.climate).

As mentioned earlier, the CNA provides two reports that have been signed by a host of retired generals and admirals addressing the dangers that climate change poses to national security. A similar organization outside the U.S. is the Royal United Services Institute, which develops papers on climate change and security for the United Kingdom and other governments around the world. These papers are bolstered by regular reports by the U.S. Department of Defense. Most recent of these are the *Quadrennial Defense Review 2014*, distributed in March of that year, and the *2014 Climate Change Adaptation Roadmap*. The Center for Climate and Security regularly provides on its website updates on administrative positions and government and nongovernmental organization reports, such as their review of *IOM Outlook on Migration, Environment, and Climate Change*, published by the International Organization for Migration, which was released in late 2014.

From a financial perspective, which many instructors may resist deploying because it puts a price tag on conservation and environmental protection, two supplementary sources stand out: economic analyses of the relative costs of mitigation versus adaptation and the perspective of the reinsurance industry on the short-term as well as long-term outlook for anthropogenically induced disasters. SwissRe has probably the most detailed website for this purpose. There are also corporations within the energy sector that take a clear stand on the need for action to mitigate climate change, including support for legislation. Duke Energy is a case in point with a section of their corporate website devoted to "Global Climate Change" (www.duke-energy.com/environment/climate-change.asp), or Shell Oil

Corporation explaining their investment in gas-to-liquids fuel production in the Emirates in terms of reducing carbon emissions (see www.shell.com/global/future-energy/natural-gas/gtl.html). The inconsistencies in Shell's approach to environmental self-regulation versus legislatively mandated regulation from country to country where they operate, such as their destructive behavior in Nigeria, might cause someone justifiably to cast a cynical eye on the company's professed commitment to green stewardship. The mere fact, nevertheless, that an increasing number of oil companies are addressing climate change as a reality requiring some kind of response facilitates the argument for scientific consensus about the phenomenal existence of ACC. The BP Corporation—notorious for the Gulf Oil disaster in the U.S., has a webpage on climate change, which has the headline, "BP believes that climate change is an important long-term issue that justifies global action." Such oil corporation greenwashing, as most would deem it, offers the opportunity in conjunction with the reading of certain primary works to question whether or not any version of business-as-usual could be capable of enabling an adequate response to the effects of ACC that have already been set in motion. In contrast to the arguments of the oil industry, there is the alternative picture presented by Oil Change International at their website, thepriceofoil.org.

For students willing to read a little more deeply, it might be worthwhile to excerpt some passages from the International Energy Agency *World Energy Investment Outlook* for 2014, where the authors discuss the need and challenges for transitioning to "a low-carbon energy system" (40). One might like to pair those excerpts with some taken from *Pathways to Deep Decarbonization, an Interim Report*, published by the Sustainable Development Solutions Network and the Institute for Sustainable Development and International Relations in July of 2014. Likewise, one of the global investment resources that has contributed to climate change through financing mega-dam projects and production of millions of tons of concrete, the World Bank, has published the rather polemical hundred-page book, *Turn Down the Heat: Why a 4°C Warmer World Must Be Avoided*, which they released back in November of 2012. They also sponsored the Policy Research Working Paper authored by Stéphane Hallegatte et al., *Investment Decision Making Under Deep Uncertainty: Application to Climate Change*, published two months earlier. Students might want to consider why the World Bank doesn't seem to implement the conclusions of the studies it funds on climate change, as well as other subjects of global concern, such as mega-dam construction.

Political parties do not have a lock on climate change platforms, although their positions on enacting legislation are easy enough to identify. The majority of efforts in Congress to block climate change mitigation legislation are led by Republicans aided by Libertarians. Democrats from coal producing states also tend to oppose such legislation as a carbon tax because of its impact on that industry. President Obama has a clear stand on climate change and hence the Democratic Party is associated with the scientific consensus. So, political supplementary materials that may most be needed for students would be ones by prominent Republicans because that is a much more surprising source than the office of a liberal Democrat. The first person to which to turn in this regard might be Henry

M. Paulson, Jr., a member of President George W. Bush's Cabinet. His editorial in *The New York Times* on June 21, 2014, "The Coming Climate Crash: Lessons for Climate Change in the 2008 Recession," is brief and to the point. Today he is chairman of The Paulson Institute at the University of Chicago, and that institute's website identifies climate change and air quality, conservation, and sustainable urbanization as three of its four programs. Former Republican mayor of New York City, Michael Bloomberg, is also a fervent proponent of both mitigation and adaptation, and now a UN special envoy for cities and climate change. Students can learn about him and his initiatives at MichaelBloomberg.com. Paulson, Bloomberg, and Thomas F. Steyer co-chair the Risky Business Project, which published *RISKY BUSINESS: The Economic Risks of Climate Change in the United States* in June of 2014. And, of course, one can turn to the website simply labeled Climate Conservative to see that not all approaches to addressing anthropogenic climate change can necessarily be defined as liberal ones.

There are also various risk assessment and adaptation reports issued by various organizations focusing on specific locations or infrastructure concerns. These are usually written for a broad audience of policy makers and non-specialist organizations and hence generally quite readable. For instance, if one has students read Kim Stanley Robinson's *Forty Signs of Rain*, which concludes with the flooding of Washington, DC, that instructor might want them to read also *Washington, D.C. and the Surging Sea: A Vulnerability Assessment with Projections for Sea Level Rise and Coastal Flood Risk*, produced by Climate Central in September of 2014. Or, for students who may have read Robinson's *2312*, with its depiction of a flooded, sea-walled, and still inhabited Manhattan, there is *Plan NYC Progress Report 2014*.

Full-length popular science books emphasizing either alternative economic models or the need to choose mitigation over adaptation provide another resource. Some of these will undoubtedly be selected as primary texts in some courses, such as Bill McKibben's *Eaarth*. But for courses that focus on fiction, video, and film, they may serve as supplementary materials. It may be that excerpts from these would work best in some courses, placing full-length books on reserve for others, or placing one text on the required reading list as background for the study examples. Some, such as Heidi Cullen's *The Weather of the Future* and Gwynne Dyer's *Climate Wars: The Fight for Survival as the World Overheats*, focus on the likely dire consequences of inaction. Other books, such as Paul Gilding's *The Great Disruption: Why the Climate Crisis Will Bring On the End of Shopping and the Birth of a New World*, devote considerable attention to a way forward through both mitigation and adaptation. The most scathing work on the impossibility of the current economic order to solve the problems it has created would be Adrian Parr's *The Wrath of Capital: Neoliberalism and Climate Change Politics*. Two books by scientists that are surprisingly accessible because of their strong narrative structure are David Archer's *The Long Thaw* and Tyler Volk's *CO$_2$ Rising*. Volk's book is particularly engaging because it creates characters out of different CO_2 molecules and narrates their life cycles and travels.

It seems to me that making a pile of climate change supplementary materials that most clearly align with an instructor's own position on the subject is the least effective way to approach persuasion. Works that merely reinforce the primary texts from the same ideological perspective may also result in a preaching-to-the-choir effect, deepening the beliefs of the students who enrolled in the course already concerned and convinced, while leaving the skeptical or the uninformed outside the sanctuary. That is why I have emphasized here materials from businesses, conservatives, military establishments, and faith-based organizations, since none of these are the sites from which people most immediately expect support for the scientific consensus on ACC or proposals for mitigation or adaptation. See also my books for the titles of other works, particularly full-length popular science studies, *Ecocritical Explorations* and *Transversal Ecocritical Praxis.*

References

2014 Cafod lecture: Argentinian bishop highlights urgency of tackling climate change. *The Tablet: The International Catholic News Weekly.* Web, 12 November 2014, accessed 5 December 2014.

American Association for the Advancement of Science. *What We Know: The Reality, Risks and Response to Climate Change.* Web PDF, 2014, accessed 2 January 2015.

Bloomberg, Michael R., Henry M. Paulson, Jr., and Thomas F. Steyer. *RISKY BUSINESS: The Economic Risks of Climate Change in the United States.* Web, June 2014, accessed 1 July 2014.

CNA Military Advisory Board. *National Security and the Threat of Climate Change.* Web, April 2007, accessed 21 June 2013.

CNA Military Advisory Board. *National Security and the Accelerating Risks of Climate Change.* Web, May 2014, accessed 1 June 2014.

Climate Central. *Washington, D.C. and the Surging Sea: A Vulnerability Assessment with Projections for Sea Level Rise and Coastal Flood Risk.* Web, September 2014, accessed 1 October 2014.

Cullen, Heidi. *The Weather of the Future: Heat Waves, Extreme Storms, and Other Scenes from a Climate-Changed Planet.* New York: Harper, 2010.

Department of Defense. *Climate Change Adaptation Roadmap.* Web, 13 October 2014, accessed 15 October 2014.

Department of Defense. *Quadrennial Defense Review 2014.* Web, 4 March 2014, accessed 9 March 2014.

Dyer, Gwynne. *Climate Wars: The fight for Survival as the World Overheats.* 2008. Oxford: OneWorld, 2011.

Gilding, Paul. *The Great Disruption: Why the Climate Crisis Will Bring On the End of Shopping and the Birth of a New World.* New York: Bloomsbury, 2011.

Hallegatte, Stéphane et al., *Investment Decision Making Under Deep Uncertainty: Application to Climate Change.* The World Bank sustainable Development Network. Web, September 2012, accessed 15 February 2014.

Hayhoe, Katherine. "Secret: Climate Change Evangelist." Nova's Secret Life of Scientists and Engineers series. YouTube, 2 May 2014, accessed 15 January 2015.

International Energy Agency. *World Energy Investment Outlook.* Web, 19 May 2014, accessed 20 May 2014.

International organization for Migration. *IOM Outlook on Migration, Environment, and Climate Change.* Web, 2014, accessed 27 January 2015.

Parr, Adrian. *The Wrath of Capital: Neoliberalism and Climate Change Politics*. New York: Columbia University Press, 2013.

Paulson, Henry M., Jr. "The Coming Climate Crash: Lessons for Climate Change in the 2008 Recession." *New York Times* 21 June 2014. Web, accessed 22 June 2014.

Plan NYC Progress Report 2014. New York: Mayor's Office of Long-Term Planning and Sustainability, 2014. Web, accessed 1 November 2014.

Public Religion Research Institute. Survey: "Believers, Sympathizers, and Skeptics: Why Americans are Conflicted about climate Change, Environmental Policy, and Science." Publicreligion.org. Web, 21 November 2014, accessed 15 January 2015.

Robinson, Kim Stanley. *2312*. New York: Orbit, 2012.

Robinson, Kim Stanley. *Forty Signs of Rain*. New York: Bantam, 2004.

Royal Society and US National Academy of Sciences. *Climate Change: Evidence and Causes*. Web, 27 February 2014, accessed 15 March 2014.

"SCOBA Statement on Global Climate Change: A Spiritual and Moral Challenge." Web, 25 May 2007, accessed 26 January 2015.

Southern Baptist Environment & Climate Initiative. "A Southern Baptist Declaration on the Environment and Climate Change." Web, n.d., accessed 14 January 2014.

Sustainable Development Solutions Network and the Institute for Sustainable Development and International Relations. *Pathways to Deep Decarbonization, an Interim Report*. Web, July 2014, accessed 8 August 2014.

World Bank. *Turn Down the Heat: Why a 4°C Warmer World Must Be Avoided*. Web, November 2012, accessed 1 December 2013.

30 Vanishing sounds

Thoreau and the sixth extinction

Wai Chee Dimock

My essay is a meditation on Thoreau in the context of climate change, the loss of biodiversity in the nineteenth century no less than in our own time. In thinking about the material that can be brought together for teaching purposes, I would like to begin at some distance from Thoreau, with a recent work by an eco-musicologist, Bernie Krause's *The Great Animal Orchestra* (2012). Krause is something of a cult figure to music fans: the last guitarist recruited by the Weavers to replace Pete Seeger, he teamed up a bit later, with Paul Beaver, to form the legendary synthesizer team, Beaver and Krause, providing electronic music for films such as *Rosemary's Baby* and *Apocalypse Now*. For the past forty years, though, his work has been primarily in bio-acoustics, focusing especially on the sound ecology of endangered habitats. Wild Sanctuary, his natural soundscape collection, now has over 4000 hours of recordings of over 15,000 species.[1]

Krause tells us that animals consistently outperform us when it comes to sound: they both hear and vocalize better than we do, and can also do more with sound than we can. One example he gives is the sound camouflage perfected by the spadefoot toad. This amphibian species, like many animals in the wild, does not vocalize separately, but does so as a group, "a synchronous chorus assuring a seamless protective acoustic texture" (Krause 2012: 178). Through this sound aggregation, they prevent predators such as foxes, coyotes, and owls from pouncing on one particular victim, since no single individual stands out.

Unfortunately, the complexity of this camouflage is such that any human interference, any artificially generated noise that falls outside the usual sound spectrum within this particular environment, is likely to disrupt it and undermine its working. Krause starts with their marvelous sound engineering, but by the time he is done it is no longer a happy story. When a military jet flew "low over the terrain nearly four miles west of the site," the sound camouflage was thrown off-kilter. It took the toads between thirty to forty-five minutes to rebuild it. Krause reports: "My wife and I watched from our nearby campsite as a pair of coyotes and a great horned owl swept in to pick off a few toads during their attempts to reestablish vocal synchronicity" (180–1).

The death of a few spadefoot toads is probably no major disaster, but the larger narrative that comes out of *The Great Animal Orchestra* is disturbing in more ways than one, with an intimated ending that probably none of us would want to hear in full. Something much larger, more systemic, and more destructive than military jets is preying on these sound ecologies, upsetting their delicate balance, making them less and less able to function as they used to. Almost half of the habitats in which Krause made his recordings have now been seriously compromised or destroyed. His audio archives are all that is left of those once sound-rich environments.

Bernie Krause is writing at a point in time when climate change is a reality, tangible in the losses that are sustained by the planet as a whole. Turning from Krause to Thoreau is not only a journey back in time; it is also a surveying of the damage done, the better to take stock of where we are now. To devise a credible way to go forward, our increasingly fragile environment needs to be seen against one that was still relatively robust, beginning to suffer to some extent, but also holding the promise of different developmental pathways, different ways of coming to terms with systemic changes to the planet.

There is no better example of these cross-currents than the boisterous frog chorus in chapter four of *Walden*:

> In the mean while all the shore rang with the trump of bullfrogs, the sturdy spirits of ancient wine-bibbers and wassailers, still unrepentant, trying to sing a catch in their Stygian lake,– if the Walden nymphs will pardon the comparison, for though there are almost no weeds, there are frogs there, – who would fain keep up the hilarious rules of their old festive tables, though their voices have waxed hoarse and solemnly grave, mocking at mirth, and the wine has lost its flavor, and become only liquor to distend their paunches, and sweet intoxication never comes to drown the memory of the past, but mere saturation and waterloggedness and distention. The most aldermanic ... quaffs a deep draught of the once scorned water, and passes round the cup with the ejaculation *tr-r-r-oonk, tr-r-r-oonk, tr-r-r-oonk!* And straightway comes over the water from some distant cove the same password repeated.
>
> (Thoreau 1971: 126)

"Repeated": this is the keyword here, perhaps the single most important word in this nineteenth-century report on the natural environment. Nothing spectacular, just the sense that there will be more, that whatever is happening now will happen again, a dilation of time that makes the future an endless iteration of the present. All of this is suggested by the croaking of the bullfrog, so natural to that particular habitat and so eternal in its recurrence that it is unimaginable there would ever be a time when that sound would not be there. And because this is Concord, Massachusetts, there are none of the predators mentioned by Krause, no coyotes or big horned owls, and no military jets. The croaking of the frog, at least as Thoreau depicts it here, can luxuriate in the present precisely because the future is not yet a cause for concern.

Walden, it is often said, is a timeless text. It is true here in one sense, in that time seems to stand still for the bullfrog, an animal that has always been there and will always be there, free from the pressures of an end date. We know, of course, that

Walden was written in the nineteenth century, but that chronological fact is not always the first thing that comes to mind for modern readers. This particular moment, though, with its sound-rich present taking for granted an unaltered future flowing from itself, does seem more "nineteenth century" than some other moments. It is a luxury to be able to feel that way, increasingly hard to sustain in the centuries to come.

Among the casualties wrought by the escalating changes to the climate since the industrial revolution, a habitable and bountiful future must rank high. The now-familiar term "Anthropocene," coined in the 1980s by ecologist Eugene F. Stoermer and atmospheric chemist Paul Crutzen, names human behavior as the chief cause for the drastically altered conditions for life on the planet, so abrupt and unprecedented as to constitute a new geological epoch. A "sixth extinction" seems well underway, the elimination of a "significant proportion of the world's biota in a geologically insignificant amount of time" (Hallam and Wignall 1971: 1). Such massive die-offs had happened only five times in the 3.6 billion-year history of life on the planet. Each time, it took millions of years for life to recover, starting from scratch with single-celled organisms such as bacteria and protozoans (see Leakey and Lewin 1996; Glavin 2007; Kolbert 2009; Marsh 2012). The sixth extinction – if that is indeed what we are headed for – promises to be even more cataclysmic than the previous five. The work of just one species, it has already resulted in 140,000 species disappearing each year, and half the life-forms on earth slated for extinction by 2100, according to E. O. Wilson (2002). In the ten years that followed, Wilson's predictions have been more than borne out. Elizabeth Kolbert now reports that "it is estimated that one-third of all reef-building corals, a third of all fresh-water mollusks, a third of sharks and rays, a quarter of all mammals, a fifth of all reptiles, and a sixth of all birds are headed toward oblivion" (Kolbert 2014: 17–8).

This is not a future Thoreau could have imagined. And yet, there is already something odd about his portrait of the frog, a noticeably archaic diction that suggests this species could be something of a relic – having a venerable past, but perhaps no longer securely inhabiting the present. The frogs are "wine-bibbers and wassailers," "quaff[ing] a deep draught" from the pond, accompanied by nymphs and the river Styx. These overdone classical allusions, rather than drawing us into the worlds of Homer and Ovid, keep us instead at arm's length, highlighting our own necessary modernity and necessary separation from the ancient world. It is in such moments, when time becomes segmented and disjointed, that the eternal present of *Walden* ceases to be eternal, and becomes more like a finite end game, points of no return, in which past and future are no longer one, in which the terminus is no longer a faithful replica of the starting point. It is worth noting in this context that, though still loudly croaking, the bullfrogs are in fact no longer what they used to be. Try as they might to "keep up the hilarious rules of their old festive tables," the wine has "lost its flavor," and their own voices have grown "hoarse and solemnly grave." Theirs is a narrative of progressive attrition, in which losses will occur as a matter of course, opening up gaps through which the growing distance between moderns and ancients would take on a significance also hitherto unimagined.

And, if this is true of Thoreau's relation to Homer and Ovid, it is even more true of his relation to the ancient authors of animal fables, a genre now almost exclusively associated with Aesop (620–560 BCE), but, for an avid reader like Thoreau, also trailing other, equally venerable traditions. These fables seemed to belong to the mythic past of humankind, passed down from times immemorial and flourishing in a variety of languages and cultures. As Laura Gibbs points out, "The animal characters of Aesop's fables bear a sometimes uncanny resemblance to those in the ancient folktales of India collected both in the Hindu storybook called the *Panchatantra*"(Gibbs 2002: xix). Aesop's fables were first translated into English and published by William Caxton in 1484; the Sanskrit stories were translated into English in 1775, as *Fables of Pilpay*. In an undated entry in his commonplace book (what he kept before he started his journals), Thoreau pays tribute to both these Greek and Sanskrit antecedents, but then proceeds to tell an animal story of his own, pulling away from both:

> Yesterday I skated after a fox over the ice. Occasionally he sat on his haunches and barked at me like a young wolf... All brutes seem to have a genius for mystery, an Oriental aptitude for symbols and the language of signs; and this is the origin of Pilpay and Aesop.... While I skated directly after him, he cantered at the top of his speed; but when I stood still, though his fear was not abated, some strange but inflexible law of his nature caused him to stop also, and sit again on his haunches. While I still stood motionless, he would go slowly a rod to one side, then sit and bark, then a rod to the other side, and sit and bark again, but did not retreat, as if spellbound.
>
> (Thoreau *Journals* 1949 Vol. 1: 470)

Pilpay and Aesop are mentioned by name, but there is in fact very little resemblance between Thoreau's encounter with the fox, and their tried and tested, and easily recognizable forms of the fable. Pilpay's and Aesop's animals typically talk, and typically do so inside a frame story, coming with morals that are clearly stated. Thoreau's fox does not. Rather than fitting comfortably into a frame story, this animal is out there running wild in more senses than one, moving according to a logic of his own, not one that readily makes sense to humans. He is not the bearer of anything edifying, for he is himself a sealed book, an unyielding mystery. And yet the disturbance that he is producing in the auditory field is such that there does seem something that is crying out to be deciphered. Without language, but in some sense not dependent on it, this fox seems to gesture toward a signifying universe that proceeds by instincts and reflexes, a "language of signs" older than civilization and older than human language itself.

Sound is crucial. For even though the fox is not saying anything intelligible to humans, the auditory field here is in fact more volatile than it would have been had he been capable of speech. For Thoreau seems to go out of his way to create a sonic anomaly: this fox does not sound like a fox at all, his bark is like that of a young wolf. And he barks only when he is sitting on his haunches, while he is playing out an extended lockstep sequence with Thoreau himself. The man and the fox move strangely in tandem, two halves of the same ritual of speeding, stopping, and starting again, a dance of pursuit and flight, making humans and nonhumans part of the same rhythmic fabric.

And yet, this rhythmic fabric notwithstanding, the man and the fox are in fact not one, separated not only by the steadily maintained physical distance between them but also by a gulf still more intractable. "The fox belongs to a different order of things from that which reigns in the village," Thoreau says, an order of things that is "in few senses contemporary with" socialized and domesticated humans (470). All that Thoreau can say about a creature so alien is that his bark is more wolf-like than foxlike, a strange sonic misalignment that seems a metaphor for just how little the fox is attuned to us, thwarting the attempts by our ears to classify him, just as he runs counter to the rationality of human settlements in general.

In fact, though not itself hunted to extinction, the fox has less in common with humans than with the wolf, a creature systemically exterminated in New England. As Christopher Benfey points out, "Among the first laws instituted by the Puritan settlers of the Massachusetts Bay Colony in 1630 was a bounty on wolves, which Roger Williams, who fled the colony for its religious intolerance, referred to as 'a fierce, bloodsucking persecutor'" (Benfey 2013). The gray wolf has been extinct in the state since about 1840, according to the Massachusetts Division of Fisheries and Wildlife.[2] Recalling that silenced species and reproducing a sound that is otherwise no longer heard, the fox points to an early loss of biodiversity in Massachusetts, one that speaks to the destructive work of humans.

This is not the only occasion where a lost world is hinted at, through a mistaken sonic identity, a disorientation of the senses. Thoreau's celebrated encounter with the loon, in the "Brute Neighbors" chapter of *Walden*, features another instance. While Thoreau is single-mindedly pursuing this bird, his soundscape is once again strangely volatile, strangely misaligned, haunted by what ought not to have been there. First of all, there is a curious expansion of the sensorium, once again conjuring up a creature not otherwise to be found on Walden Pond:

> [The loon's] usual note was this demoniac laughter, yet somewhat like that of a water-fowl: but occasionally, when he had balked me most successfully and come up a long way off, he uttered a long-drawn unearthly howl, probably more like that of a wolf than any bird; as when a beast puts his muzzle to the ground and deliberately howls.... At length having come up fifty rods off, he uttered one of those prolonged howls, as if calling on the god of loons to aid him, and immediately there came a wind from the east and rippled the surface, and filled the whole air with misty rain, and I was impressed as if it were the prayer of the loon answered, and his god was angry with me; and so I left him disappearing far away on the tumultuous surface.

(*Walden* 1971: 236)

The wolf can make an appearance here only because of an auditory conceit, a fancied likeness suggested by the ear. It might not have occurred to everyone, but Thoreau insists on it. And since this is the second time he is resorting to that conceit, it seems safe to surmise that, as with the earlier encounter with the fox, the point here seems to be to produce a disturbance, a break and a tear in the narrative fabric. The wolf-like sound, a "long-drawn-out unearthly howl," let out at just the moment when the loon has "balked [Thoreau] most successfully," could in fact be quite unnerving. Even though it is meant to be a note of triumph, an undertone of defiance, of unresolved hostility, and perhaps even of remembered pain, seems to lurk just below the surface. It reminds us that the fate of the loon is not so different, after all, from the fate of the wolf, that peaceful coexistence with humans might be close to impossible for both of them.

Indeed, by the end of the nineteenth century, the loon would become locally extinct in eastern Massachusetts. Not till 1975 would a pair of loons be sighted again, nesting at Quabbin Reservoir. Today loons are listed on the Massachusetts Endangered Species Act as a Species of Special Concern.[3] Through a haunting of the ear, Thoreau seemed to have anticipated all of this. Hearing the wolf where he is not supposed to, he injects an edginess, an intimation of harm, into an otherwise idyllic setting.

In *Walden*, though, this intimation of harm is both deliberately staged, and, just as deliberately, allowed to subside. In this world, still relatively benign, miraculous deliverances do occur, crises do get averted. And the intervening force is literally a *deus ex machina*, in the shape of the god of loons, signaling to Thoreau to leave the bird alone. The patently contrived nature of the denouement is perhaps the point: this is not meant to be entirely realistic or convincing. Any avoidance of harm that rests on this flimsy plot device is resting on a fiction that announces itself as such.

Here, then, is a story very different from those in Pilpay and Aesop. In those fables from antiquity, marked by relative harmony between humans and nonhumans, animals are there to teach us a lesson, and death is edifying, not traumatic. In a world where bad things happen only to those who are themselves at fault, harm is fully rationalized by the concept of "desert": it delivers a moral, and comes to an end when the consequences of a misdeed are embodied without fail by the culprit. If harm were to befall the loon, it is likely to take a very different form; and the precipitated response would also be savage and unappeasable, like the wolf-howl, with no edifying message to give it rational grounding, and nothing to hold it in check.

How to honor that kind of sound? Neither Pilpay nor Aesop is of much help here; the traditional animal fable cannot tell that kind of story. But Thoreau is not without alternatives, even among ancient texts. As Stanley Cavell points out, the genre closest to his temperament might turn out to be a genre regularly encountered in nineteenth-century New England, namely, the elegiac lamentations of the Old Testament prophets, especially Jeremiah and Ezekiel (Cavell 1992: 19–20). These are voices crying out in the wilderness – and doing so because their faculty of hearing is exceptional, because they have received in full what "the Lord said unto me." Hearing and lamenting are of supreme importance in the Old Testament, affirming the primacy of a sound-based environment, and providing the language, the rhetorical structure, and above all the emotional fervor to mourn publicly devastations that are large scale, that defy our common-sense reckoning. Here is Jeremiah: "For the mountains will I take up a weeping and wailing, and for the habitations of the wilderness a lamentation, because they are burned up, so that none can pass through them; neither can men hear the voice of the cattle; both the fowl of the heavens and the beast are fled; they are gone" (*The Holy Bible* 1974 *Jeremiah* 9:10).[4]

Thoreau speaks in these accents only very occasionally, and mostly outside the pages of *Walden,* as in this journal entry on March 23, 1856:

> Is it not a maimed and imperfect nature that I am conversant with? As if I were to study a tribe of Indians that had lost all its warriors. ... I listen to a concert in which so many parts are wanting ... mutilated in many places. ... All the great trees and beasts, fishes and fowl are gone; the streams perchance are somewhat shrunk.
>
> (Thoreau *Journals* 1949 Vol. 8: 21)

The Jeremiah-like sound of this lamentation shows a Thoreau increasingly aware of the natural world as one "maimed" and "mutilated" by modernity: a modernity associated in *Walden* with the railroad, the "iron horse" with massive impact on the nineteenth-century landscape. Still, environmental degradation and species loss are not yet terms available to him.

Walden is in that sense an incomplete work, with future trajectories to be charted by others. Between 2003 and 2007 a team of scientists from Boston University and Harvard University decided to measure the biodiversity in Concord, Massachusetts, using Thoreau's plant database as a reference point. Their findings were reported in the *Proceedings of the National Academy of Sciences.* Of the species seen by Thoreau in the mid-nineteenth century, 27 percent cannot be located, and an additional 36 percent persist in one or two populations where they are vulnerable to local extinction. Even more importantly, the scientists discover that the flowering time for many plant species have moved significantly earlier – by as much as 6 weeks – a change most likely triggered by global warming and strongly correlated with the extinction of some species. The article concludes: "climate change has affected and will likely continue to shape the phylogenetically biased pattern of species loss in Thoreau's woods" (see Willis et al.).

And just as there is a loss in plant species, the loss in the sound ecology is equally severe. It is this that prompts Maya Lin to build what she calls her "last memorial," a tribute to and repository of all the vanished sounds of the planet. Entitled "What Is Missing," and featuring, among other things, a huge "listening cone" filled with the sounds of loons and other birds from the Cornell Laboratory of Ornithology, this twenty-first century elegy bears emphatic witness to what Thoreau has only intimated.[5]

Notes

1   www.wildsanctuary.com
2   "State Mammal List," Massachusetts Office of Energy and Environmental Affairs. www.mass.gov/eea/agencies/dfg/dfw/fish-wildlife-plants/state-mammal-list.html.

3 "Loons, lead sinkers and Jigs," Massachusetts Office of Energy and Environmental Affairs. www.mass.gov/eea/agencies/dfg/dfw/hunting-fishing-wildlife-watching/fishing/loons-lead-sinkers-and-jigs.html.
4 *The Holy Bible* 1974 *Jeremiah* 9:10.
5 Diane Toomey, "Maya Lin: A Memorial to a Vanishing Natural World," June 25, 2012, at http://e360.yale.edu/feature/maya_lin_a_memorial_to_a_vanishing_natural_world/2545.

References

Benfey, Christopher. 2013. "The Lost Wolves of New England," *New York Review of Books,* January 22. www.nybooks.com/blogs/nyrblog/2013/jan/22/lost-wolves-new-england.

Cavell, Stanley. 1992. *The Senses of Walden: An Expanded Edition.* Chicago: University of Chicago Press.

Gibbs, Laura. 2002. Introduction to *Aesop's Fables: A New Translation by Laura Gibbs.* Oxford: Oxford University Press.

Glavin, Terry. 2007. *The Sixth Extinction: Journeys Among the Lost and Left Behind.* New York: St. Martin's Press.

Hallam, A. and P. B. Wignall. 1997. *Mass Extinctions and Their Aftermaths.* Oxford: Oxford University Press.

The Holy Bible: Revised Standard Version. London: Meridian, 1974. Print.

Kolbert, Elizabeth. 2009. "The Sixth Extinction? There have been five great die-offs in history. This time, the cataclysm is us." *The New Yorker,* May 25.

Kolbert, Elizabeth. 2014. *The Sixth Extinction: An Unnatural History.* New York: Henry Holt.

Krause, Bernie. 2012. *The Great Animal Orchestra: Finding the Origins of Music in the World's Wild Places.* Boston: Little Brown.

Leakey, Richard and Roger Lewin. 1996. *The Sixth Extinction: Patterns of Life and the Future of Humankind.* New York: Anchor Books

Marsh, Bill. 2012. "Are We in the Middle of a Sixth Mass Extinction." *The New York Times,* June 6.

Pimm, S.L., G.J. Russell, J.L. Gittleman and T.M. Brooks. 1995. The Future of Biodiversity. *Science* 269 (1995): 347–350.

Thoreau, Henry D. 1971. *Walden* ed. Lyndon Shanley. Princeton: Princeton University Press.

Thoreau, Henry D. 1949. *Journals.* Eds Bradford Torrey and Francis Allen. Boston: Houghton, Mifflin. Print.

Toomey, Diane. 2012. "Maya Lin: A Memorial to a Vanishing Natural World." June 25, at http://e360.yale.edu/feature/maya_lin_a_memorial_to_a_vanishing_natural_world/2545.

Willis, Charles G., Brad Ruhfel, Richard B. Primack, Abraham J. Miller-Rushing, and Charles C. Davis. 2008. "Phylogenetic patterns of species loss in Thoreau's woods are driven by climate change." *Proceedings of the National Academy of Sciences,* November 4, 2008, Vol. 105, No. 44: 17029-17033; published ahead of print October 27, 2008, doi:10.1073/pnas.0806446105. Available online at www.pnas.org/content/105/44/17029.full.pdf+html.

Wilson, Edmund O. 2002. *The Future of Life.* New York: Knopf.

31 Teaching climate change at the end of nature

Postcolonial Australia, Indigenous realism and Alexis Wright's *The Swan Book*

Emily Potter

> If the public is not with us yet, it means we haven't told the story of global warming well enough.
>
> Anonymous environmental journalist (cited in Tumarkin)

Responding to a 'hyperobject' (Morton) such as climate change is a complicated business. Given its implication for every aspect of human and non-human life on the planet, the reality of climate change is absolutely multiple (Mol). For this reason, the challenge of teaching climate change is the challenge of multiplicity: just as politicians, policy makers or global citizens of differing historical contexts struggle to apprehend, arrest and make provisions for the manifestations of climate change in a bewildering array of forms, so too do the designers, makers and narrators of our co-constituted technical and poetic worlds. In a literary studies context, the role of storytelling becomes a focus in this field of multiplicity, and with this, particular questions around the constitution and the success of climate change literature – what makes a 'good' climate change story?

This chapter will argue that, while this question is clearly open to debate, it is most productively posed in specific socio-historic contexts. Just as there is no single reality of climate change, there can be no totalizing story that accounts for it. Moreover the lived specificities of climate change are not just experientially contingent, they are also entangled with complex subject positions emergent from diverse historical legacies. Teaching climate change through literary studies must inevitably work with this recognition. No one text will 'represent' climate change, or its experience, but the possibilities for teaching climate change literature lie in more than offering a range of experiences in a range of texts. Rather, these possibilities are immanent to the provocations offered by literature that writes from within specific historical legacies and pushes at, and beyond, the limits of these histories in the face of climate change.

In the Australian situation from which I write, these legacies are postcolonial in a particular context of settler-colonialism. From here, the question of writing climate change must inevitably confront the implication of this history in the very conditions that have generated climate change and its impacts. A 'good' climate change story in these terms – a descriptor that will be explored further in this chapter – will be one that challenges the logic and sovereignty of Western modernity and its subjects in a postcolonial assertion of alternative historical and ontological realities. In a sense, the question in this context reorients from one concerned with story's sustaining capacities to the ongoing sustainability of certain narratives and narrative forms in a postcolonial time of climate change.

This chapter will focus on Alexis Wright's 2011 novel *The Swan Book* in response to this reorientation, a text by an Indigenous Australian woman that explicitly connects a climate-changed future to a colonial past within the world-altering parameters of Indigenous reality.

Writing climate change

The question of fiction's interventions into climate change discourse and under-standing has been raised on an international stage by literary commentators, most of whom point to the representative powers of literature as the source of its signif-icance. As the environmental journalist cited at the beginning of this chapter indicates, this manifests in the idea that a story *told well* enough will have the right kind of effects. Literary fiction is invested with the power to model the manifesta-tion of climate change in a range of contemporary and future contexts; its speculative parameters are seen to afford a realistic engagement with climate change scenarios.

UK critic Robert McFarlane demonstrated this view when he spoke of litera-ture's 'unique capacity to help us connect present action with future consequences'. One of fiction's 'special abilities', he continued, 'is that of allowing us to entertain hypothetical situations as though they were real'. George Monbiot concurred in his assessment of Cormac McCarthy's *The Road* as 'the most important environ-mental book ever written' (Monbiot). For him, it was this novel's stark representation of a lost biosphere and the consequences for human life, biophysi-cally and psycho-socially that signaled its efficacy and significance. In such assessment of the value of literary contributions, the text is configured as a kind of conduit for climate change truths.

Yet the question of multiplicity lurks here. Which realities are being conveyed, and moreover, *how*? A related critical discourse that unsettles the implied univer-sality of these assertions has focused on the *modes* of literary writing and the limitations or affordances of these. These critiques point to the tensions at play in this emphasis on the real, highlighting the ways in which climate change impels a move away from this over-invested paradigm. Indeed, in the strongest critical responses to the question of climate change genre and style we are called to see the impossibility of sustaining certain literary modes in a time of climate change. If this is the case, what modes might endure or emerge in this wake? And how does historical specificity insinuate itself in the question?

The end of nature

Timothy Clark contends that the 'trauma' of climate change is, in part, epistemo-logical. It signals, essentially, 'the deconstruction of multiple frames of reference in multiple fields and modes of thought at the same time' (Clark 132). This is because, as Clark and many others have pointed out, climate change exposes the limits of Western modernity, most centrally within this, the 'end of nature' and its hold over Western systems of meaning. The 'end of nature' trope has come to signify the 'closure' of an 'historical epoch' (133), to cite Clark, that invested in the idea of a divided 'nature' and 'culture', and of a non-human world rendered passive for the exploitation of human design. The 'end of nature' is ultimately the end of an *idea* of nature crucial to the machinations of Western humanism and industrial capitalism, and to the assertion of human sovereignty on which these histories rest.

One significant force in this reconceptualization of the Western sovereign subject is the fantasy of externality rendered untenable by climate change. With nature no longer compliantly 'outside' the human subject, and the human self consequently repositioned in dynamic relation to its wider milieu, the idea of action without consequence, or of the 'shadow places' where humans can disconnect themselves from effects, is refused (Plumwood 2008). Clark quotes David Wood on this point: 'Now there is no outside, no space for expansion, no more *terra nullius* ... When that externality is no longer available, we are in trouble' (Clark 82).

The end of externality, like the end of nature, has significance for literary forms tightly bound to dominant epistemology. If Western modernity has reached its limits, then its literary effects must have too (Clark 146). This is why Clark and others, notably the Australian writer and critic James Bradley, point to realism as a suspect mode for fictional engagements with climate change (Clark 81; Bradley 2010). Realism's naturalization of a stable, singular objective reality is wholly inadequate to convey the manifestation of climate change across dynamic spatio-temporal scales and effects, while its privileging of individualized experience runs counter to the political models of response required by climate change, as well as its refusal of externality. Experience under climate change is necessarily collectivized, even while it is multiple.

But it is the implications of the end of nature as the fall of an ascendant epistemology that really expose the limits of realism. Western modernity relies upon the externalizing of other knowledge systems, but in a world now without externality – materially and psychically – provisionality and multiplicity return as the terms of the real. Yet the unsettlement of dominant epistemology 'from within' is not the only way to approach the radical challenge of climate change to the literary imaginary. I wanted to give my students the opportunity to read climate change not through a consciously dismantled and reconfigured real (dismantled by those already invested with cultural power), but within the terms of an alternative ontology – one that never acceded to the naturalization of Western realism in the first place.

Writing postcolonial climates

As I've indicated earlier, however, the literary enactment of the end of nature will register differently, and specifically, in particular historical contexts. To return to David Wood's assertion of externality's refusal under climate change, this too has significance that echoes across located experience. The 'we' signaled by Wood ('we are in trouble') is Western and sovereign – a subject that has relied on its others as its imaginary inverse, reflecting back, out of this supposed void, the certainties of modern selfhood and the Western liberal project. This is where history comes to matter. For the postcolonial reader, in particular, the Australian postcolonial reader, the term 'terra nullius' has especial resonance, having legitimized in legal discourse the assertion of British territorial sovereignty over the continent soon to be known as Australia, in 1788. By designating this an 'empty land', without preexisting sovereign title, colonial rule and enterprise found their imaginary license. The continent's population of Indigenous inhabitants – estimated more than 300, 000 and constituting more than 250 language groups at the time of colonization, with a lineage on the continent of at least 40,000 years – were invisible in these legal terms. As such, Indigenous peoples and cultures, and their complex, more-than-human environments, became the sites of externality in the colonial machine.

The consequences of this are genocidal, and cataclysmic. They speak to the threat of a climate change future from a past that has suffered for over 200 years under the logic of modernity, and its investments in nature that underwrote the project of British colonization. Within the first 100 years of colonial occupation, the Indigenous population is estimated to have fallen by more than two thirds (Australian Government).

These deaths were profoundly enrolled with 'nature' as an idea and a legitimizing practice: dispossession from land, destruction of food and water sources, introduced disease and the state-sanctioned removal of Indigenous children from their parents, all entangle with Western ideas of the natural world, the Indigenous person's place within it, and (the fantasy of) the modern subject's capacity to control and exploit it. Darwinian notions of natural selection and species competition informed practices that targeted or justified the 'dying out' of Indigenous people, as well as the many animal and plant species lost in the wake of colonization. A creature unable to 'survive' a competitive ecology would inevitably disappear – one externality among many in the violent project of colonial modernity.

The withdrawal of externality under unfolding conditions of climate change arrests this reflex of the Western imagination. With no outside to climate change, there is no psychic or material opportunity to disconnect the consequences of Western lifestyles and their radiating historical networks, from an ecology of multispecies, cross-temporal effects. In this same vein, there is no 'outside' to the legacies of colonization. All subjects of Western modernity are enrolled in these. Of course, the impacts of colonization are variable, and inequitably dispersed, and these intersect with the same uneven distribution of climate change's effects, generated by the world's wealthy and powerful and taking a toll disproportionately on the world's poor and disenfranchised. In Australia, Indigenous Australians – most already dispossessed from their lands by colonization – face a further dispossession by the forces of climate change, and an added burden on already disadvantaged health and economic opportunities.

Yet the end of nature, and with it externality, is a vital predicate to decolonization, as it decenters Western epistemology and foregrounds ontological difference and therefore open-ness and possibility in the production of the real. The assertion that there is no 'outside', no external environment subject to human causality, is hardly radical for Indigenous Australians. Being always in relationship, always enrolled, is the pre-condition of Indigenous ontology, in which human life and culture inextricable from wider networks of more-than-human life and power, in dynamic configurations of space and time. The diversity of Indigenous cultures (every language group has its own cultural practices and histories) shares this broad commonality, which sits it in strong contrast to the Western tradition of nature, and behind this, the ontological singularity of the real. For in Indigenous accounts, the world is multi-real, and with the end of nature – the idea of nature at its limits – this multi-realism finds liberation from an oppressive and exclusionary environmental imaginary.

With this in mind, I introduced my students to Alexis Wright's 2011 novel *The Swan Book* as an example of what 'good' climate change fiction might look like in what is, at once, an emblematic but also very situated context of concern. Wright is an Indigenous Australian woman, a *Waanyi* woman, with traditional lands in the highlands of the southern Gulf of Carpentaria, in Queensland, Australia. An esteemed author of fiction and non-fiction, including powerful political essays on the significance of writing for Indigenous people, she has widely critiqued the underlying, and enduring, paternalism of governmental policies in Australia targeting Indigenous life, as a neo-colonialism that reflects the structuring force of history in the contemporary nation.

The Swan Book, Wright's third novel, is a complex and multi-stranded narrative, regarded highly by critics and challenging to many of its readers, including my students who have described their engagement with the text in terms of an epic journey towards comprehension. It is a difficult novel to summarize, but in brief, *The Swan Book* follows the experiences of young, mute Indigenous woman, Oblivia, who inhabits a community compound in remote Australia that is under lockdown by the Federal Government.[1] Oblivia's compound, sited around the ironically named 'Swan Lake', doubles as a toxic rubbish dump for military waste, and increasingly, dissolute, displaced others seeking refuge from the cataclysmic effects of climate change, which provides the broader framing of the novel. We meet Oblivia as she emerges from a period of retreat, in the darkness of a hollow tree, following a serious sexual assault.

Set almost 100 years from now, this is a text that writes into the future that is already our present, and as the reader quickly discerns, our past. This temporal through-line is Western modernity and its liberal humanist logic that informed the project of colonization and the conditions for climate change. In Wright's hands, however, 'nature' and its history are falling spectacularly apart, and temporalities converge and overlap in profoundly unsettling ways.

While there is a narrative arc that follows Oblivia on a journey from her compound to the weather-ravaged East coast of Australia, marriage to the first Indigenous Australian President, and then back to her compound in a journey of climate change exodus, the text works against a linear mode of storytelling, populated with multiple and diverse narrators, voices, species, cultural references

(Ancestors, Dreaming stories, fairy tales, William Blake, and ABBA jumble together), and most significantly for the question of time, ghosts, who co-exist, and interact, with the living characters of the text. Oblivia is increasingly surrounded by a cast of ghostly associates, who share her homes and journey across Australia in the shadow of climate events.

Ultimately, the novel concerns Oblivia's quest 'to regain sovereignty over my own brain' (Wright 4), following the assault that brought about her mute condition, but also – we must assume, given the significance of the term 'sovereignty' in postcolonial Australia – as an Indigenous subject of colonial history. Wright narrates in a periodic voice of omniscience, 'the day had come when modern man had become the new face of God and simply sacrificed the whole Earth. The swamp locals were not experiencing any terrific friendship with this new God. It was hell to pay to be living the warfare of modernity like dogs fighting over the lineage of progress against their own quiet whorls of time. Well! That just about summed up the lake people, sitting for all times in one place' (12).

Literary scholar Ann Brewster has pointed out Wright's enduring concern with sovereignty in her fiction, in which Indigenous sovereignty refers not just to the political and legal terms of statehood, ownership, and autonomy but also, relatedly, to the ontological and epistemological terms through which one lives. Essentially, Brewster argues, Indigenous sovereignty entails the 'normalization of an indigenous worldview', including 'the cosmological relationship that indigenous people have with the land, the sea and spirit beings' (Brewster 88). Sovereignty in these terms means the ability to inhabit one's own reality.

Here we see the anti-linear aspects of the text, its multi-vocality, and cross-temporal presences, as well as multi-special representation, as indicative of an Indigenous reality, a reality in which, as Wright writes elsewhere, '[a]ll times are important... No time has ended and all worlds are possible' (Wright 6). The prevalence of ghosts in the text points to a Western tradition in which specters speak of modernity's repressions – a relevant reading at the end of nature – but they point more strongly to a different cosmology entire, one on which practices of story-telling are world-making, deeply connected to the meaning and organization of life, dynamically across time. In this reality, the idea of nature as the passive material out of which humans have shaped their now-collapsing world is rejected. Instead, 'nature' becomes a multidimensional, agential force that is inseparable from cultural life.

Significantly, Wright's multi-realism, while it decenters white ontology, allows for the cohabitation of different ways of seeing the world. This is enacted, and made emblematic, through storytelling and the role of stories in *making* these multi-real worlds – this country is full of stories, Wright's characters are constantly calling up their different poetic traditions – dispossessed by colonial and climate forces, they still carry their stories with them. The text's intertextual plays (including the use of *Waanyi* language itself), as well as its non-linear loops, textual punctuation and rhythms, asserts this, too, that the real is multiply textual.

Even as climate change wreaks its effects this is evident: for instance, in the 'new story written in scrolls of intricate lacework formed by the salt crystals that the drought left behind' (Wright 54). With the end of externality, all stories, all times, matter. A 'good story', Wright argues, 'will take time to tell' (2). While climate change brings urgency to the question of response, it will unfold unevenly, according to logic outside rational human design. Ultimately, as *The Swan Book* highlights, the end of nature creates a space for the reassertion of Indigenous sovereignty, and with it, a revision of the real that we all inhabit in a time of climate change. If fiction is to matter in these conditions, and to offer sustaining modes for writing climate change, it must attend to its particular histories of emergence and to the versions of reality that cohabit there. This perhaps demands a different kind of reading practice, too. As one of my students wrote to me at the end of her studies of *The Swan Book*, it 'is one of those books I had to dream, to know ... [here] the reader must open their heart and let it break to hear the story, rather than rationalize it' (anonymous email communication 2015).

Note

1   In a mimetic move, Wright is referencing here the 2007 Northern Territory 'intervention', which was a militarized governmental incursion into remote Indigenous communities in Australia's Northern Territory, and that in some communities is still in place.

References

"Aboriginal Population Statistics". Australian Government. <www.learnline.cdu.edu.au>. Accessed 3 August 2015.

Bradley, James. "Is it Possible to Write Good Climate Fiction about Climate Change". *City of Tongues*, 22/3/10, <http://cityoftongues.com/2010/03/22/is-it-possible-to-write-good-fiction-about-climate-change>. Accessed 21 May 2015.

Brewster, Anne. "Indigenous Sovereignty and the Crisis of Whiteness in Alexis Wright's *Carpentaria*". *Australian Literary Studies*, 25.4 (2010): 85–100.

Clark, Timothy. "Some Climate Change Ironies: Deconstructions, Environmental Politics and the Closure of Ecocriticism". *The Oxford Literary Review*, 32:1 (2010): 131–149.

Clark, Timothy. "Nature, Post Nature". *The Cambridge Companion to Literature and the Environment*, edited by Louise Westling, New York: Cambridge University Press, 2014: 75–89.

McEwan, Ian. "To address global warming, we must harness rationality, good science, and enlightened globalization". 2005. <http://grist.org/article/mcewan-climate>. Accessed 4 May 2015.

McFarlane, Robert. "The Burning Question". <www.theguardian.com/books/2005/sep/24/featuresreviews.guardianreview29>. Accessed 14 April 2015.

Mol, Annmarie. *The Body Multiple: Ontology in Medical Practice*. Durham: Duke University Press, 2003.

Monbiot, George. "Civilization ends with a shutdown of human concern: Are we there already?" 2007. <www.theguardian.com/commentisfree/2007/oct/30/comment.books>. Accessed 6 March 2015.

Morton, Timothy. *Hyperobjects: Philosophy and Ecology After the End of the World*. Minneapolis: University of Minnesota Press, 2013

Plumwood, Val. "Shadow Places and the Politics of Dwelling". *Australian Humanities Review*, 44: 2008. <www.australianhumanitiesreview.org/archive/Issue-March-2008/plumwood.html>. Accessed 23 April 2015.

Tumarkin, Maria. "This Narrated Life". *Griffith Review*, 44 (2014): <https://griffithreview.com/articles/this-narrated-life>. Accessed 17 June 2015.

Westling, Louise. "Literature and Ecology", in *Teaching Ecocriticism and Green Cultural Studies*. Edited by Greg Garrard, New York: Palgrave Macmillan, 2012, 75–89.

Wright, Alexis. "Politics of Writing". *Southerly*, 62.2 (2002): 1–7. Web. Accessed 23 April 2015.

Wright, Alexis. *The Swan Book*. Artarmon, NSW: Giramondo, 2011.

32 When sea levels rise

Writing/righting climate change in Pacific Islanders' literature

Hsinya Huang

In addressing the impact of climate change on Pacific Islanders' communities or small island states, some eco-critics focus on the vulnerability of these communities while others investigate the policies, costs, sources, and locations of climate change migration. Still others put forth discourses of apocalypse and the Anthropocene, envisioning the submersion of small islands as the present and future of these islands and gesturing toward apocalyptic revelation of humankind in the face of environmental degradation of our planet. In all these critical models, nonhuman nature and the indigenous islanders are perpetually alienated into the position of the other(s).

This chapter examines the significance of the indigenous imagination in teaching climate change. In teaching climate change, I argue, it is crucial to acknowledge the significance of indigenous Pacific inscriptions of the ocean and islands. Pacific Islanders' myth, legends and stories embody the islanders' (ancestral) wisdom in righting/writing the impact of climate change. They provide an (alter)native model of resilience in the face of climate change, rendering sea-level rise as everyday life experience, or in Elizabether DeLoughrey's words, as an "ordinary future" (DeLoughrey 352). Drawing on contemporary rewriting of the islands' myths, legends and stories—Keri Hulme's *Stonefish* (New Zealand Maori) and Nequo Soqluman's *Tongku Saveq* (Taiwan Aboriginal Bunun)—I explore how indigenous ways of reckoning time (a genealogy that crosses over human and nonhuman borders) and space (the ocean, sky, islands and humans as an interconnected network) complicate the models of contemporary ecocriticism on climate change, which exclude nonhuman and indigenous others. As such, I aim to pose an alternative to the apocalyptic model of climate change and demonstrate how teaching Pacific islanders' literature may produce an ethics, aesthetics and poetics of environmental adaptation and indigenous resilience, whereby the world would be more justly constructed.

The Pacific Islands have been on the front lines of climate change. On the one hand, islands and atolls in the Pacific, Marshall Islands and Kiribati, have constantly suffered from floods and sea-level rise, which have destroyed numerous homes on the ocean sides and rendered thousands of islanders environmental refugees dispersed across the Pacific. Climate change as an apocalyptic vision thus dominates Western cultural production, Bill McKibben's much-cited book *The End of Nature* being a typical example. As Lawrence Buell puts forth, "apocalypse is the single powerful master metaphor that contemporary environmental imagination has at its disposal" (Buell 285). On the other hand, however, in "A Sea of Environmental Refugees?", Wolfgang Kempf evokes Epili Hau'ofa's signature trope of "a sea of islands" to counteract the former colonial discourse of belittlement and devaluation of the Pacific Islands and in so doing, he contends that contemporary migration flows of Pacific Islanders, due to sea-level rise contribute to "the ongoing enlargement of Oceania" (Kempf 201). As disasters and flooding propel these islanders to migrate from island space to urban settlements, according to Kempf, the world of Oceania has been expanded and the islanders provided resources to which they might otherwise have no access. This over-simplified and romanticized view of how climate change affects and enlarges islands/island chains/archipelagos omits the cultural and historical context of the indigenous Pacific. Before we create an ecologically fair world for all the planet's citizens so that "common resources" would not be walled off for the rich and privileged, we must consider how forced migration and displacement deprive Pacific Islanders of their past and history, economic base, traditions and communities, which shape and sustain their identity.[1] Furthermore, Pacific Islanders who depend on the accumulated wisdom of their ocean ancestors live mutation and adaptation as part of their everyday life. These indigenous knowledge systems, sciences and adaptive strategies have nevertheless been downgraded by modern technology as trivial, insignificant, or superstition.

By retrieving a world of Oceania as an interconnected web and cosmic/interspecies balance in teaching climate change, I dismiss both extreme, apocalyptic and romanticized views of climate change to suggest a balanced vision of climate justice, which involves the indigenous islanders' ways of imagining nature and humans' relation to it. Their stories, heavily charged with knowledge passed down to the islanders, have helped them face the water-world as day-to-day reality. Not only will the modern ecological discourse of climate change benefit from these islanders' knowledge to imagine and forge adaptive strategies and practices in the face of climate change, but their stories will also offer living materials for environmental education surrounding issues of climate change.

Keri Hulme's *Stonefish* is a collection of short stories and poems, intersecting Maori legends and modern realities, which provides an alternative to the polarized (apocalyptic or romanticized) vision of climate change and island worlds, rendering the island world cycles of mutation and transformation:

> Once upon a time, we were a community *here*, ten households of people pottering through our days. We grumbled at taxes and sometimes complained about the weather. We cheered one another through the grey time [...] We sometimes sang when we were sad. We knew—the television told us, the radio mentioned it often—that the oceans would rise, the greenhouse effect would change the weather, and there could be rumblings and distortions along the crustal plates as Gaia adjusted to a different pressure of water. And we understood it to be one more ordinary change in the everlasting cycle of life.
> (Hulme 18)

By emphasizing "here" and orienting readers toward continuous cultural connections to an original source and community, Hulme calls for indigenous resistance to Western media representations. This resistance takes the form of reclaiming a geography that has been lost elsewhere in space and time but which is powerful as a political formation of *here* and *now*. Climate change is not what is represented on the television or on the radio, but rather what happens as daily realities and experiences for the islanders. This resistance also indicates an alternative mode of thinking on a planetary scale—by evoking "Gaia" as a complex entity involving the planet's biosphere, atmosphere, oceans, and soil, she refers to the powers which emanate from the planetary body: "the totality constituting a feedback or cybernetic system which seeks an optimal physical and chemical environment for life on this planet," to borrow James Lovelock's words (Lovelock 11). Gayatri Chakravorty Spivak's differentiation of the planet from the globe is useful in this regard: "[t]he globe is on our computers. No one lives there [...]. The planet is in the species of alterity, belonging to another system; we inhabit it, on loan" (Spivak 44). This view of the planet gestures toward the species, or rather interspecies, alterity and the interrelated cycle of life that goes beyond "anthropocentric narrative of modern history" (DeLoughrey 362). Hulme inserts disasters and catastrophes as everyday life experiences, not as apocalyptic images or representations on the television or on the radio. They are ordinary experiences of the islanders. As there would be sea-level rise, there would be "rumblings and distortions along the crustal plates as Gaia adjusted to a different pressure of water" (Hulme 18). She retrieves an indigenous/island tradition of nature's law which resists submersion into (mis)representation and ideology. Her vision of climate change as "ordinary change in the everlasting cycle of life" (18) remains consistent with the Pacific ethic and tradition of genealogical connection among living beings, positing no great divide between animal and human, between nature and culture. To be precise, the "everlasting cycle of life" embodies the Maori idea of "whakapapa," which covers the descent of all living things "including the gods and humankind, birds and fish, trees, rocks, and mountains" (Allen 131). The ecological opportunity of global warming and sea-level rise resides in re-visioning climate change as part of the ordinary change(s) of everyday life. The resilience of ecosystems will be extended to human adaptation and in this way transform the ecological peril to enhance the equilibrium of the islands' social-ecological systems. Viewing climate change as "ordinary," the islanders have developed the capacity to cope with uncertainty and mutation while exploring opportunities that may arise in the uncertain future.

In a similar vein, Nequo Soqluman's *Tongku Saveq* focuses on the resilience of ecosystems and everyday practices to cope with environmental catastrophes in the island geography. "Tongku Saveq" is the transliteration of the name of the highest mountain of Taiwan, the main peak of Jade Mt., in Bunun, one of the 16 recognized tribes in Taiwan (European imaginary of Taiwan as *Ilha Formosa*, the beautiful island). In the context of Bunun flood myth, "saveq" means shelter or escape; therefore, Tongku Saveq, the Bunun sacred mountain, denotes a peak for escape or a place of shelter during the floods. There are many versions of the flood myth. One version is that there was a giant snake (or eel) whose body blocked the flow of

rivers and caused unprecedented flood. At that time, people fled from one mountain to another while the water flooded over everywhere they went and finally, the
whole world was submerged under water. The only exception was the highest
peak in the world—Tongku Saveq—which stood above the water surface, where
escaping humans and animals fortunately survived. Later on, there were legends of
some brave toads and black bulbuls who found tinder for humans and of a gigantic crab that dived underwater and cut the snake in half to release the flood.
Another version of the story touches on Taiwan before the catastrophic flooding
when it was a big flat plain which had no mountains at all. Not until the flood
came which took away large amounts of sand and stones did the terrain of Taiwan
with its mountains and valleys come into shape (Soqluman 11–12).

This Bunun mythological version of the flooding and mountain building
resonates with that of "rumblings and distortions along the crustal plates as Gaia
adjusted to a different pressure of water" in Hulme's text. Both denote the intrinsic value of a natural being, as though there could be a law defending existence *per
se*. Both refer to a cycle of life that is everlasting—forms of life that have managed
to survive in their respective environments over time, over history, i.e., in geological time beyond the human span. Both sustain the ancient tales and myths of their
individual tribes by telling them. Both stress the significance of interspecies relationship in sustaining human survival. It is "a gigantic crab that dived underwater
and cut the snake in half to release the flood" and to save the Bunun, who takes
refuge in Tongu Saveq. The mountain becomes the sacred "storied place" (Rolston
285). As Holmes Rolston III insightfully puts forth:

> What I can do is invite you as a historical subject to appreciate the objective
> story that lies in, with, and under the Earth we inhabit, to enrich the story by
> telling it. You can be a microcosm of the macrocosm and enjoy your storied
> residence here […] We ought to live in storied residence on landscapes […]
> the logic of that home place is finally narrative.
>
> (286)

Whereas Rolston's object of concentration is Earth as places in which stories are
stored in cumulative transmittable cultures, both Hulme and Soqluman demonstrate the ocean planet as the contested site of ecological crisis and opportunities.
Their method is through storytelling and narratives of their "storied residence" in
the ocean planet. In teaching climate change cultures, I include the inspiring and
transformative stories from the indigenous Pacific as living materials and invite
students not only to appreciate these stories of climate change as everyday experiences and ordinary futures but to enrich these stories by telling them and enjoying
their storied residence on the islands. Soqluman reiterates: "the way of storytelling
needs to be creative and new ways of representation need to be found in the
context of a new era" (Soqluman 13). What he accomplishes is an imaginary work
"based on [his] recognition of traditional Bunun knowledge—including mythical
legends, ancient songs and tunes, taboos, and ceremonies, etc. (13). It is, in his own
words, "my own fantastic imagination of the entire species in the tribal space when

I stand in my tribal village, watching Tongku Saveq" (13). This personal imagination nevertheless constitutes a powerful living story to transform and inspire our young students in the way they view the world commonly.

Both Maori and Taiwan indigenes belong to Austronesian-speaking peoples, who originated in Taiwan and then spread across the ocean to Easter Island in the east, to Madagascar in the west, and to New Zealand in the south. Their myths and legends are oral stories that embody a unique worldview. Or rather, they disclose a native science, an alternative knowledge system that can be more attuned to complex interdependencies between human and environment. This knowledge exists and is inherited by way of oral tales and transformed into daily practices in the face of climate change. Their narratives help translate ambiguous and abstract theoretical constructions in contemporary ecological studies and bring them into the mediated presence of their "storied residence." Another of Taiwan's indigenous tribes, Tsou, visualizes a similar story of flooding and resilience in their wall painting, forging a creative art of representing climate change.

The complex terrain of the imagination remains a way of understanding and exploring the manifestations of anthropogenic climate change in indigenous culture and community. It is a way of seeing, sensing, thinking, and interpreting that creates the conditions for human interventions in ecology. It is an expression of human sensibilities to their home places in connection with other species, landscapes, and seascapes. It plays a critical role in thinking through our representations of environmental change and offers insights to envision the future of island worlds. Ultimately in climate futures, there are visions, adaptive strategies and daily practices from the cumulative frames of indigenous cultures of the Pacific islands, which

Figure 32.1 Wall painting in Lai-ji Tsou tribe showing a gigantic crab that dived underwater and cut the snake in half to release the flood

Source: Courtesy of Yih-ren Lin.

represent "tacit acceptance of the need for adaptive strategies that can be embedded in everyday practices" (Yusoff and Gabrys 2).

The alternative worldview and knowledge system in Pacific islanders' writings provide insights for adaptation in the face of climate change and sea-level rise, which mend the abstraction of Western metaphysics and ethics in addressing today's environmental problems. Lawrence Buell contends that "environmental crisis involves a crisis of the imagination the amelioration of which depends on finding better ways of imagining nature and humanity's relation to it" (Buell 2). In his 1993 seminal essay "Our Sea of Islands," the Tongan writer Epeli Hau'ofa argues that the legacies of colonial belittlement that render the Pacific as "islands in a far sea" need to be replaced with a more accurate and world-enlarging view of "our sea of islands." Not only must we recognize the primacy of the largest ocean on the planet in facilitating both the legacies of Pacific voyaging and contemporary circuits of globalization, but the Pacific as "a sea of islands," better known as Oceania, plays a pivotal role in the protection and sustainable development of the planet (Hau'ofa 37). He represents Oceanic peoples as custodians of the sea, who "reach out to similar people elsewhere in the common task of protecting the seas for the general welfare of all living things" (55). While Hau'ofa was concerned with the ecological health of the ocean, he could not have foreseen the ways in which climate change, particularly sea-level rise, has transformed island space. Both Hulme's and Soqluman's narratives that translate the urgency of climate change mitigation through retelling their tribal myths and re-visioning climate change as day-to-day realities as well as ordinary futures complement Hau'ofa's ecological discourse. In response to climate change and the erosion of their island landscape, the Pacific island writers offer a point of view that dismisses apocalypse and inspires us to imagine adaptation and resilience as our common ecological opportunities.

Note

1   For a discussion on climate change, "common resources," and environmental justice, see Huang, "Climate Justice and Trans-Pacific Indigenous Feminisms."

References

Allen, Chadwick. *Blood Narrative: Indigenous Identity in American Indian and Maori Literary and Activist Texts.* Durham and London: Duke University Press, 2002. Print.

Buell, Lawrence. *The Environmental Imagination: Thoreau, Nature Writing, and the Formation of American Culture.* Cambridge: Belknap, 1995. Print.

DeLoughrey, Elizabeth. "Ordinary Futures: Interspecies Worldings in the Anthropocene." *Global Ecologies and the Environmental Humanities: Postcolonial Approaches.* Eds Elizabeth Deloughrey, Jill Didur, and Anthony Carrigan. New York: Routledge, 2015. Print.

Huang, Hsinya. "Climate Justice and Trans-Pacific Indigenous Feminisms." *American Studies, Ecocriticism and Citizenship: Thinking and Acting in the Local and Global Commons.* Ed. Joni Adamson and Kimberly N. Ruffin. London: Routledge, 2013, 158–72. Print.

Huang, Hsinya. "Representing Indigenous Bodies in Epeli Hau'ofa and Syaman Rapongan." *Tamkang Review* 40.2 (2010): 3–19. Print.

Hau'ofa, Epeli. "Our Sea of Islands." *A New Oceania: Rediscovering Our Sea of Islands*. Eds Vijay Naidu, Erica Waddell, and Epeli Hau'ofa. Suva: School of Social and Economic Development, The University of the South Pacific, 1993. Print.

Hulme, Keri. *Stonefish*. Wellington, NZ: Huia, 2004. Print.

Kempf, Wolfgang. "A Sea of Environmental Refugees? Oceania in an Age of Climate Change." *Macht, Differenz: Motive und Felder ethnologischen Forschens*. Eds Elfriede Hermann, Karin Klenke, and Michael Dickhardt. Gottingen: University of Gottingen, 2009: 191–205. Print.www.univerlag.uni-goettingen.de/bitstream/handle/3/isbn-978-3-940344-80-9/FormMachtDifferenz.pdf?sequence=1. Accessed 9 June 2016. Web.

Lovelock, James E. *Gaia: A New Look at Life on Earth*. New York: Oxford University Press, 1979. Print.

Mount, Amy. "When Politics Meets Poetry: What the Humanities Bring to Policymaking." *Guardian*, 29 April 2015. Web.

Rolston III., Holmes. "Down to Earth: Persons in Place in Natural History." *Philosophy and Geography III: Philosophies of Place*. Eds Andrew Light and Jonathan M. Smith. Lanham: Roman and Littlefield, 1998, 285–96. Print.

Soqluman, Nequo. *Tongku Saveq*. Paipei: INK, 2007. Print.

Spivak, Gayatri Chakravorty. *Imperatives to Re-Imagine the Planet*. Vienna: Passagen, 1999. Print.

Yusoff, Kathryn and Jennifer Gabrys. "Climate Change and the Imagination." *WIRES: Climate Change* 2.4 (2011): 516–34. Print.

33 Climate change and changing world literature

Karen Thornber

Climate fiction – often referred to as cli-fi and broadly understood as fiction that engages with climate change, the ensuing struggles for resources, and the impact of these struggles on human communities locally and globally – has proliferated in recent decades; climate fiction writers from the Americas and Europe to Africa, the Middle East, Asia, and Oceania are actively changing literature worldwide. Often traced to the British writer J. G. Ballard's *The Drowned World* (1962), climate fiction is likely to become one of the dominant forms of twenty-first century literature, while poetry and other forms of writing on climate change are likewise flourishing globally. Moreover, much climate literature itself travels beyond national and linguistic borders, circulating within and among regions both in its original language and in translations, and in so doing it has become an increasingly important part of world literature.[1] Yet not only has world literature scholarship and pedagogy remained relatively silent on climate change, as it has on other urgent matters of global concern, but also discussions of climate change, taking a scientific or social scientific approach, generally do not incorporate the many cultural products, including literature, that have addressed this global crisis.[2] These missed opportunities are regrettable, given the power of the arts to shape human consciousness and behavior.

Literature rarely offers comprehensive remedies, much less proposes official policies to prevent future or remediate current damage. But drafting policies, not to mention implementing them, requires changes in perceptions, understandings, and expectations, something literature and the study of literature – particularly in global perspective – are well placed to enhance. As Jonathan Mingle has argued, "Poets help us all process and give meaning to the changes measured by science. And they help us decide where to train our attention among a compounding profusion of data, and motivate us to act." And, as James Engell has noted, "Poetry, and literature more generally... have provided a construction of a certain consciousness about nature, without which research and knowledge cannot be knitted together into a larger kind of vision" (Mingle 14). Not necessarily a form of escapism (cf. Schulz 59), dystopian literature and other arts can better enable readers to think about, prepare for, confront, and respond to catastrophe (Pérez-Peña, cf. Trexler 220). Incorporating discussion of world literature into courses on climate change and discussion of climate change into courses on world literature not only alerts students of all fields to the deep connections between cultural products and global crises, but also provides them with a greater variety of perspectives on climate change and its likely impacts on human societies. Teaching students about the literature of climate change likewise gives them space to envision multiple future scenarios and to think imaginatively about what changes might be made to facilitate adaptation, increase resilience, lessen fear, and modulate risk.

The pages that follow introduce three prominent works of climate fiction that have circulated globally: the Japanese avant-garde writer Abé Kōbō's *Inter Ice Age 4* (Dai yon kanpyōki, 1959), the American science fiction and fantasy writer Paolo Bacigalupi's *The Windup Girl* (2009), and the Finnish crime fiction writer Antti Tuomainen's *The Healer* (Parantaja, 2010).[3] These novels – appropriate for courses on both world literature and climate change – probe the future of humanity in deluged cities and worlds. They enhance classroom discussion of the likely impacts of climate change on human societies and the steps that need to be taken to forestall even greater suffering as well as give students unparalleled insights into how individuals and communities are grappling with impending climate change.

Abé Kōbō is known worldwide for the bestseller *Woman in the Dunes* (Suna no onna, 1962), which has been translated into dozens of languages and was adapted into an award-winning film. But his earlier detective novel *Inter Ice Age 4* (1959), in addition to launching Japanese science fiction, has also received critical attention outside Japan.[4] Set in Tokyo in the late 1950s, the text is best described as "a murder mystery with a time-traveling detective [Dr. Katsumi, the first-person narrator] who discovers that he has been split into his own present and future selves to become the murderer, the detective, and the victim all at once" (Bolton, *Columbia Companion* 195). More important for our purposes, *Inter Ice Age 4* also anticipates a future where undersea volcanic eruptions have destroyed the polar ice caps, causing sea levels to rise dramatically and ultimately forcing human society underwater. As the talking computer that Katsumi and his team create in response to Soviet prediction computers itself predicts: "With the passing of time the speed of the rise in sea level increased. People continued their ceaseless migration toward higher land and in the process lost the habit of living in fixed places... People lived aimlessly on alms given by aquans" (Abé Kōbō, *Inter Ice Age 4* 216).[5]

Inter Ice Age 4 takes climate change as a given. The novel points not to how rising sea levels might be prevented, or even forestalled, but instead to how human societies might better prepare for and adapt to a drastically different physical environment. At the same time, *Inter Ice Age 4* explicitly encourages introspection. Abé writes in the afterword (atogaki), "I shall have fulfilled one of the purposes of this novel if I have been able to make the reader confront the cruelty of the future, produce within him anguish and strain, and bring about a dialogue with himself" (228). This dialogue with oneself, Abé suggests earlier in the essay, in part concerns overcoming myopia, the narrow understandings of everyday experience that preclude individuals and communities from readying themselves productively for an uncertain future. Writes Abé, "We must clearly recognize the greatest crime, which is this common order we call the everyday" (Abé Kōbō, *Nichijō* 121).[6] As is true of any number of Abé's novels, *Inter Ice Age 4* goes out of its way to expose the ultimate failure of narrow ideas of rational progress (Bolton, *Modern Japanese Writers* 8).

Paolo Bacigalupi's debut novel *The Windup Girl* (2009) – its title evoking the Japanese writer Murakami Haruki's bestselling *The Wind-Up Bird Chronicle* (*Nejimakidori kuronikuru*, 1995) – was published half a century after *Inter Ice Age 4* (1959). An instant sensation, *The Windup Girl* was named one of the best novels of 2009, and it received numerous awards, in addition to being translated into Chinese, Japanese, and a number of European languages. This work of science fiction is set in twenty-third century Bangkok. Climate change having raised oceans globally, Malaya is a morass of killing, Kowloon is underwater, China is divided, Vietnam is broken, Burma is plagued by starvation, the United States has lost much of its power, and Europe has splintered and factionalized (Bacigalupi 214). Thailand too is being swallowed by the oceans; Bangkok, a city riddled by corruption, is below sea level and is protected from complete annihilation by a system of levees and pumps. Bacigalupi's *The Windup Girl* centers on the American Anderson Lake, the corporation AgriGen's Calorie Man (the new salaryman) in Thailand.

While in Bangkok, Anderson encounters Emiko, the Windup Girl, a genetically engineered being and one of the so-called New People. Whereas in *Inter Ice Age 4* machines predict an undersea dystopian future populated by engineered beings initially created by the Japanese, *The Windup Girl* depicts an inundated dystopian future where beings engineered by the Japanese have been scattered around the world. Anderson is mesmerized by Emiko; he is one of few people in Bangkok to see her as more than a machine, as a woman with a soul who emerges from "within the strangling strands of her engineered DNA" (184). Early in the novel the narrator contrasts how the New People were treated in Japan with how they are treated in Thailand:

> [In Kyoto] New People were common... [they were] sometimes well-respected. Not human, certainly, but also not the threat that the people of this savage basic culture [Thailand] make her out to be... The Japanese were practical. An old population needed young workers in all their varieties, and if they came from test tubes and grew in crèches, this was no sin.
> *And isn't that why you* [Emiko] *sit here? Because the Japanese are so very practical? Though you look like one, though you speak their tongue, though Kyoto is the only home you knew, you were not Japanese...*
> New People serve and do not question... They [her Thai masters] have her [Emiko] strip off her clothes... Kannika speaks in Thai and tells them Emiko's life story. That she was once a rich Japanese plaything [but was discarded in Bangkok by her Japanese master]. That she is theirs now: a toy for them to play with, [to rape]... In Japan she was a wonder. Here she is nothing but a windup... If she remains silent the abuse will end soon.

(35–38)

The Windup Girl is about survival in a city and in a world turned upside down by climate change. As the narrator wryly remarks, "there is no Noah Bodhisattva now" (169), no higher power to rescue this city on the brink of annihilation.

Emiko looks to Anderson to liberate her, to help her find the New People villages up north where she no longer will be pursued by the infamous "white shirts" determined to destroy her. But ironically, it is the windups that perhaps have the greatest chance at survival. As one of the novel's characters points out, adaptation to new environments is crucial:

> We should all be windups by now. ... A generation from now, we could be well-suited for our new environment. Your children could be the beneficiaries. Yet you people refuse to adapt. You cling to some idea of a humanity that evolved in concert with your environment over millennia, and which you now, perversely, refuse to remain in lockstep with.
>
> (243)

And Emiko, too, slowly adapts to her environment, not in the sense of inuring herself to the nightly gang rapes, but instead by struggling to shed her programmed obedience and liberate herself from the terror of life as a semi-human illegal alien. Ultimately she kills many who torment her, triggering a political crisis. *The Windup Girl* concludes with water gushing into Bangkok, its levees destroyed and pumps sabotaged. The city moves north, but Emiko remains, carving out a simple life for herself in the waters of the former metropolis; the novel itself points to the violence that rising sea levels will engender as well as to possible hope for survival.

Not unlike Abé's and Bacigalupi's novels, Antti Tuomainen's dystopian thriller *The Healer* features a flooded city (Helsinki, Finland) of the near future whose residents are fleeing north, and a flooded world where disease, disputes over clean water supplies, forest fires, and other natural disasters have culminated in a complete breakdown of society. As with *The Windup Girl*, Tuomainen's novel was an instant bestseller; since its initial publication in Finland in 2010, where it was awarded the Clue Award for Best Finnish Crime Novel 2011, it has been translated into more than two dozen languages, albeit mostly in Europe. *The Healer* is narrated by Tapani Lehtinen, a writer searching desperately for his wife Johanna despite the transformed and increasingly forbidding landscape. Johanna's disappearance is connected to a story she is writing about a serial killer who calls himself the Healer; this individual believes that by murdering those responsible for climate change he is the "healer for a sick planet [*sairaan maapallon parantaja*; lit. sick earth healer]" (Tuomainen 16 [trans. 2013: 11]).

The Healer differentiates not between "human" and "engineered human" but instead between individuals of different classes. As Lehtinen observes driving through Helsinki:

> Those who had the means had moved north: those with the most means to northern Canada, the rest to Finnish, Swedish, and Norwegian Lapland. Dozens of high-security, privately owned small towns had been established in the north in recent years ... with self-contained water, sewage, and electrical systems – and, of course, hundreds of uniformed guards to keep out undesirables [*epätoivotut tulijat*; lit. unwanted entrants].
>
> (Tuomainen 34 [trans. 2013: 28])

Those with means are able to purchase security, at least for the time being, while those without are condemned to an increasingly precarious existence, *The Healer* reinforcing the fact that even though climate change is a global phenomenon, its impacts differ considerably among communities. For its part, Lehtinen's single-minded pursuit of his wife, at times making him oblivious to his surroundings, can seem irrational, but it points to the triumph, at least temporarily, of human connections, of community, to a form of adaptation that makes life more difficult but ultimately more meaningful.

Since earliest times, cultural products have engaged with the challenges facing societies. More recently, novels by Abé Kōbō, Paolo Bacigalupi, and Antti Tuomainen and countless other writers of climate literature have exposed how people have dominated, damaged, and destroyed one another and the natural world and have predicted how they will grapple with an uncertain and potentially traumatic future. Stephen Siperstein is perhaps too optimistic when he declares: "Literature can help us traverse the turbulence of feeling that is a hallmark of living in a time of global climate chaos and lead us … Towards a future worth living in, a future that we cannot control, and maybe not even imagine, but a future nonetheless filled with resilience, joy, and environmental and social justice for all." Yet, in the words of the writer Mohsin Hamid, there is little doubt that fiction "can say publicly what might otherwise appear unsayable, combating the coerced silence that is a favored weapon of those who have power... Politics is shaped by people. And people, sometimes, are shaped by the fiction they read." As Abé's *Inter Ice Age 4*, Bacigalupi's *The Windup Girl*, and Tuomainen's *The Healer* make clear, world literature can alert readers to the increased social upheaval climate change is likely to trigger and share various responses – both constructive and destructive – to such global transformations. Incorporating these and similar texts in courses on climate change as well as courses on world literature helps students better understand the multiple implications of climate change – and the many decisions that will need to be made both at present and in the coming years.

Notes

1   In the early nineteenth century, German writer Johann Wolfgang von Goethe introduced his vision of *Weltliteratur* (world literature) as the circulation of writing across national borders in Europe and of non-Western literatures into Europe. Today, world literature is thought of more comprehensively, as "all literary works that circulate beyond their culture[s] of origin, either in translation or in their original language" (Damrosch 4).

2   Goodbody and Trexler (2015) are notable exceptions. For a general introduction to teaching literature and climate change, see Gabriel and Garrard.

3   Other prominent English-language climate-change fiction includes the Australian writer George Turner's *The Sea and Summer* (1987); the American writers Octavia Butler's *Parable* novels (1990s) and Cormac McCarthy's *The Road* (2006); the Canadian/Scottish writer Hamish MacDonald's *Finitude* (2009); the American writers Barbara Kingsolver's *Flight Behavior* (2012), and Nathanial Rich's *Odds against Tomorrow* (2013); and the English writer Ian McEwan's *Solar* (2010). For more on this genre, see

Trexler and Johns-Putra (2011, 2015). Climate change is addressed as well in young
adult fiction, including Mindy McGinnis's *Not a Drop to Drink* (2013), Saci Lloyd's *The
Carbon Diaries: 2015* (2009), and Marcus Sedgwick's *Floodland* (2000). Also becoming
more prominent is climate film, with such blockbusters as *Waterworld* (1995), *The Day
After Tomorrow* (2004), *Elysium* (2013), *Wall-E* (2008), *Avatar* (2009), and *Snowpiercer*
(2014) depicting climate change as both plot point and scenery (Mark).

4   Although *Inter Ice Age 4* did not inaugurate science fiction in Japan, critics generally
identify it as Japan's first true science fiction novel.

5   Saunders's translation reads similarly to the original Japanese (165). Aquans [*suisai
ningen*; 水棲人間] are genetically engineered aquatic gilled humans, bred from aborted
mammal fetuses and reared in special factories. These beings, who live on the ocean
floor, are depicted in *Inter Ice Age 4* as struggling for equal rights until their government
is recognized internationally. Katsumi's wife unwittingly donates their son's fetus to this
project.

6   The translation is my own, from *Abé Kōbō zensakuhin*, vol. 14.

References

Abé Kōbō. "Nichijō e no senkoku: *Dai yon kanpyōki* atogaki," in *Abé Kōbō zensakuhin* 14.
Tokyo: Shinchōsha, 1973. 120–22.

Abé Kōbō. *Dai yon kanpyōki*, in *Abé Kōbō zen sakuhin* 4. Tokyo: Shinchōsha, 1973. 1–172.

Abé Kōbō. *Inter Ice Age 4*. Tokyo: Charles E. Tuttle Co., 1970. Trans. E. Dale Saunders.

Bacigalupi, Paolo. *The Windup Girl*. San Francisco: Night Shade Books, 2010.

Bolton, Christopher. "Abé Kōbō," in Jay Rubin, ed., *Modern Japanese Writers*. New York:
Charles Scribner's Sons, 2001. 1–18.

Bolton, Christopher. "Abé Kōbō," in Joshua Mostow, ed., *The Columbia Companion to Modern
East Asian Literature*. New York: Columbia University Press, 2003. 193–206.

Damrosch, David. *What is World Literature?* Princeton: Princeton University Press, 2003.

Gabriel, Hayden and Greg Garrard. "Reading and Writing Climate Change," in Greg
Garrard, ed., *Teaching Ecocriticism and Green Cultural Studies*. New York: Palgrave
Macmillan, 2012.

Goodbody, Axel H. "Melting Ice and the Paradoxes of Zero: Didactic Impulses and
Aesthetic Distanciation in German Climate Change Fiction," *Ecozone@: European Journal
of Literature, Culture and Environment* 4:1 (2013). 92–102.

Goodbody, Axel H. "Risk, Denial and Narrative Form in Climate Change Fiction: Barbara
Kingsolver's *Flight Behavior* and Ilija Trojanow's *Melting Ice*," in Sylvia Mayer and Alexa
Weik von Mossner, eds, *The Anticipation of Catastrophe: Environmental Risk in North
American Literature and Culture*. Heidelberg: Universitätsverlag Winter, 2014. 39–58.

Hamid, Mohsim and Francine Prose. "Bookends: Does Fiction have the Power to Sway
Politics?" *The New York Times Book Review* (February 22, 2015), 35.

Mark, Jason. "Climate Fiction Fantasy," *The New York Times* (December 10, 2014), A31.

Mingle, Jonathan. "Finding Poetry in Nature's Crises and Wonders," *Harvard University Center
for the Environment* 7:1 (2015). 12–17.

Pérez-Peña, Richard. "College Classes Use Arts to Brace for Climate Change," *The New York
Times* online (March 31, 2014).

Schulz, Kathryn, "The Really Big One," *The New Yorker* (July 20, 2015), 52–59.

Siperstein, Stephen. "Climate Change Fiction: Radical Hope from and Emerging Genre,"
http://eco-fiction.com. Accessed 25 May 2016.

Trexler, Adam. *Anthropocene Fictions: The Novel in a Time of Climate Change*. Charlottesville,
VA: University of Virginia Press, 2015.

Trexler, Adam and Adeline Johns-Putra, "Climate Change in Literature and Literary Criticism," *Wiley Interdisciplinary Reviews: Climate Change 2.2* (2011), 185–200.

Tuomainen, Antti. *The Healer*. New York: Henry Holt and Company, 2013. Trans. Lola Rogers.

Tuomainen, Antti. *Parantaja*. Helsinki: Helsinki-Kirjat, 2010.

34 Untangling intentions

Teaching the history of climate politics

Peder Anker

The summer of 1989 was unusually hot in Norway. And the sweltering heat provided ammunition for a parliamentary discussion about global warming. Gro Harlem Brundtland, the Prime Minister and the former Chair for the World Commission on Environment and Development, pushed hard for an ambitious program aimed at stabilizing carbon emissions by the 1990s. Her goal was to prove to the world that Norway took *Our Common Future* (1987) and its quest for sustainable development seriously.

But why global warming? History may untangle political intentions hidden behind a mountain of climate change facts. As this article will illustrate, a historical approach may uncover motives, personal ambitions, and the use (or abuse) of science for political interests. Scientific research and discoveries change over time. What is right today may be proved wrong tomorrow. Teaching students about the history of climatology will give them some insight into climate research. This can be particularly helpful to students who feel they are ill-disposed to understanding science. In the late 1980s there were still valid scientific questions being raised with respect to the evidence from climatologists (Weart 2003). This is a good starting point for discussing with students how and why sciences develop and knowledge 'hardens' over time. Norway's Prime Minister would support climatological research financially and politically. Why so? What did she try to achieve? Untangling her motivations may open up classroom discussions about climate politics, going beyond simplistic questions of whether or not politicians believe in global warming or not. Norwegian environmentalists were somewhat concerned about global warming in the mid-1980s, though they were pushing politicians to address ecological depletion and not climate change. To Brundtland, the ecological approach meant having to deal with unruly and highly vocal Deep Ecologists. Better then to start afresh with climatologists that appealed to the technocratic tradition within the Labor Party. Instead of changing the ethical and social ways of dealing with environmental problems as the Deep Ecologists were advocating, she was looking for technological and economic solutions supported by climate researchers. This move towards technocracy and cost-benefit economics reflects a post-Cold War turn towards utilitarian capitalism, but also, as I will argue, an attempt to reconcile the nation's booming petroleum industry with reduction in climate gas emissions.

The deep ecologists

In 1971 in Norway's largest tabloid newspaper, a journalist reported that global warming "may cause the polar ice to melt, that the ocean will rise above its shores, that cities and large territories of land will be under water, [and] that humans will be displaced to mountain regions" (Anonymous 1971). This alarming news was quickly buried in a host of similar stories of doom and gloom. Since Earth Day a year before, readers had become used to hearing about a fast approaching environmental Ragnarök.

The press was fed such news by an environmental organization called The Co-Working Group for the Protection of Nature and the Environment, known in the English speaking literature as the Deep Ecologists. They delivered a clear either/or dichotomy between a future of industrial doom or ecological bliss, and gained a significant following among activists seeking radicalism within acceptable socio-political boundaries of the Cold War (Anker 2007). The Deep Ecologists became a hard-hitting populist association which, at its peak in the late 1970s, was one of the largest (and certainly the most vocal) environmental organizations in Norway, attacking industrialization and economic growth in general and hydro-power developments in particular.

The Deep Ecologists would set the stage for environmental debate with non-compromising positions cast in Cold War bipolar terms as either "deep" or "shallow." They confronted Gro Harlem Brundtland head on in her capacity as Minister of the Environment between 1974 and 1979. To them, she was most definitely "shallow." With major discoveries of oil in the North Sea, the Deep Ecologists would use much ink trying to halt exploration on the grounds that oil and gas would take Norway further away from the deep eco-political path and instead towards the destructive forces of capitalism, economic growth, and exploitation of natural resources. More specifically, petroleum would cause carbon dioxide emissions and "the so-called greenhouse effect" would lead to dramatic sea-level rise as a result (Parr et al. 1974: 35). In April 1977 the chief pipeline in an oil platform called "Bravo" exploded, causing a week-long major oil spill. This put Brundtland under an unwanted spotlight with national and international media covering the evolving disaster on an hourly basis. To the Deep Ecologists the oil spill was evidence of a failed policy of economic growth endorsed by a Minster of the Environment not worthy of this title.

These tensions culminated with what became the most dramatic civil disobedience demonstration in post-war Norwegian history, namely the effort to save the Alta–Kautokeino waterway in the north of Norway from hydro-power development (Hjorthol 2006). By the summer of 1979 demonstrators were in place blocking the construction site, which they did until the fall of 1981 when the largest police operation in the nation's history removed the strictly non-violent but very determined Deep Ecologists. As Minister of the Environment and subsequently as Prime Minister from February to October 1981, Brundtland had wholeheartedly defended the project. These events occupied the country's environmental and social debates, often as front-page news. Yet for all the efforts of the demonstrators, the police operations put an effective end to the demonstrations.

The Brundtland Commission

Brundtland had won the battle but ultimately lost the war with the Deep Ecologists. The oil spill of 1977 would still haunt her, and as Prime Minister she pushed hard for developing hydro-power at the Alta River at the expense of losing her environmental credibility. The new conservative government that replaced her in the fall of 1981 would gleefully point to the failures of the callous technocratic planners within the Labor Party.

Though despised by Deep Ecologists, it is important to understand why Brundtland was regarded as a committed environmentalist among her peers. She would continue the Labor Party's technocratic tradition of handling both humans and nature, though she belonged to an emerging group of reformists within the Party expressing concerns about the social and environmental costs of economic growth. She shared with the Deep Ecologists a dream of a harmony within humankind, as well as between humans and the environment.

The opportunity to recast herself as an environmentalist came when Brundtland was asked to Chair the World Commission in 1984 (Borowy 2014). The relevance of global warming came to the forefront of the World Commission's attention in a written submission to its public hearing in Ottawa in 1986 by the climatologist Kenneth Hare (1986). What caught Brundtland's interest was not the catastrophic consequences of climate change. Environmental doom was old news to her, as Deep Ecologists for a decade had provided her with a stream of reports on the proximity of a civilizational collapse. What was intriguing, however, was the possibility of moving the environmental debate into a new science domain of climatology, and perhaps a new global political regime that spoke to the patron of the Commission, the United Nations. Thus, *Our Common Future* spelled out the dangers of global warming by pointing to the problem as one of the world's chief environmental challenges (World Commission 1987: 11, 14, 16, 20, 33, 52, 106, 128, 146–149).

Brundtland received a half-hearted applause when she presented the report at home. The bitterness from Alta still lingered among environmentalists during her second term as Prime Minister (1986–1989). That she would enjoy fame as an environmentalist abroad chairing the World Commission was seen by the Deep Ecologists as ironic, at best. Brundtland, however, made it perfectly clear in the media that she stood by the report, though few environmentalists took her seriously. They were in for a surprise.

A sustainable climate

One of Brundtland's top priorities after the publication of *Our Common Future* in 1987 was to issue a white paper for the Parliament intended to flatten criticisms at home that the Labor Party did not take the environment seriously.

At the core of *Environment and Development*, as the white paper was entitled, was a vision of Norway being "a driving force" and a "pioneer country" for environmental change (Ministry of the Environment 1989: 8). It addressed key issues related to *Our Common Future*, such as the need to protect biodiversity, the importance of public transportation, financial support of developing countries, minimizing acid rain, ending ozone layer depletion, and protecting the oceans.

Yet climate change was at the white paper's forefront labeled as "perhaps the most pressing environmental issue for the 1990s." And Brundtland was determined to do something about it. She asked the Parliament to approve a policy that would "reduce the CO_2 emissions so that they will be stabilized in the 1990s and in year 2000 at the latest" (Ministry of the Environment 1989: 10). The opposition would naturally ridicule the ambition as unnecessary and not founded on scientific facts, with the most vicious attacks coming from scholars on the political far left shocked by the "ignorance, bluff, and partly dishonest use of data" among climatologists (Rosenqvist 1989).

To counter such claims Brundtland initiated research programs, such as the Center for International Climate Environmental Research, Oslo (CICERO). Its first Chairman was Henrik Ager-Hansen. He had served as Vice-President of the all-dominating state owned Norwegian oil company Statoil ("state oil") for twenty four years, and had just stepped down to be the company's chief adviser on environmental policy. His role was to make sure that climate research at CICERO would not undermine the nation's booming petroleum industry. The Center's first Director Ted Hanisch was a keen supporter of Brundtland, serving as her Parliamentary Secretary from 1986 to 1989. This close link to the Labor Party and Statoil was not accidental. The aim of CICERO was to envision a way forward for the ambitious Norwegian climate politics to exist in harmony with oil and gas exploitation (Anonymous 2000).

Other large research programs also began investigating climate change (Braathen 2000). The Norwegian Research Council for Sciences and the Humanities (NAVF) and the European Science Foundation (ESF) arranged a large conference to kick start such research in Europe. It happened in the Norwegian city of Bergen in 1990 in lieu of the Regional Conference addressing the World Commission's *Our Common Future*. At this meeting most of the European environmental ministers would attend to prepare for the forthcoming Earth Summit in Rio in 1992. Politically the conference was a failure, as environmentalists (many of whom were Deep Ecologists) would block the bus with the ministers showcasing public transportation on their way to the hotel shouting "Bergen meeting talking and eating!"

Among the 138 scientists attending the conference it was paramount to show that they were not only "talking and eating" but actually contributing. The result was a thick anthology, produced with great speed, in which climate change was at the forefront. It included conclusions and recommendations for politicians preparing for Rio, stating that climate change was real, and that the way forward lay in the domain of international law as well as "cost effective" financial initiatives to curb emissions of greenhouse gasses (Anonymous 1990: 9).

All this was happening while Brundtland's government was in opposition for about a year. The Labor Party would, however, regain power in the fall of 1990. For her third term as Prime Minister she was determined to reach her ambitious goal of stabilizing Norway's climate emissions by the millennium. Yet the prospect of curbing the emissions that looked feasible in 1989 looked overambitious by 1990. What had changed was the gradual realization that emission reduction was not possible while at the same time dramatically increasing the nation's oil and gas production. How could one increase production and spur economic growth while at the same time reduce the emissions? Or – in the language of *Our Common Future's* definition of "sustainable development" – how could one meet "the needs of the present without compromising the ability of future generations"? (1987: 41).

Brundtland appointed the leader of the Labor Party's youth wing Jens Stoltenberg to find an answer to the difficult question. As a trained economist he knew what was worth knowing about the past, present and future of Norway's oil economy, and he was a keen proponent of exponential growth of its industry. Yet he did not take environmental issues lightly. Indeed, he would, as Norway's Prime Minister from 2005 to 2013, regard global warming (next to poverty) as "the main challenge of our time" and he would restate Brundtland's vision that Norway's environmental policy was to be a "pioneer country" for the world (Alstadheim 2010: 8, 13). How could one nurture Norway's oil and gas exploitation while at the same time curb the world's greenhouse gas emissions?

In the early 1990s a growing body of literature on environmental cost-benefit economics had emerged (Randalls 2011). Drawing on this and inspired by the US emissions trading system for sulphur dioxide quotas, Stoltenberg and his team came to the conclusion that the most cost-effective way of reducing greenhouse gasses without having to curb oil production would be to introduce a similar system for Europe, and perhaps the entire world. With plenty of money from the oil, Norway could then buy such quotas and thereby reach its millennium goal.

There was only one problem: one would first have to establish an emission market supported by an international regime. In the years leading up to the Earth Summit in Rio, Norway engaged in an intense diplomatic campaign for the plan. They met much resistance in European countries who argued that Norway should perhaps curb its own emissions instead of buying the achievement of others. The reception was not much better in newly industrialized countries such as India, Thailand, and Malaysia. When Brundtland and Stoltenberg traveled to Rio in 1992 to promote the idea, they too failed to convince the world about the virtue of carbon emission trading. Back in Oslo they concluded that they would have to show that Norway would be willing to cut some of its emissions at home while at the same time mustering support from the developing world. (Nilsen 2001; Martiniussen 2013).

At home carbon capture and storage technologies (CCS) became the approach to achieve the millennium goal. The basic idea was to replace oil with carbon dioxide when producing oil in the North Sea, and the financial incentive to do so was a government tax targeting such emissions from the petroleum industry. If Norway could capture and store climate gasses deep in the continental shelf, it should count towards climate gas reduction, Stoltenberg argued. In 1996 Statoil's Sleipner platform became the world's first offshore CCS plant injecting carbon dioxide into the oil reservoirs (though the platform would still be one of the single largest climate gas polluters in Norway). Finding technological solutions to social problems was very much in the Labor Party tradition, and CCS became the Party's most ambitious global warming initiative at home. In his new year's speech in 2007 Stoltenberg announced to the nation that Norway's "moon-landing" would be to develop CCS technologies for its petroleum industry (Alstadheim 2010: 80). The attempt failed financially, however, and then backfired on a Prime Minister who soon faced criticisms for his state-driven innovation policies along with numerous "moon-landing" jokes.

On the international scene Norway tried to muster votes from the developing world in order to get acceptance for emission trading before meeting in Kyoto in 1997. After Rio, Norwegian diplomats would spend time trying to convince the leaders of the world's poorest nations of the virtue of carbon emissions trading. What they would purpose was a system in which a rich country would pay for a carbon clean development initiative in a poor country and then get credit for that in their carbon account at home. For example, if Norway installed solar cells in sunny Burkina Faso they could get carbon emissions credit for the project in Norway. To prove their sincerity, Norway actually did install such cells and got Burkina Faso's vote in Kyoto in return. Between 1992 and 1997 Norway completed numerous projects like these in the developing world, mustering support for what eventually would be called Clean Development Mechanisms or CDMs.

By 1997 Norway had secured votes from developing nations with the help of CDM test projects, and it was confident diplomats who arrived in Kyoto. In United Nations international agreements every vote is equal, whether you represent the United States or Antigua, Belize, and Guyana (the last three being allies of Norway). As a result, in Kyoto countries would commit to reducing greenhouse gas emissions. They could do so in different ways: at home, by trading carbon dioxide equivalent quotas (TEQs), and by buying clean development mechanisms certificates (CDMs).

Soon the European Union established a market for emission trading, and the certification industry began issuing purchasable CDM certificates based on projects mostly in the developing world. Despite being a significant buyer in these new markets Norway would never meet its millennium goal from 1989 as its greenhouse gas emissions increased. Over the years, the financial cost of these tradable emission quotas have been significant, a total of €612 million between 2008 and 2012 alone (Karlsen 2014). Yet to understand this endeavor only in terms of economic efficiency would be to miss the point.

What this short essay has done is to untangle some of the intentions and motives that have driven climate politics. What was important to the Labor Party environmentalists was to showcase Norway as a virtuous "pioneer country" to its own citizens and the world. History as a pedagogical tool can move classroom debates beyond simplistic debates about supporting or not supporting climate change initiatives, by telling students about the changing nature of the politics of pure science. By following the money and political motivations over time, history can untangle the story behind the story, thus helping students to gain a deeper understanding of an important topic. Norwegian climate politics was, as this chapter has indicated, a way of reforming the Labor Party's technocratic tradition in a more environmentally friendly direction. And it was all paid for by producing the very cause of global warming—petroleum.

References

Alstadheim, K.B. (2010) *Klimaparadokset: Jens Stoltenberg om vår tids største utfordirng* Oslo: Aschehoug.

Anker, P. (2007) "Science as a Vacation: A History of Ecology in Norway," *History of Science* 45, 455–479.

Anonymous (1971) "Og havet vil stige," *VG* March 27.

Anonymous (1990) "Executive summary" in Mykletun J (ed.) *Sustainable Development, Science Policy: The Conference Report*, Oslo: Norwegian Research Council for Science and the Humanities, 9.

Anonymous (2000) *CICERO senter for klimaforskning: en evaluering*, Oslo: Norges forsknings-råd.

Borowy, I. (2014) *Defining Sustainable Development for Our Common Future: A History of the World Commission on Environment and Development (Brundtland Commission)*, London: Routledge.

Braathen, G. (2000) *Sluttrapport fra forskningsprogram om klima- og ozon spørsmål 1989–1998*, Oslo: Norsk Institutt for Luftforskning.

Hare, F.K. (1986) "Mandate for Change: The Relevance of Climate," Ottawa, May 26–27, World Commission archive.

Hjorthol, L.M. (2006) *Alta: Kraftkampen som utfordret statens makt* Oslo: Gyldendal.

Karlsen, H.T. (2014) *The cost of participating in the greenhouse gas emission permit marked*, Oslo: Statistics Norway.

Martiniussen, E. (2013) *Drivhuseffekten: Klimapolitikken som forsvant*, Oslo: Manifest.

Ministry of the Environment (1989) *St.meld. nr 46 (1988–1989): Miljø og utvikling: Norges oppfølging av Verdenskommisjonens rapport*, Oslo: Goverment Printing.

Nilsen, Y. (2001) *En felles plattform? Norsk oljeindustri og klimadebatten i Norge fram til 1998*, Oslo: TMV Senter.

Parr, H., Bryne, K.H., Hofseth, P. and Riekeles, J. (1974) *Energi, miljø og samfunn: en utredning fra Norges naturvernforbund utarbeidet av forbundets energiutvalg*, Oslo: Norges naturvernfor-bund.

Randalls, S. (2011) "Optimal Climate Change: Economics and Climate Science Policy Histories (from Heuristic to Normative)" *Osiris* 26, 224–242.

Rosenqvist, I.T. (1989) "Den store miljøbløffen" *Vegviseren* 16, 8–9.

Weart, S.R. (2003) *The Discovery of Global Warming*, Cambridge: Harvard UP.

World Commission on Environment and Development (1987) *Our Common Future*, Oxford: Oxford University Press.

Afterword

Bill McKibben

For several generations now, the lens through which we've peered at the world is primarily economic: what set of ideas and policies will produce *more*? There have been left and right takes on this question, but it's been the central preoccupation of our political and commercial life, and hence it has shaped the academy: economics and business administration are central, as are the engineering disciplines that make consumerism on our current scale possible.

But the world is encouraging us to ask a new set of questions this century. 2015 was the hottest year we've ever measured, smashing the old mark set in … 2014. So far this millennia we've watched summer sea ice in the Arctic melt away, and the great ice sheets of the Antarctic undercut by warm ocean water (and we've watched the waters of every ocean grow steadily more acidic). Even at the current level of one degree Celsius, increasing the planet's temperature is the largest thing humans have ever done—and of course we're on track for much more than that.

Which means that the preoccupations of our society are starting quickly to shift—from endless expansion to strategies for survival. And in turn that should reshape the list of things we think it's important to learn. Scientists and engineers have much work yet to do, and so do economists and business executives: every percentage increase in the efficiency of a solar panel, every percentage drop in the price of a wind turbine, betters our chances at survival. But suddenly we need everyone else too. Psychologists to understand why we're slow to react, and political scientists to trace the power of the fossil fuel industry through our societies; theologians and historians to mine our traditions for the nuggets that let us deal with new crises; artists to offer us the images that can spur action. Look at it this way: if we are suddenly living, as the scientists insist, in the Anthropocene, then the humanities by definition are central to the task at hand.

I've had the chance to see this kind of well-rounded education take root. Middlebury College, where I hang my cap, houses the oldest environmental studies department in the country, and one of the few to take the hard sciences, the social sciences, and the humanities as equal partners in the venture. In so doing, it models the kind of minds we need for this century. Instead of deep and narrow investigation of particular phenomena (which produced the scientific progress on which prosperity was built, and hence encouraged all other disciplines to mimic physics and chemistry), we now require a broad and general synthesis. We know, perhaps, enough *things*. We just don't know how they fit together. Looking at the world through the lens supplied by climate change requires true interdisciplinarity, as this fine volume shows so well.

I should caution, however, that transforming the classroom will not be enough. As academics and writers we have a natural inclination to think that words and books change the world. They certainly have their effect, but less than we sometimes think. I wrote the first book about climate change for a general audience, and was gratified by the response—it appeared in 24 languages, and was a bestseller many places. It was, I think, a real help in opening up the argument—but at a certain point I understood that we'd won the argument even as we were losing the fight. Like all serious fights, this one isn't about data points—it's about money and power, and there's an adversary, the richest industry on earth.

So a big part of our work—perhaps the biggest—comes after office hours and on weekends. It's the work of being citizens, of building the movements that can challenge the power of that industry. I was never prouder of my colleagues at Middlebury than when I watched as their students came together outside of class to start 350.org, which we've grown into the first global grassroots climate movement. They took all that they'd learned—about carbon and about social justice, about international relations and media studies—and they used it to fight, with power and effectiveness. People are doing that on most North American campuses now—demanding divestment, pushing for carbon neutrality. That may not be the proper work of the classroom, but it's the necessary work of all of us who care.

Index